From Paradise
to the Promised Land

From Paradise to the Promised Land

AN INTRODUCTION TO THE PENTATEUCH

Third Edition

T. DESMOND ALEXANDER

Baker Academic

a division of Baker Publishing Group
Grand Rapids, Michigan

Published by Baker Academic
a division of Baker Publishing Group
P.O. Box 6287, Grand Rapids, MI 49516-6287
www.bakeracademic.com

Printed in the United States of America

Library of Congress Cataloging-in-Publication Data
Alexander, T. Desmond.
    From paradise to the promised land : an introduction to the Pentateuch / T. Desmond Alexander. — 3rd ed.
        p. cm.
    Includes bibliographical references (p.   ) and indexes.
    ISBN 978-0-8010-3998-0 (pbk.)
    1. Bible. O.T. Pentateuch—Criticism, interpretation, etc. I. Title.
BS1225.52.A445 2012
222′.1061—dc23   2012002984

The internet addresses, email addresses, and phone numbers in this book are accurate at the time of publication. They are provided as a resource. Baker Publishing Group does not endorse them or vouch for their content or permanence.

14   15   16   17   18   7   6   5   4   3

In keeping with biblical principles of creation stewardship, Baker Publishing Group advocates the responsible use of our natural resources. As a member of the Green Press Initiative, our company uses recycled paper when possible. The text paper of this book is composed in part of post-consumer waste.

To
Margaret and Janet,
and in fond memory of Robert Wallace

Contents

Illustrations

Preface

The idea of writing an introductory guide to the first five books of the Bible arose following a brief period of teaching Asian theological students in Singapore in 1990. My experience there confirmed what had been evident to me in Ireland: most students of theology and religious studies have at best a very limited understanding of the basic contents of the Pentateuch. While they are vaguely familiar with the better-known stories of Genesis and Exodus, few could claim to have a clear understanding of the Pentateuch as a whole. What was lacking was a good guide to the text, a book that was suited to the needs of such students. To this end, what now appears as part 2 of this edition was published in 1995 under the title *From Paradise to the Promised Land*.

Because this former volume focused deliberately on the contents of Genesis to Deuteronomy, it provided no detailed discussion of contemporary academic approaches to the Pentateuch. To address this shortcoming, part 1 was added when the second edition was published in 2002. This third edition adds new material, with chapters revised to varying degrees. The present volume seeks to (1) guide the reader through the maze of modern approaches to the Pentateuch, and (2) focus on the main themes of the Pentateuch, viewed as a unified literary work, by drawing on the best insights of recent research into Hebrew narrative techniques.

To these a further aim has been added, which strictly speaking is not required in an introduction to the Pentateuch. I have sought to briefly outline the many ways in which the pentateuchal material is taken up and used in the New Testament. Two considerations have encouraged me to do this. First, many students of theology and religious studies approach the Pentateuch from a Christian perspective and are naturally interested in how this material relates to the beliefs and practices of the New Testament church. Second, and perhaps more important from a purely academic perspective, the New Testament documents reveal how the pentateuchal texts were understood in a period and culture much closer to that of the Pentateuch than our own. It is interesting, therefore, to compare the New Testament understanding of the Pentateuch with that of twenty-first-century readers. To what extent is there agreement on the meaning of the text?

Having stated the general aims of this study, some further comments may help clarify the overall approach adopted here. Although this volume seeks to explain the contents of the Pentateuch, it is not a verse-by-verse commentary on the text. An abundance of commentaries already exists, as noted in the recommended further reading section on pages 315–20. Yet while they are especially helpful in explaining shorter units of material—for example, individual verses or chapters—by their very nature commentaries tend to atomize the text into small units. Consequently, they sometimes fail to highlight themes that are spread across entire books, especially when such themes do not appear to be of particular importance in any single passage. Studying the biblical texts by means of commentaries can be compared to looking at the separate pieces of a jigsaw puzzle. Though we may find something of interest in each piece, it is only when all the pieces are put together that we get the complete picture. It is with this larger picture that we wish to engage in this study of the Pentateuch.

Not only may commentaries fail to give a complete picture, but they may also unintentionally give a distorted picture. By atomizing the text and considering each unit independently, there is ever present the danger of misinterpreting these shorter passages. This may be illustrated by using the jigsaw puzzle again. Examined on its own, a single piece may appear to show one thing, yet when placed alongside its matching pieces it may reveal something quite different. Obviously, knowledge of the wider context is vital for understanding the individual components of something larger. Unfortunately, scholars have not always adequately appreciated the dangers that exist in interpreting a biblical book unit by unit without sufficiently taking into account the broader context.

Alongside these shortcomings must be placed a further and much more fundamental problem. For the past two centuries the academic study of the Pentateuch has been dominated by methods that seek primarily to elucidate how the present text came into being; these methods are surveyed in part 1. Encouraged by the hope of uncovering the literary and oral prehistory of the received text, scholars have expended an inordinate amount of time and energy on developing the methodologies of *source* and *form* criticism. We observe several consequences of this practice. First, these methods have resulted in the text being dissected in a variety of ways. No longer is the Pentateuch generally considered to be a literary unity—which, regardless of how it was composed, it now is. Rather, it is commonly viewed as a collection of literary documents and/or oral accounts linked by editorial (or redactional) additions. Most scholarly research on the Pentateuch has sought to (1) discover the existence of these hypothetical sources, (2) explain the process by which they were combined to form the present text, and (3) relate the existence of these earlier sources to the history and religious development of the Israelites before the final composition of the Pentateuch in the exilic or postexilic period. While scholarly endeavors to address these issues have not been wanting, the past two decades have witnessed a substantial rejection of results that seemed assured for several immediately preceding generations of scholars. At the present time much uncertainty exists regarding how and when the Pentateuch was composed. Given our present knowledge, we could even ask if it is possible to determine with any confidence the process by which it came into being.

A second consequence of biblical scholarship's focusing its resources on the prehistory of the text has been a failure to clearly elucidate the meaning of the Pentateuch in its received form. Relatively little has been said about the final form of the Pentateuch. Most studies have focused on the sources underlying the present text. Three factors have possibly contributed to this lack of interest in the Pentateuch as received.

1. In the past source-critical studies have generally portrayed the earliest stages in the composition of the Pentateuch as the most interesting and important. In marked contrast, the contribution of the final editor or editors was considered to be insignificant. Consequently, there was little incentive to examine his work in detail. Moreover, when scholars did consider it, they generally looked only at the material assigned specifically to him. It was believed to be inappropriate or unnecessary to consider the entire Pentateuch in order to establish an understanding of the final redactor(s).

2. Many scholars appear to have assumed that a detailed explanation of the prehistory of the Pentateuch reveals all that needs to be known about the text as received. However, as R. Polzin has rightly observed: "Traditional biblical scholarship has spent most of its efforts in disassembling the works of a complicated watch before our amazed eyes without apparently realizing that similar efforts by and large have not succeeded in putting the parts back together again in a significant or meaningful way."[1] We need to recognize that the Pentateuch, as we now have it, is much more than the sum of its component parts.

3. Scholars have tended to consider the study of the Pentateuch in its final form as less demanding and therefore of less academic value than the investigation of its hypothetical sources.[2] Such reasoning is fallacious, however. The value of the final form of the Pentateuch should not be judged on the

---

1. R. Polzin, "'The Ancestress of Israel in Danger' in Danger," *Semeia* 3 (1975): 82–83.

2. A similar observation was voiced by Gerhard von Rad in 1938: "On almost all sides the final form of the Hexateuch has come to be regarded as a starting point barely worthy of discussion, from which the debate should move away as rapidly as possible in order to reach the real problems underlying it." See *The Problem of the Hexateuch and Other Essays* (Edinburgh: Oliver & Boyd, 1966), 1.

basis of the ease or otherwise of studying it. Rather, such study should be undertaken because of the inherent importance of the text as a unified literary work.[3] While some still fail to take seriously the study of the Pentateuch in its final form, it is encouraging to see that many more scholars now recognize the importance of doing so.

Even if one grants the importance of source and form criticism, various arguments strongly favor an approach that gives prominence to the final form of the Pentateuch.

First, this is the form in which the text has been received. Whatever the process by which it was composed, it is now a coherent literary work. Even if, as seems very likely, various sources were used in its composition, it must be recognized that the final editor, whoever he (or she?) may have been, appropriated all the source material as his own and used it to compose the present narrative, which begins in Genesis and continues through to the end of Deuteronomy. It therefore is essential to view the entire Pentateuch as reflecting the outlook of the final editor, not merely the portions that are normally assigned to the last editorial stage.

Second, a detailed and comprehensive study of the Pentateuch in its final form must have priority in sequence over the approaches of source and form criticism. It is methodologically unsound to explore the prehistory of the text without having established a clear understanding of how the present text is constructed as a literary work. To do otherwise is to set the cart before the horse. Similarly, on pedagogical grounds, it is surely improper to expect students to appreciate and apply critical methods before they have understood the content and literary structure of the received text. Unfortunately, students frequently are introduced to scholarly opinions regarding the process by which the text was composed, yet without knowing what the text itself is saying.

Third, new literary approaches to the study of Hebrew narrative provide fresh insights into the meaning of many pentateuchal passages. Frequently these insights offer new ways to approach problems that in the past were resolved by resorting to source- or form-critical solutions. Scholars in general are now more confident about taking seriously the present integrity of the text.

Fourth, a clear understanding of the final form of the Pentateuch is important if we are to appreciate how it influenced later writers. The writers (and earliest readers) of the New Testament were all precritical in their understanding of the Pentateuch; they did not think in terms of different literary and/or oral sources underlying the text, each reflecting a different theology. For them the Pentateuch was a single entity; this was how they understood and

---

3. By this I mean that the books of Genesis to Deuteronomy are linked in such a way that while they may be viewed as separate entities, it is clear that they have been made dependent on one another, with the later books presupposing a knowledge of the earlier ones and the earlier books being incomplete without the addition of the later ones. On this basis the Pentateuch itself is incomplete and is linked in a special way to the material in Joshua to 2 Kings.

interpreted it. All these reasons argue for an approach that treats with respect the received text of the Pentateuch.

From the preceding comments it is evident that the position adopted in part 2 of this book differs markedly from that often followed by others. The object of my study is the final form of the Pentateuch as it has been handed down to us in the Hebrew text. Little attention will be given to possible sources or the process of composition; much has been written on this elsewhere, as will be observed in part 1. Rather, it is my aim to map out the terrain of the Pentateuch as it now stands by drawing attention to its main features. To enable the reader to assimilate the contents of the Pentateuch more easily, the material is usually approached book by book. Sometimes attention is focused on major themes running through entire books. Elsewhere shorter blocks of material that deal with specific subjects are examined. The intention is to allow the text to determine the approach that seems most appropriate. For example, on the one hand, the themes of "seed," blessing, and land run throughout the book of Genesis.[4] On the other hand, the account of the building of the tabernacle dominates most of the final third of the book of Exodus. When we examine blocks of material, I have tried to follow the natural divisions of the text.

References to the rest of the Old Testament have been kept to a minimum. To have included all the relevant material would have added considerably to each chapter and shifted the focus of the book from the Pentateuch to the Old Testament as a whole.

Although I seek to include in part 2 the best insights of contemporary studies, I want to keep the presentation as straightforward as possible and thus have deliberately avoided engaging in a detailed critique of the views of other scholars. Three factors have persuaded me to adopt this approach. First, to interact meaningfully with all that has been said would take this study far beyond an introductory guide. Second, since many writers discuss the pentateuchal material from the perspectives of source and/or form criticism, it has to be recognized that they are addressing quite different issues from those being examined here. While this does not automatically exclude the possibility of meaningful interaction, it does make it much more difficult to achieve. Moreover, for every passage under consideration, it would have required a detailed discussion of past and contemporary views on the process by which it was composed, something that would have added considerably to the length of this volume. Third, the primary purpose of part 2 is to focus the reader's attention on the content of the Pentateuch itself rather than on the diverse opinions of contemporary scholars.

---

4. Though I have tended to restrict the study of particular themes to individual books, certain themes cannot easily be restricted in this way (e.g., land, descendants, blessing). Themes that may be dominant in one book (e.g., Genesis) are sometimes picked up elsewhere in the Pentateuch as important motifs echoing earlier material. As such, they are important indicators to the overall unity of the Pentateuch in its received form.

A number of chapters have appeared in print elsewhere; to varying degrees I have modified and updated these to conform to the overall presenting pattern adopted in this volume. Some of the material in chapters 3 and 5 first appeared in my book *Abraham in the Negev: A Source-Critical Investigation of Genesis 20:1–22:19*.[5] The discussion of the Passover in chapter 4 incorporates some material from my article "The Passover Sacrifice," in *Sacrifice in the Bible*, edited by R. T. Beckwith and M. Selman.[6] Chapters 5 and 9 first appeared respectively as "The Composition of the Sinai Narrative in Exodus xix 1–xxiv 11"[7] and "Genealogies, Seed and the Compositional Unity of Genesis."[8] Some of the material in chapter 6 first appeared in my article "Authorship of the Pentateuch," in the *Dictionary of the Old Testament: A Compendium of Contemporary Biblical Scholarship*, edited by T. Desmond Alexander and David W. Baker, and is used by permission of InterVarsity Press (USA). Chapter 12 was originally published as "Abraham Re-assessed Theologically: The Abraham Narrative and the New Testament Understanding of Justification by Faith," in *He Swore an Oath: Biblical Themes from Genesis 12–50*, edited by R. S. Hess, P. E. Satterthwaite, and G. J. Wenham.[9] Much of the material in chapters 13–16 was first published in 1994 in the *New Bible Commentary: 21st Century Edition*, edited by D. A. Carson and others; I am grateful to the publishers, Inter-Varsity Press (UK), for permission to reproduce this in a modified form.

Except where otherwise indicated, biblical quotations are from the NIV, and all biblical references follow the English rather than the Hebrew scheme of numeration. All Hebrew words have been transliterated according to standard practice; however, where for the ordinary reader the transliteration does not reflect the actual pronunciation of a Hebrew word, I have added this in parentheses.

For providing me with helpful observations on sections of this study, I am grateful to John Brew, Claude-Bernard Costecalde, Ian Hart, James McKeown, Alan Millard, Albert Ong, David Palmer, and Paul Williamson. Yet they can in no way be held responsible for the shortcomings that remain. I wish also to express my thanks to the staff of Baker Academic for their valuable assistance in

5. T. D. Alexander, *Abraham in the Negev: A Source-Critical Investigation of Genesis 20:1–22:19* (Carlisle: Paternoster, 1997).

6. T. D. Alexander, "The Passover Sacrifice," in *Sacrifice in the Bible*, ed. R. T. Beckwith and M. Selman (Carlisle: Paternoster; Grand Rapids: Baker, 1995), 1–24.

7. T. D. Alexander, "The Composition of the Sinai Narrative in Exodus xix 1–xxiv 11," *VT* 49 (1999): 2–20.

8. T. D. Alexander, "Genealogies, Seed and the Compositional Unity of Genesis," *TynBul* 44 (1993): 255–70.

9. T. D. Alexander, "Abraham Re-assessed Theologically: The Abraham Narrative and the New Testament Understanding of Justification by Faith," in *He Swore an Oath: Biblical Themes from Genesis 12–50*, ed. R. S. Hess, P. E. Satterthwaite, and G. J. Wenham (Cambridge: Tyndale House, 1993), 7–28; 2nd ed. (Grand Rapids: Baker; Carlisle: Paternoster, 1994), 7–28.

the final stages of this book's production. For the loving support that I receive so consistently from my wife, Anne, I am deeply grateful, not forgetting the contribution made to this by our children, Jane and David, who constantly remind me that there is more to life than books. To my mother and Anne's mother, and in memory of my father-in-law, Robert Wallace, this book is dedicated with love.

SOLI DEO GLORIA.

Abbreviations

AB	Anchor Bible	ca.	circa, approximately
ABD	*Anchor Bible Dictionary*. Edited by D. N. Freedman. 6 vols. New York, 1992	CahRB	Cahiers de la Revue biblique
		CBQ	*Catholic Biblical Quarterly*
		CBQMS	Catholic Biblical Quarterly Monograph Series
alt.	minor alteration to a quote		
AnBib	Analecta biblica	CC	Continental Commentaries
AOTC	Apollos Old Testament Commentary	CCSOT	Communicator's Commentary Series: Old Testament
ATANT	Abhandlungen zur Theologie des Alten und Neuen Testaments	chap(s).	chapter(s)
		CJT	*Canadian Journal of Theology*
		CRC	ChiRho Commentary
BA	*Biblical Archaeologist*	*CTJ*	*Calvin Theological Journal*
BAR	*Biblical Archaeology Review*	DSB	Daily Study Bible
BASOR	*Bulletin of the American Schools of Oriental Research*	EC	Epworth Commentaries
		ECC	Eerdmans Critical Commentary
BBB	Bonner biblische Beiträge		
BBC	Blackwell Bible Commentaries	EPSC	Evangelical Press Study Commentary
BETL	Bibliotheca ephemeridum theologicarum lovaniensium	*ErIsr*	*Eretz-Israel*
Bib	*Biblica*	esp.	especially
BibSem	Biblical Seminar	ESV	English Standard Version
BibS(N)	Biblische Studien (Neukirchen, 1951–)	ET	English translation
		EvQ	*Evangelical Quarterly*
BS	*Bibliotheca sacra*	FB	Focus on the Bible
BSC	Bible Student's Commentary	FOTL	Forms of Old Testament Literature
BST	Bible Speaks Today		
BTB	*Biblical Theology Bulletin*	HBM	Hebrew Bible Monographs
BWANT	Beiträge zur Wissenschaft vom Alten und Neuen Testament	HCOT	Historical Commentary on the Old Testament
BZAW	Beihefte zur Zeitschrift für die alttestamentliche Wissenschaft	HCSB	Holman Christian Standard Bible
c.	century	*HUCA*	*Hebrew Union College Annual*

IBC	Interpretation: A Bible Commentary for Teaching and Preaching	NET	The NET Bible (New English Translation)
IBD	*The Illustrated Bible Dictionary.* Edited by J. D. Douglas. 3 vols. Leicester: Inter-Varsity; Wheaton, IL: Tyndale House, 1980	*NETR*	*Near East School of Theology Theological Review*
		NIBCOT	New International Biblical Commentary Old Testament
		NICOT	New International Commentary on the Old Testament
IBS	*Irish Biblical Studies*	NIDOTTE	*New International Dictionary of Old Testament Theology and Exegesis.* Edited by W. A. VanGemeren. 5 vols. Grand Rapids, 1997
IBT	Interpreting Biblical Texts		
ICC	International Critical Commentary		
ILR	*Israel Law Review*		
Int	*Interpretation*	NIV	New International Version, 2011 (1984 if so specified)
ITC	International Theological Commentary		
		NIVAC	NIV Application Commentary
JAAR	*Journal of the American Academy of Religion*	NJPS	*The Tanakh: The Holy Scriptures; The Jewish Publication Society Translation according to the Traditional Hebrew Text,* 2nd ed., 1999
JAOS	*Journal of the American Oriental Society*		
JBL	*Journal of Biblical Literature*		
JDT	*Jahrbuch für deutsche Theologie*	NRSV	New Revised Standard Version
		NSBT	New Studies in Biblical Theology
JETS	*Journal of the Evangelical Theological Society*	NT	New Testament
		NTT	*Norsk Teologisk Tidsskrift*
JJS	*Journal of Jewish Studies*	OBO	Orbis biblicus et orientalis
JPSTC	Jewish Publication Society Torah Commentary	OBT	Overtures to Biblical Theology
		OT	Old Testament
JQR	*Jewish Quarterly Review*	OTG	Old Testament Guides
JSOT	*Journal for the Study of the Old Testament*	OTL	Old Testament Library
		OTM	Old Testament Message
JSOTSup	Journal for the Study of the Old Testament: Supplement Series	OTS	Old Testament Studies
		PIBA	*Proceedings of the Irish Biblical Association*
KJV	King James Version		
LHB	Library of Hebrew Bible	PW	Preaching the Word
lit.	literally	*PWCJS*	*Proceedings of the World Congress of Jewish Studies*
LOS	London Oriental Series		
LXX	Septuagint, Greek OT		
mg.	marginal reading or note	*RB*	*Revue biblique*
MLBS	Mercer Library of Biblical Studies	*RBL*	*Review of Biblical Literature*
		REBC	Revised Expositor's Bible Commentary
MT	Masoretic Text		
NAC	New American Commentary	RSV	Revised Standard Version
NACSBT	NAC Studies in Bible and Theology	*RTP*	*Revue de théologie et de philosophie*
		SBJT	*Southern Baptist Journal of Theology*
NCB	New Century Bible		
NCBC	New Cambridge Bible Commentary	SBLDS	Society of Biblical Literature Dissertation Series
NDBT	*New Dictionary of Biblical Theology*		

SBLMS	Society of Biblical Literature Monograph Series	TS	Texts and Studies: Contributions to Biblical and Patristic Literature
SBLSymS	Society of Biblical Literature Symposium Series	*TynBul*	*Tyndale Bulletin*
SBT	Studies in Biblical Theology	UMI	University Microfilms International, Ann Arbor, MI
ScrHier	*Scripta hierosolymitana*	*VT*	*Vetus Testamentum*
SemeiaSt	Semeia Studies	VTSup	Vetus Testamentum Supplements
ser.	series	v(v).	verse(s)
SNTSMS	Society for New Testament Studies Monograph Series	WBC	Word Biblical Commentary
SP	Samaritan Pentateuch	WEC	Wycliffe Exegetical Commentary
SSN	Studia semitica neerlandica	WestBC	Westminster Bible Companion
StudBib	Studia Biblica	WMANT	Wissenschaftliche Monographien zum Alten und Neuen Testament
TBAT	Theologische Bücherei: Altes Testament		
TD	*Theology Digest*	*WTJ*	*Westminster Theological Journal*
Them	*Themelios*	YNER	Yale Near Eastern Researches
TI	Text and Interpretation	*ZAW*	*Zeitschrift für die alttestamentliche Wissenschaft*
TJ	*Trinity Journal*		
TLJS	Taubman Lectures in Jewish Studies	*ZDPV*	*Zeitschrift des deutschen Palästina-Vereins*
TOTC	Tyndale Old Testament Commentaries		

PART 1

Pentateuchal Criticism

1

Introduction
to Pentateuchal Criticism

Since at least the third century AD, the term "Pentateuch" (derived from the Greek *pentateuchos*, "five-volume work") has been used to denote the first five books of the Bible: Genesis, Exodus, Leviticus, Numbers, and Deuteronomy. Jewish tradition has favored the designation "Torah," usually translated as "law," although "instruction" would perhaps be more accurate. Penned originally in Hebrew, the books of the Pentateuch were already important texts by at least the fourth century BC, and over the years they have had a significant influence, both knowingly and unknowingly, upon the religious outlook of Jews, Christians, and Muslims. In spite of this, most people today have only a passing familiarity with their contents, and much within them is likely to strike the modern reader as strange and/or incomprehensible.

For an introduction to the *contents* of these five books, the reader should consult part 2. The opening chapters, here in part 1, provide an introduction to contemporary academic approaches to the Pentateuch and offer a critique of them from an evangelical perspective. After almost a century of relative stability, Pentateuch criticism is currently in a state of turmoil as various theories vie with one another in an attempt to dethrone the Documentary Hypothesis as *the* explanation for the process by which these books were composed. Naturally, it is not possible to do justice to all that has been said, and I am conscious of the limitations of what follows. Nevertheless, it is hoped that this contribution may provide a basis for and a stimulus to further study.

Before focusing on the Documentary Hypothesis, it may be helpful to briefly survey how the Pentateuch has been approached in the modern period. During the past 250 years, scholarly research on the Pentateuch has developed around four main methods: *source* criticism, *form* criticism, *traditio-historical* criticism, and *literary* criticism. Since each method addresses a specific set of issues, it is important to understand how they differ from one another. Moreover, as we shall observe, the rise of each method signaled a new stage in the study of the Pentateuch.

Source Criticism

Source criticism was the first of these four methods to be employed, and it has established itself as a major tool in pentateuchal criticism. This method, which to some extent originally came into being by chance, seeks to uncover the *literary* sources that may have been used in the composition of the books of Genesis to Deuteronomy. Although pushed into the background by other methods during most of the twentieth century, it continues to exercise considerable influence, particularly in relation to the exegesis of the pentateuchal books and scholarly reconstructions of the history of ancient Israel. In chapter 2 we shall trace the development of this method from its origins in the middle of the eighteenth century to the end of the nineteenth century, by which time there evolved the influential *Documentary Hypothesis* of Graf, Vatke, and Wellhausen. For the present it is sufficient to recognize this hypothesis as proposing that four distinctive source documents were combined during a period of five or six centuries to produce the Pentateuch as we now know it, the end of this process coming in the fifth century BC.

Form Criticism

Following the almost universal acceptance of the Documentary Hypothesis, biblical scholars turned, perhaps not surprisingly, to consider the *oral* phase that was thought to lie behind the source documents. Pioneered by Hermann Gunkel in the early decades of the twentieth century, a new methodology arose, subsequently termed form criticism. This approach sought to analyze the pentateuchal material into different categories on the assumption that each had its own particular life setting (technically known as *Sitz im Leben*). By identifying the form of a particular passage, it was thought possible to recover the historical context in which the material was composed. Fundamental to the development of this method was the belief that Genesis consisted of numerous short episodes that originally circulated both orally and independently of one another. Only at a much later stage were these oral compositions brought together and committed to writing, eventually creating the four source documents from which the Pentateuch was composed. A fuller description of this method comes in chapter 3.

Traditio-Historical Criticism

Having determined (1) the earliest oral forms of the pentateuchal material and (2) the four main source documents, the next stage in the history of pentateuchal criticism was to describe the process by which the former were combined to produce the latter. Since this method was interested in the *history of the traditions* underlying the Pentateuch, it was designated traditio-historical criticism. Two of the main scholars associated with the development of this approach are Gerhard von Rad and Martin Noth. Regarding their contribution, see chapter 3.

The preceding three methods all focus on the process by which the Pentateuch was composed. Form criticism identifies the earliest oral stage, traditio-historical criticism describes the process leading up to the formation of the longer written source documents, and finally, source criticism explains how the source documents were brought together to create the Pentateuch as we now have it. In following chapters we shall outline in more detail the use and results of these methods, at the same time evaluating the success of each in achieving its objectives.

Literary Criticism

The past thirty years have witnessed the introduction of an alternative way to view the Pentateuch, known as literary criticism. While interest remains strong in uncovering the process by which the Pentateuch was composed, many scholars either have acknowledged or are gradually recognizing the need to comprehend the Pentateuch in its final form. This shift in emphasis entails a switch from a diachronic (through time) to a synchronic (at the same time) reading of the text. Instead of locating portions of the text in different historical periods, literary criticism seeks to understand the Pentateuch as a coherent, unified work composed at one specific point in time. Literary criticism recognizes that the Pentateuch cannot be understood solely on the basis of the components that have been used in its construction: the whole is much greater than the sum of its parts.

Two further dimensions of literary criticism ought to be noticed. First, the designation "literary criticism" embraces a wide range of differing approaches that may be used to interpret texts (e.g., structuralism, deconstruction, reader-response, rhetorical, narrative, feminist). Scholars primarily interested in the study of modern literature have developed many of these approaches. Second, some proponents of literary criticism adopt a very ambivalent attitude toward historical issues. They are primarily interested in the text alone, viewing questions concerning the growth of the text and its historical context as irrelevant to their particular approach. While there may be a place for adopting an ahistorical reading of some texts, it needs to be asked if this is really appropriate for the study of the Pentateuch.

In theory, the four methods outlined above are complementary, asking different questions of the Pentateuch. In practice, however, literary criticism, by revealing more clearly how the biblical text is constructed, has challenged many of the results obtained by the other methods. For this reason, in recent years literary criticism has had a major impact on the study of the Pentateuch, and it continues to do so. Nevertheless, the results obtained by the other methods still enjoy substantial support. Consequently, as we move into the twenty-first century, the academic study of the Pentateuch is marked by a greater diversity of opinions than possibly at any stage in the modern period. What follows, therefore, makes no claim to be a comprehensive description of all current views. Rather, it is designed to (1) explain how the present state of affairs came into being, (2) evaluate some of the more influential contributions, and (3) offer some tentative suggestions as to how Christians may best approach the Pentateuch as an important theological text.

2

The Rise
of the Documentary Hypothesis

Contemporary approaches to the Pentateuch have their roots in the seventeenth and eighteenth centuries. For this reason, in this chapter we shall survey, briefly and somewhat selectively, the development of source criticism as applied to the Pentateuch, from the period of the Enlightenment to the end of the nineteenth century. This historical overview provides an important introduction to the topics we shall explore in more detail throughout the rest of part 1 of this book. It will also help us to understand more clearly some of the different directions being pursued in contemporary discussions.

The origin of source criticism as a critical method may be traced back to the middle of the eighteenth century.[1] From somewhat unusual beginnings, it became the dominant tool for the study of the Pentateuch. Undoubtedly this development owed much to the new climate of intellectual freedom, associated with the Enlightenment, that permitted the questioning of traditional views. Although the source criticism of the Pentateuch developed largely through a slow process of evolution, with new ideas being introduced and refined, it is possible to distinguish a number of distinctive stages. These are helpful in highlighting various models that may be used to explain the process by

---

1. For a fuller history of pentateuchal criticism up to the 1960s, see R. J. Thompson, *Moses and the Law in a Century of Criticism since Graf*, VTSup 19 (Leiden: Brill, 1970); cf. J. W. Rogerson, *Old Testament Criticism in the Nineteenth Century* (London: SPCK, 1984).

which the Pentateuch was composed (see below under the subhead "Models for Explaining the Composition of the Pentateuch").

The Older Documentary Hypothesis

In 1753 a leading French medical professor, Jean Astruc (1684–1766), published in Brussels a work titled *Conjectures sur les mémoires originaux dont il paroit que Moyse s'est servi pour composer le livre de la Genèse*, in which he argued that Moses had compiled Genesis from older documents. Astruc made three important observations regarding Genesis: (1) certain events are recorded more than once (e.g., the creation; the flood); (2) God is designated by the names Elohim and Yahweh;[2] (3) certain events are reported before other events, although chronologically they occur later. These observations suggested to Astruc that Genesis was composed of older records, and so he proceeded to "decompose" Genesis. In one column, which he termed A, he placed passages using or linked to the divine name Elohim.[3] Next to this first column he placed a second column, B, containing passages associated with the name Yahweh.[4] However, it soon became apparent that two columns would not suffice. A third column, C, was introduced for passages that (1) were repetitions of events already included in both columns A and B, and (2) did not employ any divine designation. To this column Astruc assigned with certainty only two verses (7:20, 23). Other passages that did not contain the name of God still required attention. When Astruc noticed that the remaining passages recorded events foreign to the history of the Hebrew people, he placed them in a fourth column, D.[5] With regard to this final column, Astruc thought it unlikely that it once formed a continuous document. Rather, it consisted of fragments from other minor documents. Finally, Astruc was unable to assign certain verses to any particular column. These verses, he felt, could be common to two or three of the original documents (Gen. 7:24 to A, B, and C; Gen. 9:28–29 to A and B). Astruc proposed that Moses had originally placed these four columns side by side, but unfortunately a later copyist mistakenly combined them, thus creating the continuous narrative that now constitutes Genesis.

2. In most modern English versions of the Bible, Elohim is translated as "God," and Yahweh as "Lord." In older versions, the divine name Yahweh occasionally occurs as "Jehovah." For consistency the terms "Yahweh," "Yahwist," and "Yahwistic" are used throughout this historical survey even when writers under discussion use "Jehovah," "Jehovist," and "Jehovistic."

3. Gen. 1:1–2:3; 5:1–32; 6:9–22; 7:6–10, 19, 22; 8:1–19; 9:1–10, 12, 16, 17; 11:10–26; 17:3–27; 20:1–17; 21:2–32; 22:1–10; 23:1–20; 25:1–11; 30:1–23; 31:4–27; 31:51–32:2; 32:24–33:16; 35:1–27; 37:1–36; 40:1–48:22; 49:1–28.

4. Gen. 2:4–26; 6:1–8; 7:1–5, 11–18, 21; 8:20–22; 9:11, 13–15, 18–27; 10:1–11:9; 11:27–13:18; 15:1–17:2; 18:1–19:28; 20:18–21:1; 21:33–34; 22:11–19; 24:1–67; 25:19–26:33; 27:1–28:5; 28:10–29:35; 30:24–31:3; 31:48–50; 32:3–32; 33:17–20; 38:1–30; 39:1–23; 49:1–28.

5. Gen. 14:1–24; 19:29–38; 22:20–24; 25:12–18; 26:34, 35; 28:6–9; 34:1–31; 35:28–36:43.

Some fifteen years after the death of Astruc, Johann Gottfried Eichhorn (1752–1827) published his *Einleitung ins Alte Testament*.[6] In the second volume (1781) of this three-volume work, Eichhorn investigated the authorship and composition of the biblical books. Concerning Genesis, he maintained the orthodox view of Mosaic authorship; indeed, he argued that Moses was particularly well suited to be the author. Moses, however, had employed older written records, and Eichhorn held that it was possible, in most of Genesis, to discern two distinct documents. These documents could be distinguished (1) by the divine epithet employed and (2) by repetitions in the text. Apart from certain minor modifications Eichhorn followed the division suggested by Astruc, although he asserted that Astruc did not influence him.[7]

A further significant development in the source analysis of Genesis occurred in a work by Karl David Ilgen (1763–1834), published at Halle in 1798, titled *Die Urkunden des jerusalemischen Tempelarchivs in ihrer Urgestalt als Beytrag zur Berichtigung der Geschichte der Religion und Politik*. Ilgen, the successor of Eichhorn at Jena, suggested that Genesis comprised seventeen individual documents. These were, however, composed by merely three authors, two of whom used the divine name Elohim, whereas the third employed the epithet Yahweh. Ilgen referred to them by the terms *Sepher Eliel Harischon* (First Elohist), *Sepher Eliel Haschscheni* (Second Elohist), and *Sepher Elijah Harischon* (First Yahwist). He concluded that the First Elohist was responsible for ten sections of Genesis, the Second Elohist for five sections, and the Yahwist for two sections. Ilgen's contribution was important in that he was the first to forward the idea that more than one author used the divine name Elohim. This idea, however, did not gain recognition among scholars until it was advocated afresh by Hermann Hupfeld in 1853 (see below).

The position adopted by Astruc, Eichhorn, and Ilgen for the source analysis of Genesis is sometimes referred to as the *Older Documentary Hypothesis*. This particular approach represents the earliest phase of the source criticism of the Pentateuch. The conclusions reached by these early critics were based mainly on a consideration of the book of Genesis alone. Apart from the early chapters of Exodus, no attempt was made to extend the theory to include the other books of the Pentateuch. Furthermore, source criticism as a methodology arose more by chance than by design. It was the presence of particular phenomena in Genesis that led Astruc, Eichhorn, and Ilgen to propose the existence of earlier literary sources, and these same phenomena continued to form the basis of future scholarly research. Thus from its inception source analysis of the Pentateuch has relied heavily on the presence in Genesis of differing names for God and apparently duplicate accounts of the same events.

6. J. G. Eichhorn, *Einleitung ins Alte Testament* (Leipzig: Weidmann & Reich, 1780–83).
7. Cf. T. K. Cheyne, *Founders of Old Testament Criticism* (London: Methuen, 1893), 23.

These initial developments in source criticism were soon recognized by scholars interested in how the theology of the Old Testament developed. Especially noteworthy is the pioneering contribution of Georg Lorenz Bauer (1755–1806), who has the distinction of being the first person to produce an Old Testament theology.[8] In the "Introduction" to his *Old Testament Theology*, he writes, "We shall endeavour to place before the reader an impartial investigation of their [the ancient Israelites] ideas of God, and their notions of his Providence: to trace the history of their religion, as it is to be collected from the Books of the sacred writers, through each successive stage of its development."[9] With this aim in view, Bauer begins by noting the importance of determining the "correct chronological arrangements" of the Old Testament books. He then asserts:

> It is, however, ascertained that very few of the Books were wholly written—and some of them not even partially written—by the men whose names they bear; and that there is scarcely a Book in the Old Testament, which can be regarded as the production of but one writer. Many of the Books are compilations, composed of Hebrew documents and fragmentary histories, collected, arranged, and much interlarded by a compiler of a subsequent age; whilst other Books, which at first sight wear the appearance of individuality, are, on closer inspection, discovered to have received interpolations, additions, and appendices of different ages, and from various sources. The consequence is, that notions of earlier and later times are so woven together in the same Book, that it is a work of labour and difficulty to disentangle them.[10]

This final remark about "notions of earlier and later times [being] woven together in the same Book" is highly significant. It opens the door for Bauer to impose on the Old Testament a very distinctive view of religious development.

According to Bauer, in the time of Abraham God was a family God, one of many deities. At the time of Moses, this family God, the God of their fathers, was raised to the rank of a national God. Later the prophets and sagas expanded belief in a national God into a monotheistic faith, believing God to be the "Creator of all men." Bauer's evolutionary view of religious development is reflected in these remarks:

> The more rude man's condition, the more imperfect are his Deities. The Gods of the savage are invested by him with human forms; they act after the manner of

---

8. The full title of G. L. Bauer's book is *Theologie des Alten Testaments: Oder Abriß der religiösen Begriffe der alten Hebräer: Von den ältesten Zeiten bis auf den Anfang der christlichen Epoche; Zum Gebrauch akademischer Vorlesungen* (Leipzig: Weygand, 1796). The ET is "extracted" from the German work (see next note).

9. G. L. Bauer, *The Theology of the Old Testament: Or, A Biblical Sketch of the Religious Opinions of the Ancient Hebrews*, trans. P. Harwood (London: Charles Fox, 1838), 1.

10. Ibid.

men, and are subject to human passions. But, as man progresses in civilisation, as his intelligence increases, and his moral views grow more just, his own mind gradually exalts and perfects the object of his adoration.[11]

Starting with this theory of religious development, Bauer argues that the Old Testament contains progressively changing portraits of God and how he administered the world. This argument, however, can be sustained only on the basis that the books of the Old Testament in their present form are inconsistent. Pointing to the "fragmentary character of these Books" with their "numerous contradictions and incongruities," Bauer writes,

When the fact is once established, that portions of the same Book were written by different men, at distinct and distant periods, it no longer remains impossible to comprehend how ideas and representations of God, so inconsistent with each other, should be found in the same page—how it could have arisen, that in one sentence God is portrayed as the Creator of the universe, and in the next as the family-God of the Patriarchs, or as the national-God of the Hebrews.[12]

Later Bauer incorporates into his study the firstfruits of critical thinking on the Old Testament. Building on the work of Astruc, Eichhorn, and Ilgen, in Genesis he distinguishes two records, the Record of Jehovah and the Record of Elohim, both of which were compiled in the time of David, drawing on earlier "ancient traditions, songs, and written memorials." He even suggests, following others, that much of Deuteronomy must have been written after the time of Moses, because it reflects a view of God superior to that found in Exodus to Numbers.

Bauer's contribution to the development of modern critical thinking about the Pentateuch tends to be overlooked by modern writers. His pioneering approach dominated Old Testament studies throughout the nineteenth century, although it was taken much further by subsequent writers with all sorts of important ramifications. Compared to later studies, Bauer's discussion is quite simplistic and unrefined: much of his book is largely a collection of biblical texts, arranged to support his developmental view of religion.

It is important to recognize, however, that Bauer's prior assumptions regarding the development of Israelite religion heavily influenced his dating of the different sources that he identified within the Pentateuch. This less-than-satisfactory approach continues to be an important feature of much modern research.

11. Ibid., 2. Bauer distinguishes the family God of the patriarchs from both the national God of the exodus and the universal God of the prophets. Yet such an approach distorts what the biblical texts claim in their received form. For example, the universal nature of Yahweh's reign is clearly stated in passages associated with Abraham (e.g., Gen. 14:19, 22; 18:25).
12. Ibid.

The Fragmentary Hypothesis

The initial phase of source criticism was followed by a second, which differed in two important aspects.

1. Attention was no longer focused solely on Genesis. The Pentateuch as a whole became the object of source analysis, and this was to have an important bearing on future studies.
2. It was argued that the sources were of such a fragmentary nature that they could not be viewed as documents. The idea that Genesis was composed from extensive documents was rejected. As a result, the Older Documentary Hypothesis gave way to the *Fragmentary Hypothesis*.

The earliest exponent of the Fragmentary Hypothesis was a Scottish Roman Catholic priest, Alexander Geddes (1737–1802). In 1792 in London he published the first volume of a work titled *The Holy Bible, or the Books accounted Sacred by Jews and Christians, otherwise called the Books of the Old and New Covenants, with various readings, explanatory notes and critical remarks*. This volume contained a new translation of the Pentateuch and the book of Joshua. In 1800, Geddes published another book on the Pentateuch, *Critical Remarks on the Hebrew corresponding with a new translation of the Bible*. In both works Geddes rejected Mosaic authorship of the Pentateuch. Instead, he argued that the Hexateuch ("six volumes," Genesis to Joshua) had been composed by an editor, living in Jerusalem during the reign of Solomon, who had combined numerous fragments. Geddes suggested that these fragments originated from two separate circles of tradition, one of which used the divine name Elohim, the other Yahweh. Geddes was influenced in favor of a fragmentary explanation of the sources by what he observed concerning the legal codes in the latter part of the Pentateuch. These, especially by their independent and self-sufficient nature, supported the idea that various fragments, rather than extensive documents, had been combined to form the Pentateuch as we now have it.

In his *Commentar über den Pentateuch* (vols. 1–2 [1802], 3 [1805]), Johann Severin Vater (1771–1826) developed the position adopted by Geddes. Vater regarded the book of Deuteronomy as the nucleus around which the Pentateuch had been constructed. He separated it from the other books of the Pentateuch, arguing that certain differences between the regulations in Deuteronomy and Leviticus could be explained only by positing multiple authorship. These differences chiefly concerned the relationship between priests and Levites, and their respective incomes. Vater then proceeded to discover some thirty-nine fragments used in the compilation of the Pentateuch shortly before the exile. He also equated part of Deuteronomy with the lawbook found in the time of Josiah (2 Kings 22).

Partial support for the Fragmentary Hypothesis came from Wilhelm Martin Leberecht de Wette (1780–1849), a scholar who was to play a significant role in the development of critical thinking on the Pentateuch.[13] In his doctoral thesis of 1805, *Dissertatio Critico-Exegetica qua Deuteronomium a prioribus Pentateuchi libris diversum alius cujusdam recentioris auctoris opus esse monstratur*, de Wette proposed that Deuteronomy had been composed in the time of King Josiah (ca. 621 BC) and was to be equated with the Book of the Law mentioned in 2 Kings 22. De Wette was convinced that the books of Joshua to Kings displayed no knowledge of Deuteronomic legislation before the time of Josiah. This was especially so with regard to Deuteronomy's emphasis on a central sanctuary and its laws on kingship (Deut. 17:14–20). This view of Deuteronomy was to become very influential in future discussions.

Later, in his *Beiträge zur Einleitung in das Alte Testament* (vols. 1 [1806], 2 [1807]), de Wette further developed his thinking on the Pentateuch. Having already placed the origin of Deuteronomy in the reign of Josiah, he considered the dating of Leviticus. On the basis of its legislation, he concluded that it did not originate in the time of Moses. At the earliest, Leviticus could be dated to the reign of Solomon. De Wette also argued that the cultic history recorded in the books of Joshua and Chronicles was unreliable and thus could not be used to reconstruct the development of cultic practices. He maintained that the oldest sections of the Pentateuch came from the time of David, and that later editors drew on these fragments in order to compile the whole Pentateuch. While maintaining a fragmentary approach to the rest of the Pentateuch, de Wette rejected the position of Geddes and Vater on Genesis. He suggested that in Genesis, and as far as Exodus 6, one main Elohistic document had been supplemented by sections from a Yahwistic source, or perhaps several such sources. This view of Genesis was to find substantial support among later scholars. Finally, de Wette revised his thinking on the composition of the rest of the Pentateuch: in the final two editions of his *Lehrbuch der historisch-kritischen Einleitung in die kanonischen und apokryphischen Bücher des Alten Testamentes*,[14] he rejected the Fragmentary Hypothesis.

The Supplementary Hypothesis

In 1823 Georg Heinrich August von Ewald (1803–75) proposed that the Hexateuch was composed of an Elohistic work that formed the *Grundschrift* (basic

13. For a fuller discussion of de Wette's contribution, see J. W. Rogerson, *W. M. L. de Wette, Founder of Modern Biblical Criticism: An Intellectual Biography*, JSOTSup 126 (Sheffield: JSOT Press, 1992).
14. W. M. L. de Wette, *Lehrbuch der historisch-kritischen Einleitung in die kanonischen und apokryphischen Bücher des Alten Testamentes*, 5th ed. (Berlin: G. Reimer, 1840); 6th ed. (Berlin: G. Reimer, 1845).

document).[15] The compiler of this original Elohistic document had incorporated into it older sections, such as the Decalogue and the Book of the Covenant. Subsequently, this Elohistic document was paralleled by one employing the divine name Yahweh. Eventually this later Yahwistic source, along with certain other material, was incorporated into the original Elohistic document. This theory has become known as the *Supplementary Hypothesis*.

In 1836 Friedrich Bleek published a work on Genesis, titled *De libri Geneseos origine atque indole historica observationes quaedam contra Bohlenum*, in which he argued that a Yahwistic editor during the period of the early monarchy supplemented an earlier Elohistic document (the *Grundschrift*). Significantly, Bleek viewed this Yahwistic editor as the compiler of Genesis. He also maintained that the Yahwistic supplements were from a parallel document. Later, during the reign of Josiah, a further redaction of the Pentateuch occurred when the compiler of Deuteronomy gave the Hexateuch its present form.

In his *Geschichte des Volkes Israel bis Christ*,[16] Ewald modified his earlier position by arguing that within the Pentateuch were sections that could not be assigned to the Elohistic, Yahwistic, or Deuteronomic documents. Ewald proposed that there were two Elohistic sources, one of which he designated the Book of Origins because of its concern to explain the origins of the Sabbath, circumcision, and bloodless meat. These two continuous Elohistic sources were combined and later supplemented by the work of the Yahwistic redactor (or editor). By adopting this position, Ewald combined the approaches of the Older Documentary Hypothesis and the Supplementary Hypothesis.

The New Documentary Hypothesis

The Supplementary Hypothesis, however, did not gain many adherents. This was probably due to the impact made by an alternative theory proposed by Hermann Hupfeld (1796–1866). In his *Die Quellen der Genesis und die Art ihrer Zusammensetzung von neuem untersucht*,[17] Hupfeld returned to a purely documentary explanation for the composition of Genesis, rejecting the idea of later supplements. While Hupfeld reverted to the approach first suggested in the Older Documentary Hypothesis, he also incorporated the results of subsequent studies. His theory was based primarily on the book of Genesis. Underlying Genesis, Hupfeld suggested, were three independent continuous

15. G. H. A. von Ewald, *Die Komposition der Genesis kritisch untersucht* (Braunschweig: L. Lucius, 1823).

16. G. H. A. von Ewald, *Geschichte des Volkes Israel bis Christ*, 7 vols. (Göttingen: Dieterich, 1843–59); ET, *The History of Israel*, trans. R. Martineau, 2nd ed., 8 vols. (London: Longmans, Green, 1869–85).

17. H. Hupfeld, *Die Quellen der Genesis und die Art ihrer Zusammensetzung von neuem untersucht* (Berlin: Wiegandt & Grieben, 1853).

sources; two of these employed the divine name Elohim, and the third used Yahweh. An editor who exercised considerable freedom in his use of the sources combined these documents to form Genesis. Hupfeld called the older of the Elohistic documents the *Urschrift* (original). Significantly, two-thirds of the total *Urschrift* came in the initial nineteen chapters of Genesis and closely resembled the Elohist of Astruc and Eichhorn. With Genesis 20, the *jüngerer* or *second Elohist* commenced, and in the subsequent chapters of Genesis it was the more dominant of the two Elohistic documents. Concerning the *Urschrift*, Hupfeld observed that it had a particular interest in priestly matters; later this document became known as the *Priestly Document*, or P.

In 1854 Eduard Riehm obtained widespread support for the earlier view of de Wette that Deuteronomy had been composed independently of the other books of the Pentateuch.[18] When Hupfeld's theory of the composition of Genesis was extended to include the whole of the Pentateuch, Riehm's conclusions were incorporated. This resulted in the view, sometimes designated as the *New Documentary Hypothesis*, that the Pentateuch was composed of four documents that were combined by a redactor. Concerning the dating of the sources, it was proposed that they should be placed in the order: *Urschrift* or First Elohist (P); Jüngerer or Second Elohist (E); Yahwist (J);[19] Deuteronomy (D).[20]

The position advocated by Hupfeld gained support from a number of scholars. Two scholars in particular deserve special mention. A student of Hupfeld, Edward Böhmer, carefully separated the text of Genesis into the three sources: P, E, and J.[21] Böhmer also offered an alternative dating of the sources. He placed the *Urschrift* (P) in the reign of David, the Yahwist (J) in the time of Elisha (ninth century BC), and the Second Elohist (E) in the reign of Jeroboam (ca. 793–753 BC). Finally, a redactor combined these documents during the reign of Josiah (ca. 639–609 BC). In 1869 Theodor Nöldeke provided, in his *Untersuchungen zur Kritik des Alten Testament*,[22] what was to become accepted as the definitive outline of the *Urschrift* P. In contrast to Böhmer, however, he dated the *Urschrift* to the period shortly after the reign of Solomon.

The Documentary Hypothesis of Graf, Vatke, and Wellhausen

The assertion of the New Documentary Hypothesis that the Pentateuch was composed of four documents found general acceptance. However, a further

18. E. Riehm, *Die Gesetzgebung Mosis im Lande Moab* (Gotha: Friedrich Andreas Perthes, 1854).

19. The siglum "J" is derived from the German spelling "Jahve."

20. Cf. W. M. L. de Wette, *Lehrbuch der historisch-kritischen Einleitung*, rev. E. Schrader, 8th ed. (Berlin: G. Reimer, 1869).

21. E. Böhmer, *Das Erste Buch der Thora* (Halle: Buchh. des Waisenhauses, 1862).

22. T. Nöldeke, *Untersuchungen zur Kritik des Alten Testament* (Kiel: Schwers, 1869).

development modified the theory significantly. Although most scholars were prepared to accept the division of the Pentateuch into four documents, doubts were expressed about Hupfeld's dating of these sources. Eventually a new theory regarding the order of the documents was formulated and propagated chiefly through the labors of three scholars: Karl Heinrich Graf (1815–69), Wilhelm Vatke (1806–82), and especially Julius Wellhausen (1844–1918).

In his *Die geschichtlichen Bücher des Alten Testaments: Zwei historisch-kritische Untersuchungen* (1866), Graf adopted the view of de Wette that Deuteronomy was from the time of Josiah. By comparing the cultic legislation contained in the rest of the Pentateuch with that of Deuteronomy, Graf observed that the JE legislation was earlier than D, whereas the P material was later.[23] Like de Wette, he also rejected the historical witness of the book of Chronicles to the cultic institutions. Graf, however, took matters further by arguing that references to the tabernacle in P were merely fictional. The tabernacle itself had never existed; the detailed descriptions of it were based on the temple of the postexilic period.

Concerning the composition of the Pentateuch, Graf initially maintained a type of supplementary hypothesis, arguing that the narrative sections composing the *Urschrift* of Genesis were early. However, Graf's views were criticized by various scholars; as a result in 1869 he adopted a modified form of the New Documentary Hypothesis. In contrast to Hupfeld, Graf dated the *Urschrift*, or First Elohist (P), after Deuteronomy. Support for Graf's position came from the Dutch scholar Abraham Kuenen (1828–91). In 1869–70 he published a work titled *De godsdienst van Israël*, in which he also argued that Hupfeld's *Urschrift* ought to be dated to the postexilic period.

Vatke's contribution to the debate over the ordering of the sources arose from his interest in the work of the philosopher Hegel. Influenced by Hegel's views on the development of civilization, Vatke argued that there were three distinctive stages in the development of Israelite religion that could be aligned with the pentateuchal sources. The earliest phase, as witnessed in JE, was a religion that emphasized nature/fertility. The next stage of religious development, as reflected in D, centered on the spiritual and ethical ideas associated with the eighth-century prophets. Eventually there evolved out of these a conception of religion that was legalistic in outlook, emphasizing the importance of cultic rituals involving priests and sacrifices.

Marrying the views of Graf and Vatke, Wellhausen propagated this revised Documentary Hypothesis with remarkable skill and conviction. His

---

23. K. H. Graf, *Die geschichtlichen Bücher des Alten Testaments: Zwei historisch-kritische Untersuchungen* (Leipzig: Weigel, 1866). Graf was influenced by his teacher Eduard Reuss. According to J. Blenkinsopp, *The Pentateuch* (London: SCM, 1992), 7, "Reuss pointed out that the pre-exilic prophets betray no familiarity with the Mosaic legal system, and that the ritual law in particular, closely related as it is to Ezekiel, could not have originated earlier than the exilic period (sixth century BC)."

views appeared first in 1876–77 in a series of offprints for the *Jahrbücher für deutsche Theologie*, titled "Die Composition des Hexateuchs." These were later reprinted in the second volume of *Skizzen und Vorarbeiten*.[24] In 1878 appeared Wellhausen's *Geschichte Israels I*,[25] which was published in later editions under the title *Prolegomena zur Geschichte Israels*.[26] Relying on the work of the scholars who preceded him, Wellhausen cogently argued that the Pentateuch was composed of four distinct documents. The earliest of these was the Yahwistic source, J. The next document was the Elohistic source, E. Later these two sources were combined by an editor whom Wellhausen designated the "Jehovist" (R[JE]). For Wellhausen, this redactor played such an important role in shaping the Hexateuch that in his *Prolegomena* he focuses attention principally on the Jehovist, rather than on J and E as separate sources. Later, in the time of Josiah, the book of Deuteronomy, D, was composed.[27] This first edition of Deuteronomy was expanded by the addition of narrative, homiletic, and legal material. Since this additional material showed a knowledge of JE but not P, Wellhausen concluded that JE and D were combined before P was added. Then during the fifth century BC the Priestly Document P (Hupfeld's *Urschrift*) was composed. This occurred when an independent Priestly narrative, which recorded the covenants associated with Adam, Noah, Abraham, and Sinai, was expanded by the addition of extensive Priestly legislation. Finally, P too was combined with the earlier material. By so ordering the sources Wellhausen produced the now-famous sequence J, E, D, P. Though Wellhausen recognized the existence of four main sources, he also believed that the sources underwent redactional modifications. Consequently, the process by which the Pentateuch was composed was exceptionally complex.

Although Wellhausen was somewhat uncommitted concerning the dating of J and E, following scholars tended to favor a date for J in the second half of the ninth century BC, with E being composed about a century later. Nicholson writes, "According to the Wellhausen 'school' the documents were dated as follows:

J: c. 840 BC

E: c. 700

D: c. 623

P: c. 500–450."[28]

---

24. J. Wellhausen, *Skizzen und Vorarbeiten* (Berlin: G. Reimer, 1885); later reprinted with additional material in *Die Composition des Hexateuchs und der historischen Bücher des Alten Testaments*, 2nd ed. (Berlin: G. Reimer, 1889).

25. J. Wellhausen, *Geschichte Israels*, vol. 1 (Berlin: G. Reimer, 1878).

26. ET, J. Wellhausen, *Prolegomena to the History of Israel* (Edinburgh: A&C Black, 1885).

27. For a critique of this dating of Deuteronomy, see G. J. Wenham, "The Date of Deuteronomy: Linch-Pin of Old Testament Criticism," *Them* 10, no. 3 (1985): 15–20; 11, no. 1 (1985): 15–18.

28. E. W. Nicholson, *The Pentateuch in the Twentieth Century: The Legacy of Julius Wellhausen* (Oxford: Clarendon, 1998), 21, here using "c." for circa.

Throughout Europe, Wellhausen's views were generally well received. In his native Germany most scholars quickly adopted his approach. In Holland, Kuenen propounded the views of Wellhausen in his *Historisch-kritisch onderzoek naar het ontstaan en de verzameling van de boeken des Ouden Verbonds*.[29] In France, E. Reuss, who many years earlier had influenced Graf, supported the new theory in his *L'histoire sainte et la loi*,[30] and in Britain, William Robertson Smith became an important advocate of the new theory.[31] Indeed, the influence of the new hypothesis was such that by 1890 the views of Graf, Vatke, and Wellhausen gained almost total acceptance in the world of biblical scholarship. Although Wellhausen viewed his ideas as undermining the authority of Scripture, they were positively promoted by leading Christian theologians.[32]

Models for Explaining the Composition of the Pentateuch

Before proceeding to consider in more detail various aspects of the Documentary Hypothesis, we should briefly observe how the stages identified above reflect three different models by which the composition of the Pentateuch may be described.

The *documentary* theories may be thought of as viewing the Pentateuch like a rope made up of several colored strands. Woven together, these strands run throughout the Pentateuch, with occasionally one color being more dominant than the others. Since each strand has its own distinctive features, it is possible to distinguish it from the rest. In the case of the Documentary Hypothesis, the process by which the rope was formed initially involved two strands being combined; to these another strand was added, and then later yet another.

In contrast to the rope-model of the Documentary Hypothesis, *fragmentary* theories view the Pentateuch like a chain composed of assorted links. These links are made from different types of material and may vary greatly in their size and shape; some, however, may share common features. The Pentateuch was created when these links were joined. An important aspect of this approach

29. A. Kuenen, *Historisch-kritisch onderzoek naar het ontstaan en de verzameling van de boeken des Ouden Verbonds*, 2nd ed., vol. 1 (Leiden: Akademische Boekhandel van P. Engels, 1885); ET, *An Historico-Critical Inquiry into the Origin and Composition of the Hexateuch*, trans. P. H. Wicksteed (London: Macmillan, 1886), based on 2nd ed. of *Historisch-kritisch*.

30. E. Reuss, *L'histoire sainte et la loi* (Paris: Libraire Sandoz et Fischbacher, 1879).

31. Cf. W. R. Smith, *The Old Testament in the Jewish Church: Twelve Lectures on Biblical Criticism* (Edinburgh: A&C Black, 1881); idem, *The Prophets of Israel and Their Place in History* (Edinburgh: A&C Black, 1882).

32. E.g., H. Schultz, *Old Testament Theology: The Religion of Revelation in Its Pre-Christian Stage of Development*, trans. J. A. Paterson, 1st ed. (Edinburgh: T&T Clark, 1892), offers an exceptionally clear exposition of the Documentary Hypothesis. His work was influential in promoting the idea in the English-speaking world; a second edition of the translation was published in 1895.

is that the Pentateuch may be viewed as having been composed of blocks or sections of material that originally had nothing in common. These were later joined end to end to create a longer work.

The third model, corresponding to *supplementary* theories, views the Pentateuch as a colored string stretched out in a line. The string is then broken in various places, and other pieces of different-colored strings are knotted in, adding to the length of the original string. As a result the finished string has one dominant color, supplemented by others.

All these models seek to explain the existence within the Pentateuch of features that convey either a sense of unity or diversity. As we shall observe later, although there can be little doubt that diverse materials have been brought together to form the Pentateuch, it is also apparent that the narrative is more unified that many scholars allow.

Distinctive Vocabulary

For source criticism to work, it is necessary to have definitive criteria by which source documents can be clearly distinguished from one another. Fundamental to uncovering the source documents is the assumption that each author has a personal style of writing. Since it is not always possible to define a writer's literary style with precision, vocabulary provides the best index by which to determine authorship. As we have already observed, it was the unusual distribution of the divine names, Yahweh and Elohim, that first prompted scholars to discern the presence of two sources in the book of Genesis. Beginning here, source critics proceeded to develop vocabulary lists for each of the main source documents.[33] While in theory vocabulary is a very suitable criterion for distinguishing sources, in practice complications exist.

The presence of a particular word or phrase in various passages need not indicate a common source document; this could be due to the fact that all the relevant passages address the same subject. For example, the expression "with all your heart and with all your soul" is generally taken to be characteristic of the D source, occurring within the Pentateuch only in Deuteronomy 4:29; 6:5; 10:12; 11:13; 13:3; 26:16; 30:2, 6, 10.[34] All, however, come in Moses's exhortatory speeches addressed to the Israelites as they prepare to enter the promised land of Canaan. The context clearly determines the presence of this expression. Moreover, in the lengthy speeches in Deuteronomy we hear Moses using his own words when addressing the people of Israel; elsewhere he more

33. Examples of such lists may be found in various works. In particular, see S. R. Driver, *An Introduction to the Literature of the Old Testament*, 9th ed. (Edinburgh: T&T Clark, 1913), 116–59.

34. The only other OT occurrence of this phrase is Josh. 22:5, where the text is alluding back to Moses's exhortation to the Israelites.

often mediates God's words to the Israelites. In the light of these observations, it is reasonable to conclude that the expression "with all your heart and with all your soul" is indicative of a particular individual speaking in a distinctive context. This hardly justifies its use as a criterion for source analysis.

Two words taken by source critics to be synonyms and consequently assigned to separate sources may on closer inspection be found to have slightly different connotations; this in turn may account for the use of one term in preference to the other in certain contexts. For example, the geographical name Horeb is frequently said to be indicative of the E source; the other sources use Sinai.[35] Yet from a study of how both words are used in the Pentateuch, it is apparent that Horeb refers to a broad region, within which lies a smaller area known as Sinai. On this basis the use of the term Horeb in Exodus 17:6, for example, is determined by geographical considerations rather than the presence of the E source.

A survey of all the supposedly distinctive vocabulary terms reveals that words taken to be typical of one source occasionally come in passages assigned to another source. Clearly this completely undermines the usefulness of such terms for distinguishing source documents. Even if just one exception is noted, what guarantee can a source critic have that another exception does not exist? For example, the expression "land of Canaan" is normally taken to be typical of the P source (e.g., Gen. 12:5; 17:8).[36] Yet its presence in various verses that may be attributed to either J or E (cf. Gen. 35:6; 42:5, 7, 13, 29, 32; 44:8) clearly undermines its usefulness as a P criterion.

An element of circularity exists in the use of vocabulary to determine sources. On the basis of various occurrences, a term may be viewed as typical of a particular source document. A further occurrence of the same word may come in a passage that on other grounds might be thought to belong to a different source. In such a situation, the verse or phrase containing the term is likely to be viewed as an interpolation, with the word retained as a criterion for source analysis. However, it would surely be much more appropriate to conclude that in these circumstances the term should not be used for source analysis: the one passage in question may indicate that the term is not unique to one source.

These observations draw brief attention to the practical difficulties inherent in trying to recover the source documents of the Pentateuch on the basis of distinctive vocabulary. Given the special significance of the divine names in this regard, we shall consider them in more detail.

The Divine Names in Genesis

The divine names have been widely acknowledged as one of the main criteria for the source analysis of the Pentateuch, although strictly speaking, as we

35. Driver, *Introduction*, 82, 119.
36. Cf. J. Skinner, *Genesis*, 2nd ed., ICC (Edinburgh: T&T Clark, 1930), 289.

shall observe, their use should be confined to the whole of Genesis and the first few chapters of Exodus. Their significance is underlined by the fact that two of the pentateuchal sources are designated after them, the Yahwistic (J) and the Elohistic (E). With good reason Redford remarks that this criterion "has become virtually an article of faith among biblical scholars."[37]

Evidence supporting the claim that the peculiar arrangement of the divine names in Genesis is due to sources is drawn from a few significant passages: Genesis 4:26; Exodus 3:5–15; 6:3. Of these, Exodus 6:3, which is assigned to the Priestly Writer, is generally understood to state that the patriarchs Abraham, Isaac, and Jacob did not know God by the name Yahweh: "I appeared to Abraham, to Isaac and to Jacob as El Shaddai, but by my name Yahweh I did not make myself known to them" (NIV 1984). Although it is not explicitly expressed, Exodus 3:13–15, ascribed to E, may imply that the name Yahweh was only first revealed to Moses. Thus in the early chapters of Exodus the E and P sources apparently affirm that the patriarchs of Genesis were not familiar with the divine epithet Yahweh. This, it is suggested, is supported by the observation that "Yahweh" never appears in the E and P material preserved in Genesis. In marked contrast, the J source introduces the name Yahweh right at the beginning of Genesis, and the importance of the name is indicated in Genesis 4:26: "At that time men began to call on the name of the LORD [Yahweh]." Only by dividing Genesis into sources, it is argued, can we reconcile the apparently conflicting statements found in Exodus 6:3 and Genesis 4:26.[38]

This interpretation of the evidence, however, creates an intriguing problem. Since the time of Wellhausen it has been customary to view J as the oldest of the pentateuchal sources. Yet if J existed before E and P, why did these later sources state that the patriarchs did not know the name Yahweh? Were the authors of E and P not already aware that the patriarchs knew God as Yahweh? In its present form, the Documentary Hypothesis offers no satisfactory explanation for this problem.

Although doubts have been expressed in the past about the validity of the criterion of divine names,[39] it is still widely viewed as an important guide to the sources underlying the Pentateuch, and especially the book of Genesis.

---

37. D. B. Redford, *A Study of the Biblical Story of Joseph (Genesis 37–50)*, VTSup 20 (Leiden: Brill, 1970), 108.

38. For an outline of various attempts to harmonize the Exodus statements about the origin of the name "Yahweh" with the presence of the epithet in Genesis, see G. H. Parke-Taylor, *Yahweh: The Divine Name in the Bible* (Waterloo, ON: Wilfrid Laurier University Press, 1975), 18–62. The difficulties presented by Exod. 6:3 are discussed in T. D. Alexander, *Abraham in the Negev: A Source-Critical Investigation of Genesis 20:1–22:19* (Carlisle: Paternoster, 1997), 90–101.

39. E.g., U. Cassuto, *The Documentary Hypothesis and the Composition of the Pentateuch* (Jerusalem: Magnes, 1961), 15–41; M. H. Segal, "El, Elohim, and Yhwh in the Bible," *JQR* 46 (1955): 89–115.

Nevertheless, it is now acknowledged that a purely "mechanical application" of this criterion is unsatisfactory.[40] This is so for a number of reasons:

- Whereas Yahweh is a personal name, Elohim is a common noun. While there are many occasions in Genesis where it is possible to interchange these terms, there are contexts that permit only the use of Elohim as a common noun meaning "deity."[41]

- There are some obvious instances where the use of a particular divine name is determined by the context. For example, in Genesis 3:1–5 the serpent and the woman use the designation Elohim, rather than Yahweh Elohim, which is used elsewhere throughout Genesis 2:4–3:24. As his adversary, it is hardly surprising that the serpent avoids using God's personal name, Yahweh.

- "The name for God is not as stringent a criterion for J as it is for P (or E)."[42] Given that in E and P the divine name Yahweh was first revealed to Moses, we would clearly not expect to find "Yahweh" appearing in E or P passages occurring in Genesis. There is, however, no reason why Yahweh should not appear in E or P narratives describing events after the revelation of this new name to Moses; indeed, we would expect this to be the case. Similarly, there is no reason why the epithet Elohim may not be present in any J passage.[43] Thus, strictly speaking, in Genesis only the presence of "Yahweh" in a text can be viewed as a decisive indicator for source analysis; the presence of Elohim in a particular verse does not automatically require that it should be assigned to either E or P.

- An examination of biblical material outside Genesis reveals that "variation in the name for God is certainly possible in a literary unity."[44] The presence of both divine names in a single passage does not necessarily imply that two separate accounts have been integrated. It is possible for one author to use both divine epithets.

- We should be alert to the possibility that the biblical texts may have been modified as a result of editorial activity. Thus, for example, J. Skinner, supporting the Documentary Hypothesis, argues that the presence of

40. C. Westermann, *Genesis 1–11: A Commentary*, trans. John J. Scullion (Minneapolis: Augsburg, 1984), 579; cf. R. N. Whybray, *The Making of the Pentateuch: A Methodological Study*, JSOTSup 53 (Sheffield: Sheffield Academic Press, 1987), 63–72.

41. E.g., Gen. 9:26; 17:7, 8; 24:3, 7, 12, 27, 42, 48; 26:24; 27:20; 28:13 (2x), 21; 31:5, 19, 29, 30, 32, 34, 35, 42 (2x), 53 (2x); 32:9 (2x); 33:20; 35:2, 4; 43:23 (2x); 46:1, 3; 50:17.

42. Westermann, *Genesis 1–11*, 579.

43. Cf. Skinner, *Genesis*, l–li.

44. Westermann, *Genesis 1–11*, 579; cf. Segal, "El, Elohim, and Yhwh," 94–97; Whybray, *Making of the Pentateuch*, 67–68.

Yahweh in Genesis 22:11, 14; 28:21; and 31:49 is "due to the intentional action of a redactor."[45]

- It is not inconceivable that in some instances a divine name was changed merely by accident in the transmission of the Genesis text. We cannot be completely certain that the Masoretic Text accurately preserves the arrangement of the divine names following the amalgamation of the supposed sources J, E, and P. This possibility is supported by the different textual traditions found in the Samaritan Pentateuch and the Septuagint.[46]

All these observations underline the danger of adopting a purely mechanical application of the divine-names criterion for source analysis.

In spite of these difficulties, the idea that Genesis is comprised of sources that use different divine names still attracts support, and many scholars appear content to accept the Documentary Hypothesis explanation for the distribution of the divine epithets in Genesis. As Westermann observes, "None of the attempts to explain the variation in the name for God in another way have [sic] so far led to any convincing result."[47] While this may be so, the criterion of divine names cannot, in the light of the facts observed above, be relied on to provide a definitive source analysis of Genesis.

Doublets

Alongside vocabulary, the source analysis of the Pentateuch has relied heavily on the idea that the text contains duplicate accounts of the same events, often described as "doublets." These fall into two main types:

1. The same event may be described in two quite separate episodes. Thus, for example, there are two accounts of Abraham pretending that his wife is his sister (Gen. 12:10–20; 20:1–18; a similar incident involving Isaac comes in Gen. 26:1–11). In each episode Sarah is taken by a foreign ruler and only after divine intervention is returned to Abraham. According to the Documentary Hypothesis, Genesis 12:10–20 represents J's version of this event, and Genesis 20:1–18 is E's version.

45. Skinner, *Genesis*, l–li. See also the suggestion of G. J. Wenham, "The Religion of the Patriarchs," in *Essays on the Patriarchal Narratives*, ed. A. R. Millard and D. J. Wiseman (Leicester: Inter-Varsity, 1980), 157–88, that the name Yahweh was inserted into the Genesis material by a Yahwistic redactor. For a critique of Wenham's position, see Alexander, *Abraham in the Negev*, 93–96.
46. For a fuller discussion of the textual evidence, see J. Skinner, *The Divine Names in Genesis* (London: Hodder & Stoughton, 1914). The SP differs from MT in some nine cases (7:1, 9; 14:22; 20:18; 28:4; 31:7, 9, 16a; 35:9b). The LXX manuscripts preserve over sixty readings where the divine names differ from the MT.
47. Westermann, *Genesis 1–11*, 578.

2. Some doublets involve a single episode that is dissected into two separate accounts. Thus, for example, it is argued that the flood narrative
in Genesis 6–9 is an amalgam of two versions, one deriving from J and
the other from P. The existence of doublets is an important factor in
support of the Documentary Hypothesis, for they indicate that the
different source documents used in the composition of the Pentateuch
parallel one another in terms of contents.

Space does not permit a detailed critique of all the supposed doublets found
within the Pentateuch.[48] It is my experience that under close inspection
many of these doublets do not support the existence of once-independent
parallel sources.[49] Thus, for example, the account of Sarah's abduction by
Abimelech in Genesis 20 presupposes that the reader is already familiar with
a similar incident that has occurred previously. Without a prior knowledge
of the events described in Genesis 12:11–15, it is impossible to make sense
of Genesis 21:2. This strongly suggests that the account in Genesis 20 was
composed as part of a document that already contained the material in Genesis 12:10–20 (or something very similar). This suggestion argues against
a *documentary* solution to the presence of these two incidents in Genesis;
possibly Genesis 20 was composed as a supplement to an already-existing
document. When, however, all the source-analysis criteria are considered
in Genesis 12:10–20 and 20:1–18, it is highly likely that the same writer
composed both episodes.[50]

The issues involved in determining the presence of true doublets within the
Pentateuch are complex. Occasionally the arguments are so finely balanced
that it is difficult to be confident that parallel source documents exist. This is
certainly the case with regard to the flood narrative.[51]

In the preceding paragraphs we have focused on distinctive vocabulary
and doublets. While these represent the mainstays of the Documentary
Hypothesis, other criteria are often discussed (e.g., contradictions, theological outlook). The latter, however, are of much less importance in terms
of supporting the Documentary Hypothesis, for they do not automatically
support the existence of parallel source documents. These other criteria were

48. For a fuller list of "doublets" of both types, see R. E. Friedman, "Torah (Pentateuch),"
ABD 6:609.

49. For a much fuller discussion of the main doublets found within the Abraham narrative
in Genesis 11:27–25:11, see Alexander, *Abraham in the Negev*, 32–69.

50. See ibid., 32–51.

51. The arguments for and against the source analysis of the flood narrative are debated in
a series of articles by Wenham and Emerton: cf. G. J. Wenham, "The Coherence of the Flood
Narrative," *VT* 28 (1978): 336–48; J. A. Emerton, "An Examination of Some Attempts to Defend
the Unity of the Flood Narrative in Genesis," *VT* 37 (1987): 401–20; 38 (1988): 1–21; and G. J.
Wenham, "Method in Pentateuchal Source Criticism," *VT* 41 (1991): 84–109.

recognized only after the various sources were isolated by using distinctive vocabulary and doublets.[52]

Implications for the History of Israelite Religion

An important aspect of the Documentary Hypothesis is the impact that it has had on the study of Israelite religion. No longer was the Pentateuch viewed as providing evidence of religious practices dating from before the period of the monarchy. Rather, it consisted of four source documents, J, E, D, and P, dated respectively to the tenth–ninth, ninth–eighth, seventh, and sixth–fifth centuries BC. Since each source supposedly provides a snapshot of the religious customs being practiced at the time of its composition, it was possible by comparing them to see how Israelite religion evolved from the tenth century through to the fifth century BC.[53] The impact of this development can be seen, for example, in the modern assessment of the history of Passover.[54]

By comparing Exodus 23:15–16 and Exodus 34:18–22 (both J) with Deuteronomy 16:1–17 (D), Wellhausen concluded that in ancient Israel there were three main feasts: Unleavened Bread, Weeks, and Tabernacles/Booths.[55] On the basis of their earliest titles (Unleavened Bread, Harvest, and Ingathering, as reflected in Exod. 23 and 34), they were clearly agricultural in origin, probably taken over by the Israelites from the Canaanites. Furthermore, because the J sections of the Pentateuch never mention it, the Passover could not have existed when J was composed.[56] Wellhausen then suggested, on the basis of Deuteronomy 16:1–8 (D), that the Passover and the Feast of Unleavened Bread were amalgamated about the time of Josiah's reforms in 621 BC. Before this they were totally unconnected. Subsequent developments, as revealed in the Priestly Writer's portrayal of the Passover (as found in Exod. 12:1–20, 28, 43–49; 13:1–2; Lev. 23:5–8; Num. 9:1–14; 28:16–25), confirmed this major innovation.[57] By concluding that the Passover and the Feast of Unleavened Bread were unrelated before about 620 BC, Wellhausen overturned the long-standing tradition, highlighted especially in Exodus 12–13, that both originated as commemorations of the Israelite exodus from Egypt. So cogent were

52. For a much fuller critique of the criteria used in support of the Documentary Hypothesis, see Whybray, *Making of the Pentateuch*, 43–131.

53. For this reason Wellhausen's influential study was titled *Prolegomena to the History of Israel*.

54. For a fuller discussion, see T. D. Alexander, "The Passover Sacrifice," in *Sacrifice in the Bible*, ed. R. T. Beckwith and M. Selman (Carlisle: Paternoster; Grand Rapids: Baker, 1995), 1–24.

55. Wellhausen, *Prolegomena*, 83–120.

56. To support this idea Wellhausen, ibid., 85n1, emends the expression *ḥag happāsaḥ*, "feast of the Passover," in Exod. 34:25, to *ḥaggî*, "my feast," on the basis of Exod. 23:18.

57. E.g., the precise dating of the Passover; more exact specifications regarding the offerings.

his arguments for the original independence of the Passover and the Feast of Unleavened Bread that Wellhausen's work heralded a new era in the study of the early history of these sacred feasts.

If the Passover was unconnected to the Feast of Unleavened Bread before the time of Josiah, how did it originate, and what form did it take? For his part, Wellhausen suggested that the Passover developed in a pastoral rather than an agricultural setting, as the offering of the firstfruits of sheep and cattle.[58] Expressing gratitude to God for fruitful flocks and herds, it was the oldest of the feasts and was not tied to any particular time in the year. Although the offering of firstfruits originated in Israel's nomadic past, it was rarely observed during the early monarchy; hence it is not mentioned in the Book of the Covenant (Exod. 22:29–30). It was revived in Judah after the fall of the northern kingdom in 721 BC, to be amalgamated almost a century later with the Feast of Unleavened Bread. Only at this stage was the name *pesaḥ*, Passover, introduced.

Other writers, accepting the validity of Wellhausen's general approach, revised substantially his picture of the Passover's origin. G. B. Gray sought to isolate various ancient features of the Passover by focusing on its later customs.[59] He concluded that the Passover was originally observed by nomadic Israelites on the night of the full moon nearest the spring equinox. In its earliest form it consisted of a sacrificial meal in which the entire victim was eaten raw, with the blood still in it.[60] This custom was later modified: the victim was now cooked and its blood smeared on the doorposts. The blood ritual had an apotropaic purpose: to protect those within from some power outside by providing a "re-inforced closed door."[61] With the centralization of sacrificial worship in Jerusalem in 620 BC, the practice of smearing the blood on the door was abandoned; the sacrificial meal alone continued to be observed.

According to R. de Vaux, the Passover began as the springtime sacrifice of a young animal, not necessarily the firstborn, by nomadic or seminomadic shepherds in order to guarantee the prosperity of the flock.[62] It occurred before

58. The inadequacy of this reconstruction is highlighted by M. Haran, "The Passover Sacrifice," in *Studies in the Religion of Ancient Israel*, ed. G. W. Anderson, VTSup 23 (Leiden: Brill, 1972), 94–95.

59. G. B. Gray, *Sacrifice in the Old Testament: Its Theory and Practice* (Oxford: Clarendon, 1925), 337–82.

60. Gray, in ibid., 368, observes that in Exod. 12:9 and 12:46 it is forbidden to eat the victim raw or to break any of its bones. He concludes, "A legal prohibition is commonly directed against what is, or has been, actual practice. It has therefore been inferred that at one time the Paschal victim was eaten raw, and that the bones, having been broken and pounded for the purpose, were eaten as well as the flesh."

61. Ibid., 362.

62. R. de Vaux, *Ancient Israel: Its Life and Institutions*, 2nd ed. (London: Darton, Longman & Todd, 1965), 484–93. He appears to follow L. Rost's comparative study of the customs of nomadic Arabs, "Weidewechsel und altisraelitischer Festkalendar," *ZDPV* 66 (1943): 205–16;

the tribal migration and required neither a priest nor an altar. An important feature of the feast, which took place at the full moon, was the smearing of blood on the tent poles in order to drive away evil powers. Various features of the later Passover celebration reflect its nomadic origin:

> The victim was roasted over a fire without any kitchen utensils; it was eaten with unleavened bread (which is still the normal bread of Bedouin to-day), and with bitter herbs (which does not mean vegetables grown in the garden, but the desert plants which Bedouin pick to season their food). The ritual prescribed that those eating it should have their belts already fastened, sandals on their feet (as if they were going to make a long journey on foot), and a shepherd's stick in one hand.[63]

Before the Israelite settlement of Canaan, the Passover was a common feast celebrated at the central sanctuary of the tribal federation. With the decentralization of cultic worship after Israel's occupation of Canaan, it became a family feast. Much later, as a result of Josiah's decision to have all cultic worship centralized in Jerusalem, it reverted to a common feast.

The speculative nature of such histories has been highlighted by J. Van Seters. On methodological grounds he rejects these attempts to reconstruct the Passover's origin through either the backward projection of later features or the use of comparative customs.

> For all its ingenious reconstructions the disadvantages of the traditio-historical method are considerable. Since it speculates about the shape of the pre-literate tradition[,] its theories cannot be falsified by an appeal to the present texts. There is also no way to make any judgment between radically different proposals and thus theories about the cult have greatly proliferated. Furthermore, those who follow this method have never demonstrated by comparative literature that tradition-history is anything but a completely artificial construction of biblical scholars.[64]

Because they cannot be substantiated, traditio-historical theories about the Passover's origin must be treated with the utmost caution. They clearly do not provide a very secure foundation on which to base a reconstruction of the history of Passover. (For a fuller discussion of the traditio-historical method,

---

reprinted in L. Rost, *Das kleine Credo und andere Studien zum Alten Testament* (Heidelberg: Quelle & Meyer, 1965), 101–12. B. N. Wambacq has queried the relevance of Rost's study; see "Les origines de la *Pesaḥ* israélite," *Bib* 57 (1976): 206–24, 301–26. In particular he observes that the blood rite among nomadic Arabs concerns their arrival and settlement in a new location, whereas the Passover ritual in Exod. 12 focuses on the Israelites' departure from Egypt.

63. De Vaux, *Ancient Israel*, 489.

64. J. Van Seters, "The Place of the Yahwist in the History of Passover and Massot," *ZAW* 95 (1983): 169–70.

see chap. 3 under the headings "Traditio-Historical Criticism" and "The Limitations of Traditio-Historical Criticism Illustrated.")

Although Van Seters emphatically affirms the priority of source analysis for uncovering the true history of the Passover, he rejects Wellhausen's approach on a number of specific points:

1. He is convinced that the J material should be dated to the period of the exile, making D the earliest source, with J coming midway between D and P.
2. Although Wellhausen maintained that the Passover and the Feast of Unleavened Bread were first amalgamated in Deuteronomy 16, Van Seters views all the references to Unleavened Bread in Deuteronomy 16 as later additions.
3. He supports the view of J. Halbe that the Feast of Unleavened Bread did not originate as an ancient Canaanite agricultural festival.[65] Rather, he dates it to the exilic period, when the eating of the Passover sacrifice could no longer be observed due to the destruction of the temple; the eating of unleavened bread became the basis of a substitute festival.
4. He reassigns some of the material in Exodus 12–13 to different sources; 12:29–39 and 13:3–16 come from J; the remaining verses (12:1–28 and 13:1–2) are the product of P.[66]

In the light of these considerations, Van Seters proposes the following reconstruction of the Passover's history. As implied in the earliest source, D, the Passover was a one-day festival in the spring at a local sanctuary. After the slaughter of an animal from the flock or herd, there was a meal, eaten at night without unleavened bread. Then D restricted the celebration of the festival to a central sanctuary and introduced the idea that it was a commemoration of the exodus. About a century and a half later, with the destruction of the temple, it was no longer possible to celebrate the Passover. As a result, J instituted the Feast of Unleavened Bread as a substitute. However, this new feast lasted for a week, and prominence was given to the eating of unleavened bread, the one significant element retained from the Passover celebration. With the restoration of the temple after the exile, further modifications occurred, as witnessed in P.

65. J. Halbe, "Erwägungen zu Ursprung und Wesen des Massotfestes," *ZAW* 87 (1975): 325–34. Among the reasons listed by Halbe, the following are the most convincing: (1) the month of Abib (March–April) is too early for a harvest festival; (2) it is strange that a harvest celebration should be marked by the eating of unleavened bread; (3) a seven-day festival is hardly likely to have occurred at the beginning of the harvest; (4) a special reason, the exodus from Egypt, needs to be provided for celebrating the Feast of Unleavened Bread; this is not so for the true harvest feasts of Harvest (Weeks) and Ingathering (Tabernacles/Booths).

66. Van Seters's source analysis may be compared with the more traditional position adopted by Driver, *Introduction*, 28. He assigns Exod. 12:1–20, 28, 37a, 40–51; 13:1–2 to P; Exod. 12:29–30 to J; Exod. 12:31–36, 37b–39, 42a to E; and Exod. 12:21–27; 13:3–16 to JE.

The revived Passover celebration was combined with the Feast of Unleavened Bread. Yet this presented a problem for Jews living in the Diaspora. How could they, far removed from the sanctuary, participate in the new combined feast? To resolve the problem, each household was sanctified by means of a blood rite: "A small animal could be slaughtered as a sacrifice, its blood used to purify the house, and the animal cooked in such a way as to resemble an offering by fire."[67] To legitimize this activity, the Priestly Writer created the etiology of the blood rite of the exodus story.[68]

The contrasting proposals of Wellhausen and Van Seters highlight the variety of reconstructions possible for the history of the Passover. Their differing conclusions depend heavily on the source analysis of the relevant pentateuchal passages and their dating in relation to one another. Since space does not permit us to critique in detail here these differing views of Passover, several observations must suffice.

First, at the present time the whole question of the source analysis of the Pentateuch is in a state of flux. As we shall discover in chapter 3, the once-assured results of the Documentary Hypothesis no longer enjoy widespread acceptance. Recent studies have challenged both the validity of the criteria used to distinguish sources and the order in which they should be dated. In the light of these developments, we should be wary of reconstructing the history of the Passover on the basis of source-critical theories that lack widespread support.

Second, in the past it has generally been assumed that if a pentateuchal source shows no knowledge of a custom or practice, that feature did not exist when the source was composed. Yet conclusions drawn from the silence of the text may prove unwarranted. Two factors make this likely. On the one hand, some passages about the Passover are exceptionally brief (e.g., Exod. 34:25; Lev. 23:5; Num. 28:16). The absence of particular details may be due entirely to the succinct nature of the material.[69] On the other hand, if two sources have been combined, specific details in one source may be omitted for editorial reasons.[70] This is especially relevant regarding the narrative in Exodus 12–13, which is generally taken to be comprised of two or more sources. Little allow-

---

67. Van Seters, "Place of the Yahwist," 180–81.

68. This proposal raises a number of problems. The smearing of blood on the doorposts is mentioned only in connection with the original Passover night in Egypt. There is no hint that the blood was used in this way during later commemorations of the Passover. In view of the uniqueness of the original occasion, the Exodus narrative hardly provides a suitable etiology for justifying the adoption of this practice on future occasions. Furthermore, would the Priestly Writer have supported a practice that involved the offering of sacrifices by nonpriests? Finally, Van Seters offers no evidence of its having been practiced in the exilic or postexilic period, and no explanation as to why it ceased, presumably soon afterward, to be observed.

69. This difficulty is not overcome when scholars deliberately remove evidence from a passage on the basis that it is a later interpolation.

70. The source analysis of the flood narrative in Gen. 6–9 illustrates this possibility. Although the Yahwistic material contains no reference to the building of the ark, it clearly presupposes

ance is made for the fact that the editor(s) who combined the supposed sources may have deliberately omitted details already present in one source in favor of parallel details found in another of the sources. For example, while J alone mentions the use of a basin for catching the blood and of hyssop for smearing it on the doorposts (Exod. 12:21–27), we should not suppose that P's silence about these matters means that he had no knowledge of them. We must allow for the possibility that some material became redundant when the sources were combined.[71] Unfortunately, we have no way to know how little or how much material has been lost in the editorial process, assuming that parallel sources were once combined, an assumption widely made but impossible to prove.

In the light of these observations, it is apparent that the task of reconstructing the history of the Passover will continue to present a major challenge, even if scholars arrive at a new consensus regarding the source analysis of the Pentateuch. Two factors, however, suggest that greater reliability should be placed on the present synchronic account of the Passover's history.

First, almost every passage that refers to the Passover associates it with either the Feast of Unleavened Bread or the eating of unleavened bread.[72] Although Wellhausen and Van Seters maintain that the two feasts were originally unconnected in J and in D, respectively, their arguments are not convincing. M. Haran has demonstrated, contra Wellhausen, that J knew of both feasts, and there is no reason to delete the term *pesaḥ*, Passover, in Exodus 34:25.[73] Nor is it necessary to remove, as Van Seters suggests, all references to the Feast of Unleavened Bread in Deuteronomy 16.[74] Given the unanimity of the biblical tradition, there is surely good ground for believing that the feasts were united from their inception. The evidence to the contrary is not compelling.

Second, all the pentateuchal sources link the Passover with the Israelite exodus.[75] The evidence does not support the assumption that later writers cre-

that one was constructed. If the present account is the product of J and P material having been combined, the editor has adopted the P version of the ark's construction in preference to that of J.

71. As Haran, "Passover Sacrifice," 88, observes, "The J passage (Exod. xii 21–27) in no way contradicts the description given in P. . . . Both refer to the same happening, only neither of them embraces all the details, which means that they actually complement each other." Indeed, such is the unity of the present narrative that Van Seters assigns all of Exod. 12:1–28 to P.

72. Only two passages mention the Passover without making any reference to unleavened bread: Num. 33:3, a brief chronological remark, and 2 Kings 23:21–23, a short description of the Passover celebrated by Josiah. Passover and the Feast of Unleavened Bread are linked in Exod. 12:1–13:16; 23:15–18; 34:18–25; Lev. 23:5–6; Deut. 16:1–16; 2 Chron. 30:1–21; 35:1–19; Ezra 6:19–22. Passover and the eating of unleavened bread are associated in Exod. 12:1–13:16; 23:18; 34:25; Num. 9:2–14; 28:16–17; Deut. 16:1–8; Josh. 5:10–11; Ezek. 45:21.

73. Haran, "Passover Sacrifice," 96–101.

74. Cf. J. G. McConville, *Law and Theology in Deuteronomy*, JSOTSup 33 (Sheffield: JSOT Press, 1984), 99–123; Alexander, "Passover Sacrifice," 11–14.

75. Among all the references to the Passover in the Pentateuch, only in Lev. 23:5–6 is there no mention of the exodus. Apart from Exod. 12:1–13:16, the two events are linked in Exod. 23:15; 34:18; Num. 9:1–2; 33:3; Deut. 16:1, 3, 6.

ated a historical etiology. No alternative explanation for the designation *pesaḥ*, Passover, has gained widespread support; although scholars have expressed reservations concerning the explanation given in Exodus 12–13, it is by far the most suitable.[76]

Conclusion

In the opening section of this chapter, we surveyed the chain of developments that led to the formulation of the Documentary Hypothesis toward the end of the nineteenth century. We next considered the two main criteria used to isolate the source documents thought to underlie the Pentateuch, focusing in particular on the divine names. Finally, we observed how the Documentary Hypothesis has had a telling impact on the history of Israelite religion, radically challenging the traditional understanding of the Pentateuch. Only a limited critique of various aspects of the Documentary Hypothesis has been offered here. In chapter 4 we shall observe more recent developments, some of which have seriously questioned the validity of the Documentary Hypothesis. Before doing so, it is necessary to consider the impact of both form and traditio-historical criticism on the study of the Pentateuch.

76. H.-J. Kraus, *Worship in Israel: A Cultic History of the Old Testament* (Oxford: Basil Blackwell, 1966), 45–46; cf. J. B. Segal, *The Hebrew Passover, from the Earliest Times to A.D. 70*, LOS 12 (London: Oxford University Press, 1963), 95–101.

3

Going behind the Documents

Following the widespread acceptance of the Documentary Hypothesis as *the* definitive explanation for the source documents underlying the Pentateuch, toward the end of the nineteenth century a few scholars began to consider the preliterary stage in the growth of the Pentateuch. This led to the development of two new methods of studying the Old Testament texts: form criticism and traditio-historical criticism. These methods sought to move backward from written texts to oral accounts. Compared with source criticism, however, this involves a greater degree of speculation, for we can never expect to recover the original oral forms of the pentateuchal materials. The best we could perhaps hope for is a written transcript of an oral presentation, and even this is unlikely to be totally accurate.

Of these two methods, form criticism was the first to be developed in detail, yet as we shall see below, the origins of both methods may be traced back to one scholar, Hermann Gunkel.

Form Criticism

The scholar identified with pioneering form criticism is Hermann Gunkel. He sought to go beyond the work of earlier source critics by examining the development of the Israelite traditions in their oral stage. To achieve this he introduced a method of research now generally known as form criticism (*Formgeschichte*), although Gunkel himself referred to it as *Gattungsforschung* (research into literary types) or *Literaturgeschichte* (history of literature).

In his approach Gunkel broke free from the limits imposed by the older source-critical method, which had restricted scholars to examining the growth of the Pentateuch at the purely literary level. Stressing the part played by oral transmission, Gunkel sought to write a history of the preliterary development of the traditions underlying the Pentateuch, and in particular the book of Genesis.

According to Gunkel, in Genesis one can observe different types or forms of material: etiological stories describing how a custom or institution came into being, cultic legends explaining the origin of a sanctuary, ethnological legends outlining the relationship between different groups of people, etymological stories setting out how a person or place received its name. Gunkel believed that many of these were much older than the literary sources in which they are preserved. As a result, Gunkel was able to move back behind the documentary sources that comprise the Pentateuch. Moreover, Gunkel maintained that each type or form of material originated from a particular life setting (*Sitz im Leben*) in ancient Israelite society, which when analyzed pointed toward an oral rather than a literary origin.

In his commentary on Genesis,[1] first published in 1901, Gunkel set out his reasons for believing that the narratives in Genesis had originally circulated orally. First, he observed that the book of Genesis consists of numerous episodes that appear to have been collected to form a longer narrative. Second, he argued that these episodes represented short, separate stories, which he called *Sagen* (legends, fables, myths, tales; sing., *Sage*). In Gunkel's opinion, any piece of narrative that belonged to the category of *Sage* must have been transmitted orally. Three important features distinguished a *Sage* from other forms: (1) unlike real "history" (*Geschichte*), a *Sage* has a poetic tone; (2) a *Sage* recounts supernatural or incredible events; (3) the subject matter of a *Sage* differs from that found in historiography; whereas, for example, the former may focus on family affairs, the latter is interested in national events. As these features reveal, Gunkel distinguished *Sagen* from "history." He believed that within an ancient society, storytelling initially involved the use of *Sagen*, short oral accounts, and only later did this primitive form develop into "history" writing. Although the material compiled in Genesis belongs to the earliest period within the evolution of Israelite society, the books of Samuel and Kings, for example, reflect a much later phase. This distinction between *Sagen* and "history" confirmed for Gunkel his belief that the material in Genesis originated orally.

Gunkel, however, not only argued that Genesis was composed of short episodes that had once circulated orally; he also sought to date the individual episodes. S. M. Warner summarizes well Gunkel's approach:

1. J. F. H. Gunkel, *Genesis: Übersetzt und erklärt*, 3rd ed. (Göttingen: Vandenhoeck & Ruprecht, 1910); ET, based on 3rd German ed., *Genesis* (Macon, GA: Mercer University Press, 1997).

His [Gunkel's] argument was simple. The more primitive (ancient) a society was, the less moral, ethical, and spiritual awareness it would possess. Thus, for example, he believed that the older stories, lacking in religious sophistication, had a "naive" (p. L) way of mixing the religious and profane elements within their narratives, while later stories emphasized only the religious element. He similarly thought that all those stories about the patriarchs which revealed them as flesh and blood people, warts and all, had to be earlier than those which emphasized only their religious qualities (p. LI). He also believed that the way in which the patriarchal stories depicted theophanic events could be used as an indicator of their age (p. XLII). Later, more sophisticated people would take offence at any story which could take seriously the idea that a deity would reveal itself in the flesh. In the same way the age of the narrative could be revealed from the extent to which it dissociated the deity from its sanctuary. Older stories could only depict a deity with influence in the area immediately surrounding its sanctuary. Later stories allowed a deity a far greater freedom of movement and influence (pp. XLII–XLIII).[2]

In both his general approach and his dating of the individual episodes, Gunkel relied heavily on a developmental theory of history in which things evolve from being simple and primitive to being complex and sophisticated. As Warner observes, the fallacy of such a contrast between primitive and modern man has been recognized by those engaged in the study of "primitive" societies in Africa and elsewhere; even so-called primitive peoples have very elaborate and involved societies. Regarding Genesis, the narrative techniques used in the writing of the book reflect the work of an author (or authors) who employed well-developed literary skills.[3] It is a mistake, therefore, to think of the material in Genesis as "primitive."

Fundamental to Gunkel's approach is the belief that the episodes in Genesis were composed orally. While this assumption is commonly made, it remains to be clearly demonstrated. In spite of attempts to define the nature of oral material, we have no way to show that even one episode in Genesis was composed orally. As Warner observes, "At present we see no reason to assume that the narratives of Genesis bear any close resemblance to orally transmitted data at all. If biblical scholars wish to argue such a thesis, they must develop new criteria with which to establish it."[4] Warner's comments highlight one of the main unresolved issues in the study of the Pentateuch. Our knowledge of the oral stage is likely to remain minimal for years to come, and theories based on it rest on uncertain foundations.[5]

2. S. M. Warner, "Primitive Saga Men," *VT* 29 (1979): 329.
3. E.g., M. A. Fishbane, "Composition and Structure in the Jacob Cycle (Gen. 25:19–35:22)," *JJS* 26 (1975): 15–38.
4. Warner, "Primitive Saga Men," 335.
5. For a fuller critique of form criticism, see R. N. Whybray, *The Making of the Pentateuch: A Methodological Study*, JSOTSup 53 (Sheffield: JSOT Press, 1987), 133–85.

In time, Gunkel's form-critical approach was adopted and developed by other scholars, mainly in Germany. Albrecht Alt produced influential studies on the religion of the patriarchs[6] and Israelite law.[7] In the former he sought to explain the evolution of Israelite religion before the time of the monarchy, and in the latter he distinguished between two main types of law found in the Pentateuch: casuistic (If a man . . .) and apodictic (Thou shalt [not] . . .). Alt's approach had a profound influence on two of his students, Gerhard von Rad and Martin Noth, both of whom became leading exponents of the traditio-historical method.

Traditio-Historical Criticism

We have already noted how source criticism seeks to determine the documents underlying the present text of the Pentateuch, and form criticism concentrates on the initial oral stage of the individual episodes. Traditio-historical criticism tries to explain what happened between these two stages. It aims to account for the process by which the once-independent oral episodes were united to form the documents that, according to the Documentary Hypothesis, comprise the Pentateuch.

The origins of traditio-historical criticism can be traced back to Gunkel, particularly to his views on how the book of Genesis developed from once-independent oral stories.[8] While Gunkel acknowledged that the different types of material found in Genesis originally existed as independent oral stories, he also proposed that during the oral stage of transmission, some of them were collected to form larger units. Consequently, he suggested that it was possible to uncover in Genesis "cycles of legends" (*Sagenkränze*). Gunkel drew attention to several examples of such cycles. Once-independent stories about Abraham and Lot were brought together at the oral stage to form a longer account, comprising various episodes. Two similar "cycles of legends" were composed using stories about Jacob-Esau and Jacob-Laban. As a further development, these two cycles were combined to form a single Jacob-Esau-Laban cycle. Gunkel also proposed that the Joseph story in Genesis 37–50 was another example of a cycle of legends, although he noted that in this case the

6. A. Alt, *Der Gott der Väter: Ein Beitrag zur Vorgeschichte der israelitischen Religion*, BWANT 12 (Stuttgart: Kohlhammer, 1929); reprinted in *Kleine Schriften zur Geschichte des Volkes Israels*, vol. 1 (Munich: C. H. Beck, 1953), 1–78; ET in *Essays on Old Testament History and Religion* (Oxford: Blackwell, 1966). For a helpful summary of Alt's views on early Israelite religion, see E. W. Nicholson, *The Pentateuch in the Twentieth Century: The Legacy of Julius Wellhausen* (Oxford: Clarendon, 1998), 54–58.

7. A. Alt, *Die Ursprünge des israelitischen Recht*, 1934; reprinted in *Kleine Schriften zur Geschichte des Volkes Israels*, vol. 1; ET in *Essays on Old Testament History and Religion*, 80–132.

8. Nicholson, *Pentateuch*, 31–43.

episodes making up the cycle were less self-contained. As a result, he classified the Joseph story as a *Novelle*.

An important implication of Gunkel's approach was that he came to view the sources J and E as collections of oral material. Consequently, it was no longer appropriate to think of the Yahwist and Elohist as "authors": they were merely collectors who brought together material that was not entirely homogeneous.[9]

Gunkel's views on traditio-historical criticism did not immediately gain the same recognition as his form-critical ideas. It was some years before traditio-historical criticism emerged as a separate method, and even then the shadow of form criticism was present.

Although presented as a form-critical study, von Rad's book *Das formgeschichtliche Problem des Hexateuch*[10] was influential in establishing the importance of the traditio-historical method. Von Rad suggested that J was composed along the lines of an outline of Israel's history contained in early creedal forms and used in cultic celebrations. Examples of these early credos are preserved in Deuteronomy 6:20–24; 26:5b–9; and Joshua 24:2b–13. In these credos von Rad isolated three main themes: (1) Aramaean origin, (2) rescue from Egypt, (3) possession of the land. According to von Rad, these credos were first used in cultic worship related to the Feast of Weeks held at Gilgal during the initial period of Israel's settlement in Canaan. As such, they celebrated the gift of land to the Israelites.

For von Rad's thesis to be valid, these credos must have existed before the composition of J. However, the evidence points in the opposite direction. In each instance the credo occurs in a passage that is normally dated later than J. As Nicholson rightly observes, "Such brief recapitulations of the story of Israel's origins probably stand much more towards the end of the development of the Pentateuch than at its beginnings."[11] It therefore is impossible to prove that J was based on such creedal confessions.

In a similar fashion, von Rad argued that the tradition of theophany and covenant making at Sinai, recorded in Exodus 19–24 and the book of Deuteronomy, originated from a festival held in the autumn at Shechem, an important cultic center in the premonarchic period. Associating this autumnal festival with the Feast of Tabernacles, von Rad maintained that its origin was to be clearly distinguished from that of the credos linked to Gilgal.

Having argued for separate origins for the traditions associated with Gilgal and Shechem, von Rad proceeded to suggest that these were later combined by

9. In marked contrast, Gunkel viewed P as an "author" who clearly shaped into his own mold any traditional material that he received.

10. G. von Rad, *Das formgeschichtliche Problem des Hexateuch*, BWANT 24 (Stuttgart: Kohlhammer, 1938); ET, *The Problem of the Hexateuch and Other Essays* (Edinburgh: Oliver & Boyd, 1966), 1–77.

11. Nicholson, *Pentateuch*, 89; for a fuller discussion, see idem, *Exodus and Sinai in History and Tradition* (Oxford: Oxford University Press, 1973), 20–26.

an author and theologian of some genius to form J.[12] While von Rad followed others in assigning authorship to the Yahwist, he viewed him as much more than a collector or editor of existing stories. Although the Yahwist drew on existing traditions, he gave them a totally new dimension by creating a larger, unified picture of divine activity that was no longer directly tied to cultic institutions.

One further aspect of von Rad's approach should be noticed. Whereas scholars of the Wellhausen school were strongly inclined to date the origin of J to the middle of the ninth century BC, von Rad argued that the Yahwist was to be dated earlier, to the period of David. In the context of the nation being unified under David and taking possession of the land, the Yahwist was able to develop his distinctive understanding of God and create the J document in the latter part of the tenth century BC.[13]

Von Rad's approach was developed more fully by Noth in his study *A History of Pentateuchal Traditions*.[14] Noth presents his aim as follows: "The chief task . . . is to ascertain the *basic themes* from which the totality of the transmitted Pentateuch developed, to uncover their roots, to investigate how they were replenished with individual materials, to pursue their connections with each other, and to assess their significance."[15] To determine the history of the traditions used in the Pentateuch, Noth accepted the usual source analysis of the Documentary Hypothesis. However, he proposed that on account of the similarities between J and E, they must have derived from a common origin, or *Grundlage*, "foundation" (G). Where J and E contain similar elements, it is possible to trace the influence of G.

Noth modified von Rad's position by arguing that five major themes could be uncovered in J:

1. Guidance out of Egypt
2. Guidance into the arable land
3. Promise to the patriarchs
4. Guidance in the wilderness
5. Revelation at Sinai

He proposed that these themes were brought together to form the framework of J. Various factors suggested that the themes were originally unconnected.

12. In addition to the traditions associated with Gilgal and Shechem, von Rad believed that various other originally independent traditions were also taken over by the Yahwist and used in the composition of J. These included episodes from the Primeval History in Gen. 1–11, much of the patriarchal material in Gen. 12–50, the exodus account in Exod. 1–15, and the Balaam story in Num. 22–24.

13. For a fuller discussion of von Rad, see Nicholson, *Pentateuch*, 63–74.

14. M. Noth, *Überlieferungsgeschichte des Pentateuch* (Stuttgart: Kohlhammer, 1948); ET, *A History of Pentateuchal Traditions* (Englewood Cliffs, NJ: Prentice-Hall, 1972).

15. Noth, *History of Pentateuchal Traditions*, 3.

For example, the theme of "guidance out of Egypt" presupposes entry into the land of Canaan from the west. In contrast, "guidance into the arable land" assumes that the land of Canaan is invaded from the east. According to Noth, these two themes arose in different groups of people.

Although Noth viewed these five themes as having circulated independently, he believed that they were united at an early stage in Israel's history, when the separate tribes joined in what Noth described as an *amphictyony*. This term is used to describe an association of twelve (or six) tribes in ancient Greece and Italy who met at a central shrine for worship. The tribes had the responsibility of maintaining the shrine and did so on a monthly or bimonthly rotation. Noth suggested that the Israelite tribes were associated in the same way around a central shrine, and that this bound them together. After the amphictyony was formed, the distinctive traditions of the separate tribes were combined to form the five main themes that comprised the *Grundlage* (G).

Various assumptions underlie Noth's approach. He assumes that the bulk of the Pentateuch originally circulated orally. He also accepts the source analysis of the Pentateuch as proposed in the Documentary Hypothesis. As we have noted, both of these are currently disputed issues.

Noth also assumes that the earliest narrative traditions were short and concise; later traditions did not exhibit the same brevity of form. Thus, for example, he views Genesis 24 as late due to its discursive style. Again, this is an assumption that modern scholars reject. Length cannot be a guide to age. Unfortunately, Noth's whole approach relies heavily on his being able to distinguish early from late traditions.

Another of Noth's assumptions is worth mentioning. He believes that in the process of oral transmission, stories may change their main characters. In particular, less well-known individuals may be replaced by better-known figures. This idea lies at the very heart of Noth's view of Moses. Although Moses is the main character in the books of Exodus to Deuteronomy, Noth maintains that he had no connection with the stories when they were first told and that he was introduced only at a later stage. He argues, for example, that Moses did not appear in the earliest traditions about the Israelites coming out of Egypt as recorded in the first half of the book of Exodus. In the earliest traditions it was the elders (cf. 3:16, 18; 4:29) and foremen (5:6–19) who negotiated with Pharaoh. To support this thesis, Noth holds that 5:3–19 represents the most original tradition concerning the departure of the Israelites from Egypt. Since Moses does not appear in this scene (v. 4, which mentions Moses, is designated a later insertion), Noth concludes that he had no part in the earliest tradition of the people leaving Egypt. Similarly, in the making of the covenant at Sinai, the presence of Moses was not part of the original tradition. Here also Moses has been introduced in place of the elders of the people. Noth offers no detailed arguments as to why Moses was introduced into these traditions. He merely assumes that this was the process by which the traditions developed. Finally, we should note that for Noth the most authentic element concerning Moses was the account of his burial.[16]

16. For a fuller critique of Noth's work, see Whybray, *Making of the Pentateuch*, 185–98.

Although in Germany scholars like von Rad and Noth developed their form and traditio-historical criticism within the framework of the Documentary Hypothesis, a different approach was adopted in Scandinavia. The origins of this alternative approach can be traced back to the studies of S. Mowinckel on the Psalms,[17] H. S. Nyberg's emphasis on the importance of oral transmission before the exile,[18] and the negative reaction of P. Volz[19] and J. Pedersen[20] to the Documentary Hypothesis. By combining the views of these various scholars, a new methodology for the study of the Pentateuch suggested itself, the leading exponent being I. Engnell.[21]

While Engnell referred to his approach as the traditio-historical method (*traditionshistorisk metod*) on account of similarities with the *überlieferungsgeschichtliche Methode* used in Germany, the two approaches are not identical.[22] Engnell rejected the idea that one could discover separate literary sources underlying the present text. He maintained that a Priestly Writer who drew on both preexilic and postexilic material composed Genesis to Numbers. By rejecting the possibility of preexilic literary sources, Engnell was obliged to dismiss the Documentary Hypothesis. Oral strata replaced literary sources.

The attempts of Engnell and other Scandinavian scholars to dismiss the usual source analysis of the Pentateuch by emphasizing the oral transmission of the traditions have gained little support. However, the oral-versus-written distinction continues to influence some source-critical studies.[23]

The Limitations of Traditio-Historical Criticism Illustrated

Traditio-historical criticism seeks to recover the process of composition that lies behind the source documents. Since extrabiblical texts provide no direct evidence, scholars have had to reconstruct this process from the text of the

17. S. Mowinckel, *Psalmenstudien*, vol. 2, *Das Thronbesteigungsfest Jahwäs und der Ursprung der Eschatologie* (Kristiania: J. Dybwad, 1922); *Psalmenstudien*, vol. 3, *Kultprophetie und prophetische Psalmen* (Kristiania: J. Dybwad, 1923).

18. H. S. Nyberg, *Studien zum Hoseabuche* (Uppsala: A. B. Lundequistska, 1935).

19. P. Volz, *Der Elohist als Erzähler: Ein Irrweg der Pentateuchkritik?* BZAW 63 (Giessen: A. Töpelmann, 1933).

20. J. Pedersen, "Die Auffassung vom Alten Testament," *ZAW* 49 (1931): 161–81; in this article Pedersen expresses his rejection of the Documentary Hypothesis; cf. idem, "Passahfest und Passahlegende," *ZAW* 52 (1934): 161–75.

21. I. Engnell, *Gamla Testamentet: En traditionshistorisk inledning* (Stockholm: Svenska Kyrkans Diakonistyrelses Bokförlag, 1945); idem, "Methodological Aspects of Old Testament Study," in *Congress Volume: Oxford, 1959*, by International Organization for the Study of the Old Testament, VTSup 7 (Leiden: Brill, 1960), 13–30.

22. Cf. R. Rendtorff, "Traditio-Historical Method and the Documentary Hypothesis," *PWCJS* 5 (1969): 5–6.

23. Cf. J. Van Seters, *Abraham in History and Tradition* (New Haven: Yale University Press, 1975).

Pentateuch as finally composed. This, however, opens the door to a wide variety of theories. Something of this may be observed by considering how several prominent scholars have approached the short passage in Genesis 14:18–20 featuring Abraham's encounter with Melchizedek.[24]

The following observations are normally made regarding Genesis 14: (1) It is generally accepted that the chapter as a whole does not come from one of the main source documents, J, E, D, or P; there are no clear criteria by which to identify it with one of these sources. (2) The style of verses 1–11 differs somewhat from that found in verses 12–24. (3) Abraham's meeting with the king of Sodom is interrupted by the unexpected arrival of the previously unmentioned king of Salem, Melchizedek. This has led many scholars to suggest that verses 18–20 are a later addition to the text and that originally verse 21 directly followed verse 17.

To explain the makeup of the chapter, C. Westermann suggests that the three sections come from separate periods in Israel's history.[25] Section 1 (vv. 1–11 [12]) is analogous to ancient Near Eastern accounts of military successes. Section 2 (vv. 12–17, 21–24) is a narrative of liberation, similar to those found in the book of Judges, in which a hero rescues people from foreign oppressors. Section 3 (vv. 18–20) comes from the time of the first temple (before 586 BC) and was told to encourage the bringing of tithes to Jerusalem. In support of this, Westermann observes that (1) Salem is another designation for Jerusalem (see Ps. 76:2 [3], a psalm of Zion), and (2) the name Melchizedek resembles that of Zadok, a high priest in the time of king David (cf., e.g., 2 Sam. 15:24–29). Westermann dates the final form of the story to the postexilic period due to the elevation of Abraham to the position of a world figure; this conforms to a pattern found in the books of Judith and Daniel.

In his reading of Genesis 14, J. A. Emerton links Melchizedek with David and sees the insertion of verses 18–20 as designed to support the claim of David to rule over the Israelites and other peoples of Canaan.[26] Like Melchizedek, David is king over Jerusalem. Emerton, however, rejects links between Melchizedek and Zadok. He also rejects the suggestion that the purpose of the narrative was to encourage the bringing of tithes to Jerusalem.

A third approach is offered by J. Van Seters.[27] He dates the Melchizedek incident to the postexilic period, in a time when the priesthood of the second

24. The discussion that follows relies heavily on J. G. McConville, "Abraham and Melchizedek: Horizons in Genesis 14," in *He Swore an Oath: Biblical Themes from Genesis 20–50*, ed. R. S. Hess, P. E. Satterthwaite, and G. J. Wenham, 2nd ed. (Grand Rapids: Baker; Carlisle: Paternoster, 1994), 93–118.

25. C. Westermann, *Genesis 12–36: A Commentary*, trans. John J. Scullion (London: SPCK; Minneapolis: Augsburg, 1985), 198–99.

26. J. A. Emerton, "The Riddle of Genesis xiv," *VT* 21 (1971): 403–39.

27. Van Seters, *Abraham in History and Tradition*, 296–308.

temple aspired to royal office. He finds evidence for this in the claim of the Hasmoneans to be both kings and "high priests of God Most High."[28]

J. G. McConville provides a helpful critique of these three views.[29] Regarding the purposed analogies for the first two sections of Genesis 14, McConville highlights the inadequacy of the parallels suggested. The campaign account cannot be easily identified with a specific form of ancient Near Eastern material. The proposal that the second section resembles hero-liberation accounts found in the book of Judges is also questionable. The similarities are very superficial, and Abraham's actions do not parallel those of judges like Gideon or Samson. Moreover, the Genesis context presents Abraham as a figure of some standing, and it is not surprising to find him having contact with kings (cf. 12:10–20; 20:1–18; 21:22–34); elsewhere the inhabitants of Hebron call him a "prince of God" (23:6).

Regarding Genesis 14:18–20 McConville rejects the traditio-historical explanations of Westermann, Emerton, and Van Seters. The postexilic setting suggested by Van Seters is highly unlikely. Would a postexilic author introduce a tradition about an ancient Canaanite priest-king in order to support the claims of Jewish priests? Westermann's proposal that the narrative encouraged the bringing of tithes to Jerusalem is not really appropriate. Likewise, Emerton's suggestion that it was intended to justify David's rule over both Israelites and non-Israelites is also dubious; David is more likely to be associated with the warrior Abraham than with Melchizedek.

Adopting a different approach to Genesis 14, McConville makes the following observations:

1. In Genesis, Abraham is commonly portrayed as a figure of some importance. Outside Genesis 14, he encounters foreign rulers: Pharaoh of Egypt and Abimelech of Gerar. The inhabitants of Hebron also acknowledge his special status. It is not surprising, therefore, that in Genesis 14 he should have dealings with two other kings, the kings of Salem and Sodom.
2. He notes the importance of Genesis 14 in the development of the Lot/Sodom motif, which is prominent in Genesis 13 and 18–19.
3. He argues that the Melchizedek incident, while interrupting the narrative flow of Genesis 14, is not an intrusion. Various links exist with the surrounding text. Melchizedek knows that Abraham has won a victory (v. 20). Abraham's refusal to be made rich by the king of Sodom (v. 23) involves a wordplay with the term for "tithe" in verse 20. When Abraham refers to "Yahweh, El-Elyon, Creator of heaven and earth," he echoes the expression used by Melchizedek in verse 19.

28. Ibid., 308.
29. McConville, "Abraham and Melchizedek," 93–118.

On the basis of these observations, McConville proceeds to ask, What effect does the inclusion of the Melchizedek incident have on our reading of the chapter? He observes that Abraham's meetings with the kings of Salem and Sodom provide two contrasting pictures of how Abraham might take possession of the land of Canaan. With the king of Sodom the emphasis is on human strength: through exercising military power, one comes to possess what belongs to others. The king of Salem, however, gives a very different answer. Abraham's victory is a gift from God (v. 20). By giving a tenth of the booty to Melchizedek, Abraham acknowledges the truthfulness of what he has said. Abraham underlines this by refusing to accept anything from the king of Sodom. Thus the Melchizedek incident is significant since it implies that Abraham will receive the land as a gift from God, not by using his military muscle.

Several general comments may be made in the light of the preceding discussion. First, by its very nature traditio-historical criticism may give rise to conflicting theories concerning the process by which a text was composed. This underlines the speculative nature of traditio-historical criticism. Second, in the past many scholars have been quick to offer traditio-historical explanations for features in the text that they have been unable to explain by other means. While traditio-historical reconstructions may occasionally appear to solve perceived difficulties within a text, we should always be alert to the possibility that other explanations may yet be forthcoming. As we have observed with regard to Genesis 14:18–20, the synchronic reading proposed by McConville makes excellent sense of the text as it stands, without recourse to a traditio-historical reconstruction.

4

The Documentary Hypothesis under Threat

The Documentary Hypothesis has dominated the source criticism of the Pentateuch throughout most of the twentieth century. For many scholars the theory has been so convincing that it is merely assumed and used as the basis for further research on other issues. Some scholars, however, have continued to investigate the literary origins of the Pentateuch and as a result have proposed modifications of different kinds. Others, however, have completely rejected the Documentary Hypothesis. We shall now consider these modifications and rejections.

Modifications to the Documentary Hypothesis

Given the complex nature of the Documentary Hypothesis, it is hardly surprising that various modifications to it have been proposed during the past hundred years. To a large extent these have arisen out of more detailed investigations of the individual sources and their relationship to one another. Even among those who accept the basic tenets of the Documentary Hypothesis, there are many differences of opinion; for example, it is common for scholars to disagree over the assignment of individual verses or passages to a particular source. No attempt shall be made here to explore all these differences. Rather, we shall focus on some of the more significant ways in which some scholars have sought to modify the Documentary Hypothesis.

The J Source

Once it was accepted that the Pentateuch was composed of four main sources, and the extent of these sources agreed on, it was only natural that questions should be asked about the composition of the individual sources.[1] Wellhausen himself drew attention to this question by noting that in the early chapters of Genesis, J displayed inconsistencies.[2] This suggested that J was composite in nature, and if this were so, then it ought to be possible to determine the sources underlying it. (Similar views were expressed by Wellhausen about E and P.) A variety of studies have focused on the composite nature of J.

In 1883 K. Budde in his *Die biblische Urgeschichte (Gen. 1–12, 5)*[3] argued that the J material in the early chapters of Genesis consisted of two documents, J[1] (tenth century BC) and J[2] (later ninth or possibly eighth century BC), which were combined by a Yahwistic editor in the eighth century BC. Budde's views were extended in 1885 by C. Brunston to include the whole of the Pentateuch.[4] Gunkel also maintained that the J material was composite.[5] However, he limited his views to the Primeval History[6] and the Abraham narratives. Whereas in the Primeval History J was comprised of two documents, J[e] and J[i], in the Abraham narratives J consists of two collections of traditions, J[a] and J[b], which originated from the regions of Hebron and Beersheba respectively.[7] On the relationship of these latter two traditions, Gunkel held that J[b] supplemented J[a].

In 1912 R. Smend, in his *Die Erzählung des Hexateuch auf ihre Quellen untersucht*,[8] gave fuller expression to the view that the Hexateuch contains not one but two J documents, J[1] and J[2], which were the oldest sources used in the compilation of the Hexateuch; he placed the documents in the sequence J[1], J[2], E, D, P. Support for Smend's approach came from O. Eissfeldt, who reverted to the idea of two J documents combined by a later editor.[9] Eissfeldt, however, referred to J[1] as the "Lay source" (*Laienquelle*), which he denoted

---

1. A fuller survey of the J source is provided by A. de Pury, "Yahwist ('J') Source," *ABD* 6:1012–20.

2. J. Wellhausen, *Die Composition des Hexateuchs und der historischen Bücher des Alten Testaments*, 3rd ed. (Berlin: G. Reimer, 1899); first published as "Die Composition des Hexateuchs," *JDT* 21 (1876): 392–450, 531–602; 22 (1877): 407–79.

3. K. Budde, *Die biblische Urgeschichte (Gen. 1–12, 5)* (Giessen: J. Ricker, 1883).

4. C. Brunston, "Les deux jéhovistes (de la Genèse à 1 Rois)," *RTP* 18 (1885): 5–34, 499–528, 602–37.

5. J. F. H. Gunkel, *Genesis: Übersetzt und erklärt*, 3rd ed. (Göttingen: Vandenhoeck & Ruprecht, 1910).

6. The term "Primeval History" is often used to describe the material in Gen. 1:1–11:26.

7. J. Skinner, *Genesis*, 2nd ed., ICC (Edinburgh: T&T Clark, 1930), 240–42, followed the view of Gunkel but labeled the sources J[h] and J[b].

8. R. Smend, *Die Erzählung des Hexateuch auf ihre Quellen untersucht* (Berlin: G. Reimer, 1912).

9. O. Eissfeldt, *Hexateuch Synopse* (Leipzig: J. C. Hinrich, 1922); support came also from W. Eichrodt, *Die Quellen der Genesis von neuem untersucht* (Giessen: A. Töpelmann, 1916).

by the symbol L; as the name suggests, this source has little interest in cultic or priestly affairs. Having designated J[1] as L, Eissfeldt was able to label J[2] as J. Then G. Fohrer followed the position advocated by Eissfeldt.[10] However, Fohrer rejected the designation "Lay source" because he considered the document to have a theology as developed as J or E. Instead, he referred to it as the Nomadic source (*Nomadenquelle*) N. Since Fohrer dated it later than J but earlier than E, the sequence of the sources became J, N, E, D. Likewise, P. R. Kilian has advocated the view that J is not completely homogeneous.[11] In a detailed investigation of the prepriestly Abraham traditions, Kilian sought to demonstrate that the author of J employed both written and oral sources, which he shaped according to his own theological outlook. Other scholars who oppose the concept of a single J source will be considered later in this chapter. Yet while some scholars discovered sources underlying J, it must be recognized that the majority of scholars continued to view J as a unified source.[12]

Although Wellhausen argued that J was the earliest of the four main sources, he remained somewhat vague regarding the nature and date of J. Though he believed that J was an author (*Schriftsteller*), Gunkel later proposed that J was merely a collector and editor of existing traditions. It was left to von Rad to propose that J was a theologian of some brilliance who, during the "golden age" of Solomon (ca. 950–930 BC), produced a history of Israel that included the following elements: Primeval History, patriarchal stories, Joseph, Moses, exodus, Sinai, conquest. While von Rad saw J as extending into the book of Joshua, Noth believed that the final part of J was lost when the Tetrateuch ("four volumes," Genesis to Numbers) was linked to the Deuteronomistic History. Although Noth modified aspects of von Rad's approach (see "Traditio-Historical Criticism" in chap. 3), he strongly supported a tenth-century-BC date for the composition of J.

While the significance of J as the earliest biblical writer of importance continues to find support,[13] two quite different developments have occurred in recent years. On the one hand, various scholars have challenged the concept of the Yahwist as Israel's first great theologian, arguing that there is insufficient evidence to support the existence of a continuous J document throughout the

10. G. Fohrer, *Überlieferung und Geschichte des Exodus* (Berlin: A. Töpelmann, 1964); idem, *Introduction to the Old Testament* (London: SPCK, 1970).

11. P. R. Kilian, *Die vorpriesterlichen Abrahamsüberlieferungen*, BBB 24 (Bonn: Hanstein, 1966).

12. S. R. Driver, *An Introduction to the Literature of the Old Testament*, 9th ed. (Edinburgh: T&T Clark, 1913), 116–26, provides a description of the vocabulary, style, and grammar of J. For a discussion of the theology of J, see H. W. Wolff, "The Kerygma of the Yahwist," *Int* 20 (1966): 131–58; P. F. Ellis, *The Yahwist: The Bible's First Theologian* (London: G. Chapman, 1969); W. Brueggemann and H. W. Wolff, *The Vitality of Old Testament Traditions* (Atlanta: John Knox, 1975).

13. E.g., R. E. Friedman, *Who Wrote the Bible?* (Englewood Cliffs, NJ: Prentice Hall, 1987); R. Coote and D. Ord, *The Bible's First Historian: From Eden to the Court of David with the Yahwist* (Philadelphia: Fortress, 1989).

Pentateuch.[14] Also, J's role in joining together the once diverse traditions now found in the Pentateuch is variously attributed to D and P (see discussion below on Rendtorff and Blum). On the other hand, there has been a trend toward dating J to the exilic period. Since 1970 there has been a sustained attempt to dissociate J from the Solomonic "enlightenment." H. H. Schmid suggested that various features pointed to a date for J well after the time of Solomon: various J texts display Deuteronomistic ideas; J reflects a time of national crisis, not success.[15] On the basis of a detailed study of the Abraham narrative, J. Van Seters also argued that J should be dated later. Nevertheless, his late J is not completely identical in content to the J source of the Documentary Hypothesis. (Van Seters's approach is discussed more fully below.) According to Van Seters, J is to be dated to the exilic period, being a post-Deuteronomistic, but pre-Priestly source.[16] The idea of dating J late is also advocated by M. Rose, who argues that J was composed as a "prologue" to the Deuteronomistic History (Deuteronomy–Kings).[17] Rose maintains that various J texts show signs of having been composed after the corresponding episodes in the Deuteronomistic History. A late dating of J is also supported by C. Levin, who suggests that the author of the work was a member of the courtly upper class who had been deported to Babylon in about 597 BC.[18] It must be recognized, however, that these proposals to date J late are not entirely homogeneous, and as J. L. Ska rightly points out, the Yahwist has become a man "with a thousand faces."[19]

The E Source

Of the various documents believed to underlie the Pentateuch, the source E has probably received the least attention from scholars. However, various

14. See in particular the collection of essays in *Abschied vom Jahwisten: Die Komposition des Hexateuch in der jüngsten diskussion*, ed. J. C. Gertz, K. Schmid, and M. Witte, BZAW 315 (Berlin: de Gruyter, 2002). In these essays various texts previously considered to belong to J are viewed as originating elsewhere, and some are dated post-P.

15. H. H. Schmid, *Der sogenannte Jahwist: Beobachtungen und Fragen zur Pentateuchforschung* (Zurich: Theologischer Verlag, 1976).

16. Cf. J. Van Seters, "The Report of the Yahwist's Demise Has Been Greatly Exaggerated!" in *A Farewell to the Yahwist? The Composition of the Pentateuch in Recent European Interpretation*, ed. T. B. Dozeman and K. Schmid, SBLSymS 34 (Atlanta: Society of Biblical Literature, 2006), 143–57.

17. M. Rose, *Deuteronomist und Jahwist: Untersuchungen zu den Berührungspunkten beider Literaturwerke*, ATANT 67 (Zurich: Theologischer Verlag, 1981).

18. C. Levin, "The Yahwist: The Earliest Editor in the Pentateuch," *JBL* 126 (2007): 209–30; cf. idem, "The Yahwist and the Redactional Link between Genesis and Exodus," in Dozeman and Schmid, *A Farewell to the Yahwist?*, 131–41.

19. J. L. Ska, "The Yahwist, a Hero with a Thousand Faces: A Chapter in the History of Modern Exegesis," in Gertz, Schmid, and Witte, *Abschied vom Jahwisten*, 1–23; cf. T. C. Römer, "The Elusive Yahwist: A Short History of Research," in Dozeman and Schmid, *A Farewell to the Yahwist?*, 9–27.

writers have considered in detail the extent and nature of E and its relationship to J. Before 1890 A. Kuenen had already suggested that E was composite in character.[20] He proposed that E comprised two documents, E^1 and E^2. E^1 originated in the northern kingdom during the eighth century BC. A century later E^1 underwent a revision in the southern kingdom and was expanded by the inclusion of new material, E^2. Later C. H. Cornill[21] and O. Procksch[22] adopted Kuenen's position. Generally, however, scholars have rejected the view that E is composite in character.

In 1930 S. Mowinckel questioned the concept of an independent E document.[23] Instead, he viewed E as supplementing and expanding earlier traditions. Later, in *The Two Sources of the Pre-deuteronomic Primeval History (JE) in Gen 1–11*,[24] Mowinckel proposed that the pre-P material in Genesis 1–11 was composite, and identified the sources as J and E.[25] Earlier most scholars had maintained that there was no E material in Genesis before chapter 15. Mowinckel later revised his opinions on the extent of E and suggested that while it was present to a limited extent in the Pentateuch, it was absent from the Primeval History, the Jacob and Joseph stories, and Exodus 1–15.[26] Rather than refer to JE, Mowinckel spoke of J^v (J *variatus*) because he regarded J as having been supplemented by material that had circulated mostly in oral form.

Another major challenge to the existence of an independent E document came from P. Volz and W. Rudolph. In a joint study on Genesis, *Der Elohist als Erzähler: Ein Irrweg der Pentateuchkritik?*[27] Volz and Rudolph questioned the existence of a continuous E document. Examining Genesis 1–35, Volz concluded that there was a basic J narrative, mainly a collection of earlier traditions, that was eventually expanded by E and P material. According to Volz, neither E nor P had existed as an independent document, a conclusion supported by the lack of substantial narrative material from these sources. Volz also assigned to J some sections that had previously been designated E or P, such as Genesis 22–23. Rudolph, concentrating on the Joseph narrative, concluded that there was no need to posit an independent E document for

20. A. Kuenen, *An Historico-Critical Inquiry into the Origin and Composition of the Hexateuch*, trans. P. H. Wicksteed (London: Macmillan, 1886), 248–62.

21. C. H. Cornill, *Einleitung in das Alte Testament*, 2nd ed. (Freiburg: Mohr, 1892).

22. O. Procksch, *Das nordhebräische Sagenbuch: Die Elohimquelle* (Leipzig: J. C. Hinrichs, 1906).

23. S. Mowinckel, "Der Ursprung der Bil'āmsage [Balaam saga]," *ZAW* 48 (1930): 233–71.

24. S. Mowinckel, *The Two Sources of the Pre-deuteronomic Primeval History (JE) in Gen 1–11* (Oslo: J. Dybwad, 1937).

25. G. Hölscher, *Die Anfänge der hebräischen Geschichtsschreibung* (Heidelberg: C. Winter, 1942), followed Mowinckel in suggesting that E occurred in the Primeval History.

26. S. Mowinckel, "Erwägung zur Pentateuch Quellenfrage," *NTT* 65 (1964): 1–138; cf. idem, *Tetrateuch-Pentateuch-Hexateuch*, BZAW 90 (Berlin: A. Töpelmann, 1964).

27. P. Volz and W. Rudolph, *Der Elohist als Erzähler: Ein Irrweg der Pentateuchkritik?* BZAW 63 (Giessen: A. Töpelmann, 1933).

this part of Genesis. He rejected the criterion of divine names by arguing that whereas the author used Yahweh in narrating the story, his characters used El Shaddai and Elohim when speaking in Palestine and Egypt respectively. In a later work on the books of Exodus to Joshua, Rudolph again challenged the idea of a continuous independent E document.[28]

More recently the existence of a parallel E source in the Joseph narrative has come under attack from various scholars. R. N. Whybray has argued (1) that the obvious literary qualities of the narrative cannot be adequately explained by supposing that the final account was produced by the conflation of two earlier parallel sources, and (2) that von Rad's dating of the story to the early monarchy excludes the possibility of two sources being combined.[29] This latter argument presupposes an acceptance of von Rad's contention that the Joseph story is an example of Wisdom literature, a view not accepted by all scholars.[30]

In his book *A Study of the Biblical Story of Joseph (Genesis 37–50)*, D. B. Redford investigates the Joseph story in considerable detail. Demonstrating the literary qualities of the narrative, he argues, like Whybray, against dividing the account into separate J and E sources. Nevertheless, Redford does discover two sources underlying the present story. He suggests that an original "Reuben" version of the Joseph story was subsequently expanded by a "Judah" version. However, he emphatically rejects the idea that this "Judah" version existed as an independent account paralleling the "Reuben" version.

G. W. Coats has also subjected the Joseph story to a thorough investigation in his monograph *From Canaan to Egypt: Structural and Theological Context of the Joseph Story*.[31] Like Redford and Whybray, he questions the traditional source analysis of the story. However, he is much more emphatic than Redford in asserting the unity of the narrative. Redford's suggestion that

---

28. W. Rudolph, *Der "Elohist" von Exodus bis Josua*, BZAW 68 (Berlin: A. Töpelmann, 1938).

29. R. N. Whybray, "The Joseph Story and Pentateuchal Criticism," *VT* 18 (1968): 522–28. Whybray restricts himself to discussing the position adopted by G. von Rad, "The Joseph Narrative and Ancient Wisdom," in *Problem of the Hexateuch and Other Essays*, trans. E. W. T. Dicken (Edinburgh: Oliver & Boyd, 1966), 292–300, first published as "Josephsgeschichte und ältere Chokma," in *Congress Volume: Copenhagen, 1953*, by International Organization for the Study of the Old Testament, VTSup 1 (Leiden: Brill, 1953), 120–27; cf. G. von Rad, *Die Josephsgeschichte*, BibS(N) 5 (Neukirchen: Neukirchener Verlag, 1954). Von Rad considered the Joseph narrative, which he termed a "novel," to be an example of Wisdom literature from the period of the early monarchy.

30. Cf. J. L. Crenshaw, "Method in Determining Wisdom Influence upon 'Historical' Literature," *JBL* 88 (1969): 129–42; D. B. Redford, *A Study of the Biblical Story of Joseph (Genesis 37–50)*, VTSup 20 (Leiden: Brill, 1970), 100–105; G. W. Coats, "The Joseph Story and Ancient Wisdom: A Reappraisal," *CBQ* 35 (1973): 285–97. Whereas Crenshaw and Redford reject von Rad's position, Coats favors a wisdom background for Gen. 39–41, which he terms a "political legend."

31. G. W. Coats, *From Canaan to Egypt: Structural and Theological Context of the Joseph Story*, CBQMS 4 (Washington, DC: Catholic Biblical Association of America, 1976); cf. idem, "Redactional Unity in Genesis 37–50," *JBL* 93 (1974): 15–21.

a later author expanded the story is rejected. For Coats, the Joseph story is an "artistic masterpiece." On the question of authorship and date, Coats remains cautiously undecided, although he does not exclude the possibility that the Yahwist composed the story during the time of Solomon.

Another recent objector to the concept of a parallel E narrative source is C. Westermann. In his massive commentary on Genesis,[32] he argues that E never existed as a separate source in the Abraham narrative. Yet although Westermann rejects the idea of an E document, he accepts that other traditions apart from J and P were incorporated into the final form of the Abraham narrative. Thus he views Genesis 20:1–18 and 21:22–34 as supplements to the main J narrative.[33]

In spite of a growing body of opinion against viewing E as an independent source paralleling J, various scholars still defend the traditional Documentary Hypothesis understanding of E. The suggestion that E narratives were produced as "deliberate corrective supplements to J" is rejected by A. W. Jenks.[34] R. E. Friedman offers support for the view that E was once an independent source.[35] He argues that (1) during the process of being combined with J, much of the beginning of E was lost, and (2) some E material in the books of Exodus to Numbers has been wrongly assigned to other sources, especially J. A consequence of these factors is that E has mistakenly been perceived as shorter and more fragmentary than J. Thus Friedman concludes: "E is a well-represented source, originally continuous prior to its being combined with J, and that E and J are approximately equal in quantity of text now preserved in the Pentateuch."[36]

From this brief survey it is obvious that scholarly opinion is divided over the extent and nature of the E source. While some scholars still maintain the traditional Documentary Hypothesis view of E as a continuous literary source paralleling J, a growing number question the validity of this position.[37]

The D Source

In many ways the D source stands apart from J, E, and P. Whereas the latter sources are found running throughout the books of Genesis to Numbers

32. C. Westermann, *Genesis: A Commentary*, 3 vols. (Minneapolis: Augsburg, 1984–86).
33. Ibid., 2:347, 571–72.
34. A. W. Jenks, "Elohist," *ABD* 2:479.
35. R. E. Friedman, "Torah (Pentateuch)," *ABD* 4:619; idem, *Who Wrote the Bible?*
36. Friedman, "Torah (Pentateuch)," *ABD* 4:619.
37. To add to an already confusing picture, R. G. Kratz (*The Composition of the Narrative Books of the Old Testament*, trans. J. S. Bowden [London and New York: T&T Clark, 2005], 281–82) uses the classical siglum "E" to denote "a tradition of Israel extending from the exodus from Egypt under Moses (Exodus–Numbers) to the entry into the promised land under Joshua (Joshua)." This "exodus narrative," which he calls "E," must be distinguished from the Primeval History and the Patriarchal History of Genesis, which Kratz labels "J." This E is a most unfortunate choice of siglum, for it needs to be recognized that Kratz's E bears no resemblance to the E source of the Documentary Hypothesis.

(and possibly also in Joshua, according to some early source critics), D is confined largely to the book of Deuteronomy. R. E. Friedman, for example, observes that "the joining of D with JEP required little more than moving the accounts of the promoting of Joshua and the death of Moses to the end of Deuteronomy."[38]

Though the early proponents of the Documentary Hypothesis suggested that the book of Joshua ought to be considered in conjunction with the Pentateuch, Noth challenged this view in 1943. He proposed that the book of Deuteronomy was the first part of a larger literary work, which included the books of Joshua, Judges, Samuel, and Kings. Noth designated this account of Israel's time in Canaan a "Deuteronomic History"; later writers have preferred the title "Deuteronomistic History," retaining the term "Deuteronomic" for the book of Deuteronomy itself. According to Noth, an exilic author (the Deuteronomist) took over an already-existing law code (most but not all of the book of Deuteronomy) that had been composed in the time of Josiah; here Noth adopts the Documentary Hypothesis dating of the D source. Adding a historical introduction (Deut. 1:1–3:29) to the Deuteronomic law code, the Deuteronomist created the opening book of his history. Since the Deuteronomistic History concludes with the account of King Jehoiachin's release from prison in 562 BC (2 Kings 25:27–30), the whole work must have been composed shortly after this date. Noth proposed that this "History" was originally unconnected to the books of Genesis to Numbers. With the widespread acceptance of Noth's theory of a Deuteronomistic History, it became appropriate to speak of a Tetrateuch rather than a Pentateuch. As a result, recent research on Deuteronomy has tended to focus mainly on its relationship to the books that come after it rather than those that come before it.[39]

Noth's idea of a "historian" who penned the books of Deuteronomy to Kings is taken up by Van Seters. In his study *In Search of History: Historiography in the Ancient World and the Origins of Biblical History*,[40] Van Seters argues that the Deuteronomistic Historian may be best compared with the Greek historians of the Persian period. However, Van Seters differs from Noth in two significant ways. First, he believes that the Deuteronomistic Historian did not incorporate earlier compositions into his work, but with little recourse to existing sources, relied mainly on his own imagination. Second, he argues

38. Friedman, "Torah (Pentateuch)," *ABD* 4:618.

39. For a review of modern approaches to the Deuteronomistic History, see S. L. McKenzie, "Deuteronomistic History," *ABD* 2:160–68; J. G. McConville, *Grace in the End: A Study of Deuteronomic Theology* (Carlisle: Paternoster, 1993); idem, "The Old Testament Historical Books in Modern Scholarship," *Them* 22, no. 3 (1997): 3–13.

40. J. Van Seters, *In Search of History: Historiography in the Ancient World and the Origins of Biblical History* (New Haven: Yale University Press, 1983).

that J was composed after the Deuteronomistic History, an idea that has found support with a number of other scholars.[41]

H. H. Schmid[42] and Rendtorff have also argued that the books of Genesis to Numbers are influenced by Deuteronomic/Deuteronomistic thinking. Indeed, Rendtorff goes some way to arguing that the final redaction of the Pentateuch was "deuteronomically stamped," although he acknowledges that "criteria for what is 'deuteronomic' . . . have not yet been adequately worked out."[43] T. B. Dozeman[44] and W. Johnstone[45] have expressed somewhat similar views regarding the book of Exodus; both suggest that there is evidence of a major Deuteronomistic redaction in Exodus, although they believe, unlike Rendtorff, that this was followed by a further priestly redaction. Blum also notes Deuteronomistic influence in the composition of Exodus,[46] as does H.-C. Schmitt.[47]

In spite of growing support (1) for finding Deuteronomic/Deuteronomistic influence in the Tetrateuch and (2) for dating the composition of the Tetrateuch after the Deuteronomistic History, the issue is far from settled, with other scholars observing that many passages in Deuteronomy display clear signs of having been composed in the light of material found elsewhere in Genesis to Numbers. M. Weinfeld argues that the Deuteronomic version of the Decalogue is based on that found in Exodus 20, and that Deuteronomy 7 presupposes Exodus 23:23–33.[48]

---

41. Cf. A. D. H. Mayes, *The Story of Israel between Settlement and Exile: A Redactional Study of the Deuteronomistic History* (London: SCM, 1983), 141; R. N. Whybray, *The Making of the Pentateuch: A Methodological Study*, JSOTSup 53 (Sheffield: JSOT Press, 1987), 225; J. Blenkinsopp, *The Pentateuch* (London: SCM, 1992), 233–37; E. T. Mullen, *Ethnic Myths and Pentateuchal Foundations: A New Approach to the Formation of the Pentateuch*, SemeiaSt (Atlanta: Scholars Press, 1997), 317–18. J. Van Seters develops this further in his books *Prologue to History: The Yahwist as Historian in Genesis* (Louisville: Westminster/John Knox, 1992) and *The Life of Moses: The Yahwist as Historian in Exodus–Numbers* (Louisville: Westminster/John Knox, 1994).

42. H. H. Schmid, *Der sogenannte Jahwist*.

43. R. Rendtorff, *The Problem of the Process of Transmission in the Pentateuch*, JSOTSup 89 (Sheffield: JSOT Press, 1990), 197.

44. T. B. Dozeman, *God on the Mountain: A Study of Redaction, Theology, and Canon in Exodus 19–24*, SBLMS 37 (Atlanta: Scholars Press, 1989), 37–86; cf. idem, "The Commission of Moses and the Book of Genesis," in Dozeman and Schmid, *A Farewell to the Yahwist?*, 107–30; idem, *Commentary on Exodus*, ECC (Grand Rapids: Eerdmans, 2009).

45. W. Johnstone, *Exodus*, OTG (Sheffield: JSOT Press, 1990), 75–86; cf. idem, "Reactivating the Chronicles Analogy in Pentateuchal Studies, with Special Reference to the Sinai Pericope in Exodus," *ZAW* 99 (1987): 16–37; idem, "The Decalogue and the Redaction of the Sinai Pericope in Exodus," *ZAW* 100 (1988): 361–85.

46. E. Blum, *Studien zur Komposition des Pentateuch*, BZAW 189 (Berlin: de Gruyter, 1990); cf. idem, "Die Literarische Verbingung von Erzvätern und Exodus: Ein Gespräch mit neueren Endredaktionshypothesen," in Gertz, Schmid, and Witte, *Abschied vom Jahwisten*, 119–56.

47. H.-C. Schmitt, "Das sogenannte jahwistische Privilegrecht in Ex 34, 10–28 als Komposition der spätdeuteronomistischen Endredaktion des Pentateuch," in Gertz, Schmid, and Witte, *Abschied vom Jahwisten*, 157–71.

48. M. Weinfeld, *Deuteronomy 1–11*, AB 5 (New York: Doubleday, 1991), 242–319, 367; cf. R. G. Kratz, "Der Dekalog im Exodusbuch," *VT* 44 (1994): 205–38.

Consideration must also be given to the views of those who argue that P must be dated earlier than D (see next section). J. Milgrom, for example, notices that D is often dependent on P, but P is never dependent on D.[49]

The P Source

The P source has also come under close scrutiny in ways that resemble closely the discussion over the extent and nature of the E source. In 1924 M. R. H. Löhr argued that P never existed as an independent document.[50] Reverting to a type of fragmentary hypothesis, Löhr suggested that Ezra and his companions combined various collections of narratives and laws to form the Pentateuch as we now have it. His position found support in the later work of Volz, who also denied the existence of a separate P document.[51]

Von Rad discussed the unity of the P material in detail in his book *Die Priesterschrift im Hexateuch literarisch untersucht und theologisch gewertet.*[52] He proposed that P consisted of two parallel narrative strands, P^a and P^b, and an independent work comprising genealogical lists (*Toledothbuch*). Although P^b had a greater interest in priestly affairs than the less complex P^a, both works were sufficiently similar to allow themselves to be easily combined. This view, however, has received little support.

I. Engnell has also questioned the existence of P as an independent document.[53] He preferred to consider P as a compiler and editor of the books Genesis to Numbers. Although Noth agreed with Engnell that P ended in Numbers and not in Joshua, as some scholars maintained, he accepted the traditional position that P was originally a separate document.[54] For Noth, P was a narrative history into which collections of laws and cultic regulations were later inserted.[55]

Support for Engnell's view that P never existed as an independent document has come from F. M. Cross. In an essay titled "The Priestly Work,"[56]

---

49. J. Milgrom, *Leviticus 1–16: A New Translation with Introduction and Commentary*, AB 3 (New York: Doubleday, 1991), 9–13.

50. M. R. H. Löhr, *Untersuchungen zum Hexateuchproblem: Der Priesterkodex in der Genesis*, BZAW 38 (Giessen: A. Töpelmann, 1924).

51. Volz, *Der Elohist als Erzähler*.

52. G. von Rad, *Die Priesterschrift im Hexateuch literarisch untersucht und theologisch gewertet*, BWANT 65 (= 4th ser., 13) (Stuttgart: Kohlhammer, 1934).

53. I. Engnell, *Gamla Testamentet: En traditionshistorisk inledning*, vol. 1 (Stockholm: Svenska Kyrkans Diakonistyreles Bokförlag, 1945); cf. idem, "The Pentateuch," in *Critical Essays on the Old Testament*, ed. I. Engnell, J. T. Willis, and H. Ringgren (London: SPCK, 1970), 50–67.

54. M. Noth, *Überlieferungsgeschichte des Pentateuch* (Stuttgart: Kohlhammer, 1948); ET, *A History of Pentateuchal Traditions* (Englewood Cliffs, NJ: Prentice-Hall, 1972).

55. In Leviticus, Noth assigned only chaps. 8–10 to the original P narrative. He regarded the Holiness Code (chaps. 17–26) as a later insertion into P. Also, P is limited to Genesis–Numbers by A. Bentzen, *An Introduction to the Old Testament*, 7th ed. (Copenhagen: G. E. C. Gad, 1967), 271.

56. In F. M. Cross, *Canaanite Myth and Hebrew Epic* (Cambridge, MA: Harvard University Press, 1973), 293–325.

Cross concludes that "the Priestly strata of the Tetrateuch never existed as an independent narrative document."[57] He proposes that toward the end of the exile, the Epic (JE) tradition was expanded by a priestly tradent, or possibly a narrow priestly school, to provide "the Tetrateuch in its penultimate form." According to Cross, the lack of substantial P narratives throughout the Tetrateuch casts serious doubts on the idea that P first circulated as an independent narrative document; what we know of P points to its being merely a revision and expansion of earlier material. R. Rendtorff adopts a similar position, arguing that the P material never formed an independent source, but was employed by a redactor to combine various traditions.[58]

As regards the legislative material associated with P, it has become widely accepted that Leviticus 17–26 represents a separate source, designated the *Heiligkeitsgesetz*, Holiness Code (H).[59] While early critics believed that H was taken over by the Priestly Writer and incorporated into his work, Milgrom and I. Knohl have recently argued that P existed before H.[60]

Apart from difficulties over defining the exact nature of P, attention has also focused on the dating of the source. Though most scholars have been content to accept a postexilic date for P, allowing for the possible incorporation of some preexilic material, a growing number have tried to date P considerably earlier. In a series of articles and books, Y. Kaufmann argued at length that P was earlier than D and not later, as Wellhausen maintained.[61] Substantial support for dating P early has come from A. Hurvitz, who has in detail compared

57. Ibid., 324.
58. Rendtorff, *Problem of the Process of Transmission*.
59. This title was first proposed by A. Klostermann ("Ezechiel und das Heiligkeitsgesetzes," in *Der Pentateuch*, pp. 368–418 [Leipzig, 1893]) and is now commonly used. For a survey of recent research on the Holiness Code, see the article "Holiness Code" by H. T. C. Sun in *ABD* 3:254–57.
60. Milgrom, *Leviticus 1–16*, 3–51; idem, "Priestly ('P') Source," *ABD* 5:454–61; I. Knohl, *The Sanctuary of Silence: The Priestly Torah and the Holiness School* (Minneapolis: Fortress, 1995). Notice, however, the proposal of R. Rendtorff ("Two Kinds of P? Some Reflections on the Occasion of the Publishing of Jacob Milgrom's Commentary on Leviticus 1–16," *JSOT* 60 [1993]: 75–81) that the cultic material assigned to P should be distinguished from the narrative material normally associated with the same source, and the response of Milgrom ("Response to Rolf Rendtorff," *JSOT* 60 [1993]: 83–85).
61. Y. Kaufmann, "Probleme der israelitisch-jüdischen Religionsgeschichte," *ZAW* 48 (1930): 23–43; 51 (1933): 35–47; *Toledot ha-Emunah ha-Yisre'elit* (Tel-Aviv: Dvir, 1937–57). The first seven volumes of this eight-volume work were condensed and translated into English by M. Greenberg in *The Religion of Israel* (Chicago: University of Chicago Press, 1960). Kaufmann's views exercised a considerable influence on subsequent Jewish scholarship; cf. S. Sandmel, *The Hebrew Scriptures: An Introduction to Their Literature and Religious Ideas* (New York: Knopf, 1963); M. Weinfeld, *Deuteronomy and the Deuteronomic School* (Oxford: Clarendon, 1972); M. Haran, *Temples and Temple-Service in Ancient Israel* (Oxford: Clarendon, 1978); idem, "Behind the Scenes of History: Determining the Date of the Priestly Source," *JBL* 100 (1981): 321–33. A late date for P is also rejected by S. R. Külling, *Zur Datierung der "Genesis-P-Stücke"* (Kampen: Kok, 1964). As early as 1886, A. Dillmann, *Die Bücher Numeri, Deuteronomium und Josua*, 2nd ed. (Leipzig: Hirzel, 1886), 593–690, defended the idea that P was earlier than D.

the "instructional" vocabulary of P with that of the exilic book of Ezekiel;[62] differences suggest that P must be dated to the preexilic period. In the recent studies of Milgrom and Knohl, these observations are developed further; H is dated toward the end of the eighth century BC, with P having been composed no later than 750 BC.[63] The impact of these new developments can be observed in Friedman's article "Torah (Pentateuch)" in the *Anchor Bible Dictionary*. While in every other respect Friedman follows the Documentary Hypothesis as formulated a century ago, he dates P earlier than D.[64]

With all these proposed alterations to the Documentary Hypothesis, we must wait to see what their impact will be on the scholarly consensus that develops during the next two decades. Alongside these modifications, however, scholars will also have to evaluate other recent developments that strongly challenge the very validity of the Documentary Hypothesis.

Alternatives to the Documentary Hypothesis

The past hundred years have also witnessed a variety of studies critical of the Documentary Hypothesis. Initially, many of these originated from scholars who, as a result of their conservative theological convictions, were hostile to a theory that challenged the long-standing tradition of Mosaic authorship of the Pentateuch.[65] These attacks on the Documentary Hypothesis tended to be ignored or dismissed by the majority of biblical scholars. Yet as time has progressed, an increasing number of mainstream scholars have joined this chorus of dissent. As a consequence during recent decades, criticisms of the Documentary Hypothesis have been taken more seriously. Recent critics cannot all be dismissed as being theologically motivated in their opposition to the Documentary Hypothesis.

Winnett, Wagner, Redford, and Van Seters

There have been few sustained attempts to produce an alternative source analysis for the Pentateuch. However, during the past sixty years a small group

62. A. Hurvitz, "Evidence of Language in Dating the Priestly Code: A Linguistic Study in Technical Idioms and Terminology," *RB* 81 (1974): 24–56; idem, *A Linguistic Study of the Relationship between the Priestly Source and the Book of Ezekiel*, CahRB 20 (Paris: J. Gabalda, 1982); idem, "Dating the Priestly Source in Light of the Historical Study of Biblical Hebrew a Century after Wellhausen," *ZAW* 100 (1988): 88–99. For a recent critique of Hurvitz, see J. Blenkinsopp, "An Assessment of the Alleged Pre-Exilic Date of the Priestly Material in the Pentateuch," *ZAW* 108 (1996): 495–518; cf. M. S. Smith, *The Pilgrimage Pattern in Exodus*, JSOTSup 239 (Sheffield: Sheffield Academic Press, 1997), 165–71.

63. See footnote 53 above.

64. See also Friedman, *Who Wrote the Bible?*

65. For a brief survey, see T. D. Alexander, *Abraham in the Negev: A Source-Critical Investigation of Genesis 20:1–22:19* (Carlisle: Paternoster, 1997), 17–20.

of North American scholars have developed a new approach to the composition of the Pentateuch, focusing in particular on the book of Genesis. These scholars are F. V. Winnett and his students, N. E. Wagner, D. B. Redford, and J. Van Seters.

In 1949 Winnett suggested that the books of Exodus and Numbers formed one source, the Mosaic tradition, which eventually was revised by P.[66] Since this source originated in the northern kingdom, Winnett somewhat reluctantly designated it J. Instead of four main sources in the Pentateuch, he discovered only three: J, D, P. Later Winnett developed his views on Genesis in an article titled "Re-examining the Foundations."[67] In it he divided Genesis into three main sections: the Primeval History, the patriarchal narratives, and the Joseph story. Following an opinion first expressed by J. Morgenstern,[68] he dated the J material of the Primeval History to the early postexilic period. In the Abraham cycle, Winnett developed a suggestion of S. Sandmel[69] and argued that E supplemented the J material in order to create a more favorable impression of Abraham. Viewed in this light, E could never have existed as an independent, parallel account of the life of Abraham. Winnett then proceeded to question the usual source analysis of the Jacob narrative; he concluded that the evidence in favor of an extensive E version of the story was extremely weak. As for J, Winnett believed that one could detect the use of both early and late material in its composition. To explain this, he suggested that an Abraham-Jacob cultic document (K) underwent two official revisions; the first of these was by E, and the second by "Late J," who significantly developed the divine promises. In the Joseph story Winnett argued that a basic E story was supplemented by J material. These J additions, however, did not form part of a larger J narrative but were merely a retelling of part of the E narrative. Winnett linked these J supplements with the J material of the Primeval History and the J revision of the patriarchal narratives. However, he believed that the basic E Joseph story differed markedly from the E supplements to the patriarchal narratives and so must be viewed as having different origins.

Wagner also offered an analysis of the patriarchal narratives along the lines suggested by Winnett.[70] For the Abraham narrative (Gen. 11:26–25:18) he concluded that the material usually assigned to J consisted of a basic J narrative that was later supplemented by a compiler E. This expansion by E

---

66. F. V. Winnett, *The Mosaic Tradition* (Toronto: University of Toronto Press, 1949).

67. F. V. Winnett, "Re-examining the Foundations," *JBL* 84 (1965): 1–19.

68. J. Morgenstern, "The Mythological Background of Psalm 82," *HUCA* 14 (1939): 29–126.

69. S. Sandmel, "The Haggada within Scripture," *JBL* 80 (1961): 105–22. Sandmel rejects the idea of an ancient unified J document.

70. N. E. Wagner, "A Literary Analysis of Genesis 12–36" (PhD dis., University of Toronto, 1965); cf. idem, "Pentateuchal Criticism: No Clear Future," *CJT* 13 (1967): 225–32; idem, "Abraham and David?" in *Studies on the Palestinian World*, ed. J. W. Wevers and D. B. Redford (Toronto: University of Toronto Press, 1972), 117–40.

occurred during the time of Jeremiah and Ezekiel. Finally, C, who developed the theme of divine promises to the patriarch, supplemented the JE narrative. After considering Genesis 25:19–36:43, Wagner observed that the basic J narrative about Jacob appeared to have an Israelite origin, whereas the primary J material about Abraham came from Judah. He concluded that two J authors were responsible for these differences: J^a (Abraham) and J^j (Jacob). Wagner also maintained that there was no trace of E in Genesis 25:19–36:43. Then J^j, unlike J^a, was expanded only by C, a Judean author from the sixth century BC who was responsible for the pre-P form of Genesis. Finally, in about 400 BC, P supplemented C's work to produce the present book of Genesis.

Wagner's approach to Genesis 12–36 was extended by Redford, another of Winnett's students, to embrace the Joseph narrative. He cautiously suggested that the final redaction of the Joseph story (his "Judah" version) might be equated with Winnett's "Late J" or Wagner's source C.

By far the most significant attempt to produce a new source analysis for part of Genesis comes from Van Seters in his book *Abraham in History and Tradition*. Through an investigation of the relationship between the wife/sister incidents in Genesis 12, 20, and 26, Van Seters concludes that there were three important stages in the development of the Abraham cycle. Genesis 12:10–20 originally formed part of a pre-Yahwistic first stage, which consisted of three episodes linked by a brief framework.[71] To this were added Genesis 20:1–17 and 21:25–26, 28–31a, which Van Seters labels as a pre-Yahwistic second stage and equates with the source E. This material constituted a single unified story, originally following immediately after the account of Abraham's stay in Egypt (12:10–13:1). The third stage in the growth of the Abraham cycle involved the Yahwist (J), who added (1) brief secondary additions to the earlier material[72] and (2) larger episodic units,[73] which "were skillfully incorporated into the older literary work with some new arrangement of the materials."[74] The Yahwist's work was later supplemented by the priestly author (P), who incorporated certain genealogical and chronological material,[75] as well as chapters 17 and 23. Van Seters identifies this as the fourth stage of development. The fifth and final stage in the growth of the Abraham cycle, the post-priestly stage, occurred when chapter 14 was incorporated into the overall narrative. Concerning the dating of these various stages, Van Seters argues that the important Yahwistic stage occurred during the time of the exile. Significantly, Van Seters adopts a supplementary approach toward the composition of the Abraham cycle;

71. Gen. 12:1, 4a, 6a, 7, 10–20; 13:1–2; 16:1–3a, 4–9, 11ab, 12; 13:18; 18:1a, 10–14; 21:2, 6–7; however, all references to Lot were added at a later stage.

72. Gen. 12:2–3, 6b, 8–9; 16:7b, 10, 11c, 13–14; 20:1a; 21:1.

73. Gen. 13:3–5, 7–17; 15; 18:1b–9; 18:15–19:38; 21:8–24, 27, 31b–34; 22; 24; 25:1–6, 11; 26.

74. J. Van Seters, *Abraham in History and Tradition* (New Haven: Yale University Press, 1975), 313.

75. Gen. 11:26–32; 12:4b–5; 13:6; 16:3b, 15–16; 21:3–5; 25:7–10.

rather than being composed of continuous parallel documents, it consists of one basic narrative supplemented by later additions.

In subsequent writings Van Seters has supported his dating of J to the exilic period. In *Prologue to History* and *The Life of Moses*, he examines the Yahwistic materials of Genesis and Exodus–Numbers respectively, concluding that during the exilic period the Yahwist, who was familiar with eastern (Mesopotamian) and western (Greek) antiquarian traditions, produced a comprehensive prologue to the Deuteronomistic History. Though Van Seters ascribes to the Yahwist the shaping of the Tetrateuch, especially the bringing together of the patriarchal and exodus traditions, this has not gone unchallenged: some recent writers attribute this role to a Deuteronomistic or priestly editor.[76]

Rendtorff and Blum

In 1969 R. Rendtorff drew attention to what he perceived to be an irreconcilable conflict between the Documentary Hypothesis and more recent developments in form and traditio-historical criticism.[77] In particular, he argued that the existence of a continuous J or E document in Genesis is excluded by the observation that within Genesis are larger independent literary units—such as the Joseph story, the Jacob-Esau cycle, and the Jacob-Laban cycle—that were produced by different "authors."

Rendtorff continued his attack on the Documentary Hypothesis in *The Problem of the Process of Transmission in the Pentateuch*.[78] Building on a number of important observations, Rendtorff contends that the time has now come to abandon the Documentary Hypothesis as the best way of explaining the composition of the Pentateuch. Various factors have led him to this conclusion. First, a survey of the relevant literature reveals that there is considerable disagreement among scholars regarding the precise formulation of the Documentary Hypothesis. What is often assumed to be a scholarly consensus is far from such, and the existence of diverse opinions clearly challenges the validity of the entire theory. Second, traditio-historical investigations of the Pentateuch have suggested that it is composed of a number of larger units that

---

76. See next section. In favor of a priestly editor are K. Schmid, "The So-Called Yahwist and the Literary Gap between Genesis and Exodus," in Dozeman and Schmid, *A Farewell to the Yahwist?*, 29–50; and J. C. Gertz, "The Transition between the Books of Genesis and Exodus," in Dozeman and Schmid, *A Farewell to the Yahwist?*, 73–87. Support for a "late pre-Priestly author/ editor" comes from D. M. Carr, "What Is Required to Identify Pre-Priestly Narrative Connections between Genesis and Exodus? Some General Reflections and Specific Cases," in Dozeman and Schmid, *A Farewell to the Yahwist?*, 159–80; cf. Dozeman, *Commentary on Exodus*, 40.

77. R. Rendtorff, "Traditio-Historical Method and the Documentary Hypothesis," *PWCJS* 5 (1969): 5–11.

78. Cf. R. Rendtorff, "The 'Yahwist' as Theologian? The Dilemma of Pentateuchal Criticism," *JSOT* 3 (1977): 2–10.

originally existed independently of one another (e.g., the Primeval History, the patriarchal narratives, the account of the exodus from Egypt, the Sinai passage, Israel's stay in the desert, the occupation of the land). Rendtorff believes that it is impossible to reconcile the existence of these larger units with the concept of continuous documents that extend throughout the Pentateuch. Third, drawing from the material assigned to the Yahwistic and Priestly Writers, it is impossible to reconstruct continuous, coherent documents. Fourth, there are too many inconsistencies in the use of linguistic criteria to assign material to a particular source. Various words and expressions generally taken to be typical of one source may also occur in passages assigned to one of the other sources. Fifth, it is questionable whether material so disparate in form—such as Genesis 12:10–20 ("brief" narrative style), 24:1–67 ("detailed" narrative style), and the Joseph story ("novelistic" style)—could have originated from the same source. Form-critical considerations suggest that these passages derive from different settings and therefore cannot be the product of a single author. Yet all three narratives are normally assigned to J. In the light of these differing arguments, Rendtorff views the Documentary Hypothesis as untenable.

While rejecting the idea that continuous parallel documents were used to compose the Pentateuch, Rendtorff offers an alternative explanation. Focusing on the divine promises found in Genesis 12–50, he concludes that it is possible to detect the redactional stages by which the patriarchal stories involving Abraham, Isaac, Jacob, and Joseph were united. He argues, for example, that one can discern different redactional phases on the basis of the expressions "to you," "to you and your descendants," "to your descendants."[79] Yet, though Rendtorff's analysis of the divine promises is detailed and his reconstruction of the redactional process closely reasoned, the whole approach rests on the highly questionable assumption that minor variations within the divine-promise speeches reflect different stages of composition. Nowhere, however, does he allow for the possibility that these variations may have arisen due to factors other than editorial reworking. In many instances it is possible that minor differences are little more than stylistic variations of expression, a natural feature of everyday speech. Consequently, we must express reservations about the basis for Rendtorff's reconstruction of the editorial process by which the patriarchal stories were united.

Although Rendtorff's critique of the Documentary Hypothesis is trenchant, especially his arguments against the existence of continuous documents extending throughout the Pentateuch, a word of caution must be expressed. Rendtorff places considerable weight on the traditio-historical observation that the Pentateuch consists of larger units. However, he does not discuss the extent and content of these units: their general existence is assumed rather than demonstrated. Furthermore, the supposition that they were originally

---

79. Rendtorff, *Problem of the Process of Transmission*, 55–84.

independent requires investigation. Not only are some of the units more closely linked than Rendtorff allows, but it is also apparent that in a variety of ways later units presuppose the existence of earlier units (e.g., Exod. 1–14 assumes a knowledge of the events recorded in the concluding chapters of Genesis in order to explain why the Israelites are in Egypt). Moreover, even if we in principle allow for the existence of once-independent units, these have now been integrated. However, there is no way of knowing how much or how little editorial reworking has occurred in this editorial process. All proposals are entirely speculative and should be viewed with extreme caution, especially when some scholars claim to be able to detect the presence of several distinctive editorial layers.

Rendtorff's rejection of the existence of J and E is developed further by one of his students, E. Blum, in a lengthy study titled *Die Komposition der Vätergeschichte*.[80] Focusing on Genesis 12–50, Blum argues for a process of composition that differs significantly from that proposed under the Documentary Hypothesis. In essence, he rejects the existence of parallel sources in favor of a supplementary approach. Starting with material drawn from Genesis 25–33, Blum uncovers a story about Jacob (*Jakoberzählung*; 25:9–34; 27:1–33:20) that focuses on the importance of Bethel as a cultic center and on the theme of reconciliation between brothers. According to Blum, this narrative was composed in the northern kingdom to address the political situation that existed in the time of Jeroboam I following the breakup of the Solomonic kingdom. Sometime later, before the downfall of the northern kingdom, the *Jakoberzählung* was expanded by the addition of the Joseph story to form the *Jakobgeschichte* ("the Jacob history," most but not all of Gen. 25–50), a biography of Jacob from birth to death. Later a Judean author who wished to emphasize the importance of Judah further expanded this narrative and thus added chapters 34, 38, and 49, as well as 35:21–22a.

After the collapse of the northern kingdom, the *Jakobgeschichte* was yet again expanded, this time by adding the Abraham-Lot story (Gen. 13, 18–19). This new document, centered on the divine promises found in 13:14–17 and 28:13–15, formed the first Patriarchal History, or *Vätergeschichte* (Vg[1]). A new version of this history (Vg[2]) was produced during the Babylonian exile; it was built around the divine speeches in 12:1–3; 26:2–3; 31:11, 13; 46:1–5a and focused on the topics of nationhood, territory, and blessing. Other material reflecting a similar outlook was also added at this stage (i.e., 12:6–9, 10–20; 16; 21:8–21; 22; 26).

In the postexilic period an important redaction occurred at the hands of a Deuteronomistic editor who, apart from adding chapters 15 and 24, linked the Patriarchal History to the rest of the Pentateuch. This was then followed

---

80. E. Blum, *Die Komposition der Vätergeschichte*, WMANT 57 (Neukirchen-Vluyn: Neukirchener Verlag, 1984).

by another revision, undertaken by a Priestly Writer, which for the book of Genesis involved the creation of the *tôlĕdōt* framework and the inclusion of various other texts (e.g., Gen. 17). While links with the Documentary Hypothesis are observable, particularly for the final stages of this process, Blum's reconstruction of the way in which the patriarchal narratives developed represents a major break with past approaches.

To his credit, Blum seeks to uncover the process of composition by undertaking a detailed study of the text itself, thereby avoiding the more speculative type of traditio-historical research undertaken by Noth. Yet his approach, like that of Wellhausen, assumes that early and late material can be distinguished with considerable certainty even though the material had gone through a number of significant redactional stages. Finally, regarding the Abraham narrative, Blum relies heavily on Rendtorff's analysis of the divine promises, which, as we have noted above, rests on highly questionable premises.[81]

In his more recent work *Studien zur Komposition des Pentateuch*, Blum's observations of the Patriarchal History have been extended to include the rest of the Pentateuch. Abandoning the Documentary Hypothesis model, Blum argues that the Pentateuch underwent two major stages in its composition. The first of these, D-Komposition (K^D), was undertaken by editors influenced by the Deuteronomistic History in the early postexilic period. These editors integrated two blocks of already-existing material: an earlier form of Genesis 12–50 dating from the exilic period and a "Life of Moses," which included much of the material presently in Exodus to Numbers. The process of integrating these two blocks of material involved the creation, by the K^D editors, of the promise texts in Genesis.[82] The importance of these promise texts is underlined by the fact that Blum views K^D as having started with Genesis 12:1–3. A second stage took place when Priestly Writers reworked K^D; not surprisingly, Blum designates this final redactional stage P-Komposition (K^P). With this final redaction the Primeval History of Genesis 1–11 was added, creating the Pentateuch as we now know it. However, more recently Blum has revised his thinking about the process by which the Genesis and Exodus materials were combined. He is now of the opinion that this occurred only at the K^P stage.[83]

Central to Blum's approach is the idea that the pentateuchal materials came into being through a number of distinctive stages: early written traditions,

---

81. Regarding this, Van Seters rightly observes, "Rendtorff had concluded (to my mind on dubious grounds) that Genesis 13:14–17 contained the earliest form of the land promise theme. This is what really dictates Blum's choice of the Abraham-Lot stories as the earliest level of the Abraham tradition. Rendtorff's complex scheme of promises development governs the other levels of Blum's composition history as well. But if one cannot accept the arguments for a multiplicity of levels in the nonpriestly promise texts, then the whole scheme may be reconstructed in quite a different way" ("Review of *Die Komposition der Vätergeschichte*, by E. Blum," *JBL* 105 [1986]: 707).

82. Gen. 15; 22:15–18; 24:7; 26:3b–5, 24; cf. Exod. 13:5, 11; 32:13; 33:1; Num. 11:12; 14:16, 23.

83. Blum, "Die Literarische Verbingung von Erzvätern und Exodus," 119–56.

Deuteronomy, the Deuteronomistic History, K^D, and finally K^P. Fundamental to the ordering of these is the idea that K^D was composed after the Deuteronomistic History. Though this general idea finds support among some scholars, it has also invited serious criticism.[84] The issue of the relationship between the Tetrateuch and the Deuteronomistic History, as well as the relationship between Genesis and Exodus, will continue to figure prominently in future scholarly discussion. Yet the weight of evidence seems to argue strongly against Blum's approach.[85]

Whybray

In his book *The Making of the Pentateuch: A Methodological Study*, R. N. Whybray provides one of the most recent, detailed assessments of the Documentary Hypothesis. Focusing principally on the narrative sections of the Pentateuch, he evaluates (1) the presuppositions underlying the theory (i.e., philosophical and religio-historical, linguistic, literary, cultural); (2) the criteria used to distinguish the different documentary sources (i.e., language and style; repetitions, duplications, and contradictions; differences of culture, religion, and theology); (3) the application of the criteria; and (4) the role of the redactors.

Whybray's especially effective criticisms of the Documentary Hypothesis include the following:

1. Proponents of the Documentary Hypothesis assume "a consistency in the avoidance of repetitions and contradictions which is unparalleled in ancient literature (and even in modern fiction), and which ignores the possibility of the deliberate use of such features for aesthetic and literary purposes."[86]
2. The Documentary Hypothesis often breaks up narratives into different sources, destroying their literary and aesthetic qualities, while at the same time creating texts that lack such qualities.
3. Variations in language and style need not result solely from the existence of different sources. They may arise equally well from "differences of subject-matter requiring special or distinctive vocabulary, alternations of vocabulary introduced for literary reasons, and unconscious variation of vocabulary."[87]

84. For example, E. W. Nicholson, *The Pentateuch in the Twentieth Century: The Legacy of Julius Wellhausen* (Oxford: Clarendon, 1998), 194, comments, "The evidence does not support the notion of a systematic Deuteronomistic editing of the Tetrateuch, much less the view that the first Tetrateuch was the work of a Deuteronomistic author."

85. See, e.g., the discussion of Deuteronomistic influence in the composition of Exod. 19–24 in chap. 5 (below).

86. Whybray, *Making of the Pentateuch*, 130.

87. Ibid.

4. There is inadequate evidence to support "the presence *throughout* each of the documents of a single style, purpose and point of view or theology, and of an unbroken narrative thread."[88]

While others have already noted many of the shortcomings of the Documentary Hypothesis highlighted by Whybray, his work is noteworthy for two reasons. First, his rejection of the Documentary Hypothesis is not motivated by an underlying theological conservatism. Indeed, he concludes that the narrative sections of the Pentateuch were probably composed in the sixth century by a single author who, while drawing on some recent traditions, relied mainly upon his own imagination.[89] Second, Whybray offers a generally comprehensive assessment of the Documentary Hypothesis. While some issues are dealt with briefly, he demonstrates that the Documentary Hypothesis rests on unacceptable presuppositions, inadequate criteria for distinguishing the different sources, and a method of literary composition for which there is no analogy elsewhere.

Although Whybray's criticism of the Documentary Hypothesis is compelling, he nowhere tries to demonstrate the literary unity of the Pentateuch by a detailed exposition of the entire text, or even part of it. Thus, while he may have gone some way to demolishing the idea that the Pentateuch was composed of continuous, parallel documents, his study does not exclude the possibility of either a fragmentary or supplementary explanation for the composition of the Pentateuch.

Conclusion

As we move further into the twenty-first century, there can be little doubt that pentateuchal criticism is in something of a crisis. The opponents of the Documentary Hypothesis are no longer limited to those of a conservative theological outlook. While some scholars remain committed to the basic concept of the Documentary Hypothesis, others seek to modify it substantially, and still others launch a fresh approach to the whole issue of the Pentateuch's composition. Even staunch supporters of the Documentary Hypothesis concede that it is presently in decline. With good reason E. W. Nicholson remarks:

> As a result, pentateuchal research since the mid-1970s has become a mirror image of what it was in the years following the publication of Wellhausen's study of the composition of the Pentateuch in the mid-1870s: whereas at that time the Documentary Theory which he had so persuasively argued was in the ascendant,

88. Ibid.
89. R. N. Whybray briefly restates this position in his more recent book, *Introduction to the Pentateuch* (Grand Rapids: Eerdmans, 1995).

commanding ever increasing support, today it is in sharp decline—some would say in a state of advanced rigor mortis—and new solutions are being argued and urged in its place.[90]

While the time has certainly come for the Documentary Hypothesis to be abandoned, no new consensus has emerged to take its place. The present state of pentateuchal studies is captured well in a brief comment by B. Sommer:

> For more than a century beginning in the mid-1800s, the Documentary Hypothesis represented a near-consensus among critical scholars who studied the composition of the Pentateuch. . . . The hypothesis in its broadest outlines commanded widespread respect, and it was assumed as the starting point for almost all discussions of the Pentateuch and the development of Israelite religion. In the last quarter of this century, however, this consensus has broken down. . . . The verities enshrined in older introductions have disappeared, and in their place scholars are confronted by competing theories which are discouragingly numerous, exceedingly complex, and often couched in an expository style that is . . . "not for the faint-hearted."[91]

This final sentence captures well the present state of play regarding scholarly attempts to explain how the Pentateuch was composed. No single theory has arisen to replace the Documentary Hypothesis, and this situation is likely to remain so into the foreseeable future.

In spite of all that has been written during the past 250 years, we need to acknowledge that today we cannot unravel how the Pentateuch was composed. We simply do not know enough to say with any certainty how these books were put together. Different scholars looking at the same texts can arrive at very different conclusions. Current theories are based on speculation and circular argumentation. Unless we actually discover new documents that shed direct light on the prior history of the books of Genesis to Deuteronomy, we should resign ourselves to the idea that it is impossible to confidently reconstruct the process by which they were composed. While earlier sources were undoubtedly used, we cannot recover these with any degree of certainty from the present texts alone. Those who think otherwise are pursuing a chimera.

90. Nicholson, *Pentateuch*, 95–96.
91. B. D. Sommer, "Review of *The Pentateuch in the 20th Century: The Legacy of Julius Wellhausen*, by E. Nicholson," *RBL* 2 (2000): 184.

5

The Sinai Narrative—A Test Case

As we have observed in the preceding chapter, recent developments in pentateuchal criticism have challenged the validity of the Documentary Hypothesis, prompting a variety of alternative approaches. Among these newer developments has arisen the idea that the material in the books of Genesis to Numbers underwent several redactional stages, one of which resembles the literary style of the writer(s) responsible for the Deuteronomistic History (the books of Deuteronomy to Kings).[1] As a result, some scholars now argue that the books of Genesis to Numbers were composed to form a prologue to the Deuteronomistic History.

In the light of these developments, in this chapter we shall examine afresh the composition of the Sinai Narrative in Exodus 19:1–24:11. This provides us with an opportunity (1) to test the validity of the Documentary Hypothesis as applied to a particular text and (2) to evaluate claims of Deuteronomistic influence in the composition of Genesis to Numbers. Not only does Exodus 19–24 lend itself well to both of these issues; it also merits attention because scholarly efforts to uncover the source(s) of these chapters have proved less than satisfactory. As J. I. Durham observes, "Though many helpful observations may be harvested from the critical work of more than a century, the sum total of that work is a clear assertion that no literary solution to this complex narrative has been found, with more than a hint that none is likely to be found."[2] Although Durham's assessment reflects well the current state of

1. See under the heading "The D Source" in chap. 4.
2. J. I. Durham, *Exodus*, WBC 3 (Waco: Word Books, 1987), 259.

play regarding Exodus 19:1–24:11, there are perhaps grounds for hoping that a new approach, freed from some of the constraints of previous studies, may yet yield a better understanding of the process by which these chapters were composed. It will be argued below that Exodus 19:1–24:11 displays greater signs of literary unity than has been recognized in the past; the key to this unity rests in the narrative framework that surrounds the divine speeches in Exodus 19:3–6 and 20:22–24:2.

Narrative Framework of Divine Speeches in 19:3–6; 20:22–24:2

As presently constituted, Exodus 19:1–24:11 describes the ratification of a covenant between Yahweh and the Israelites, involving a divine theophany at Mount Sinai. Central to these events are a number of important divine speeches. While the best known of these is the Ten Commandments or Decalogue (Exod. 20:2–17), we shall first focus on the addresses in Exodus 19:3–6 and 20:22–24:2. As D. Patrick has observed, these latter speeches, in spite of their very differing lengths, share a common narrative framework.[3] Expanding slightly on Patrick's observations, the parallels between Exodus 19:2b–8a and 20:21–24:3 are set out in table 5.1 (my trans.).

Among the most striking aspects of these parallels are the following. A contrast is made between Moses's ascent to Yahweh (Exod. 19:3; 20:21) and the people remaining at the foot of the mountain (19:2b; 20:21).[4] After Moses separates from the Israelites, Yahweh takes the initiative and speaks to him (19:3; 20:22). Each speech begins with the expression, "This is what you are to say," emphasizing that Moses is to convey Yahweh's remarks to the people "word for word."[5] In both instances Yahweh's opening words for the Israelites are "YOU yourselves have seen"; these introduce brief comments about prior divine activities witnessed by the people. Later, after hearing what Yahweh has to say, Moses returns and, as instructed, reports all that he has been told (19:7; 24:3). Finally, the people respond positively, affirming their willingness to do all that Yahweh has said (19:8; 24:3; cf. 24:7). Although minor variations in wording exist, the strong similarities between the narrative frameworks and the introductory words of the divine speeches in Exodus 19:3–6 and 20:22–24:2 suggest common authorship.[6] We shall return to the issue of the identity of this author.

---

3. D. Patrick, "The Covenant Code Source," *VT* 27 (1977): 145–57; cf. idem, *Old Testament Law* (London: SCM, 1986), 64.

4. In both cases this contrast is marked by a break in the *vav*-consecutive sequence of the Hebrew text, and by naming the subject, Moses, before a perfect verb.

5. B. Jacob, *The Second Book of the Bible: Exodus* (Hoboken, NJ: Ktav, 1992), 525.

6. Although a later author could have modeled the narrative framework and opening words of one divine speech on an already-existing account, it is much more likely that a single author was responsible for composing both.

Table 5.1
Common Elements in Exodus 19:2b–8a and Exodus 20:21–24:3

Exodus 19:2b–8a	Exodus 20:21–24:3
[19:2b]There Israel camped in front of the mountain. [3]But Moses went up to God,	[20:21]The people remained at a distance, but Moses approached the thick darkness where God was.
and the LORD called to him from the mountain, saying,	[22]Then the LORD said to Moses,
"This is what you shall say to the house of Jacob and what you shall tell the children of Israel:	"This is what you are to say to the children of Israel:
[4]"YOU* yourselves have seen what I did to Egypt, and how I carried YOU on eagles' wings and brought YOU to myself. . . .'"	'YOU yourselves have seen that I have spoken to YOU from heaven. . . .'"
[The main part of the divine speech.]	[The main part of the divine speech.]
[7]So Moses came and summoned the elders of the people and put before them all these words that the LORD had commanded him.	[24:3]So Moses came and told the people all the LORD's words and all the laws.
[8]The people replied all together, "All that the LORD has said we will do."	All the people replied with one voice, "All the words that the LORD has said we will do."

*Here "YOU" stands for the second-person plural in MT; "you" translates the second-person singular.

While Yahweh's words in Exodus 19:3–6 are normally assigned to the same source as the narrative that follows in verses 7–8,[7] source critics have generally not observed any connections between the speech in 20:22–24:2 and its narrative framework. Since the time of Wellhausen, 20:22–23:33 has generally been viewed as coming from an independent source,[8] having nothing in common with 24:1–11. In the light of this, and given that the parallels noted above include only the very opening words of Yahweh's speech (i.e., 20:22), can other evidence be found to link 20:22–23:33 with 24:1–11?

To address this question, some general observations must be made briefly regarding the content and structure of the speech in Exodus 20:22–24:2. As it stands, Yahweh's address to Moses falls into a number of distinct sections:[9]

7. The source analysis of Exod. 19 will be discussed later.
8. Here it is not possible to consider the process by which Exod. 20:22–23:33 was composed. For four recent but differing approaches, see E. Otto, *Wandel der Rechtsbegründungen in der Gesellschaftsgeschichte des antiken Israel: Eine Rechtsgeschichte des "Bundesbuches" Ex XX 22–XXIII 13*, StudBib 3 (Leiden: Brill, 1988); L. Schwienhorst-Schönberger, *Das Bundesbuch (Ex 20,22–23,33)* (Berlin: de Gruyter, 1990); Y. Osumi, *Die Kompositionsgeschichte des Bundesbuches: Exodus 20,22b–23,33*, OBO 105 (Göttingen: Vanderhoeck & Ruprecht, 1991); J. M. Sprinkle, *"The Book of the Covenant": A Literary Approach*, JSOTSup 174 (Sheffield: JSOT Press, 1994).
9. Patrick, *Old Testament Law*, 63–96.

20:22–26	instructions concerning the making of cultic objects
21:1–22:20	regulatory principles (*mišpāṭîm* [*mishpāṭîm*])
22:21–23:9	moral imperatives
23:10–19	instructions concerning the Sabbath and religious festivals
23:20–33	promises and warning concerning the land of Canaan
24:1–2	instructions for Moses and other individuals to come up to Yahweh

On the basis of content and form, the boundaries between these sections are relatively clear. The reference to *mišpāṭîm* (regulations) in 21:1 introduces the material in 22:2–23:19, setting 20:22–26 apart as the first unit in the speech. A new section comes in 22:20–23:9, framed by 22:20 and 23:9, which together form an *inclusio*;[10] this section consists of exhortations concerned mainly with protecting the weaker members of society and safeguarding the judicial system. Exodus 23:10–19 consists of cultic instructions relating to the Sabbath and festivals; this material is bound together by the use of the numbers "six" (vv. 10, 12) and "three" (vv. 14, 17). The next section, 23:20–33, is distinguished from the rest by both its paraenetic style and subject matter; directions are given as to how the Israelites must behave in order to be assured of Yahweh's help in taking possession of the land of Canaan. Finally, 24:1–2 is set apart from the rest of the address by the inclusion of the brief narrative comment "and to Moses he said." For the purpose of this present study, detailed attention will be given to 20:22–26 and 24:1–2 since both passages provide evidence linking the divine speech to 24:3–11.

Although it is often suggested that the so-called altar laws (Exod. 20:22–26) have been separated from 22:17–23:19 by the later insertion of the *mišpāṭîm* in 21:1–22:16, a number of factors support the originality of the present arrangement. First, the prohibition against making idols and the instructions for building altars both focus on the important subject of how God's presence is to be experienced by the Israelites in the future. Yahweh's blessing will come to the people when they worship him through the offering of sacrifices on altars, but not through the construction of golden or silver images. Since the whole thrust of the Sinai covenant is the establishment of a special relationship between God and the Israelites, through which the people will continue to know and experience the divine presence, these instructions form an appropriate introduction to the covenant document. Second, the directions concerning the building of altars relate in a direct way to the ratification of the covenant in 24:3–11. The narrative in Exodus 24 describes the construction of an altar and the making of whole-burnt offerings and fellowship offerings, the two types

---

10. An *inclusio* is a literary device whereby a section of material is framed by using similar expressions as the beginning and end. In this instance, the text repeats comments about not oppressing aliens because the Israelites themselves were aliens in Egypt.

of sacrifices specified in 20:24. While there are prior references in Genesis and Exodus to the building of altars and the making of sacrifices, Exodus 20:24 and 24:4–5 are the first passages in the Pentateuch to mention side by side both whole-burnt offerings and fellowship offerings. Third, the prohibition in 20:23 against having gods of either gold or silver takes on a special significance in the light of the "golden calf" incident recorded later, in 32:1–6. Close parallels exist between the ratification of the covenant in Exodus 24 and the account of its undoing in Exodus 32.[11] Both passages describe the making of an altar (24:4; 32:5), the sacrificing of whole-burnt offerings and fellowship offerings (24:5; 32:6), and the people eating and drinking in Yahweh's real or supposed presence (24:11; 32:6). Moreover, in Exodus "gods of gold" are mentioned only in 20:23; 32:4, 31. All these observations suggest that 20:22–26 is integrated more fully into the Sinai narrative than is usually supposed. Further evidence in support of this is provided below.

Regarding Exodus 24:1–2, there has been a strong tendency to discuss these verses apart from 20:22–23:33. However, verses 1–2 are obviously intended to be understood as a continuation of the preceding divine speech. Unfortunately, the present chapter division exacerbates the apparent break between 23:33 and 24:1. The continuity between 23:33 and 24:1 is immediately evident in that the identity of the speaker is not specified; it is assumed that he has already been introduced (cf. 20:22). B. S. Childs rightly observes that Exodus 24:1 forms an unusual opening,[12] for it marks not the beginning of a new episode, but merely a minor break in the divine speech that commences in 20:22. Through the inclusion of the brief narrative comment at the start of 24:1, Yahweh's concluding words to Moses are deliberately set apart from what has gone before. Although the content of 20:22–23:33 concerns all the Israelites (cf. 20:22), the instructions addressed to Moses in 24:1–2 relate only to him and a selected group of Israelite leaders.[13]

By viewing Exodus 24:1–2 as the conclusion to Yahweh's speech to Moses, we see the structure of 24:1–11 much more clearly and observe signs of careful composition. This is evident from the way in which the overall structure of the divine speech in 20:22–24:2 is reflected in the events described in 24:3–11. After returning to the people, Moses reports "all Yahweh's words and regulatory principles" (24:3), fulfilling the instruction given to him in 20:22. Then

11. Cf. A. Phillips, "Fresh Look at the Sinai Pericope," *VT* 34 (1984): 51.

12. B. S. Childs, *The Book of Exodus: A Critical, Theological Commentary*, OTL (Philadelphia: Westminster; London: SCM, 1974), 499–500.

13. Ibid., 502–4; Durham, *Exodus*, 342–43. Although the third-person references to Yahweh in Exod. 24:1–2 might suggest that the speaker is someone other than Yahweh (cf. M. Noth, *Exodus: A Commentary*, OTL [London: SCM, 1962], 196–97), it is not uncommon within the Sinai narrative for God to refer to himself in this way (e.g., Exod. 19:21–22, 24; 20:7, 10–11).

Moses records this material in writing.[14] The next day he constructs an altar and oversees the offering of whole-burnt offerings and fellowship offerings (24:4–5), activities that in a striking way parallel the instructions given in 20:24–26. Moses then reads to the Israelites the "Book of the Covenant" (presumably the contents of 20:23–23:33) before sealing the covenant by sprinkling blood upon the people (24:7–8). Finally, in obedience to Yahweh's concluding instructions (24:1–2), Moses and the elders ascend the mountain, bringing the covenant ratification ceremony to an end by eating and drinking in Yahweh's presence (24:9–11). These parallels between the lengthy divine speech (20:22–24:2) and the subsequent account of ratifying the covenant (24:3–11), in conjunction with our earlier observations concerning the narrative framework in 20:21–22 and 24:3, suggest that the narrative from 20:21 to 24:11 has been skillfully constructed.

Before leaving Exodus 24:1–11, it should be recognized that previous attempts to uncover the sources underlying this section have not proved particularly satisfactory. In general there has been a trend toward finding in these verses two or even three distinctive sources, but no consensus exists. Noth attributes verses 1–2, 9–11 to E, with verses 1–2 then undergoing redactional changes, and verses 3–8 originating from a once-independent "Book of the Covenant" source.[15] In marked contrast, J. P. Hyatt assigns verses 1–2, 9–11 to J; verses 3, 4b–6, 8 to E; and verses 4a, 7 to a Deuteronomistic redactor.[16] Childs assigns verses 3–8 to E, with the surrounding verses lacking any clear criteria by which their source(s) may be determined.[17]

While diverging over the precise identity of the sources in Exodus 24:1–11, critical scholars generally agree that verses 1–2, 9–11 differ in origin from verses 3–8. This belief rests largely on the fact that the former verses record both a command for Moses and others to ascend to Yahweh (vv. 1–2) and its fulfillment (vv. 9–11), whereas verses 3–8 focus on a covenant-ratification ceremony. Consequently, while acknowledging the lack of decisive criteria for source analysis, Childs takes recourse to the preliterary stage and concludes that verses 3–8 go back to an oral account of a "covenant renewal ceremony," whereas verses 1–2, 9–11 reflect "a covenant meal following a theophany."[18] Although this proposal neatly circumvents the inadequacy of the criteria for source analysis, it is entirely speculative.

Support for the unity of Exodus 24:1–11 may be deduced from Deuteronomy 27:1–8, which contains instructions for the renewing of the covenant at Mount

14. Since the "regulatory principles" make up only part of Exod. 20:22–24:2, the expression "all Yahweh's words" probably refers here to the remaining sections of the Book of the Covenant and not the Decalogue.
15. Noth, *Exodus*, 194–99.
16. Ibid., 254–57.
17. Ibid., 500–502.
18. Ibid., 501.

Ebal (cf. Josh. 8:30–35). Deuteronomy 27:1–8 describes a series of closely related activities: recording the covenant obligations; building a stone altar without using iron tools (cf. Exod. 20:25); offering whole-burnt offerings and fellowship offerings; and eating in the presence of "the LORD." From a form-critical perspective, these features obviously comprise a covenant-ratification ceremony. Significantly, the same elements come in Exodus 24:1–11, taken as a whole.[19] Moreover, as Childs observes, "the covenant meal [Exod. xxiv 9–11] is now seen as a culmination of the rite in 3–8, and not as a rival ceremony."[20] Since verses 1–2, 9–11 and verses 3–8 taken together form a coherent account, no justification exists for maintaining that more than one source is present in Exodus 24:1–11.

Exodus 20:22 and the Decalogue

Thus far we have argued that the divine speeches in Exodus 19:3–6 and 20:22–24:2, together with the narratives immediately surrounding them (19:2a, 7–8a; 20:21; 24:3–11), display evidence of having been constructed as a unified work. Central to our argument have been the parallels noted in table 5.1, especially the similar introductions to the two divine addresses. Now we must turn to consider the relationship between the proclamation of the Decalogue (Exod. 20:1–17) and Yahweh's speech in Exodus 20:22–24:2.

As we have already briefly noted, a common element in Exodus 19:3 and 20:22 is the expression, "YOU yourselves have seen." In both speeches this phrase draws attention to divine activities personally witnessed by all the Israelites. Exodus 19:3 refers to the deliverance of the people from Egypt and their journey to Mount Sinai; significantly, 20:22 focuses not on the exodus from Egypt but on the fact that Yahweh has spoken to the Israelites "from heaven." In view of the parallels between the introductions to the two speeches, this latter activity is obviously presented as being comparable to the divine rescue of the Israelites from slavery in Egypt. The mention of Yahweh's speaking

19. Though clear parallels exist between Exod. 24:3–11 and Deut. 27:1–8, the ratification of the covenant at Mount Sinai represents a unique occasion; future covenant ceremonies take place (1) after the construction of the tabernacle, and (2) within the promised land. Thus, in Exod. 24:3–11 Moses and the seventy elders ascend Mount Sinai to eat and drink in Yahweh's presence; when the covenant is later renewed at Mount Ebal, the people, having been instructed to eat and rejoice in "the presence of Yahweh" (Deut. 27:7), gather around "the ark of the covenant of Yahweh," the symbol of God's presence in their midst (Josh. 8:33). Similarly, whereas Moses records the terms of the covenant in a scroll, elsewhere they are inscribed on large stones coated with plaster (cf. Deut. 27:2, 4; Josh. 8:32). The use of different writing materials is explicable in terms of the Israelites' location. A scroll enables the details of the covenant obligations to be transported to the land of Canaan. These variations between the Sinai covenant and later renewals are explicable, therefore, in terms of the differing settings in which the covenant ratification ceremonies occur.

20. Childs, *Exodus*, 502.

"from heaven" must refer to the giving of the Decalogue (20:2–17), for all the other divine speeches recorded in Exodus 19–24 are mediated through Moses to the Israelites. This indicates that the author who penned 20:22 had already incorporated 20:1–17 (or its equivalent) into his composition.

Exodus 20:22 also provides further evidence supporting the present location of 20:18–21 after the Decalogue. If Yahweh has indeed spoken directly to the Israelites, as he claims, why does he now in verse 20 instruct Moses to convey his words to the people? The obvious answer to this question comes in 20:18–21, which records how the people, out of fear, no longer desire that Yahweh should address them directly. Consequently, they ask Moses to act once more as Yahweh's spokesman. A careful reading of 20:22 strongly suggests that it was penned as the sequel to 20:1–21.

Since Exodus 20:22 both presupposes a speech uttered directly by Yahweh to the people and introduces a divine address delivered via Moses, there seems every reason to believe that the Decalogue and the Book of the Covenant were incorporated into the Sinai narrative by the author responsible for composing the narrative frameworks that presently surround the divine speeches in 19:3–6 and 20:22–24:2.

Deuteronomistic Redaction and the Sinai Narrative

Several recent studies have already drawn attention to the importance of Exodus 20:22 for understanding the process by which the Sinai narrative was composed, although differing somewhat in their conclusions. The two earliest studies both appeared in volume 27 of *Vetus Testamentum*, the first by Patrick[21] and the second by E. W. Nicholson.[22] Although these originated independently of each other, their findings are taken up and developed at some length by A. Phillips in volume 34.[23]

As noted above, Patrick draws attention to the common authorship of Exodus 19:3b–8; 20:22–23; and 24:3–8, which were "composed for the purpose of setting the [Covenant] Code in the context of the revelation at Sinai."[24] According to Patrick, this independent source was inserted into E before the latter was combined with J. While acknowledging "points of contact" between the narrative framework of the Covenant Code and Deuteronomy/Deuteronomistic literature, Patrick sees the latter as having been influenced by the former, and not vice versa.

Approaching Exodus 20:22–23 from a different perspective, E. W. Nicholson, in reference to Yahweh's speaking from heaven, finds evidence of a

---

21. Patrick, "Covenant Code Source," 145–57.
22. E. W. Nicholson, "The Decalogue as the Direct Address of God," *VT* 27 (1977): 422–33.
23. Phillips, "Fresh Look at the Sinai Pericope," 39–52, 282–94.
24. Patrick, "Covenant Code Source," 156.

Deuteronomistic redaction of the Sinai narrative that involved the interpolation of both the Decalogue and Exodus 20:22–23. As his starting point he
takes the tradition in Deuteronomy 4–5 concerning the "Decalogue as God's
direct address to Israel" and observes similarities between Exodus 20:23 and
Deuteronomy 4:16–28. Then he argues that Exodus 20:1–17, 22–23 was composed after Deuteronomy 4:1–40 and added by a Deuteronomistic redactor
to an existing version of the Sinai narrative, which already included the Book
of the Covenant.

Responding to Nicholson's discussion, Phillips highlights a number of
factors that argue against Exodus 20:1–17, 22–23 coming from a Deuteronomistic redactor. In particular, he observes that the Deuteronomic version of
the Decalogue "shows clear signs of having been altered from the Exodus version in order to comply with Deuteronomic legal concerns."[25] Consequently,
he favors a pre-Deuteronomic date for the redaction of the Sinai narrative.
Moreover, he maintains that Exodus 20:24–26 ought to be included in any
discussion of 20:22–23 and that the former was relocated and placed alongside
20:22–23 when these verses, with the rest of the Book of the Covenant, were
inserted into the Sinai narrative. Significantly, Phillips argues that Exodus
20:22–26 reflects "a purification of Israel's sanctuaries to a much simpler and
primitive form," and derives "from a pre-Deuteronomic attempt to reform
Israel's worship."[26] Phillips dates these reforms to the time of Hezekiah (cf.
2 Kings 18:4) and gives those responsible for redacting the Sinai narrative the
label Proto-Deuteronomists. For the first time these theologians introduce
the concept of the Decalogue as being spoken by Yahweh from heaven, although, according to Phillips, they did not see this as having any theological
significance.[27]

The arguments presented by both Patrick and Phillips against a Deuteronomistic redaction of the Sinai narrative are more convincing that those offered by
Nicholson in favor of such; several recent studies have also come out strongly
in support of the priority of the Exodus version of the Decalogue.[28] Yet while
Phillips's case for a pre-Deuteronomistic redaction is skillfully argued, two
major modifications are necessary. The first of these concerns the dating of this
redaction to the time of Hezekiah and its description as Proto-Deuteronomic.
The second involves a more radical assessment of the redactional process that
Phillips believes took place.

25. Phillips, "Fresh Look at the Sinai Pericope," 43–44.
26. Ibid., 41.
27. Phillips views Exod. 20:18–21 as originally having come immediately after Exod. 19:19,
with the Decalogue following both passages. According to Phillips, the Proto-Deuteronomists
were also responsible for inserting the Book of the Covenant into the Sinai narrative, as well as
introducing Exod. 32–34.
28. Cf. M. Weinfeld, *Deuteronomy 1–11*, AB 5 (New York: Doubleday, 1991), 242–319; R. G.
Kratz, "Der Dekalog im Exodusbuch," *VT* 44 (1994): 205–38.

On dating the redaction involving Exodus 20:22, Phillips, like Patrick, is undoubtedly correct in placing this before the composition of Deuteronomy. However, by labeling the redaction Proto-Deuteronomic and locating it in the time of Hezekiah, he obviously implies that those responsible were not far removed from the Deuteronomic activities normally associated with King Josiah (2 Kings 22–23). Yet one major factor suggests that this redaction of the Sinai narrative took place at a much earlier time.

An important component of Phillips's discussion is the present location of material concerning idols and altars at the very start of the Book of the Covenant. For Phillips, the prominence given to these ideas in Exodus 20:23–26 reflects a concern to purify Israelite sanctuaries, as occurred in the time of Hezekiah. However, he fails to observe the close link, noted above, that exists between 20:24–26 and the preliminary activities concerned with the ratification of the covenant in 24:4–5. This connection has important implications for dating the redaction, for Phillips himself views Exodus 24:4–6, 8 as reflecting "an early covenant ritual which must pre-date the monarchy."[29] Taken together, Exodus 20:23–26 and 24:4–6, 8 display no awareness of either a special priesthood or a central sanctuary. Indeed, this material implies that any Israelite could build an altar and offer whole-burnt offerings and fellowship offerings to Yahweh.[30] Such an outlook can hardly come from theologians who, as Phillips's designation Proto-Deuteronomic implies, were the immediate predecessors to a reform movement that favored the restriction of worship to a central sanctuary. Both the content of Exodus 20:23–26 and the prominence given to these verses suggest a much earlier date of composition than that advocated by Phillips.[31] In the light of this, the term Proto-Deuteronomic seems inappropriate.

29. Phillips, "Fresh Look at the Sinai Pericope," 285. In addition to the reference to "young men," Phillips (285) notes that D. J. McCarthy, "Běrît in Old Testament History and Theology," *Bib* 53 (1972): 117, describes the phrase "blood of the covenant" as "very un-Deuteronomic." Also, Phillips (285) draws attention to how E. W. Nicholson, "The Interpretation of Exodus xxiv 9–11," *VT* 24 (1974): 77–97, dates Exod. 24:1–2, 9–11 as "pre-Yahwistic."

30. In support of this, it is noteworthy (1) that no special skills are required to construct the altar, which can be made from easily found materials, and (2) that the reason given for the prohibition against steps leading up to an altar in 20:26 would not apply to Aaronic priests, who are expected to wear undergarments (Exod. 28:42–43). Furthermore, the fact that these instructions are expressed in the second-person singular suggests that they are intended for all the Israelites and not merely a selected few.

31. Further evidence, in keeping with an earlier date for this redaction of the Sinai narrative, comes in a study on the dating of the Book of the Covenant by J. W. Marshall, *Israel and the Book of the Covenant: An Anthropological Approach to Biblical Law*, SBLDS 140 (Atlanta: Scholars Press, 1993). Though it is clear that an early date for the Book of the Covenant does not automatically mean an early date for the redaction of the Sinai narrative, the redaction cannot be dated before the composition of the Book of the Covenant. By dating the Book of the Covenant to the premonarchic period, Marshall's study leaves open the possibility of an early redaction. A similar argument may be applied regarding the dating of the Decalogue, for

The second aspect of Phillips's approach that requires modification is the issue of the nature and extent of the redaction associated with Exodus 20:22. This issue is not really addressed by Phillips, who tends to work within the framework established by Nicholson. However, once the existence of Deuteronomic/Deuteronomistic material within the Sinai narrative is rejected in favor of the Sinai narrative's having been composed prior to Deuteronomy, the presence of redactional activity within Exodus 19–24 can no longer be automatically assumed. Unfortunately, Phillips fails to appreciate the implications of his own redating of the supposed redactional material and continues to assume that the narrative framework associated with Exodus 20:22 originates from an editor who modified an earlier version of the Sinai narrative. Yet, once Deuteronomic/Deuteronomistic influence is rejected, the redactional nature of Exodus 20:22 and the verses associated with it must be demonstrated afresh; it cannot be merely assumed.

At this stage it is necessary to bring into consideration Exodus 19:2b–8, which, as we noted at the start of our study, closely parallels the narrative framework surrounding the divine speech in 20:22–24:2. If Phillips is correct in finding evidence of redactional activity in 20:22–26, this ought to be reflected also in 19:2b–8. Unfortunately, Phillips pays little attention to the source analysis of 19:2b–8.

The Source Analysis of Exodus 19

As the Sinai narrative comes to us, Exodus 19:2b–8 introduces the account of the theophany that dominates Exodus 19:1–25. Any attempt to understand the process by which 19:2b–8 was composed must take into consideration the whole chapter. For convenience we shall examine 19:1–15 and 19:16–25 separately, observing the natural break in the narrative that comes between verses 15 and 16.

Since the end of the nineteenth century, scholars interested in the source analysis of Exodus 19:1–15 have tended to assign verses 3b–8 to a Deuteronomic editor, and verses 1–2a to P, with the remaining verses (2b, 9–15) being attributed to J and E, the precise allocation of these latter verses being uncertain. Though this analysis has been widely followed, its tentative nature is demonstrated by J. Van Seters, who suggests that verses 2–11, 13b–15 originate from J (as he understands it) and verses 1, 12–13a from P.[32]

---

its existence is presupposed by Exod. 20:22. However, the very nature of the Decalogue makes it exceptionally difficult to date.

32. J. Van Seters, "Comparing Scripture with Scripture: Some Observations on the Sinai Pericope in Exodus 19–24," in *Canon, Theology, and Old Testament Interpretation: Essays in Honor of Brevard S. Childs*, ed. G. M. Tucker, D. L. Petersen, and R. R. Wilson (Philadelphia: Fortress, 1988), 112–14.

Exodus 19:1–2a, which provides the chronological and geographical settings for the events narrated in 19:1–15, is normally assigned to P. The initial verse dates the arrival of the Israelites at Sinai in relation to their departure from Egypt; verse 2 picks up the itinerary of the Israelites' journey by briefly noting their progress from the last named campsite at Rephidim (17:1; cf. 17:8). Since each verse performs a different function, there is no reason to view them as coming from separate sources (contra, on the one hand, Van Seters,[33] who views the chronological statement of verse 1 as an addition from P, and on the other hand, Durham,[34] who considers verse 2 to have been inserted later). Under the Documentary Hypothesis, chronological notices are normally attributed to P. However, the formula in Exodus 19:1 is unique: the date is reckoned in terms of the time elapsed since the departure of the Israelites from Egypt, and not from the start of the calendar year, as is normally the case.[35] Given the distinctiveness of the chronological formula in verse 1, little weight should be assigned to it as a criterion for ascribing the origin of this verse to P.[36]

In spite of widespread support for finding Deuteronomic influence in Exodus 19:3b–8, none of the terms used to describe Israel's future status is found in exactly the same form in Deuteronomy. This is especially true of the expressions "kingdom of priests" and "holy nation," which occur only here in the whole of the Old Testament. Although the term *sĕgullâ*, "treasured possession," is found in Deuteronomy 7:6; 14:2; 26:18, it comes in the distinctive expression "*'am sĕgullâ*," "treasured people." Even the comment about God's carrying the Israelites on "eagles' wings" (v. 4) is sufficiently different from that used in Deuteronomy 32:10–12 to suggest that they are not necessarily the product of a single author. Given the lack of clearly identifiable Deuteronomic language in Exodus 19:3b–8, the possibility of an alternative origin for these verses should not be dismissed.[37] This is supported by three further observations. First, as the Sinai narrative stands, verses 3b–8a perform an important function, at the outset establishing the Israelites' willingness to accept Yahweh's covenant. In spite of suggestions to the contrary, verses 3–8a are an integral part of the present section, and there is no reason to view them as secondary. The divine speech is merely an invitation to enter into a covenant relationship and as such lacks a detailed presentation of the obligations that the Israelites are expected to keep.[38] Second, the parallels (noted above) between the introductions to the

---

33. Ibid., 112.

34. Durham, *Exodus*, 261.

35. Within the context of the book of Exodus as a whole, the phrase "in the third month of the Israelites' going out from Egypt" (19:1, my trans.) must refer to (the day of) the third new moon since the Passover; this would then be the first day of the fourth month of the year, since the Passover took place on the fourteenth day of the first month (12:2–6).

36. Cf. R. Rendtorff, *The Problem of the Process of Transmission in the Pentateuch*, JSOTSup 89 (Sheffield: JSOT Press, 1990), 157–63.

37. Cf. Patrick, "Covenant Code Source," 145–57, esp. 154–56.

38. Cf. ibid., 148–49.

divine speeches in Exodus 19:3–6 and 20:22–24:2, and their narrative settings, suggest that the source analysis of 19:3b–8 cannot be decided in isolation. Significantly, however, the narrative framework surrounding Exodus 20:22–24:2 displays no obvious Deuteronomic characteristics. Third, Weinfeld observes that Deuteronomy 7:6 is "dependent on Exodus 19:5–6."[39] These observations suggest that any similarities between Exodus 19:3b–8 and Deuteronomy are best explained by maintaining the priority of the Exodus material, rather than vice versa.

The account of Moses's return to Yahweh (Exod. 19:8b) and his subsequent reporting of the people's reply (v. 8c) clearly presuppose the events of verses 3–8a. Having received a favorable response, Yahweh instructs Moses regarding the preparations necessary for the theophany that will occur before the sealing of the covenant (19:10–13). The detailing of these preparations is clearly contingent on the people's having expressed their willingness to accept their role as outlined in 19:4–6. Though verses 8b–15 have usually been assigned to J and E, no consensus has emerged regarding individual verses. As they stand, verses 8b–15 form a coherent account, and there is no need to attribute the material to two or more sources.[40] Moreover, these verses build well upon verses 3–8a, suggesting that they should all be assigned to the same source.

The second half of Exodus 19 falls into two main scenes: verses 16–19 are a vivid description of the divine theophany as observed by the people from below the mountain; verses 20–25 record a brief conversation between Yahweh and Moses that takes place at the top of the mountain. Both scenes build upon verses 1–15. The chronological notice in verse 16, referring to "the third day," not only marks the beginning of a new episode, but also immediately links this section to the preceding (cf. vv. 11, 15) by indicating that God's promise to come to Moses (v. 9) is about to be fulfilled. Similarly, Moses's reply in verse 23 clearly presupposes God's earlier instructions in verses 10–13.

Regarding the source analysis of this section, only a very general consensus exists, with verses 16–20, 25 being assigned between J and E, and verses 21–24 being viewed as a later addition. Thus, Noth attributes verses 16aα, 18, 20 to J; and verses 16aβb, 17, 19 to E; with verses 21–25 being "secondary additions."[41] Hyatt assigns verses 16a, 18 to J and verses 16b–17, 19, 25 to E, with verses 20–24 coming from the "J supplementer."[42] The uncertainty of this analysis is highlighted by Van Seters's willingness to attribute verses 16–19 to

39. Weinfeld, *Deuteronomy 1–11*, 367. According to Weinfeld, Deut. 7 also presupposes Exod. 23:23–33.

40. The general assumption, fostered especially by the Documentary Hypothesis, that parallel sources extend throughout most of the Pentateuch has tended to drive the quest for finding at least two sources in many passages.

41. Noth, *Exodus*, 154–60.

42. J. P. Hyatt, *Exodus*, NCB (London: Oliphants, 1971), 199–203.

J and verses 20–25 to P.[43] While some scholars[44] find two separate accounts of a divine theophany here—a thunderstorm and a volcanic eruption—this is quite unnecessary. As Durham observes: "The storm and fire imagery of vv. 16–19a is one part of an attempt to describe the indescribable experience of the coming of Yahweh. It is language recurrent in OT theophany accounts, and language rooted in Canaanite descriptions of the arrival of deity."[45] Given the coherence of verses 16–19 and the lack of decisive criteria for distinguishing between J and E, there seems to be no reason for positing two sources here. Finally, since verses 16–19 presuppose the preceding episode, there is every reason to assign Exodus 19:1–19 to a single source.

This leaves the issue of the source analysis of Exodus 19:20–25 to be resolved. These verses form a coherent scene that is framed by comments about Moses's ascending (v. 20) and descending (v. 25) the mountain. The unit forms a neat palistrophe:

  A Moses goes up (v. 20)
    B Yahweh speaks to Moses (vv. 21–22)
      C Moses replies (v. 23)
    B′ Yahweh speaks to Moses (v. 24)
  A′ Moses goes down (v. 25)

These verses, however, are widely viewed as a later insertion, interrupting the climax of the theophany and containing material that appears somewhat secondary to the account of Exodus 19. Why, it may be asked, should Moses at this stage be called up the mountain again, and why does God warn him yet again concerning the people coming up? To these questions may be added the following observations:

1. Verses 20–25 contain no mention of the various signs of the theophany (e.g., cloud, lightning, fire) found in verses 16–19.
2. The dialogue between Yahweh and Moses appears to be concerned with preparations for the theophany.
3. According to Van Seters, "There is no public legitimization of Moses as suggested in verse 9 as the point of Moses' role in the theophany, only a reprimand."[46]

43. Van Seters, "Comparing Scripture with Scripture," 113–14.
44. E.g., M. L. Newman, *The People of the Covenant* (Nashville: Abingdon, 1962), 39–51; J. K. Kuntz, *The Self-Revelation of God* (Philadelphia: Westminster, 1967), 72–100.
45. Durham, *Exodus*, 270; cf. R. J. Clifford, *The Cosmic Mountain in Canaan and the Old Testament* (Cambridge, MA: Harvard University Press, 1972), 107–20; J. J. Niehaus, *God at Sinai* (Grand Rapids: Zondervan, 1995), 17–141.
46. Van Seters, "Comparing Scripture with Scripture," 113.

4. The warning that the people are not to approach the mountain in verses 21–22 seems to be at odds with the later reaction of the people in standing at a distance in Exodus 20:18–21.[47]

5. Noth[48] and Hyatt[49] suggest that Exodus 20:18–21 forms a better sequel to verses 16–19, with both 19:20–25 and 20:1–17 being considered to be later additions to the narrative. Rejecting the idea that the Decalogue is a later insertion, Durham views only 19:19b–25 as secondary, and 20:1 as the natural sequel to 19:19a.[50]

These arguments in favor of the secondary nature of Exodus 19:20–25 must be weighed against a number of considerations that support the originality of this passage:

1. Verses 20–25 presuppose knowledge of Yahweh's earlier instructions to Moses concerning the preparations necessary for the theophany; Moses's reply in verse 23 obviously alludes to the divine commands in verses 10–13. This indicates that verses 20–25 are unlikely to have had an independent existence outside their present context; they make sense only in the light of verses 9–15.

2. Verses 20–25 are linked to the earlier part of Exodus 19 by two important motifs. First, Moses's mediating role in verses 20–25 is in keeping with God's earlier remarks in verse 9, which assume that Moses will continue to convey Yahweh's instructions to the Israelites. Verses 20–25 provide (contra Van Seters) a public legitimization of Moses's role. Second, the dominant issue in the dialogue between Yahweh and Moses is the holiness of the mountain. Remarkably, while the theme of holiness is prominent in verses 10–15, it is completely absent from the description of the theophany in verses 16–19. Without verses 20–25 the narrative contains no mention of the mountain's becoming holy as a result of Yahweh's presence.[51] Since the holiness of the mountain cannot be perceived by ordinary senses—in 3:5 Moses has to be told that the ground is holy—it is not surprising that 19:16–19 makes no mention of the mountain's holy state. Verses 20–25 clearly complement the description of the theophany by focusing on the motif of holiness. The complementary nature of the two scenes probably also explains why verses 20–25 contain no reference to the signs of the theophany. While the first scene abounds in narrative details and records no direct

47. Cf. G. C. Chirichigno, "The Narrative Structure of Exodus 19–24," *Bib* 68 (1987): 472.
48. Noth, *Exodus*, 168.
49. Hyatt, *Exodus*, 217.
50. Durham, *Exodus*, 283, 302.
51. This would be a remarkable omission in the light of the way Exod. 19 parallels the earlier theophany in Exod. 3:1–4:17.

speech, the second has a bare minimum of narrative details and consists mainly of dialogue. This, however, does not necessarily mean that verses 16–19 and 20–25 come from different sources.

3. The dialogue in verses 20–25 highlights another theme that lies at the very heart of the covenant relationship being established at Sinai. This concerns the obedience of the people. By commanding Moses to warn the Israelites against ascending the mountain, God implies that some of them at least tend toward disobedience rather than compliance. This will be highlighted later, when they construct the golden calf (Exod. 32:1–8). God's warning in verses 20–25 casts a dark shadow across the positive response of the people in verse 8.

4. Although the divine commands in verses 20–25 clearly echo those of verses 10–13, an important difference is introduced regarding the way in which those who transgress the boundary around the mountain will be punished. Whereas in verses 10–13 Moses is ordered to put to death by stoning or shooting those who touch the mountain, in verses 20–25 it is Yahweh himself who will "break out" against anyone coming up the mountain. Since Yahweh will now punish any transgressors, this suggests that he has descended upon the mountain. Before the theophany, the responsibility for punishment rests with Moses and the people.

In the light of these considerations, the case for viewing Exodus 19:20–25 as secondary is not as strong as often suggested, and several recent commentators lean toward this conclusion. Childs suggests that verses 20–25 are a fitting part of the narrative, focusing on the preparations necessary "for the deliverance of the law."[52] In a similar vein, Fretheim appears to accept that verses 20–25 are an integral part of Exodus 19, forming "an interlude between 19:19 and 20:1."[53]

The preceding discussion highlights the ambiguous nature of scholarly attempts to uncover the sources underlying Exodus 19:1–25. In spite of frequent assertions to the contrary, the narrative displays substantial unity, and, but for an a priori belief that parallel sources were combined to form much of the Pentateuch, there is little evidence to suggest that the present narrative was composed through either several sources being combined or an early text being expanded by later redactional activity. As the chapter stands, it may be read as a continuous account, with later verses building upon those that have gone before. Consequently, since the divine speech in 19:3–6 and its narrative framework (19:2b, 7–8) cannot be excised from its present context without destroying the whole account, Exodus 19:2b–8 argues against, rather than for, the occurrence of redactional activity in the composition of the Sinai narrative.

52. Childs, *Exodus*, 370.
53. T. E. Fretheim, *Exodus*, IBC (Louisville: John Knox, 1991), 219–20.

Conclusion

At the outset of our investigation into the sources underlying Exodus 19:1–24:11, we observed the remarkable similarities between the narrative sections framing the divine speeches in 19:3–6 and 20:22–24:2. These, together with the parallels between Yahweh's speech in 20:22–24:2 and the following episode in 24:3–11 suggest that 20:21–24:11 was composed by a single author.[54] Building upon this, we proceeded to observe that 20:22 presupposes Yahweh's direct proclamation of the Decalogue to the Israelites in 20:1–17 and the subsequent short episode in 20:18–21. Next, in the light of the parallels between the narrative frameworks surrounding the divine speeches in 19:3–6 and 20:22–24:2, we turned to consider the composition of Exodus 19. No evidence of redactional activity was found in connection with 19:2b–8. Rather, the whole of Exodus 19 displays signs of having been composed as a unified account.

These observations suggest that the narrative framework surrounding the divine speeches in Exodus 19:3–6 and 20:22–24:2 comes from the author who shaped the entire Sinai narrative in 19:1–24:11. Regarding the composition of the Decalogue and the Book of the Covenant, this author may have taken over existing material. However, if he did so, he fully incorporated these two blocks of material into this account. Consequently, in spite of numerous statements to the contrary, the Sinai narrative in Exodus 19:1–24:11 appears to have been skillfully composed. On the date of composition, the limited evidence considered above indicates (1) that Exodus 19:1–24:11 already existed before the book of Deuteronomy was composed, and (2) that it could have been penned as early as the premonarchic period.

In spite of its restricted scope, the preceding discussion has important implications for current developments in pentateuchal criticism. First, our study of the Sinai narrative provides no evidence to support the existence of the sources associated with the Documentary Hypothesis. While previous writers have sought to analyze the text on the basis of criteria relating to the sources J, E, D, and P, this approach has failed to provide a consensus view.

54. In saying this, it must be acknowledged that no evidence has been presented regarding Exod. 21:1–23:33. Our concern, however, is primarily with the composition of the narrative within which the Book of the Covenant is placed. A detailed discussion of the process by which the Book of the Covenant was composed would require much more space than is currently available, as evidenced by the various works cited in footnote 9. To these could be added the more recent studies of J. Van Seters, *A Law Book for the Diaspora: Revision in the Study of the Covenant Code* (Oxford and New York: Oxford University Press, 2003); B. S. Jackson, *Wisdom-Laws: A Study of the Mishpatim of Exodus 21:1–22:16* (Oxford: Oxford University Press, 2006); and D. P. Wright, *Inventing God's Law: How the Covenant Code of the Bible Used and Revised the Laws of Hammurabi* (Oxford: Oxford University Press, 2009). See also B. M. Levinson, "Is the Covenant Code an Exilic Composition? A Response to John Van Seters," in *In Search of Pre-Exilic Israel: Proceedings of the Oxford Old Testament Seminar*, ed. J. Day, JSOTSup 406 (London: T&T Clark, 2004), 272–325.

Moreover, adherence to the Documentary Hypothesis has prevented scholars from observing the main compositional features of the text. These, as we have observed, suggest that a single author has skillfully composed the entire narrative. Second, while links have been observed with the book of Deuteronomy, these are best explained in terms of the priority of the Sinai narrative. Our analysis of the Sinai narrative has shown there is no evidence of a Deuteronomistic revision having occurred; everything points toward Deuteronomy's having been influenced by Exodus 19–24. On the basis of the Sinai narrative, there is no reason to suppose that the books of Genesis to Numbers were penned as a prologue to an already-existing Deuteronomistic History.

6

The Future of Pentateuchal Studies

Looking to the Future

At this stage there is no telling how pentateuchal studies will develop. Without new evidence, possibly from yet-to-be-discovered extrabiblical sources, it is highly unlikely that biblical scholars will be able to uncover with any certainty the process by which the Pentateuch was created. For the present we can but hope that contemporary scholars will learn from the shortcomings of their predecessors and be more willing to acknowledge the tentative nature of their theories regarding how the Pentateuch came into being. Surely the time has arrived to seriously acknowledge the limitations of source and form criticism and to avoid the construction of theories regarding the development of Israelite history and religion that rest primarily on the supposed sources of the Pentateuch.

Regarding future developments, the following issues ought to receive consideration:

1. Since the introduction of source criticism in the mid-eighteenth century, the study of the Pentateuch has been dominated by diachronic considerations. As a result, considerable effort has been expended, first on trying to explain how the Pentateuch was composed, and then on applying these results to shed new light on the history of Israelite religion. The diachronic methods have had such a bewitching effect that most scholars have completely ignored a synchronic reading of the text. Indeed, many scholars find it difficult to read the Pentateuch as a unified

continuous narrative. Moreover, the impression is strongly given that such a reading is not merely naive, but also involves reverting from a two-dimensional view of the text to a one-dimensional view. However, as we have observed, the diachronic methods are not completely satisfactory, and their hypothetical results possibly provide no better a picture of Israelite history and religion than that available from a synchronic reading of the Pentateuch. The time has come to take more seriously a synchronic approach, especially given recent progress in understanding how biblical narratives are constructed.[1]

2. The issue of historical accuracy must remain open. Various studies have rightly highlighted the inadequacy of some attempts to support an early date for parts of the Pentateuch.[2] While this has had the effect of increasing historical skepticism toward the books of Genesis to Deuteronomy, it ought to be recognized that the dismissal of poor arguments for the historicity of these books does not prove that the Pentateuch records fiction rather than fact. Unfortunately, many scholars have become so acclimatized to dating the pentateuchal material in the monarchic or postmonarchic periods that attempts to date it earlier are generally dismissed without being given adequate consideration. Moreover, the nature of the material in Genesis to Deuteronomy makes it highly unlikely that we shall find reports of these events in the relatively few contemporary nonbiblical documents that have so far been uncovered by archaeologists. For example, the biblical narrative places the patriarchs in approximately the twenty-first to nineteenth centuries BC and portrays them as seminomadic herdsmen who may have engaged in limited agriculture. After almost four millennia, there is little reason to expect that we shall uncover archaeological evidence that relates directly to their existence. In these circumstances, "absence of evidence is no evidence of absence."[3] Unfortunately, for their own reasons some scholars exploit the inadequacy of the very limited evidence that is available. Such an

---

1. Cf., e.g., J. Licht, *Storytelling in the Bible* (Jerusalem: Magnes Press / Hebrew University, 1978); R. Alter, *The Art of Biblical Narrative* (New York: Basic Books, 1981); M. Sternberg, *The Poetics of Biblical Narrative: Ideological Literature and the Drama of Reading* (Bloomington: Indiana University Press, 1985); S. Bar-Efrat, *Narrative Art in the Bible* (Sheffield: Almond, 1989); H. C. Brichto, *Toward a Grammar of Biblical Poetics* (Oxford: Oxford University Press, 1992); D. M. Gunn and D. N. Fewell, *Narrative in the Hebrew Bible* (Oxford: Oxford University Press, 1993).

2. E.g., T. L. Thompson, *The Historicity of the Patriarchal Narratives*, BZAW 133 (Berlin: de Gruyter, 1974); J. Van Seters, *Abraham in History and Tradition* (New Haven: Yale University Press, 1975). See also the series of articles in *Essays on the Patriarchal Narratives*, ed. A. R. Millard and D. J. Wiseman (Leicester: Inter-Varsity, 1980); and more recently G. J. Wenham, *Genesis 16–50*, WBC 2 (Dallas: Word Books, 1994), xx–xxviii.

3. K. A. Kitchen, "The Patriarchal Age: Myth or History?" *Biblical Archaeology Review* 21 (1995): 50.

approach is ultimately as defective as that which claims more than the available evidence supports.[4]

3. In spite of the long-standing tradition that the first five books of the Bible belong together, it needs to be recognized that they are intimately connected to the books that follow them. As they stand, the books of Genesis to Kings form a continuous narrative. This is apparent from both the overall picture provided and the way in which individual books are linked. Viewed as a whole, Genesis to Kings records selected events from the creation of the earth to the demise of the Davidic monarchy at the time of the Babylonian exile. Later books in the sequence presuppose that the reader is already familiar with those that have gone before. For example, the opening verses of Exodus presuppose that the reader is already familiar with the main details of the Joseph story in Genesis 37–50. Exodus 13:19 refers back to Joseph's comments in Genesis 50:25 concerning his bones being taken up out of Egypt. The account of the appointment of Aaron and his sons as priests in Leviticus 8:1–36 presupposes the instructions given in Exodus 29:1–46. God's comment in Numbers 20:12 regarding the death of Moses outside the promised land is fulfilled in Deuteronomy 34:1–8. References to the deaths of Moses and Joshua at the very start of the books of Joshua and Judges respectively serve the purpose of linking these books with those immediately preceding. The description of David as a frail old man at the start of 1 Kings presupposes the account of his earlier life in the books of 1 and 2 Samuel. Whatever the prior oral and/or literary history of the individual books, it is obvious that they have been deliberately linked to form a continuous narrative. On the basis of content and language, we may with reasonable confidence assume that all this material was brought together to form this continuous narrative shortly after 562 BC, the date of Jehoiachin's release from prison in Babylon (2 Kings 25:27–30).[5] Given the unity of Genesis to Kings, the composition of the Pentateuch must be discussed in conjunction with that of the books of Joshua to Kings.[6] This, however, does not imply that the contents of the Pentateuch came into being only during the exilic period.

4. A very helpful discussion of the whole subject of biblical historiography is provided by V. P. Long, *The Art of Biblical History* (Leicester: Apollos, 1994).

5. For a recent defense of this dating based on linguistic considerations, see A. Hurvitz, "The Historical Quest for 'Ancient Israel' and the Linguistic Evidence of the Hebrew Bible: Some Methodological Observations," *VT* 47 (1997): 301–15.

6. Cf. J. G. McConville, "The Old Testament Historical Books in Modern Scholarship," *Them* 22, no. 3 (1997): 3–13; C. Westermann, *Die Geschichtsbücher des Alten Testaments: Gab es ein deuteronomistisches Geschichtswerk?* TBAT 87 (Gütersloh: Chr. Kaiser, 1994). Westermann argues that there was a pre-Deuteronomistic narrative extending from Exodus to Kings, which associated the beginning of the nation's history with the exodus from Egypt.

When Was the Pentateuch Composed?

During the past two centuries the quest to identify the author(s) of the Pentateuch has become one of the most complex and provocative issues in biblical studies.[7] For some, to doubt the long-standing tradition of Mosaic authorship is the greatest heresy. For others, to unquestioningly support the belief that Moses wrote the whole Pentateuch is the hallmark of blind, uncritical thinking. As a prelude to entering this minefield, we shall briefly and somewhat selectively review the history of biblical scholarship as it relates to the composition of the Pentateuch.

Recent History of Scholarship

Before the Enlightenment in the eighteenth century, Jewish and Christian scholars were mostly unanimous in affirming Mosaic authorship of the Pentateuch. The origin of the first five books of the Bible was clearly associated with Moses, who consequently was venerated as one of the most outstanding figures in the history of ancient Israel. While a few scholars, like the medieval Jewish writer Ibn Ezra (1092/93–1167), were conscious that the Pentateuch contained material that appeared to contradict the concept of Mosaic authorship, the authority of synagogue and church on this issue was never seriously challenged.

All this gradually changed when the intellectual ideas associated with the Enlightenment elevated human reason over divine revelation. Those adopting this new approach distrusted other authorities, believing that the road to truth lay through reason, observation, and experiment. In this climate some scholars began more openly to express reservations about religious traditions and dogmas, often in the context of exploring new approaches to other areas of human life. The English philosopher Thomas Hobbes (1588–1679) epitomizes this in *Leviathan*, a lengthy treatise on human government, in which he argues against the divine right of kings to rule over others. Hobbes devotes several pages to various arguments against Mosaic authorship of the Pentateuch.[8] While the Enlightenment introduced a new willingness to question traditional ideas, there was initially little momentum toward rejecting Mosaic authorship of the Pentateuch. Yet the door was opened for further developments to occur.

During the final quarter of the eighteenth century and throughout the nineteenth century, various scholars experimented with the idea that the Pentateuch displayed signs of multiple authorship. In particular, the use of two different

7. This section is taken in part from *Dictionary of the Old Testament: Pentateuch; A Compendium of Contemporary Biblical Scholarship*, ed. T. Desmond Alexander and David W. Baker, copyright © 2003 by InterVarsity Christian Fellowship/USA, and used by permission of InterVarsity Press, PO Box 1400, Downers Grove, IL 60515, www.ivpress.com.

8. T. Hobbes, *Leviathan* (1651; repr., New York: Penguin, 1968), 417–18.

divine names in Genesis (Elohim [God] and Yahweh [LORD]) led some scholars to suggest that either several documents or numerous fragments had been combined to form the present text. In 1792 Alexander Geddes (1737–1802) argued that during the reign of Solomon, the books of Genesis to Joshua had been composed from fragmentary sources, some of which favored the name Elohim and others Yahweh. A few years later, in 1796, G. L. Bauer dated the editing of the materials in Genesis to the time of David and considered much of Deuteronomy to have been written after the time of Moses. A more radical approach was advocated by W. M. L. de Wette (1780–1849) in 1805, when he suggested that the composition of the book of Deuteronomy should be linked directly to the religious reforms undertaken by King Josiah in about 621 BC. Building on this, de Wette proposed that the oldest parts of the Pentateuch came from the time of David, at the earliest.

The dating of Deuteronomy to Josiah's reign became an integral part of further theories regarding the composition of the Pentateuch. Building on the concept of multiple authors, many scholars came to the opinion that the Pentateuch was composed of four main documents. Eventually the theory evolved that these four sources—known today by the terms Yahwistic (J), Elohistic (E), Deuteronomic (D), Priestly (P)—had been combined to form the Pentateuch. Although many scholars contributed to the debate regarding the nature of these four source documents, Julius Wellhausen (1844–1918) did more than most in shaping and promoting the idea of dating the sources in this order: J (ca. 840 BC), E (ca. 700 BC), D (ca. 623 BC), P (ca. 500–450 BC). On the basis of these dates, the Documentary Hypothesis, as it came to be known, clearly placed the composition of the Pentateuch long after the time of Moses. The impact of this new approach was such that by 1890 all but the most conservative of biblical scholars had rejected the concept of Mosaic authorship.

After establishing a framework for future pentateuchal (and OT) studies, biblical scholarship proceeded to explore related issues. In the early twentieth century Hermann Gunkel pioneered studies in the oral traditions that lay behind the source documents, raising the possibility that traditions contained in J, E, D, and P might have been composed some time before their inclusion in these sources. With attention now focused on the origin of the source documents, Gerhard von Rad proposed that existing cultic traditions had been collected and edited by the Yahwist. Modifying slightly the Documentary Hypothesis, von Rad dated the Yahwist's activity a century earlier, to the time of David, arguing that the Yahwist had been an author and theologian of some genius.

Although further developments occurred, many scholars accepted that the Yahwist, more than anyone else, had established the basic shape of the Pentateuch as we now know it. While biblical scholarship generally applauded the contribution of the Yahwist, the role of the Priestly Writer, who was viewed as the one responsible for the final editing of the Pentateuch, received considerably less attention and almost no acclaim.

In spite of the broad support given to it, the Documentary Hypothesis was never without detractors, although initially they came chiefly from the ranks of conservative Christian and Jewish scholars. However, by the final quarter of the twentieth century a new generation of scholars began to reexamine the process by which the Pentateuch was composed. Prominent among the advocates of a new approach are Rolf Rendtorff, John Van Seters, Jacob Milgrom, and Norman Whybray.[9]

Influenced by what he saw to be irreconcilable incompatibilities between the approaches of source and form criticism, Rendtorff has forcefully argued that there never was a Yahwist. In a different vein, Van Seters has redefined the nature of the Yahwist, arguing that he was a figure of the exilic period. Milgrom belongs to a growing band of scholars who, though broadly sympathetic to the idea of various sources, challenge Wellhausen's dating of them; in particular he proposes that P is to be dated before D. Rejecting the criteria by which the different source documents are distinguished, Whybray favors placing the composition of the entire Pentateuch in the exilic/postexilic period. While proponents of the Documentary Hypothesis still exist, there is an ever-growing unease that it fails to provide the best explanation for the composition of the Pentateuch. As Whybray has recently remarked: "There is at the present moment no consensus whatever about when, why, how, and through whom the Pentateuch reached its present form, and opinions about the dates of composition of its various parts differ by more than five hundred years."[10]

Main Issues Arising from a Survey of Scholarship

Although biblical scholarship is deeply divided on the issue of how the Pentateuch was composed, there is widespread agreement that the Pentateuch, as it now stands, is an edited work and not a piece of literature that was penned ab initio by one individual. Various factors strongly indicate that the Pentateuch was created through a process involving the editing of already-existing materials, regardless of whether the editor was Moses or someone else. The Pentateuch itself occasionally refers to the existence of other documents that were presumably written down before the whole of Genesis through Deuteronomy was composed (e.g., Gen. 5:1; Exod. 17:14; 24:4, 7; 34:27; Num. 21:14–15; 33:2; Deut. 31:9, 22, 24).

Furthermore, biblical scholarship has struggled to explain the composition of the Pentateuch by using various models: fragmentary, documentary, supplementary, or a complex mixture of these. Central to all these is the idea

9. For a fuller discussion of these writers, see chap. 4 above; cf. G. J. Wenham, "Pondering the Pentateuch: The Search for a New Paradigm," in *The Face of Old Testament Studies: A Survey of Contemporary Approaches*, ed. D. W. Baker and B. T. Arnold (Grand Rapids: Baker; Leicester: Apollos, 1999), 116–44.

10. R. N. Whybray, *Introduction to the Pentateuch* (Grand Rapids: Eerdmans, 1995), 12–13.

that different kinds of material have been united. Whereas a fragmentary approach stresses the disparate nature of the materials that have been edited together, documentary and supplementary approaches emphasize a degree of unity running throughout much of the material. In Genesis, for example, the presence of the *tôlĕdōt* headings ("These are the generations of . . ."; Gen. 2:4; 5:1; 6:9; 10:1; 11:10, 27; 25:12, 19; 36:1, 9; 37:2) at the start of new sections within the book suggests that they have been used by the book's editor to give it a distinctive structure. In this process, the editor may well have taken over some already-existing headings that were attached to genealogical lists (e.g., Gen. 5:1). Given that the contents of Genesis span a long period of time and consist of different kinds of writing (e.g., genealogical lists, short narrative episodes [e.g., the tower of Babel incident], longer narratives [e.g., the Joseph story]), it seems only reasonable to assume that one person was not responsible for composing everything. This would also seem to be the case for the different poetic portions found in Genesis (4:23–24; 9:25–27; 27:27–29, 39–40; 48:20; 49:2–27). Genesis 14 displays peculiar features that point to the incorporation of an ancient text into the account of Abraham's life (e.g., the use of explanatory notes to provide updated names for several places, although this could also have occurred at a later stage involving the transmission of the whole Pentateuch). When we move beyond Genesis to the rest of the Pentateuch, it becomes even clearer that different blocks of material, each with its own distinctive features, have been united to form the whole.

All these factors point in the direction of preexisting material having been taken over and edited to form the Pentateuch as we now know it. This best explains features within the Pentateuch that point on the one hand toward the overall unity of the narrative plot and on the other hand toward a clear lack of homogeneity in the contents of the books of Genesis to Deuteronomy. In the light of these contrasting features, the Pentateuch is best understood as a literary collage. What remains in dispute, however, is the nature of the editorial process, the identity of the one (or those) responsible, and the dating of it.

Throughout the final decades of the nineteenth century and most of the twentieth century, the Documentary Hypothesis was the dominant explanation for the process by which the Pentateuch was composed. However, the history of pentateuchal criticism reveals that the solution proposed by the Documentary Hypothesis evolved over a long period of time. Today many of the assumptions accepted toward the end of the nineteenth century are no longer considered valid.[11]

Furthermore, given our present knowledge and the lack of relevant external evidence, serious doubts exist regarding the ability of scholars to uncover the process by which the Pentateuch was composed. While New Testament

11. R. N. Whybray, *The Making of the Pentateuch: A Methodological Study*, JSOTSup 53 (Sheffield: JSOT Press, 1987).

scholarship is almost unanimous in supporting the idea that Matthew had before him a copy of Mark's Gospel, it is highly unlikely that scholars could begin with Matthew and thereby uncover, using internal evidence alone, a source document identical to Mark. In the light of such considerations, we ought to ask seriously: Is it possible for contemporary scholars to have any certainty in recovering the process by which the Pentateuch was composed, especially when no other relevant texts are available?[12]

Accepting that the Pentateuch is a literary collage, the question of the date of final editing becomes even more complex since editing allows for the possibility that different parts may have been composed over a wide range of time and by different writers.

Before asking what date should be assigned to the final composition of the Pentateuch, a number of general observations should be made. First, it is not possible to assign a date of writing to all the individual components that make up the Pentateuch. Scholars differ greatly in the dates they give to particular portions, and often these dates tend to be relative rather than absolute. Second, even if it were possible to claim categorically that every passage in the Pentateuch existed in the time of Moses, this would not of itself prove that Moses was the final editor. While it allows for this possibility, it is equally feasible that an editor long after the time of Moses may have been responsible for the present shape of the Pentateuch. Third, even if it could be demonstrated beyond doubt that the date of final editing was late (e.g., exilic or postexilic), this does not automatically indicate that everything contained in the Pentateuch must also be dated to the exilic/postexilic period. It is always possible that traditions going back many centuries were brought together at a later time. Fourth, due to the very limited scope of extrabiblical sources from Palestine, our knowledge of the preexilic period in ancient Israel is limited, and scholars diverge greatly in their assessment of it. Much depends on the historical reliability that scholars assign to the relevant biblical material found mainly in the books of Genesis to Kings. Yet even if one accepts that this material provides an accurate picture of this period, the picture is far from comprehensive, and there are many gaps in our knowledge. These observations highlight the complexity of the issues surrounding the authorship of the Pentateuch.

Date of Final Editing

If the Pentateuch is a literary collage that was formed to a greater or lesser extent through the bringing together of disparate materials, what can we discover about the final date of composition? Three different approaches may help to determine the date of editing, although, as we shall observe, they all present problems. First, if we can isolate and date the latest tradition preserved

---

12. T. D. Alexander, *Abraham in the Negev: A Source-Critical Investigation of Genesis 20:1–22:19* (Carlisle: Paternoster, 1997), 126–33.

in the Pentateuch, then we may conclude that the final editing must have taken place after this date. Second, by discovering specific references to the Pentateuch in other writing, it may be possible to establish the date at which it came into being. Third, if we can ascertain the purpose behind the writing of the Pentateuch, this may guide us to when it was composed.

LATEST TRADITION

It goes without saying that the final editing of the Pentateuch cannot be earlier than the date of composition of the latest tradition preserved in the books of Genesis to Deuteronomy. This, however, leads us into the very complex issue of determining the actual date at which every tradition within the Pentateuch was committed to writing. Given that the Pentateuch consists of a large number of traditions, representing a variety of literary genres, the task of dating each tradition is far from easy. Unfortunately, many of the individual traditions preserved in the Pentateuch lack criteria by which an absolute date may be assigned to them. Moreover, opinions may differ significantly regarding the date of a particular tradition: different scholars may assign the same passage to quite different periods of time.

The narratives in Genesis concerning Abraham and his immediate descendants provide many examples of the complexities of trying to determine the date of individual traditions. Toward the end of the nineteenth century and into the twentieth century, due to the influence of the Documentary Hypothesis, it was widely held that the stories about the patriarchs were invented by scribes living at the time of the Israelite monarchy. This view, however, was challenged during the middle of the twentieth century by various biblical archaeologists, the most prominent being W. F. Albright, who saw the patriarchal traditions as reflecting early second-millennium customs. Then, in the final quarter of the twentieth century, due largely to the influence of T. L. Thompson and J. Van Seters, the pendulum started to swing back in favor of the idea that the stories concerning the patriarchs should be viewed as literary creations from the middle of the first millennium BC, having no links with the early second millennium BC. Although the overall approach of Thompson and Van Seters has not gone uncontested,[13] some of their criticisms are valid regarding the way in which extrabiblical parallels have been used to justify the historicity of patriarchal traditions.

The problem of dating individual traditions may be illustrated using the following example based on Genesis 23. In 1953 M. R. Lehmann argued that the account of Abraham's purchase of the cave at Hebron reveals an intimate knowledge of Hittite law and custom dating from the second millennium BC. According to Lehmann, the bargaining between Abraham and Ephron was concerned not merely with the possession of a piece of land but also with

---

13. Millard and Wiseman, *Essays on the Patriarchal Narratives.*

obligations to the king entailed through ownership of land. Abraham wanted to avoid these obligations, but Ephron was keen to rid himself of them. Basing his argument on several statutes from a Hittite law code found at Boghazköy in Asia Minor, Lehmann concluded:

> We have thus found that Genesis 23 is permeated with intimate knowledge of intricate subtleties of Hittite laws and customs, correctly corresponding to the time of Abraham and fitting in with the Hittite features of the Biblical account. With the final destruction of the Hittite capital of Hattusas about 1200 BCE, these laws must have fallen into utter oblivion. This is another instance in which a late dating must be firmly rejected. Our study again confirms the authenticity of the "background material" of the Old Testament, which makes it such an invaluable source for the study of all aspects of social, economic and legal aspects of the periods of history it depicts.[14]

Given Lehmann's suggestion, however, that Abraham wished to avoid feudal services due to the Hittite king, it is surely strange that no reference, either direct or indirect, is made to the monarch.

A very different approach has been suggested by G. M. Tucker, who develops the idea that the account of Abraham's purchase of the cave resembles in form a Neo-Babylonian dialogue document, used in about 700–500 BC in transferring property or other possessions. "The similarities between this type of contract and Genesis 23 are striking, though the OT narrative preserves a much fuller account of the negotiations. The dialogue document's pattern is reflected in Ephron's quoted 'offer' (vs. 15), Abraham's acceptance described in the third person (vs. 16aα), the payment clause (vs. 16aβb), and the transfer clause (vss. 17–18) which includes a description of the property."[15] While Thompson[16] and Van Seters[17] have embraced Tucker's claim that the legal details found in Genesis 23 reflect best Neo-Babylonian customs, several difficulties arise. First, Tucker's suggestion that a "dialogue document" underlies Genesis 23 is restricted to only verses 15–18. Second, "dialogue documents" are attested in the early second millennium BC.[18] This undermines the suggestion that the legal aspects of the narrative are necessarily late.

An alternative approach to the legal features outlined in Genesis 23 has been proposed by R. Westbrook, based upon what he terms "a legal fiction of double transfer." Westbrook reports that in land transactions from Ugarit, "a number take the curious form of a tripartite transaction whereby the king intervenes not merely as a witness but [also] as an intermediary through whose

14. M. R. Lehmann, "Abraham's Purchase of Machpelah and Hittite Law," *BASOR* 129 (1953): 18.

15. G. M. Tucker, "The Legal Background to Genesis 23," *JBL* 85 (1966): 82.

16. Thompson, *Historicity of the Patriarchal Narratives*, 295–96.

17. Van Seters, *Abraham in History and Tradition*, 98–100.

18. M. Selman, "The Social Environment of the Patriarchs," *TynBul* 27 (1976): 117–24.

hands the property passes from one party to the other."[19] Similar transactions are found in Hittite documents from Boghazköy and in Elamite documents dated in about 1600 BC. Westbrook suggests that the part played by the Hittites in Abraham's purchase of the cave from Ephron can be explained best by this "double transfer" (cf. Gen. 23:17, 20; 25:9–10). In the light of this, the account in Genesis 23 may possibly reflect a practice in existence long before the development of Neo-Babylonian dialogue documents.

As this example illustrates, it is possible to uncover various ancient Near Eastern customs that may parallel the events recorded in Genesis 23. While the views of Lehmann and Tucker are less compelling than that of Westbrook, it may well be that none of the above suggestions is applicable.

In the light of this, some general observations should be made. Any attempt to date a particular tradition is hampered by the limited and sporadic nature of the evidence available. On the basis of past and current archaeological discoveries, it is not possible to reconstruct a continuous, detailed picture of life within every society throughout the ancient Near East. This is especially so for Israel/Palestine during the whole of the second millennium and the first half of the first millennium BC. While much archaeological evidence has been uncovered, it represents, relatively speaking, only a few tracks in the sand, and many gaps in our knowledge exist. For this reason, due to the absence of more appropriate materials, scholars have often been forced to compare biblical traditions with customs found in Mesopotamia, hundreds of miles away. Not surprisingly, such parallels occasionally prove to be less than satisfactory.

A further complication is that new archaeological evidence does not come to light in a uniform manner. On the one hand, a chance find may provide an abundance of artifacts relating to a specific site. On the other hand, a systematic survey of part of a major site may uncover relatively little. As archaeologists have long acknowledged, "Absence of evidence is not evidence of absence."[20] This becomes an even greater factor when we are dealing with the early second millennium BC. Moreover, we need to have realistic expectations as to what kind of evidence is likely to be discovered after three thousand or four thousand years. Is it likely, for example, that extrabiblical documents or artifacts will ever be found documenting the lives of seminomadic people like the patriarchs of Genesis?

In addition, it is always dangerous to assume that a particular social custom may be dated to a narrowly defined period of time. We now know that the custom of a wife's giving her husband a slave girl (see Gen. 16:1–4; 30:3–5, 9–10) was practiced during a period of one thousand years, ranging from the early second millennium BC through to the middle of the first millennium BC.

19. R. Westbrook, "Purchase of the Cave of Machpelah," *ILR* 6 (1971): 36.
20. Kitchen, "Patriarchal Age," 50.

Care also needs to be taken that we are not guilty of eisegesis regarding the biblical text. Often the biblical description of a custom is exceptionally brief and open to various interpretations (e.g., as noted above with Abraham's purchase of the cave of Ephron). The danger is ever present that an extra-biblical custom is "read into" the biblical text. E. A. Speiser's analysis of the wife-sister incidents in Genesis exemplifies the hazard of such an approach.[21]

All these factors make the task of dating the pentateuchal traditions, especially those associated with Genesis, exceptionally difficult. When scholars noticeably differ in their estimation of the date of a particular tradition, the reasons for doing so are often quite tentative. Although it is clearly beyond the scope of this chapter to consider the dating of every tradition found within the Pentateuch, a number of general observations shall be made in support of the idea that greater weight ought to be given to the view that the pentateuchal traditions are authentic rather than later fictional creations, as some scholars have recently argued.[22]

Regarding the book of Genesis, various social customs and religious practices stand at odds with what developed in the time of Moses and afterward. The freedom with which the patriarchs built altars at different locations and offered sacrifices (Gen. 12:7–8; 13:4, 18; 22:9; 26:25; 33:20; 35:1, 3, 7) stands in marked contrast to the religious practices associated with Mosaic Yahwism, with its emphasis on the role of priests and the importance of a central sanctuary.[23] This contrast is even greater when we move to the postexilic period.

Similarly, as shown in several prominent examples, the patriarchs act in ways that would have been abhorrent to those living under the legislation and customs associated with the Sinai covenant. According to Genesis 20:12 Abraham married his half-sister Sarah, yet this practice is forbidden in Leviticus 18:9, 11; 20:17; and Deuteronomy 27:22. Similarly, whereas Leviticus 18:18 prohibits a man from marrying two sisters, Jacob married Leah and her sister Rachel (Gen. 29:15–30).

The Pentateuch also contains traditions that stand strangely at odds with later attitudes. For example, as Nicholson highlights, Esau's firstborn status in Genesis is unlikely to have been invented by a Jewish writer of the exilic/postexilic period.[24] On the contrary, this would have been a major embarrass-

---

21. See E. A. Speiser, "The Wife-Sister Motif in the Patriarchal Narratives," in *Oriental and Biblical Studies*, ed. J. J. Finkelstein and M. Greenberg (Philadelphia: University of Pennsylvania Press, 1967), 62–88; and the critique by S. Greengus, "Sisterhood Adoption at Nuzi and the 'Wife-Sister' in Genesis," *HUCA* 46 (1975): 5–31.

22. E.g., E. T. Mullen, *Ethnic Myths and Pentateuchal Foundations: A New Approach to the Formation of the Pentateuch*, SemeiaSt (Atlanta: Scholars Press, 1997).

23. See R. W. L. Moberly, *The Old Testament of the Old Testament: Patriarchal Narratives and Mosaic Yahwism*, OBT (Minneapolis: Fortress, 1992); A. Pagolu, *The Religion of the Patriarchs*, JSOTSup 277 (Sheffield: Sheffield Academic Press, 1998).

24. E. W. Nicholson, *The Pentateuch in the Twentieth Century: The Legacy of Julius Wellhausen* (Oxford: Clarendon, 1998), 159–60.

ment to Jews, who viewed the Edomites as archenemies (e.g., Jer. 49; Lam. 4:22; Ezek. 25:12–13; 35:15; Obadiah). The same argument could also be applied to the prominence given to Joseph in Genesis, over against the less-important role played by his older brother Judah. If this latter tradition was created by a Judean writer, it is hard to imagine that he would have given pride of place to Joseph, from whom the Ephraimites, associated with the northern kingdom of Israel, claimed a royal lineage. This would suggest that the traditions concerning Esau and Joseph are preserved due to their authenticity rather than their appeal to contemporaries living in the exilic/postexilic age. Why invent traditions that give a special standing to those who were later viewed with some disdain?

Whereas the preceding comments have focused on Genesis, A. P. Ross makes a similar point regarding the traditions concerning the tabernacle. If these traditions were created in the exilic or postexilic period, it "yields the improbable scenario in which the nation in exile longs to return to their land but instead receives instructions to build a portable shrine for the desert."[25]

Alongside the difficulty of explaining why various traditions should have been invented in the exilic or postexilic period, other features point to the antiquity of various elements within the Pentateuch. For example, F. M. Cross and D. N. Freedman's study of the poetic sections embedded in the books of Genesis to Deuteronomy points to an early date of composition for these.[26] Given that poetry, in contrast to narrative, is less likely to be modified by later editors, the dating of these materials is highly significant. Rendsburg observes that within the Pentateuch the Hebrew personal pronoun *hû'*, which normally denotes the third-person masculine "he," occasionally refers to the third-person feminine "she." According to Rendsburg, this is best explained as reflecting an early linguistic feature.[27] From a different perspective, Wenham observes the absence of personal names in Genesis that have been formed using a theophoric element derived from the divine name YHWH.[28] This evidence points toward a date of composition before the first millennium BC, when it became very common for personal names to incorporate elements from YHWH.[29]

Over against these indicators of ancient material, we should also observe that there are various features in the Pentateuch that point toward a date of composition after the time of Moses. For example, the use of the name "Dan"

25. A. P. Ross, *Holiness to the Lord: A Guide to the Exposition of the Book of Leviticus* (Grand Rapids: Baker Academic, 2002), 35.

26. F. M. Cross and D. N. Freedman, *Studies in Ancient Yahwistic Poetry* (Missoula, MT: Scholars Press, 1975).

27. G. A. Rendsburg, "A New Look at Pentateuchal HW'," *Bib* 63 (1982): 351–69.

28. G. J. Wenham, "The Religion of the Patriarchs," in *Essays on the Patriarchal Narratives*, ed. A. R. Millard and D. J. Wiseman (Leicester: Inter-Varsity, 1980).

29. For further linguistic evidence supporting an early date for the pentateuchal traditions, see R. S. Hess, "Language of the Pentateuch," in Alexander and Baker, *Dictionary of the Old Testament: Pentateuch*, 491–97.

in Genesis 14:14 is anachronistic; according to Judges 18:29 the designation "Dan" was given to the city of Laish after the Israelites entered the land of Canaan. In addition, would Moses have written of himself, "Now Moses was a very humble man, more humble than anyone else on the face of the earth" (Num. 12:3)?[30] Significantly, some of the features that are viewed as clearly post-Mosaic are in keeping with the idea that older traditions were edited at a later date.

EXTERNAL EVIDENCE

Another way by which we may try to date the composition of the Pentateuch is to find references to it in other documents. Though at first sight such an approach may seem straightforward, various difficulties arise for the Pentateuch.

There is a limited range of materials from which to glean evidence. Through to the postexilic period, we must rely almost exclusively on the biblical books of Joshua to Kings, alongside the writings of the preexilic prophets. These writings provide a very limited picture of a period of history that spans about eight hundred years.[31]

The identification of references to the entire Pentateuch in the earliest relevant extant documents is complicated by the fact that no single title appears to have been used to denote the books of Genesis to Deuteronomy. The designation "Pentateuch" (derived from the Greek *pentateuchos*, "five-volume work") came into use in about the third century AD. Prior to this, various expressions were used, often involving one or both of the terms "Moses" and "Torah" (usually translated as "Law," although "Instruction" would convey better the sense of the Hebrew word in English). Thus, in the prologue of Ecclesiasticus, the Greek translation of Sirach written about 132 BC, the author refers to the threefold division of the Old Testament by using the following expressions (NRSV): "the Law and the Prophets and the others that followed them"; "the Law and the Prophets and the other books of our ancestors"; "the Law itself, the Prophecies, and the rest of the books." Here the term "Law" is clearly used to denote the Pentateuch.

Yet a survey of earlier materials reveals that the term "law" is first used in a more restricted manner. According to the book of Deuteronomy, Moses set before the people "the law," a body of material that is introduced by the narrator in 4:44 and extends from 5:1 to 26:19 (or possibly 30:20). Later Moses gave a written copy of this law to the priests (31:9), instructing them to read it to the people regularly (31:11). In the meantime they were to place it beside the ark of the covenant (31:26). Within the "book of the law," Moses gave

---

30. For a fuller list of post-Mosaic traditions, see D. W. Baker, "Source Criticism," in Alexander and Baker, *Dictionary of the Old Testament: Pentateuch*, 799–800; cf. G. C. Aalders, *A Short Introduction to the Pentateuch* (London: Tyndale, 1949), 105–10.

31. For a discussion of several important extrabiblical texts, see E. Waaler, "A Revised Date for Pentateuchal Texts? Evidence from Ketef Hinnom," *TynBul* 53 (2002): 29–55.

instructions that the future king should make for himself a copy of "this law" in order that he would be guided by its contents (17:18–20). This same "book of the law" is referred to in Joshua 1:7–8: "Be strong and very courageous. Be careful to obey all the law my servant Moses gave you; do not turn from it to the right or to the left, that you may be successful wherever you go. Keep this Book of the Law always on your lips; meditate on it day and night, so that you may be careful to do everything written in it. Then you will be prosperous and successful." In the light of Deuteronomy, there can be no doubt, although this is not always appreciated, that the Book of the Law mentioned at the start of Joshua is *not* the Pentateuch as we know it. Rather, the expression "Book of the Law" denotes the contents of Deuteronomy 5–26 (or perhaps 5–30).

From this starting point, it becomes clear that further references to the "book of the law of Moses" (e.g., Josh. 8:31; 23:6; 2 Kings 14:6; Neh. 8:1), "the law of Moses" (e.g., Josh. 8:32; 1 Kings 2:3; 2 Kings 23:25; 2 Chron. 23:18; 30:16; Ezra 3:2; 7:6; Dan. 9:11, 13), "the book of Moses" (e.g., 2 Chron. 25:4; 35:12; Ezra 6:18; Neh. 13:1), the "Book of the Law" (e.g., 2 Kings 22:8, 11; 2 Chron. 17:9; cf. 2 Chron. 34:14), and "the law" (e.g., 2 Kings 21:8; 2 Chron. 25:4) all probably refer to the material now preserved in Deuteronomy 5–26 (or 5–30). On some occasions, there can be no doubt that the text of Deuteronomy 5–26 is in view. Quoting Deuteronomy 24:16, the author of 2 Kings 14:6 (cf. 2 Chron. 25:4) states that Amaziah (ca. 800–783 BC) "did not put the sons of the assassins to death, in accordance with what is written in the Book of the Law of Moses where the LORD commanded: 'Fathers shall not be put to death for their children, nor children put to death for their fathers; each is to die for his own sins.'" Although no quotation is provided, Nehemiah 13:1 unmistakably alludes to Deuteronomy 23:3, which states that Ammonites and Moabites should be excluded from the assembly of God. On other occasions dependence on Deuteronomy 5–26 (or 5–30) is more difficult to prove. For example, Joshua 8:31, which states, "according to what is written in the Book of the Law of Moses—an altar of uncut stones, on which no iron tool has been used," would seem at first sight to be alluding to Exodus 20:25. However, there is no mention of "iron" in Exodus 20. Alternatively, Deuteronomy 27:5, which itself depends on Exodus 20:25, specifically uses the term "iron." It may be, therefore, that the author of Joshua 8:31 is alluding to Deuteronomy 27:5.

While the earliest Old Testament evidence strongly suggests that the designation "the Book of the Law of Moses" and its related variants denote the core chapters of Deuteronomy alone, an important development takes place in the postexilic period. At this stage, the designation "Law" comes to embrace more than the material contained in Deuteronomy 5–26 (or 5–30). Thus, for example, a subtle change in wording by the Chronicler in 2 Chronicles 25:4 (cf. 2 Kings 14:6) suggests that he may have viewed the "Book of Moses" as a subset of "the Law." More significantly, the reference in Nehemiah 8:13–14 to the written "Law" probably relates to Leviticus 23:34–43, although H. G. M. Williamson observes that at least one feature depends on Deuteronomy 16:13–15.[32] A similar observation is applicable to Nehemiah 10:34–36, which presupposes a knowledge of Exodus 13:13; 34:20; Numbers 18:15–18; and Deuteronomy 15:19–23. In these latter two examples, the name of Moses is not associated with the "Law"; the "Law of the LORD" encompasses the "Law of Moses" yet goes beyond it to include materials found in Exodus and Leviticus.

The evidence considered above does not go far toward supporting the idea that the Pentateuch, as we know it, existed in the preexilic period. The most that we can conclude is that much of the book of Deuteronomy existed in written form. However, even here we need to take into account the incident recorded in 2 Kings 22 concerning Hilkiah's discovery of the "Book of the Law" during the reign of Josiah. While, as we have noticed earlier, many biblical scholars from the time of de Wette onward have mistakenly dated the composition of Deuteronomy to this event, in about 620 BC, a different implication may be drawn from the narrative. Josiah's reaction to the discovery of this document reveals that the detailed contents of this "Book of the Law" must have been largely unknown at the start of the final quarter of the seventh century BC. This indicates that for some period of time it could not have been read. Indeed, apart from brief references to the "Book of the Law" in the time of David/ Solomon (1 Kings 2:3) and Amaziah (2 Kings 14:6), little mention is made of it before 620 BC. (Another brief reference to the law is found in 2 Kings 17:13, although it is not clear that this is the "Book of the Law." The "Book of the Law of the LORD" is also mentioned by 2 Chron. 17:9 in connection with the reign of Jehoshaphat [ca. 873–849 BC].)

It is no surprise, however, that knowledge of the "Book of the Law" should have been neglected, if not deliberately suppressed, by the Judean and Israelite monarchies. As the book of Kings reveals, the contents of Deuteronomy offer a serious indictment of the practices of many kings. To take but one example, Solomon's desire for wealth (1 Kings 9:10–10:29), horses from Egypt (10:28–29), and many wives (11:1–8) stands in marked contrast to the advice given in Deuteronomy 17:16–17. Given the overall spiral of spiritual and moral decline that followed on from the reign of Solomon and eventually led to the destruction of the Jerusalem temple by the Babylonians, it is hardly unexpected that specific references to the "Book of the Law" are few and brief.

While this is so, clear evidence exists that the "Book of the Law" (i.e., Deut. 5–26 [or 5–30]) was composed well before the time of Josiah. We see this in the writings associated with the prophets. In particular, the book of Hosea presupposes that the prophet's contemporaries knew the "Law of Moses" and accepted its authority. As Andersen and Freedman state, "Hosea's discourses are threaded with Deuteronomic ideas in a way that shows they were already

32. H. G. M. Williamson, *Ezra, Nehemiah*, WBC 16 (Waco: Word Books, 1985), 294–95.

authoritative in Israel."[33] Hosea, however, is not the only prophet to have been influenced by the legal traditions found within the Pentateuch. As Tucker, writing about the eighth-century-BC prophets, observes, "The law, in the sense of authoritative and binding expectations for behavior, comes before even the earliest prophets."[34] Marshall's study of the dating of the legal materials in the Book of the Covenant (Exod. 21–22) also points toward a premonarchic date.[35]

Although there is a clear absence of external sources to confirm the composition of the whole of the Pentateuch as we know it before the postexilic period, the lack of evidence needs to be treated cautiously. Moreover, considerable evidence indicates that many traditions found within the Pentateuch were clearly known in the preexilic period. Consequently, we must ask, are these traditions known from a preexisting Pentateuch, or was the Pentateuch composed later, on the basis of much earlier traditions? Given our present knowledge, the weight of evidence probably favors the latter of these options.

WHY WAS THE PENTATEUCH COMPOSED?

What prompted the bringing together of the various traditions that now make up the Pentateuch? If this can be determined, it may prove to be a helpful guide toward the date of final editing.

Although scholars have expended considerable energy in seeking to determine the origins of the Pentateuch, it has to be acknowledged that they have tended to ignore a key question: Why was the Pentateuch composed? Yet this is as important as the issue of how the Pentateuch came into being, if not more so. The "why" question is also likely to be of greater interest to those who seek to read the Pentateuch from a theological perspective. What follows is a tentative step toward addressing this issue afresh.

As we have observed, the Pentateuch cannot be easily separated from the books of Joshua to Kings. While Noth's theory of a Deuteronomistic History is not without problems, it highlights the close links that exist between the book of Deuteronomy and the books that come after it. Unfortunately, Old Testament scholars rarely read and comment on the books of Genesis to Kings as a unified narrative; attention is usually given to either the Tetrateuch/Pentateuch or the Deuteronomistic History. Those who do comment on Genesis to Kings as a whole are inclined to describe it as a record of the history of the people of Israel. This is implied by R. N. Whybray, who remarks that

33. F. I. Andersen and D. N. Freedman, *Hosea: A New Translation with Introduction and Commentary*, AB 24 (New York: Doubleday, 1980), 75; cf. W. Brueggemann, *Tradition for Crisis: A Study in Hosea* (Richmond: John Knox, 1968), 38–40.

34. G. M. Tucker, "The Law in the Eighth-Century Prophets," in *Canon, Theology, and Old Testament Interpretation: Essays in Honor of Brevard S. Childs*, ed. G. M. Tucker, D. L. Petersen, and R. R. Wilson (Philadelphia: Fortress, 1988), 214.

35. J. W. Marshall, *Israel and the Book of the Covenant: An Anthropological Approach to Biblical Law*, SBLDS 140 (Atlanta: Scholars Press, 1993).

the Pentateuch is "a history of the origins of the people of Israel, prefaced by an account of the origins of the world," which may have been intended as a "supplement (i.e., a prologue) to the work of the Deuteronomistic Historian, which dealt with the more recent period of the national history."[36] According to C. Houtman, Genesis to Kings "presents itself as a description of Israel's history from the perspective of its calling and its continual unfaithfulness."[37] E. T. Mullen has recently proposed that the Tetrateuch was composed as a prologue to the Deuteronomistic History in order to provide "a narrative foundation for the reformulation and maintenance of 'Israelite' ethnic and national identity in the Second Temple period."[38]

The idea that the books of Genesis to Kings were brought together to provide an account of Israel's history seems to be an obvious explanation for their redactional unity. Beginning in Genesis, we trace the growth of Israel from the initial call of Abraham through to the establishment of his descendants as a nation in the land of Canaan. Years of struggle and frustration eventually give way to a time of stability and splendor during the reigns of David and Solomon. Thereafter the nation's history is marked by decline, leading eventually to the Babylonians' overthrowing the kingdom of Judah.

Central to the development of the theme of nationhood in Genesis to Kings are the divine promises announced to Abraham (strictly speaking, Abram) in Genesis 12:1–3. These play a major role in linking the books of Genesis to Kings by setting the agenda for most of what follows. Summoning Abraham to leave his family and homeland, "the LORD" promises, "I will make you into a great nation" (Gen. 12:2). Several chapters later this promise of nationhood is developed more fully and confirmed by a covenant that focuses on two areas: numerous descendants (Gen. 15:1–6) and land (Gen. 15:7–21).

The divine promise of land is renewed with Abraham's immediate descendants, Isaac and Jacob (cf. Gen. 26:3; 28:13; 35:12; cf. 28:4; 48:4; 50:24). In Exodus, God's promise of land to Abraham, Isaac, and Jacob is mentioned on various occasions (2:24; 6:4, 5; 13:11; 34:11; cf. Lev. 26:42; Deut. 34:4), and there are several allusions to the covenant of Genesis 15 (Exod. 3:8, 17; 13:5; 23:23; 33:2; in these passages the peoples of Gen. 15:19–21 are named; cf. Deut. 1:7; 7:1; 20:17). In the light of the specific references to slavery and release in Genesis 15:13–14, it is hardly surprising that this covenant features prominently in Exodus. Indeed, in Exodus 2:24 God's deliverance of the Israelites from Egypt is directly linked to his covenant with Abraham. Later, after the Israelites are punished for making the golden calf, the renewal of the Sinai covenant is once again based on the promises made to Abraham, Isaac, and Jacob concerning land (cf. Exod. 32:13). Preparations for taking

36. Whybray, *Making of the Pentateuch*, 242.
37. C. Houtman, "The Pentateuch," in *The World of the Old Testament*, ed. A. S. van der Woude (Grand Rapids: Eerdmans, 1989), 2:200.
38. Mullen, *Ethnic Myths and Pentateuchal Foundations*, 327.

possession of the land are prominent in the book of Numbers. Occupation is delayed, however, through the unbelief and rebellion of the people. Nevertheless, after the death of all the adult Israelites who left Egypt, except for Joshua and Caleb, the imminent fulfillment of the promise of land is anticipated in the later chapters of Numbers and the book of Deuteronomy. The books of Joshua, Judges, and Samuel, up to the reigns of David and Solomon, record the gradual completion of this process.

The promise of land and its fulfillment is clearly important in the books of Genesis to Samuel. The same is true regarding the promise of descendants, the other aspect of becoming a great nation. A recurring theme in the patriarchal narratives is God's role in overcoming the barrenness of the matriarchs Sarah, Rebekah, and Rachel (Gen. 21:1; 25:21; 30:22–24). In the opening chapter of Exodus, the remarkable increase of the Israelites causes resentment in Egypt and leads to the repressive policy of Pharaoh (Exod. 1:6–10). Later, as the Israelites prepare to enter the land of Canaan, Moses acknowledges that the promise of Genesis 15:5 has been fulfilled: "The LORD your God has increased your numbers so that today you are as numerous as the stars of the sky" (Deut. 1:10; cf. 10:22; 28:62; Neh. 9:23). Though the topic of population growth is less prominent in the books of Joshua to Kings, it is specifically noted that during the reign of Solomon "the people of Judah and Israel were as numerous as the sand on the seashore" (1 Kings 4:20; cf. 2 Sam. 17:11).

Although the books of Genesis to Samuel describe the gradual fulfillment of the divine promise of nationhood to Abraham, Kings charts the reversal of this process. Beginning with Solomon, the narrative describes how the failure of both monarchy and people leads to the loss of territory and the deportation of many citizens. Of significance is the fact that these later events are anticipated even before the Israelites enter the promised land (cf. Deut. 28:64–68; 30:1, 4). However, there are indications that the loss of land and population is not the final chapter in God's dealings with Israel (cf. Deut. 30:1–5; 1 Kings 8:46–51).

This brief survey reveals that the theme of nationhood plays a major role in linking the books of Genesis to Kings. While we in no way wish to diminish the importance of this theme, it is paralleled by another concept that is as important, if not more so, for understanding the redactional unity of the books of Genesis to Kings. This parallel theme concerns a king through whom the nations of the earth will be blessed.

Scholars have long recognized the importance of the promise of nationhood in Genesis, yet they have mostly failed to observe that Genesis also focuses on a divinely promised royal "seed." This failure results, at least in part, from a general tendency to neglect the final form of Genesis in favor of source- and form-critical approaches. When Genesis is viewed as a literary unity, however, there can be little doubt that it is especially interested in pointing toward the coming of a unique king. Viewed against this background, the theme of kingship in the books of Exodus to Kings takes on a new dimension.

Although the promise of nationhood (i.e., land and descendants) is a central feature of the patriarchal narratives in Genesis, it is not the only promise highlighted. "The LORD" says to Abraham: "Leave your country, your people and your father's household and go to the land I will show you, so that I may make you into a great nation and bless you and make your name great. Be a blessing, so that I may bless those who bless you, and curse the one who disdains you, and so that all the families of the ground may be blessed through you" (Gen. 12:1–3, my trans.). This statement falls naturally into two halves, each introduced by an imperative. The first part focuses primarily on the promise of nationhood; the second centers chiefly on the blessing of others. The entire speech comes to a climax in the statement "so that all the families of the ground may be blessed through you." The promise that Abraham will become a "great nation" is of secondary importance to God's principal desire to bless all the families of the ground.[39] Thus the primary motive behind the call of Abraham is God's intention to bless, rather than curse, humanity. By commanding him to leave his homeland and be a blessing, God places the onus on Abraham to obey in order that the promises concerning nationhood and blessing may be fulfilled.

As we have already observed, the fulfillment of the promise of nationhood is later guaranteed through the divine covenant made with Abraham in Genesis 15. A further covenant is introduced in Genesis 17.[40] Most commentators, unfortunately, focus on the sign of the covenant, circumcision, without noticing that the essence of this covenant lies in the promise that Abraham will be the "father of many nations" (17:4–5). Since this promise is later associated with Sarah—"She will be the mother of nations" (17:16)—it is unlikely that it includes the nations descended from Abraham through his relationships with Hagar (cf. 17:20) and Keturah (25:1–4). The Old Testament, however, is remarkably silent concerning the idea that Abraham would be the biological ancestor of different nations. In the light of this, we should observe that the Hebrew word 'āb ('āv), "father," is sometimes "used of a variety of social roles that carried authority or exercised a protective or caring function. It could be used of a prophet (2 Kings 6:21), priest (Judg. 18:19), king (1 Sam. 24:11), or governor (Isa. 22:20–21)."[41] By taking 'āb in this nonbiological sense, we may

39. On the importance of the promise of blessing, see V. P. Hamilton, "Genesis: Theology of," *NIDOTTE* 4:667; P. R. Williamson, *Abraham, Israel and the Nations: The Patriarchal Promise and Its Covenantal Development in Genesis*, JSOTSup 315 (Sheffield: Sheffield Academic Press, 2000), 220–34.

40. Although the covenant of Gen. 15 focuses primarily on nationhood (land and descendants), the covenant in Gen. 17 highlights Abraham's special status in relation to the nations. Unfortunately, biblical scholars have tended to blur the differences between these two covenants, some viewing them as parallel accounts of the same covenant, preserved in different sources. For a fuller discussion of the Abraham narrative, see chap. 12 below and the study by Williamson, *Abraham, Israel and the Nations*.

41. C. J. H. Wright, "אב ('āb)," *NIDOTTE* 1:219.

understand Genesis 17:4–5 as stating that Abraham will be the "father of many nations" not because these nations are his physical descendants but because he will be for them a channel of divine blessing.[42] As N. M. Sarna observes, the phrase "father of many nations" "has a more universal application in that a large segment of humanity looks upon Abraham as its spiritual father."[43] This nonbiological understanding of *'āb*, "father," is supported by the fact that Abraham is instructed to circumcise those who are not his offspring, which includes those born in his "household or bought with money from a foreigner" (17:12–13). This suggests that circumcision, and the covenant associated with it, was never intended to be a sign of racial purity. Later in Genesis the men of Shechem undergo circumcision in order to establish a bond of kinship with Abraham's descendants (34:14–17). This makes their subsequent slaughter by Simeon and Levi all the more reprehensible.

Although all the male members of Abraham's household are circumcised, including Ishmael, the LORD emphasizes that the covenant will be established with Isaac, and him alone (Gen. 17:19, 21). The uniqueness of Isaac's position regarding this covenant is underlined by the exclusion of Ishmael even though he is also circumcised.[44] This introduces an important distinction between those who may enjoy the benefits of this covenant and the one through whom the covenant will be established. Whereas the former includes all who are circumcised, the latter appears to be restricted to a single line of descendants. On this we shall have more to say below.

The Abraham narrative moves toward an important climax in Genesis 22. After relating God's testing of Abraham's obedience by demanding that he sacrifice his much-loved son, Isaac, the episode concludes with a divine oath (Gen. 22:16–18). This oath corresponds closely with the initial divine speech in Genesis 12:1–3, framing the main section of the Abraham narrative, and possibly also marking the ratification of the covenant announced in Genesis 17.[45] As it stands, the LORD's proclamation to Abraham falls into two distinctive parts; whereas the first half affirms that Abraham's "seed" will become very numerous, the second half asserts that Abraham's "seed" will defeat his enemies and mediate blessings to the nations of the earth. While

---

42. This understanding of "father" is probably reflected in the unusual comment that Joseph is "father to Pharaoh" (Gen. 45:8). Furthermore, when God blesses Jacob in 35:11, echoing an earlier blessing by Isaac on Jacob (28:3), a distinction is drawn between "a nation" and "a community of nations" coming from him. The implication seems to be that although many nations will be closely associated with him, only one nation will be directly descended from him.

43. N. M. Sarna, *Genesis*, JPSTC (Philadelphia: Jewish Publication Society, 1989), 124.

44. Cf. Gen. 21:12. A similar pattern may be observed concerning Esau and Jacob. The covenant is established with Jacob, but not with Esau. The importance of Abraham, Isaac, and Jacob as successive recipients of the divine covenant is reflected in the way that they are mentioned together in later passages.

45. See T. D. Alexander, "Genesis 22 and the Covenant of Circumcision," *JSOT* 25 (1983): 17–22; Williamson, *Abraham, Israel and the Nations*, 234–59.

each half of the oath refers to "seed," syntactical considerations strongly suggest that in the second half, in contrast to the first, the term "seed" denotes a single descendant of Abraham.[46] In other words, God swears that the nations will be blessed through one of Abraham's descendants rather than through all of them collectively. Moreover, this individual will be victorious over his enemies.[47]

This emphasis on a single descendant takes on special significance when viewed against the whole of Genesis. Several distinctive literary features reveal that the book of Genesis traces the development of a unique line of "seed," beginning with Adam and ending with Jacob/Israel and his twelve sons.[48] One of these features is the *tôlĕdōt* formula ("These are the generations of . . ." [KJV]),[49] which functions somewhat like the zoom lens on a camera by focusing attention on a single individual and his immediate descendants. Used in conjunction with the linear genealogies found in Genesis 5 and 11, the *tôlĕdōt* formula enables the Genesis narrative to follow the progress on a unique family line that includes Enoch, Methuselah, Noah, Abraham, Isaac, and Jacob.

Linked to the *tôlĕdōt* formula in terms of purpose is the Hebrew word *zera'*, "seed," which is used in Genesis as a keyword; it occurs throughout Genesis 59 times compared to 170 times in the rest of the Old Testament. Genesis draws attention to the existence of a distinctive line of "seed" that begins with Seth, the third-born son to Adam and Eve (cf. Gen. 4:25), and concludes by highlighting in particular the importance of both Perez, the son born as a result of Judah's unusual relationship with Tamar (Gen. 38:27–29), and Ephraim, the younger of Joseph's two sons (Gen. 48:1–22).[50] Throughout Genesis, and especially in the patriarchal narratives, special care is taken to establish the identity of those who belong to this line of seed; occasionally this results in a firstborn son being passed over in favor of a younger sibling.[51]

When due attention is given to the *tôlĕdōt* formula and the keyword *zera'*, it becomes evident that the book of Genesis in its final form anticipates the coming of a royal savior through whom God's blessing will be mediated to all

46. See T. D. Alexander, "Further Observations on the Term 'Seed' in Genesis," *TynBul* 48 (1997): 363–67; this builds on C. J. Collins, "A Syntactical Note (Genesis 3:15): Is the Woman's Seed Singular or Plural?" *TynBul* 48 (1997): 139–48.

47. These ideas are developed in Ps. 72, which clearly associates the blessing of the nations with the universal rule of a future Davidic king.

48. See T. D. Alexander, "From Adam to Judah: The Significance of the Family Tree in Genesis," *EvQ* 61 (1989): 5–19; idem, "Genealogies, Seed and the Compositional Unity of Genesis," *TynBul* 44 (1993): 255–70. These ideas are developed more fully in chap. 8 below.

49. Gen. 2:4; 5:1; 6:9; 10:1; 11:10, 27; 25:12, 19; 36:1, 9; 37:2.

50. See chap. 9 below for a fuller discussion of the significance of the terms *tôlĕdōt* and *zera'* in Genesis.

51. Seth takes priority over Cain (Gen. 5:3), Isaac over Ishmael (Gen. 21:12), and Jacob over Esau (Gen. 27:36).

the nations of the earth.[52] The existence of such an individual is first intimated in Genesis 3:14–15 (NIV, alt), when the LORD God tells the serpent:

> Cursed are you above all the livestock
> and all the wild animals!
> You will crawl on your belly
> and you will eat dust
> all the days of your life.
> And I will put enmity
> between you and the woman,
> and between your seed and her seed;
> he will crush your head,
> and you will strike his heel.

Although modern trends in Old Testament scholarship have led many writers to reject the idea that the "seed of the woman" refers to an individual, the case for such an interpretation remains strong,[53] especially if one takes into account Collins's recent observations on the syntax of Genesis 3:15.[54] While 3:15 does not explicitly state that this individual will be of royal status, W. Wifall notes interesting links with various expressions found in "royal" psalms, and these he takes as indicating a Davidic or royal background to 3:15.[55]

The linear genealogies in Genesis 5 and 11 trace the "seed of the woman" to Abraham, through whom God promises to bless all the families of the ground (12:1–3). This same promise probably underlies the covenant of circumcision and the idea that Abraham will be the "father of many nations." Although this covenant is made first with Abraham, it is clearly oriented toward the future. The LORD states that it will be established with Abraham's "seed" "for the generations to come" (Gen. 17:7 KJV/NIV). Furthermore, the establishment of the covenant is linked specifically to Isaac. Later, as we have already observed, the LORD swears an oath to Abraham, presumably in Isaac's presence, that all the nations of the earth will be blessed through his "seed" (Gen. 22:18 KJV). The fulfillment of this divine oath, which is unique within the Pentateuch, also lies in the future.

---

52. A fuller discussion of this comes in chaps. 9 and 10 below.

53. Cf. T. D. Alexander, "Messianic Ideology in the Book of Genesis," in *The Lord's Anointed: Interpretation of Old Testament Messianic Texts*, ed. P. E. Satterthwaite, R. S. Hess, and G. J. Wenham (Grand Rapids: Baker; Carlisle: Paternoster, 1995), 27–32.

54. Collins, "A Syntactical Note."

55. According to W. Wifall, "David is addressed as God's 'anointed' or 'messiah' (Ps. 89:21, 39 [20, 38]; 2 Sam. 22:51) whose 'seed' will endure forever under God's favor (Ps. 89:5, 30, 37 [4, 29, 36]). As Yahweh has crushed the ancient serpent 'Rahab' (Ps. 89:11 [10]), so now David and his sons will crush their enemies in the dust beneath their feet (Ps. 89:24 [23]; 2 Sam. 22:37–43). . . . In Psalm 72:9, the foes of the Davidic king are described as 'bowing down before him' and 'licking the dust.' In the familiar 'messianic' Psalms, God is described as having placed 'all things under his feet' (Ps. 8:6) and will make 'your enemies your footstool' (Ps. 110:1)"; see "Gen 3:15—A Protevangelium?" *CBQ* 36 (1974): 363.

The Abraham narrative clearly builds on the divine promise given in Genesis 3:15 regarding the "seed of the woman" overcoming the "seed of the serpent." The motif of blessing is prominent in Genesis 12:1–3 and stands in marked contrast to that of cursing, which dominates the divine judgments announced in Genesis 3. In addition, the "royal" nature of the line of seed becomes more explicit within the Abraham story. At the outset this is reflected in the promise that Abraham's name will "become great."[56] Although he is nowhere designated a king, Abraham is presented in various episodes as enjoying a status similar to that of contemporary monarchs (Gen. 14:1–24; 21:22–34; 23:6). Furthermore, the LORD specifically promises Abraham that "kings will come from you" (Gen. 17:6; cf. 17:16).

The theme of royalty is less evident in Genesis 25–36. Isaac, like his father Abraham, enters into a covenant with Abimelech, king of Gerar (26:26–31). On his return from Paddan Aram, Jacob receives the divine promise that "kings will come from your body" (35:11). The existence of a future monarchy in Israel is also suggested by the brief comment in 36:31: "These were the kings who reigned in Edom before any Israelite king reigned."

In marked contrast, kingship is important in the account of Joseph's life, being the dominant motif in the two dreams that he experiences (Gen. 37:5–11). His brothers, filled with jealousy and hatred, remark, "Do you intend to reign over us? Will you actually rule us?" But Joseph's father "kept the matter in mind." In spite of the brothers' attempt to rid themselves of Joseph, he later emerges from an Egyptian prison to become second only to Pharaoh in authority over the kingdom of Egypt (41:39–43). Ironically, when some years later Joseph's older brothers travel to Egypt, the narrative records how they bow before him with their faces to the ground (42:6). In due course, however, Joseph reveals his identity to them and remarks how God has made him "father to Pharaoh, lord of his entire household and ruler of all Egypt" (Gen. 45:8; cf. 45:9, 26).

In the light of Genesis as a whole, Joseph clearly plays a major role by being one of the "firstborn" through whom God's blessing is imparted to others.[57] The importance of his family line is further underlined when Joseph brings his two sons, Manasseh and Ephraim, to the elderly and frail Jacob in order to have them blessed. As has happened previously in Genesis, the younger of the two boys, Ephraim, receives the superior blessing, in this way confirming the importance of his family line for the fulfillment of God's purposes. Later, when the Israelites come to take possession of the promised land, it is an Ephraimite, Joshua, who successfully leads the twelve tribes across the Jordan to their new home.[58]

56. Cf. G. J. Wenham, *Genesis 1–15*, WBC 1 (Waco: Word Books, 1987), 275–76; V. P. Hamilton, *The Book of Genesis: Chapters 1–17*, NICOT (Grand Rapids: Eerdmans, 1990), 372–73.
57. On the status of Joseph as Jacob's firstborn, see chap. 9 below.
58. Although Joshua is never given the title of king, his success as a leader is directly associated with his obedience to the "Book of the Law" (Josh. 1:8). According to Deut. 17:18–19, the king is expected to "write for himself on a scroll a copy of this law" and "to read it all the days of his life."

The account of Joseph's life dominates Genesis 37–50. Yet when in old age Jacob gathers his sons around him to tell them what will happen in days to come (cf. 49:1), kingship appears to be associated with the descendants of Judah (cf. 49:8–12), and not Joseph (cf. 49:22–26). While the poetic language of Genesis 49 makes it possible for differing interpretations to be placed on Jacob's remarks, viewed against the background of Genesis as a whole, these verses clearly point to a powerful future ruler to whom the nations will submit in obedience.[59]

In the light of this, the earlier description of the birth of Judah's son, Perez, takes on added significance. Recorded in Genesis 38, the story of Judah's unseemly relationship with Tamar unexpectedly interrupts the account of Joseph's arrival in Egypt. Not only does Genesis 38 divert attention away from Joseph, but also it significantly picks up the important theme of the continuation of the family line.[60] Remarkably, the story concludes with a brief description of the birth of twins, during which the younger, Perez, breaks out in front of the firstborn, Zerah (Gen. 38:28–30). Taking into account the location and central theme of Genesis 38, the symbolism of this birth account should not be overlooked, especially given, as we shall observe below, the much later divine rejection of the line of Joseph-Ephraim in favor of the line of Judah.

The account of the Israelites' divine deliverance from bondage in Egypt and their journey toward the promised land dominates the books of Exodus to Deuteronomy. Though the theme of kingship surfaces only rarely in these books (e.g., Num. 24:17–19; Deut. 17:14–20), it becomes much more prominent in Joshua and Judges. These books anticipate the establishment of a monarchy in Israel by focusing on the divine provision of spirit-empowered deliverers. Although those appointed by God as leaders fulfill many of the tasks of a king, they are prohibited from creating royal dynasties, as highlighted in the story of Gideon's son, Abimelech (Judg. 9:1–57). The picture in Judges of ever-increasing moral and spiritual decline comes to a climax in the final four chapters of the book. These are framed by the significant refrain "in those days Israel had no king; everyone did as they saw fit" (Judg. 17:6; 21:25; cf. 18:1; 19:1).

Although the books of Genesis and Joshua give prominence to the line of Joseph, traced through Ephraim, thereafter things appear to fall apart for the Ephraimites. As the book of Judges reveals, during the time of Jephthah the Ephraimites not only fail to take the lead in delivering the Israelites from their enemies; they also aggressively oppose others for doing so successfully (Judg. 12:1–7). As a consequence, 42,000 Ephraimites are slaughtered at the fords of the Jordan.

59. Cf. Alexander, "Messianic Ideology in the Book of Genesis," 32–37. In passing, we should observe that the reign of this destined king will be marked by a time of abundant fruitfulness, a sign of divine blessing.

60. This is developed more fully in chap. 9 below.

God's eventual rejection of Ephraim as the anticipated royal line comes to the fore in the early chapters of Samuel. Here the narrative focuses on events associated with the temple at Shiloh in the region of Ephraim, describing how God distances himself from the hereditary priesthood associated with the sanctuary. The final stage, in what appears to have been a long process, comes when the ark of the covenant is taken in battle by the Philistines. The significance of this event is poignantly captured by the dying remarks of Eli's daughter-in-law when she names her son Ichabod because "the Glory has departed from Israel" (1 Sam. 4:21).

Although 1 Samuel goes on to describe the appointment of Saul as the first king of Israel, due to his own shortcomings, he is soon replaced by David, the youngest son of Jesse, a descendant of Judah.[61] When David is eventually enthroned as king over all Israel, he establishes Jerusalem as his capital and in due course brings there the ark of the covenant. This event, among other things, confirms God's choice of David as king. Soon afterward the LORD makes a covenant with David in which he promises to establish David's dynasty forever (2 Sam. 7).

The reign of David's son Solomon provides an interesting picture of the kind of rule that God intends to establish through the promised "seed" of Abraham. Under Solomon the people experience peace, justice, and prosperity. Unfortunately, Solomon fails to remain loyal to the LORD, and following his death the kingdom is partitioned, with the house of David keeping control of only the region of Judah. Throughout the book of Kings, God's promise to establish David's dynasty forever stands in tension with his warning that he will punish the disobedience of David's descendants. Eventually Kings records the destruction of the Jerusalem temple and the removal of King Jehoiachin to Babylon. Though this marks the end of the Davidic dynasty's rule over Jerusalem, the final episode in the book of Kings focuses on the release of Jehoiachin from prison, an event that clearly symbolizes the possibility that the throne may be restored to David's line.

The preceding survey reveals, if somewhat sketchily, that within the books of Genesis to Kings the divine promise of a royal savior plays a more important role than the promise of nationhood.[62] Yet in spite of this, the pledge of a royal savior remains unfulfilled by the end of Kings. Nevertheless, some progress toward fulfillment occurs as the line of "seed" introduced in Genesis is traced through to the creation of the Davidic dynasty. Furthermore, following the establishment of David as king over Israel, God makes a covenant with him, confirming that through his lineage the nations of the earth will be blessed

---

61. The significance of David's ancestry for the fulfillment of the divine promises announced in Genesis is highlighted in the book of Ruth; cf. E. H. Merrill, "The Book of Ruth: Narration and Shared Themes," *BS* 142 (1985): 130–39.

62. Although the promises of nationhood and royal savior are distinctive, it would be a mistake to divorce them from each other.

(2 Sam. 7:5–16; 1 Chron. 17:4–14).[63] As the book of Kings reveals, however, the cumulative disobedience of David's descendants appears to thwart the fulfillment of God's promise to bless the nations. There are, however, strong indications in Kings that the removal of the house of David from the throne in Jerusalem is not the end of the story. Although God with complete justification punishes David's descendants for their sins, the hope remains that there will yet be a "son of David" through whom the nations will experience God's favor.[64]

Since the books of Genesis to Kings, as a coherent narrative, cannot have existed before the exilic period, the events of the exile may well have been catalytic in bringing these books together into a continuous account. This does not automatically mean, however, that the tradition of a divinely promised royal savior originated after 587 BC. The eighth-century prophets were already familiar with this idea, as reflected, for example, in the final chapter of Amos and in Isaiah 7–11. From a different perspective, it is worth observing that it would require an author of exceptional genius and religious optimism to compose these books ab initio after the demise of the Davidic monarchy and the destruction of the temple in Jerusalem.

In the light of the coherent narrative plot that runs from Genesis through Kings, which cannot be easily broken at either the end of Numbers or Deuteronomy, it seems best to assume that all the material in Genesis to Kings was brought together at one time to form the extended narrative that comprises these books. Given the diversity of materials and styles of presentation contained in Genesis to Kings, earlier traditions were clearly used to compose this complex literary collage.

The books of Genesis to Kings were probably given their present shape shortly after 562 BC, the date of Jehoiachin's release from prison (2 Kings 25:27). While the process by which these books were compiled remains obscure, they were probably written to give hope to those adversely affected by the destruction of Jerusalem and the temple, the demise of the Davidic dynasty, the deportation of many leading Judean citizens to Babylon, and the flight of others to Egypt. The books of Genesis to Kings not only offer an explanation for the occurrence of these traumatic events by focusing on the nation's failure to be faithful to Yahweh (see esp. Deut. 28:15–68; 29:16–28); they also preserve the hope that God will one day raise up a descendant of David through whom

---

63. For a fuller discussion of the Davidic covenant and in particular the expression "and this is the instruction of humanity" (2 Sam. 7:19, my trans.), see T. E. McComiskey, *The Covenants of Promise: A Theology of Old Testament Covenants* (Grand Rapids: Baker, 1985), 21–35. O. P. Robertson, *The Christ of the Covenants* (Phillipsburg, NJ: P&R, 1980), 33–34, observes that the bringing of the ark to Jerusalem is linked by David to the covenant promised to Abraham (1 Chron. 16:15–18). Further links between David and Abraham are discussed by R. E. Clements, *Abraham and David: Genesis XV and Its Meaning for Israelite Tradition*, SBT, 2nd ser., 5 (London: SCM, 1967).

64. This hope is articulated in many of the prophetic books of the OT. Cf. T. D. Alexander, *The Servant King: The Bible's Portrait of the Messiah* (Leicester: Inter-Varsity, 1998), 89–120.

God will bless all the nations of the earth. Similar optimism comes in other writings, some of which originate before the exile (e.g., Isa. 9:1–7; 11:1–5; Jer. 23:5–6; 30:8–9; Ezek. 17:22–24; 34:23–24; 37:24; Amos 9:11–12).

Conclusion

Since the Pentateuch itself offers no clear statement regarding the one responsible for creating it, we should exercise extreme caution before stating that its author can be identified with certainty. While the long-standing tradition of Mosaic authorship is based on clear statements that Moses was responsible for writing substantial parts of the Pentateuch, the weight of evidence suggests that Moses probably did not compose the Pentateuch as we now have it.[65] This is not to say that the Pentateuch's claims concerning Moses's literary activity should be rejected. On the contrary, such assertions ought to be respected and given serious consideration, which unfortunately all too rarely happens.

As we have recognized, two conflicting factors complicate the task of trying to identify the author of the Pentateuch. As a literary work, the Pentateuch displays evidence of both unity and disunity. Unity of overall composition, involving a narrative plot that binds disparate materials together, has to be balanced against the fact that the pentateuchal writings lack homogeneity, with different styles and types of writing having been placed side by side. These factors suggest that the Pentateuch was composed through a process of editing that involved the bringing together of already-extant documents.

The task of determining when this editorial task was undertaken is far from straightforward. As we have noticed, early traditions may be brought together at a much later date, leaving open the possibility that many centuries could pass between the original composition of traditions found within the Pentateuch and their incorporation into a single work. Acknowledging that any conclusion reached must be based on very limited evidence, it seems best to conclude that the Pentateuch as a literary whole, which was linked to the books of Joshua to Kings, eventually took shape in the exilic period. Though the traditions contained within the Pentateuch clearly existed before this time and were obviously viewed as both ancient and authoritative by the final editor of the Pentateuch, it is exceptionally difficult to demonstrate that the Pentateuch itself existed in its entirety as a literary unity before the sixth century BC. As we have suggested, it may have been the dramatic events surrounding the fall of Jerusalem that prompted the bringing together of the traditions that are now embedded not just in the books of Genesis to Deuteronomy but also in Genesis to Kings.

It is open to debate whether substantial parts of the Pentateuch already existed as literary works before this final editing. Evidence from Kings and

65. Cf. Aalders, *Short Introduction to the Pentateuch*, 105–58.

the prophetic writings indicates that much of Deuteronomy already existed. Whether the same is true, for example, of Genesis is difficult to determine; Wenham has recently argued that the rhetorical features of Genesis point to a date of composition in the early monarchy.[66] Certainly the editor of Genesis appears to have been aware of the establishment of the Davidic dynasty, associated with the line of Perez, and the rejection of the line of Ephraim.[67] However, the complex relationship between the royal lines that descended from Joseph and Judah, anticipated in Genesis 37–50, would hardly have led to Joseph's being given prominence at the very time when David and Solomon were seeking to establish their claim to the throne of Israel. A later date of editing, well beyond the division of the Solomonic empire, and possibly after the fall of the northern kingdom of Israel, would seem to offer the best time for composing a work that gives greater prominence to Joseph/Ephraim over against Judah/Perez. That this should happen at such a late period, when there was little to be gained by advancing the cause of Joseph/Ephraim, suggests that the editor of these traditions was committed to preserving them accurately.

To suggest, even tentatively, that the Pentateuch reached its present form long after the time of Moses may appear to some readers to undermine its authority and challenge the concept of divine inspiration. Yet such is not the case. A late date of editing does not automatically deny the authenticity of the traditions contained in the Pentateuch, especially when, as we have noted, earlier written documents have been used in its composition. By linking the books of Genesis to Kings, the final editor of this material produced an important metanarrative that provides a unique perspective on God's dealing with humanity. This ancient metanarrative not only recounts events that have taken place; it also significantly offers an authoritative explanation of them. Furthermore, as Sternberg has observed, the narrator of these events comes across as omniscient, knowing, for example, not only what various characters in the story are thinking but, more important, what God is thinking. For Sternberg, such knowledge displayed by the narrator points toward divine inspiration.[68]

66. G. J. Wenham, *Story as Torah: Reading the Old Testament Ethically*, OTS (Edinburgh: T&T Clark, 2000).

67. See Ps. 78:59–72; T. D. Alexander, "The Regal Dimension of the תלדות־יעקב: Recovering the Literary Context of Genesis 37–50," in *Reading the Law: Studies in Honour of Gordon J. Wenham*, ed. J. G. McConville and K. Möller, LHB/OTS 461 (Edinburgh: T&T Clark, 2007), 196–212.

68. Sternberg, *Poetics of Biblical Narrative*, 23–35.

PART

The Main Themes
of the Pentateuch

7

An Overview of the Pentateuch

Before embarking on a fuller study of the individual books that compose the Pentateuch, it may be helpful to provide a brief overview of the whole, in the process highlighting the themes that will be examined in more detail in following chapters.

As presently constituted, the Pentateuch consists of five books that have been composed in the light of one another to form a single unit. Various factors reveal the interdependence of the individual books. Primary among these is the plot, which begins in Genesis and flows logically through to the end of Deuteronomy. Certain threads run through this plot, uniting the different books. Genesis introduces the idea that the land of Canaan is promised to the descendants of Abraham, Isaac, and Jacob. The fulfillment of this promise sets the agenda for the books of Exodus to Deuteronomy and beyond. Although the land is promised to Abraham, Isaac, and Jacob, it is anticipated that their descendants will take possession of it only after a long stay in Egypt (Gen. 15:13–16; cf. Exod. 12:40–41). The Joseph story records how the first small group of Israelites leave Canaan to settle temporarily in Egypt. Yet here, as the opening chapters of Exodus reveal, they are enslaved by the Egyptians until through divine intervention the Israelites are enabled to flee the country. Thus their journey through the wilderness toward Canaan is narrated in Exodus, Leviticus, and Numbers. The account of this journey ends in Deuteronomy, with the people located on the plains of Moab, east of the Jordan. Central to the account of the Israelites' divine rescue from Egypt is the figure of Moses, with the opening chapters of Exodus describing his birth and the final chapter of Deuteronomy recording his death.[1]

Apart from thematic threads that run through a number of books, adjacent books are also linked through the presence of shared motifs. For example, Genesis concludes with Joseph's making the sons of Jacob swear that they will carry his bones up from Egypt (Gen. 50:25); the exact fulfillment of this request is picked up in Exodus 13:19. Instructions for the setting apart of priests are given in Exodus 29; their appointment is narrated in Leviticus 9. While Numbers 20:12 anticipates the death of Moses outside the promised land, the account of this happening comes in Deuteronomy 34.

Even Genesis, often viewed as being quite different in character from the remaining books of the Pentateuch, is clearly integrated into the overall plot. The divine promises to the patriarchs set the agenda for developments in the books of Exodus to Deuteronomy and beyond. The whole of the Joseph story provides an essential link between the stories of Abraham, Isaac, and Jacob living in Canaan and the account of their descendants being rescued from Egypt. In the light of these general observations, it is important not to lightly dismiss the present unity of the Pentateuch. Although the books of Genesis to Deuteronomy are made up of very diverse components, which may superficially give the impression of lacking unity, someone has skillfully brought them together to form a narrative that exhibits considerable cohesion and harmony. In its present form the Pentateuch is clearly a unified work.

The basic plot of the Pentateuch may be outlined as follows. At the outset humans are created in order to enjoy a special relationship with God and to exercise authority on his behalf over the earth. Commissioned to fill the earth, they are to create a temple-city that will become God's earthly residence. However, the disobedience of Adam and Eve alienates them from God, and as a result they are punished through divine curses and expelled from Eden. By betraying God, they disqualify themselves from serving as his vice-regents and so fulfilling their role as temple-city builders. Moreover, their subsequent actions not only pollute the earth, making it unfit for divine habitation, but they also use their divinely given abilities to construct cities that are the antithesis of the temple-city that God intends to be his residence. The city of Babel-Babylon[2] exemplifies human aspirations to control not only the earth, but heaven as well.

While the early chapters of Genesis concentrate mainly on the terrible consequences of these initial developments, the rest of Genesis, from chapter 12 onward, moves forward with the hope that humanity may yet be reconciled to God. Central to this hope of reconciliation are the divine promises made

---

1. In the light of the importance of Moses, it is hardly surprising that an early and enduring title for the Pentateuch has been "The Books of Moses."
2. On Babel-Babylon, see chap. 8 below.

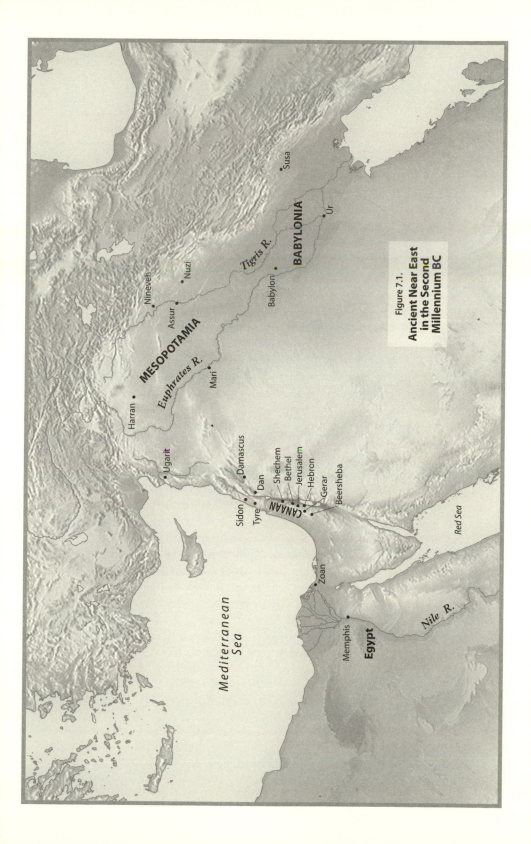

Figure 7.1.
Ancient Near East in the Second Millennium BC

Susa

BABYLONIA

Ur

Nineveh

Nuzi

Tigris R.

Assur

Babylon

MESOPOTAMIA

Euphrates R.

Mari

Harran

Ugarit

Damascus

Shechem
Bethel
Jerusalem
Hebron
Gerar
Beersheba

Dan

CANAAN

Sidon

Tyre

Mediterranean
Sea

Zoan

Red Sea

Memphis

Egypt

Nile R.

to Abraham. The importance of these should not be underestimated: they set the agenda for all that follows in the rest of the Pentateuch and beyond. From a careful study of the Abraham narrative, it is clear that there are two main dimensions to these promises. First, there is the promise that through the "seed" of Abraham "all nations on earth will be blessed" (Gen. 22:18). Although of primary importance for reversing the consequences of what took place in the Garden of Eden, this promise remains unfulfilled by the conclusion of the Pentateuch. Within Genesis this promise is specifically linked to a future royal lineage that will be descended from Abraham, in the first instance, through his great-grandson Joseph. This line is then traced via Ephraim to Joshua. However, Genesis anticipates that the future monarchy associated with Joseph-Ephraim will be replaced by one that will come from the line of Judah, through his son Perez.

The other divine promises to Abraham center on the establishment of a great nation. These promises generally emphasize two aspects of this: descendants and land. God through a special covenant guarantees Abraham that his descendants will be given the land of Canaan some four centuries later (Gen. 15). For this promise of nationhood to be fulfilled, various developments must occur, and these are recorded in the rest of the Pentateuch. Yet the promise of nationhood, like the promise of blessing for the nations of the earth, remains unrealized by the end of Deuteronomy.

The promises of blessing and nationhood are closely linked. The blessing of the nations can occur only after the promise of nationhood has been fulfilled and a monarchy is created. This explains why the Pentateuch concentrates on the establishment of Abraham's descendants as a nation in the land of Canaan. Indeed, because so much attention is given in the Pentateuch to it, this latter promise tends to overshadow the promise of blessing for the nations through a royal descendant of Abraham.

The setting apart of Israel as a nation distinct from all others dominates the books of Exodus to Deuteronomy. The primary purpose behind this is that Israel should initiate the process by which God's temple-city will one day dominate the earth. Although the book of Exodus begins by emphasizing how the Israelites are fulfilling the creation mandate (Exod. 1:7; cf. Gen. 1:28), opposition comes from the king of Egypt. The Israelites soon find themselves enslaved and forced to become city builders for the Egyptian pharaohs. Against this background, they are eventually rescued and invited to enter into a unique relationship with God, with the potential to become a "kingdom of priests and a holy nation" (Exod. 19:6). At the heart of this is the idea that Israel will experience the unique presence of God as he takes up residence among them.

The Pentateuch anticipates in part a return to the kind of divine-human relationship enjoyed in Eden, with the Israelites living in harmony with the LORD on land blessed by him. Yet, although God comes to dwell in the midst

116

of Israel, the people still do not experience the same intimate communion with him that Adam and Eve originally enjoyed. While the making of the Sinai covenant and the building of the tabernacle bring about an important advance in God's relationship with one section of humanity, this does not give the Israelites immediate and unhindered access to the divine presence. Barriers still exist between God and the people. Only Moses enjoys what might be described as intimate contact with God, but even this is limited. God's relationship with Israel as a people merely anticipates what is yet to come in conjunction with the blessing of the nations of the earth.

Another aspect of Israel's role as a holy nation is that it should exemplify the kind of righteousness required by God. To this end Israel is to be governed by God's decrees and laws. The importance of this is highlighted in the covenant obligations given first at Sinai and repeated later on the plains of Moab. Israel as a nation is expected to reflect God's holy and perfect nature to the other nations of the earth.

Although the Pentateuch emphasizes that the Israelites are especially privileged by the fact that the Lord has revealed himself to them through signs and wonders in Egypt and then later through verbal communication at Sinai, it also highlights their waywardness in failing to trust and obey God completely. In spite of all that he does for them, their shortcomings are a recurring feature of the narrative in Exodus to Numbers. Moreover, even as they stand poised to possess the promised land, the Lord reminds them that, although they will initially enjoy his blessing, they will eventually be unfaithful and, as a result, be exiled from the land. No longer will they know God's presence in their midst.

This latter observation highlights another important idea within the Pentateuch. The enjoyment of the benefits of the divine promises is linked to a trust in God's ability to fulfill them. Faith in God, marked by obedience, is highlighted in a variety of ways, both positively and negatively. The absence of faith was responsible for the disobedience of Adam and Eve in the Garden of Eden. Faith was central to the life of Abraham, who is presented as a model for others to follow. Similarly, it was important in the experience of the Israelites in the wilderness. Here, however, it is their frequent lack of faith that is highlighted. Later, Deuteronomy shows how Moses encourages the people to trust and obey the Lord in order that they may take possession of the promised land. While the benefits of the divine promises may be forfeited temporarily due to human failure, the promises will ultimately be realized because they originate with God.

Although the Pentateuch gives a very distinctive history of the world from its creation to the arrival of the Israelites on the borders of Canaan, it is much more than a history of what has taken place. The divine promises of blessing and nationhood, which are so important to the development of the plot, remain unfulfilled by the end of Deuteronomy. As a result, the Pentateuch is oriented toward the future. What will become of these promises? To answer this we must look beyond the concluding chapters of Deuteronomy.[3] As it stands, the Pentateuch is an unfinished story.

3. In the light of this observation, it is important to note that the books of Joshua to 2 Kings provide a vital sequel to the Pentateuch. See T. D. Alexander, "Genesis to Kings," in *NDBT*, 115–20.

8

God's Temple-City

Interpreted against their ancient Near Eastern background, the opening chapters of Genesis anticipate that God's plans for the earth center on the creation of an extraordinary temple-city where God will dwell in harmony with humanity. To this end, humans are given a royal and a priestly status, with the expectation that they will be God's vice-regents on the earth. However, tempted by the serpent, Adam and Eve betray their Creator, resulting in their expulsion from Eden and the loss of their special status. The following narrative comes to a significant climax with an account of humanity's attempt to construct an alternative city to the holy temple-city planned by God. These initial events set the scene for the call of Abraham and all that develops thereafter.

Introduction

The opening chapters of Genesis are exceptionally important for understanding the rest of the Pentateuch. Apart from setting the initial scene, Genesis 1–3 determines the trajectory for all that follows. For this reason, it is vitally important to clearly comprehend the essence of these chapters within their present literary context. Unfortunately, discussions of Genesis 1–3 are too often hijacked by those who are almost exclusively preoccupied by the modern debate on the relationship between the biblical view of creation and that of contemporary science. Though this issue needs to be addressed, we should constantly remember that the author of these chapters penned them as an introduction to the narrative that unfolds in the books of Genesis to Kings. As we shall presently see, this narrative begins with the expectation that humans were created to build for God a temple-city on the earth. Unfortunately, God's plans are almost immediately thrown into chaos as Adam and Eve betray their Creator and subsequently their descendants pursue their own agenda by constructing God-less cities.

To understand how the opening chapters of Genesis introduce the larger narrative that extends to the end of the book of Kings, we must begin by observing that Genesis 1–3 provides two complementary descriptions of creation, a panoramic overview (1:1–2:3) followed by a zoomed-in close-up (2:4–3:24). The shift from the initial overview to the close-up is achieved by the special heading that comes in 2:4: "These are the generations of the heavens and the earth when they were created . . ." (NRSV). Similar headings recur throughout Genesis, often functioning like the zoom lens on a camera, enabling the narrator to focus in on a smaller part of a larger scene.[1] While Genesis 1:1–2:3 provides a panoramic description of creation, Genesis 2:4–3:24 concentrates on the creation of the first human couple, Adam and Eve, and their activity within the Garden of Eden.

This zooming-in effect explains why the literary style of Genesis changes significantly between 1:1–2:3 and 2:4–3:24. Certain differences are very obvious. Genesis 1 is "repetitious, tabular, and formal."[2] By producing a highly structured account, the author reflects the order underlying the whole creation event. As M. A. Fishbane remarks:

> The text thus provides a reflection of an orderly, harmonious creation. The alternation of the narrator's voice with divine speech, of description with prescription, serves to present "the creation" as a dispassionate recitation recurrently punctuated with vital divine energy. The text shifts rhythmically between actions and results which utilize the same words ("separate" . . . "call" . . . "see" . . . "make") and sequences. Its economy of vocabulary and technique produces a dictum of controlled energy and force.[3]

In marked contrast, 2:4–3:24 has a quite different narrative style. No longer is the narrative shaped by a formal structure based on a seven-day scheme; gone is the repetition of chapter 1. "Here . . . we meet concise and vivid stories told in a masterful fashion."[4]

This change in literary style is also accompanied by differences in vocabulary, the most noteworthy of these being the names used for God.

---

1. These headings—in Gen. 2:4; 5:1; 6:9; 10:1; 11:10, 27; 25:12, 19; 36:1, 9; 37:2—all contain the Hebrew word *tôlēdōt*, often translated "generations." The word itself is associated with "giving birth" and, when linked to a person or object, refers to what that person or object produces.
2. N. C. Habel, *Literary Criticism of the Old Testament* (Philadelphia: Fortress, 1971), 19.
3. M. A. Fishbane, *Text and Texture: Close Readings of Selected Biblical Texts* (New York: Schocken Books, 1979), 8.
4. Habel, *Literary Criticism of the Old Testament*, 21.

Throughout 1:1–2:3 the Creator is always referred to by using the Hebrew term Elohim, which means "God." From 2:4 through to 3:24, the divine designation is Yahweh Elohim (usually translated "LORD God"), although there is a noteworthy departure from this pattern in 3:1b–5, where Elohim (God) alone occurs.

The variation in divine names also coincides with another interesting feature of the text. When we analyze how God is described in Genesis 1–3, we discover that he is portrayed in two distinct ways.

> In Genesis 1 the majestic transcendence of a powerful cosmic organizer is primary. In line with this basic viewpoint Elohim creates and orders the universe by a series of decrees. He issues his command and the results are automatic. God appears as a being who stands outside of his cosmos and controls it with his mighty word. Hence the possible "anthropomorphic" expressions of Genesis 1 ("God said," "God saw," and "God rested") are reserved in character and tend to preserve the transcendence of God. They do not suggest the close proximity of a God who acts and looks like men.[5]

By way of contrast, the description of God in Genesis 2–4 is quite different.

> Here his immanence, personal nearness, and local involvement on the human scene are basic features. Yahweh is not a detached sovereign overlord but a God at hand as an intimate master. He is a God with whom man has ready contact and immediate responsibility. Accordingly the anthropomorphisms of Genesis 2–4 are so bold that they almost seem to depict Yahweh in terms of human limitations. He moulds with his hands as a potter, he breathes into the mouth of a clay model, he plants a garden, he searches for a man, he has private conversations with man, woman, and beast, and he places a mark on yet another man.[6]

Given these differences between 1:1–2:3 and 2:4–3:24, it is hardly surprising that many scholars conclude that two different writers must have been responsible for producing such contrasting accounts.[7]

Undoubtedly, there is a clear difference between the style and theological outlook of 1:1–2:3 and 2:4–3:24. With this there can be no disagreement. But, we must ask, why is this so? Why are two distinctive accounts of creation found at the beginning of the book of Genesis?

By way of addressing this question, we need to recognize that the two descriptions of creation complement each other in a most remarkable way. This is

5. Ibid., 24; cf. Fishbane, *Text and Texture*, 8.
6. Habel, *Literary Criticism of the Old Testament*, 25.
7. It is usually maintained that 1:1–2:4 comes from the Priestly Writer (P) because of its interest in the Sabbath (2:1–3), and 2:5–3:24 is assigned to the Yahwist (J) because it uses the divine name Yahweh.

121

especially so regarding their characterization of the Creator. In 1:1–2:3 God is revealed as separate and distant from his creation. In theological terms, he is transcendent. However, 2:4–3:24 pictures God as very close to humanity, walking and talking with Adam and Eve in the garden. In theological terms, God is immanent. By placing these accounts side by side, the opening sections of Genesis present a two-sided but complementary view of God. He is both transcendent and immanent.

This carefully balanced, two-sided picture of God is also brought out by the narrator's choice of divine names. In 1:1–2:3 we find repeatedly the designation Elohim (God). However, in 2:4–3:24 the name Yahweh is introduced. Whereas Elohim is the general designation for a deity, Yahweh is a personal name. The use of Yahweh after 2:4 emphasizes the personal nature of God's relationship with humanity, something reflected in the contents of the narrative itself. For this same reason, in 3:1–5 the serpent always refers to God as Elohim and never as Yahweh; as his archenemy the serpent refuses to use God's personal name in the presence of Adam and Eve.

Although the two descriptions of creation in 1:1–2:3 and 2:4–3:24 are quite dissimilar, they should be viewed as complementary rather than contradictory. By having two accounts, Genesis enables us to see creation from two perspectives, enriching our understanding of what is going on. Remarkably, in spite of differing in content and literary style, the two accounts are united by the idea that the earth has been created to become God's dwelling place (see below).

The Earth as God's Temple-City

Most readers of Genesis 1 concentrate on the six days of creation. However, the opening section of Genesis comes to a climax with the seventh day. Unfortunately, this tends to be largely ignored due to the chapter division that separates day seven from days one to six. The present chapter divisions, however, were not there in the earliest form of Genesis.

The dominant motif in day seven involves God's resting (2:1–3). This could imply that the Creator was tired from so much creating. But such an interpretation seems somewhat banal, especially when in Genesis 1 God merely speaks and things are brought into being. Why the emphasis on rest?

The most plausible explanation for this unusual interest in rest comes from J. H. Walton:

> On the seventh day we finally discover that God has been working to achieve a rest. This seventh day is not a theological appendix to the creation account, just to bring closure now that the main event of creating people has been reported. Rather, it intimates the purpose of creation and of the cosmos. God does not set up the cosmos so that only people will have a place. He also sets up the cosmos

to serve as his temple in which he will find rest in the order and equilibrium that he has established.[8]

Walton arrives at this conclusion by reading Genesis in its ancient Near Eastern context. He observes that in extrabiblical accounts when gods become involved in creative activity, they do so in order to make for themselves a resting place. Normally this involves the creation of a temple that stands at the heart of a city. Divine rest is associated with temple building.[9]

Approaching the text of Genesis 1 independently of Walton, J. R. Middleton concludes that in this chapter God is portrayed as a cosmic builder:

> Suppose we press the question, *what sort of building* is God making in Genesis 1? Although not immediately obvious, the unequivocal answer given from the perspective of the rest of the Old Testament is this: God is building a *temple*. The notion of the cosmos as temple has its roots in the ancient Near Eastern worldview, in which temples were commonly understood as the royal palaces of the gods, in which they dwelled and from which they reigned. Furthermore, creation, followed by temple building and then divine rest, is a central theme in Mesopotamian, and perhaps Ugaritic, mythology (both Marduk and Baal have temples built for them after their conquest of the chaos monster).[10]

For both Walton and Middleton, the opening creation account in Genesis contains subtle allusions to temple-building. As we shall see, the narrative in 2:4–3:24 reinforces this idea.

The Garden of Eden as Sanctuary

While 1:1–2:3 alludes to the creation of a temple, in 2:4–3:24 the Garden of Eden has every appearance of being a garden attached to a temple. Thus G. J. Wenham comments:

> The garden of Eden is not viewed by the author of Genesis simply as a piece of Mesopotamian farmland, but as an archetypal sanctuary, that is[,] a place where God dwells and where man should worship him. Many of the features of

8. J. H. Walton, "Creation," in *Dictionary of the Old Testament: Pentateuch*, ed. T. D. Alexander and D. W. Baker (Downers Grove, IL: InterVarsity; Leicester: Inter-Varsity, 2003), 161. Cf. J. H. Walton, *The Lost World of Genesis One: Ancient Cosmology and the Origins Debate* (Downers Grove, IL: IVP Academic, 2009), 72–86.

9. The Hebrew term for temple, *hêkāl*, may also be translated as "palace." A temple was a divine palace. Consequently, temple and kingdom are intimately connected concepts.

10. J. R. Middleton, *The Liberating Image: The Imago Dei in Genesis 1* (Grand Rapids: Brazos, 2005), 81; cf. R. P. Gordon, "The Week That Made the World: Reflections on the First Pages of the Bible," in *Reading the Law: Studies in Honour of Gordon J. Wenham*, ed. J. G. McConville and Karl Möller, LHB/OTS 461 (Edinburgh: T&T Clark, 2007), 234–37.

the garden may also be found in later sanctuaries, particularly the tabernacle or Jerusalem temple. These parallels suggest that the garden itself is understood as a sort of sanctuary.[11]

Interesting parallels exist between Eden and the later Israelite sanctuaries, in particular the tabernacle and Jerusalem temple.[12]

1. The LORD God walks in Eden as he later does in the tabernacle (Gen. 3:8; cf. Lev. 26:12; Deut. 23:15; 2 Sam. 7:6–7).
2. Eden and the later sanctuaries are entered from the east and guarded by cherubim (Gen. 3:24; Exod. 25:18–22; 26:31; 1 Kings 6:23–29).
3. The tabernacle menorah (or lampstand) possibly symbolizes the tree of life (Gen. 2:9; 3:22; cf. Exod. 25:31–35).
4. The river flowing from Eden (Gen. 2:10) resembles Ezekiel 47:1–12, which envisages a river flowing from a future Jerusalem temple and bringing life to the Dead Sea.
5. Gold and onyx, mentioned in Genesis 2:11–12, are used extensively to decorate the later sanctuaries and priestly garments (e.g., Exod. 25:7, 11, 17, 31).[13] Gold in particular is associated with the divine presence.

Another fascinating pointer to the Garden of Eden as being part of a divine sanctuary may be seen in the duties that God gives the man in Genesis 2:15. The man's responsibilities in the garden are encapsulated by using two verbs: ʿābad (ʿāvad), "to serve," "to work," "to till"; šāmar (shāmar), "to keep," "to observe," "to guard."[14] When used independently of one another, these verbs can refer to a wide range of activities. However, when used together they tend to be linked to activities associated with the tabernacle or temple. The book of Numbers uses them in tandem to describe the duties of the Levites in the sanctuary (cf. Num. 3:7–8; 8:26; 18:5–6). This strongly suggests that the man's work is priestly in nature rather than agricultural. The man is appointed first and foremost as a guardian of sacred space; he was not created simply to be a gardener.

The overall picture in Genesis 1–2 suggests that the creation of the earth is closely associated with the construction of God's temple, although this is merely the start of the process, not its completion. In this context humans are

11. G. J. Wenham, "Sanctuary Symbolism in the Garden of Eden Story," *PWCJS* 9 (1986): 19.
12. These parallels are set out by Wenham in ibid., 19–25.
13. About one hundred references to gold and seven to onyx appear in the Exodus account of building the tabernacle.
14. The Hebrew verb *šāmar* is used in Deut. 5:12 concerning the Sabbath. The Israelites are to "observe, guard, keep" the Sabbath by preserving its sanctity. In all likelihood, Adam was commissioned to keep or guard the garden in order that it should remain holy as part of God's temple on earth.

created not only to serve within this temple, but also to extend its boundaries outward so that it fills the whole earth. To enable them to do this, they are given royal authority alongside their priestly status.

Humanity's Royal Status

Genesis 1 stands in marked contrast to other ancient Near Eastern accounts when it describes the status of human beings. Whereas the main Babylonian story of creation, *Enuma Elish,* presents the destiny of humans in terms of providing food for the gods, Genesis ascribes to people a divinely given royal authority to rule over the earth. This is highlighted in two ways. First, they are directly instructed by God to exercise dominion over all other creatures.

> Then God said, "Let us make mankind in our image, in our likeness, so that they may rule over the fish in the sea and the birds in the sky, over the livestock and all the wild animals, and over all the creatures that move along the ground."
>
> So God created mankind in his own image,
>   in the image of God he created him;
>   male and female he created them.
>
> God blessed them and said to them, "Be fruitful and increase in number; fill the earth and subdue it. Rule over the fish of the sea and the birds in the sky and over every living creature that moves on the ground." (Gen. 1:26–28)

These verses emphasize that people are to govern all land animals, birds, and fish; the point is repeated twice within three verses. At the heart of the divine plan for humanity is the idea that they should rule over the earth as God's vice-regents.

Second, the concept of royalty is associated with the expression "image of God." In ancient Egypt and Mesopotamia, the phrase "image of God" is frequently linked to kings. The king was the living "image of a god." The Egyptian king Ramses II (1290–1224 BC) describes his divine image status in this way:

> Utterance of the divine king, Lord of the Two Lands, lord of the form of Khepri, in whose limbs is Re, who came forth from Re, whom Ptah-Tatenen begat, King Ramses II, given life; to his father, from whom he came forth, Tatenen, father of the gods: "I am thy son whom thou hast placed upon thy throne. Thou hast assigned to me thy kingdom, thou hast fashioned me in thy likeness and thy form, which thou hast assigned to me and hast created."[15]

15. J. H. Breasted, *Ancient Records of Egypt: The Nineteenth Dynasty*, vol. 3 (Chicago: University of Chicago Press, 1906), 181.

To be made in the "image of God" is to be given regal status. As Middleton remarks,

> The writer of Genesis 1 portrays God as king presiding over "heaven and earth," an ordered and harmonious realm in which each creature manifests the will of the creator and is thus declared "good." Humanity is created *like* this God, with the special role of representing or imaging God's rule in the world.[16]

Although the expression "image of God" has been the subject of much debate, it makes good sense to see it as denoting humanity's regal status.

Underlying the creation of the earth is God's desire to make a dwelling place for himself. In the light of this aspiration, the opening two chapters of Genesis reveal that humans are created with the intention that they should participate in transforming the earth into a divine dwelling. To this end, they are given a holy or priestly status that enables them to be in God's presence and serve in his sanctuary. God also delegates to people authority to rule on the earth as his vice-regents. In line with this, they are instructed to be fruitful and multiply and fill the earth (1:28). Behind these commands lies the expectation that an ever-growing human population of royal priests will create a magnificent temple-city, which will eventually fill the earth.[17]

Such an expectation should not surprise us, especially when we view the book of Genesis in its original cultural context. In the ancient Near East, individual gods were often associated with particular cities. The inhabitants of the city worshiped the god whose temple stood at the heart of their community. The earliest readers or listeners to Genesis would have automatically associated the creation of God's sanctuary on the earth with a city. They would have quickly realized that Eden was the greenfield site designated by God to be the location for his temple-city.[18]

The Great Betrayal

In the light of the divine plan for the earth, Genesis 3 recounts how the human couple tragically abandon the special responsibility entrusted to them by God. The significance of Genesis 3 cannot be overestimated, though as a selective account of what took place it leaves many questions unanswered. In reading

16. Middleton, *Liberating Image*, 26.

17. W. J. Dumbrell, "Genesis 2:1–17: A Foreshadowing of the New Creation," in *Biblical Theology: Retrospect and Prospect*, ed. S. J. Hafemann (Downers Grove, IL: InterVarsity; Leicester: Apollos, 2002), 53–65, develops the idea that Adam is a king-priest with the role of expanding Eden into a worldwide sanctuary.

18. This comparison does not necessarily mean that the Israelites derived the concept of the temple-city from other nations. It is equally possible that polytheistic ideas about temple-cities have their origin in and are perversions of beliefs concerning the one and only true God.

this chapter, we need to restrain our curiosity in order to hear clearly what the writer wishes to communicate.

Without unpacking the intriguing dialogue that takes place between the serpent[19] and the woman, let us observe how the human couple willfully abandon their principal duties as priestly vice-regents. First, Genesis 3 reveals that by letting in the serpent, they neglect to guard the sanctity of the garden. As G. K. Beale remarks, "When Adam failed to guard the temple by sinning and letting in a foul serpent to defile the sanctuary, he lost his priestly role, and the cherubim took over the responsibility of 'guarding' the Garden temple: God 'stationed the cherubim . . . *to guard* the way to the tree of life' (so Gen. 3:24; see also Ezek. 28:14, 16)."[20] As priests the human couple should have expelled the serpent from the garden.

Second, although God intended the human couple to rule over all the other creatures, on this occasion they obey one of the animals. By following the serpent's promptings, they fail to exercise authority over it. Their failure not only overturns the divinely instituted order of creation, but also significantly is a blatant betrayal of God. By siding with the serpent, they reject God and his ordering of the world. Ironically, their treachery occurs in the context of the serpent's saying to them that they shall become "like God, knowing good and evil" (3:5). Unlike the serpent, the human couple have been made in the "image of God." However, by obeying the serpent instead of God, they forfeit their position as God's vice-regents. If they image anyone now, it is the serpent. Tragically, the authority delegated to them by God now passes to the serpent.

By siding with the serpent, the human couple lose their royal and priestly status. This has major consequences. For now we shall mention only two of these. Almost immediately Adam and Eve are expelled from the garden and no longer enjoy an intimate relationship with God. As J. H. Walton observes, "In the aftermath of the fall, the greatest loss was not paradise; it was God's presence."[21] Responsibility for keeping the garden is given to cherubim who are stationed to guard the way to the tree of life (3:24).

Excluded from having access to the "tree of life," Adam and Eve come under the power of death. Although they have been told by God that the punishment for eating from the "tree of the knowledge of good and evil" is death (2:17), they have ignored this warning. Some scholars argue that this punishment was

---

19. The serpent is clearly no ordinary animal. Apart from being described as being "more crafty than any of the wild animals the LORD God had made" (3:1), it is portrayed by its actions as opposing God's sovereign rule over the earth. While later biblical texts identify the "ancient serpent" as "the devil and Satan" (cf. Rev. 20:2), Gen. 3 does not explicitly say this.

20. G. K. Beale, *The Temple and the Church's Mission: A Biblical Theology of the Dwelling Place of God*, NSBT 17 (Leicester: Apollos, 2004), 70; cf. Middleton, *Liberating Image*, 59.

21. J. H. Walton, "Eden, Garden of," in Alexander and Baker, *Dictionary of the Old Testament: Pentateuch*, 205.

not enforced by God because the human couple did not die immediately after eating from the tree of the knowledge of good and evil. However, "death" in this context need not necessarily imply the end of life; rather it indicates spiritual separation from the one who is the source of all life.[22]

Since the opening chapters of Genesis anticipate the construction of a city that will be inhabited by both God and people, the disobedience of Adam and Eve throws God's creation project into chaos. In spite of being authorized and instructed to rule over all other creatures, they fail to exercise dominion over this cunning wild animal (3:1). By succumbing to the serpent's temptations, the human couple betray their Creator. Consequently, their authority to rule over the earth is transferred to the serpent, and they themselves become subject to it. Of necessity God expels them from Eden and strips them of their royal and priestly status.

The tragic outcome of Adam and Eve's rebellion against God is reported in Genesis 4–11 through a series of specially chosen episodes. The last of these quite significantly involves the construction of a city.

The Tower of Babel

Against the background of God's plan to construct a temple-city on the earth, the account of the building of the city of Babel-Babylon[23] takes on special significance. In spite of its brevity, it brings the opening chapters of Genesis to a notable climax. Having turned away from God, people intuitively set about building a city exclusively for themselves.[24] The Babel-Babylon episode highlights two contrasting aspects of human existence: the capacity of people to achieve great things and the hubris of humans who have rejected God's sovereignty over them.

> What a wealth of human meanings converge in the single image of Babel! It is an ambivalent image, evoking powerful feelings of a wide range. On one side we can see the human longings for community, achievement, civilization, culture, technology, safety, security, permanence and fame. But countering these

22. Cf. R. P. Gordon, "The Ethics of Eden: Truth-Telling in Genesis 2–3," in *Ethical and Unethical in the Old Testament: God and Humans in Dialogue*, ed. K. J. Dell, LHB/OTS 528 (London and New York: T&T Clark, 2010), 11–33.

23. In most English versions of the Bible, the city in Gen. 11:1–9 is called Babel. This name is derived from its Hebrew name, *babel* (11:9). However, *babel* is also the Hebrew designation for Babylon. In English translations of the OT, the Hebrew word *babel*, which occurs over two hundred times, is almost always consistently translated by the name "Babylon." In the whole OT, there are generally only two exceptions to this rule, Gen. 10:10 and 11:9, and even here a few English translations replace Babel in Gen. 10:10 with Babylon (e.g., NIV, NJPS). The use of the name Babel in Gen. 11:9 is really an anomaly and should be replaced by Babylon, as done in HCSB.

24. In line with this, it is worth observing that the first city builder is Cain (Gen. 4:17).

aspirations we sense the moral judgment against idolatry, pride, self-reliance, the urge of material power and the human illusion of infinite achievement.[25]

While in one sense the construction of Babel-Babylon is a natural consequence of people using divinely given abilities, they do so without regard for the one who gifted them. Their aspirations are to dethrone God, not only on earth, but in heaven as well. Constructed by people for people alone, Babel-Babylon is a mockery of what God intended when he created humans and commissioned them to be his temple-city builders. Babel-Babylon typifies every human enterprise that seeks to exalt the creature over the Creator.

Although the Genesis report of the building of Babel-Babylon is exceptionally brief, nine verses in all, this city casts a long shadow over the whole of the Bible. It does so for a number of reasons. Babel-Babylon is the archetypal God-less city. In Babel-Babylon we see people uniting as one to make a name for themselves by building a tower that reaches up to heaven itself (11:4). While Adam and Eve aspired to become like God in Genesis 3:4–5, the inhabitants of Babel-Babylon seek to establish themselves as supreme not only on earth but in heaven as well. With incredible arrogance they try to build a tower that will enable them to access heaven and take control of it.

The antagonism of the human city builders toward God takes on added significance when we observe that Babel-Babylon is also associated with aggressive human leadership or kingship. This link may not appear immediately obvious, for Genesis 11:1–9 contains no reference to any king. However, Babel-Babylon is first mentioned in Genesis 10 in association with the powerful hunter Nimrod.

> Cush was the father of Nimrod, who grew to be a mighty warrior on the earth. He was a mighty hunter before the LORD; that is why it is said, "Like Nimrod, a mighty hunter before the LORD." The first centers of his kingdom were Babylon, Erech, Akkad and Calneh, in Shinar. From that land he went to Assyria, where he built Nineveh, Rehoboth Ir, Calah and Resen, which is between Nineveh and Calah—which is the great city. (Gen. 10:8–12)

Within Genesis 10, this passage stands apart. It focuses on one person, about whom a few selected details are recorded. In the light of what is said concerning Nimrod, two aspects are especially noteworthy. First, Nimrod is linked to Babel-Babylon; this is where his kingdom begins. However, from there it extends to include cities located in Assyria. In this short summary Nimrod is credited with building the "great city"—a title that appears to cover a number of locations, including Nineveh, Resen, and Calah. Nimrod is a city builder of renown.

25. Anon., "Babel, Tower of," in *Dictionary of Biblical Imagery*, ed. L. Ryken, J. C. Wilhoit, and T. Longman (Downers Grove, IL: InterVarsity; Leicester: Inter-Varsity, 1998), 67.

Second, apart from his link with cities, Nimrod is also designated a powerful or mighty man, a hunter in the sight of "the LORD." This description ought to be viewed negatively. While the Hebrew text in 10:9 may legitimately be translated "in the sight of the LORD," it could also mean "opposite the LORD," "facing the LORD," or "facing up to the LORD." This latter sense seems more appropriate in the context of all that is said in Genesis 1–11. Nimrod's aggression as a person runs counter to what God intended when at creation he commissioned people to rule the earth on his behalf. The early chapters of Genesis underline God's abhorrence of the prevalent human violence (cf. 6:11–13).

Although God originally intended humanity to rule over the earth in peace, Nimrod uses power to establish a kingdom that is a distortion of the one that God wished to have on the earth. Through force, Nimrod founds an extensive kingdom that includes both Babylon and Nineveh. Undoubtedly the tradition of kingdom building through aggression, initiated by Nimrod, lived on in these cities. Later in history the inhabitants of Nineveh and Babylon descended in destructive power on the kingdoms of Israel and Judah. Late in the eighth century BC the Assyrians destroyed the northern kingdom, Israel; early in the sixth century BC the Babylonians decimated the southern kingdom, Judah.

By linking Nimrod to Babel-Babylon, the author of Genesis introduces the idea of two contrasting cities and kingdoms. Due to the rebellion of Adam and Eve, God's desire to establish his kingdom on the earth through the construction of a holy temple-city is thwarted. Instead of ruling as his vice-regents, humans oppose God and establish an alternative kingdom and city. Within Genesis 10 and 11, Nimrod and Babel-Babylon function as negative archetypes of what God intends people to be and do respectively.

Old Testament Summary

The opening chapters of Genesis introduce themes that will be central in the subsequent narrative. Principal among these is the expectation that the earth is to become God's dwelling place through the construction of a holy temple-city. As God's vice-regents, humans are to extend his authority over the earth, at the same time ensuring its sanctity as sacred space. Tragically, tempted by the serpent, Adam and Eve betray their Creator and thereby lose their royal and priestly status. Expelled from Eden and alienated from God, human beings try to establish a name for themselves by using their God-given ability to build an alternative city. Though their initial attempt is thwarted by God, the aspirations of those who built Babel-Babylon live on. Against this background, the book of Genesis records the call of Abraham, with whom God will begin the long process of reversing the consequences of humanity's rebellion against its Creator.

Special consideration needs to be given to how the short description of the building of Babel-Babylon precedes the much longer account of Abraham's life. God's promise to make Abraham's name great (12:2) obviously mirrors the aspiration of the people of Babel-Babylon, who wished to make a name for themselves (11:4). Moreover, God's provision of a particular land for Abraham and his descendants has the appearance of being a deliberate response to the scattering of the city builders over the whole earth. More important, Abraham is set apart to be the one through whom God will advance the process of establishing his kingdom and temple-city. To this end, Abraham's descendants will become a great nation and will include a royal line.

Beyond Genesis, the book of Exodus describes how God rescues the Israelites from building cities for a despotic Egyptian king in order that they may begin the process of constructing God's dwelling place on the earth (1:11; 25:8). Rescued from death and given both royal and priestly status, the Israelites have the opportunity to live as God's holy nation (19:6). Although serious shortcomings still remain, with the making of the tabernacle an important step is taken toward the fulfillment of God's creation project. This is, however, merely part of a long process that will later include, among other things, the establishment of Jerusalem/Zion as God's temple-city and its destruction by the Babylonians. In the light of these events, which are deeply imbedded in much of the Old Testament writings, the opening chapters of Genesis take on a deeper significance when we observe their particular interest in the relationship between the anticipated temple-city of God and its human antithesis, Babel-Babylon.[26]

New Testament Connections

In tune with the overall movement in the book of Genesis, the author of Hebrews links the patriarchs—Abraham, Isaac, and Jacob—with the divine construction of a unique city. Accordingly, in Hebrews 11 Abraham's faith is reflected in the fact that he looked forward to "a better land," a "heavenly one," a city with foundations, designed and built by God.

> By faith Abraham, when called to go to a place he would later receive as his inheritance, obeyed and went, even though he did not know where he was going. By faith he made his home in the promised land like a stranger in a foreign country; he lived in tents, as did Isaac and Jacob, who were heirs with him of the same promise. For he was looking forward to the city with foundations, whose architect and builder is God. . . . All these people were still living by

26. From Genesis to Revelation, Babel-Babylon features prominently as the symbol of humanity's attempt to construct a universal city without reference to God. Babel-Babylon is the archetypal God-less city, which stands in opposition to the creation of God's city on the earth.

faith when they died. They did not receive the things promised; they only saw them and welcomed them from a distance, admitting that they were foreigners and strangers on earth. People who say such things show that they are looking for a country of their own. If they had been thinking of the country they had left, they would have had opportunity to return. Instead, they were longing for a better country—a heavenly one. Therefore God is not ashamed to be called their God, for he has prepared a city for them. (Heb. 11:8–10, 13–16)

Particularly striking is the emphasis given here to Abraham's anticipation of a city. The author of Hebrews stresses that Abraham's journey to a foreign land was motivated by his "looking forward" to this city. Although some scholars find little evidence for this in Genesis, when the call of Abraham in Genesis 12:1–3 is read against the background of Genesis 1–11, and especially the building of Babel-Babylon, the interpretation adopted in Hebrews 11 makes good sense.

The author of Hebrews is convinced that the future experience of all believers involves a city. In 12:22 he refers once more to this city, describing it as "the city of the living God, the heavenly Jerusalem," and later he states, "For here we do not have an enduring city, but we are looking for the city that is to come" (Heb. 13:14).

When we consider this "city that is to come," it is difficult not to think about the vision the apostle John describes in Revelation 21–22. At the start of Revelation 21, John speaks of seeing "the Holy City, new Jerusalem, coming down out of heaven from God, prepared as a bride beautifully dressed for her husband" (Rev. 21:1–2). He then describes the city in some detail, with its enormous size and splendor. This is no ordinary city. Remarkably, not only does it fill the entire earth, but it also is constructed largely of gold. For John, this exceptional city is the goal toward which everything in creation is moving. It is the fulfillment of what God initiated in Genesis 1.

Apart from the grandeur and splendor of the architecture, John's vision of the city highlights other things of significance. The city is inhabited by people drawn from many nations, who are able to experience the intimate presence of God in such a way that they see his face. Nothing stands between God and those who dwell with him in the city. There is an intimacy here that is almost unique in the whole of the Bible. Since the whole city is a holy temple, each inhabitant is a priest. There is no one in the city who is not holy. Every citizen without exception serves and worships God.

John's vision of the new Jerusalem also emphasizes that God rules over the temple-city as its king. His throne is at the heart of the metropolis. As its sole divine sovereign, he reigns unchallenged, and everyone and everything is subject to him. Yet right at the end of his vision, John comments that those who serve God will also reign forever and ever (Rev. 22:5). Everyone within the city enjoys a royal status.

With good reason, the Holy City is portrayed as a utopia, a paradise. Not only does John observe that all evil and suffering are banished from the metropolis, but in the city stands the "tree of life" "for the healing of the nations" (Rev. 22:2; cf. Gen. 2:9). As a holy city under the absolute control of a perfect deity, the new Jerusalem provides a perfect environment for its inhabitants.

Although John's vision gives a remarkable insight into a unique holy city, it is noteworthy that this future new Jerusalem is contrasted in the book of Revelation with another city that already exists on the earth. Not surprisingly, perhaps, it is called Babylon. In Revelation 14–18, Babylon is portrayed as both the alternative God-less city and the great enemy of those who belong to the kingdom of God.

While the initial chapters of Genesis give us an insight into God's purposes in creating the world, the concluding chapters of Revelation enable us to envisage the outcome of all that God has planned. Tragically, those who stand in opposition to God continue to create their own cities and kingdoms, often through violence and the exploitation of others. As the archetypal God-less city, the existence of Babel-Babylon reveals that many people aspire for total security and lasting fame apart from God. However, ultimate reward will come only to those who in faith seek the city that has God as its architect and builder.[27]

27. For a fuller discussion of the relationship between Gen. 1–11 and the book of Revelation, see T. D. Alexander, *From Eden to the New Jerusalem: An Introduction to Biblical Theology* (Grand Rapids: Kregel, 2009).

9

The Royal Lineage in Genesis

T he book of Genesis has been carefully composed to focus on a unique family line, starting with Adam and continuing down to the twelve sons of Jacob. This line of "seed" includes various individuals who all enjoyed a special relationship with God: Noah, Abraham, Isaac, Jacob, and Joseph. With great import, Genesis anticipates that a royal dynasty will arise from the descendants of Abraham. Although this future dynasty is initially associated with Joseph and his son Ephraim, it is also linked in a subtle way to Judah and his son Perez.

Introduction

For many readers Genesis is a collection of unconnected stories, interrupted here and there by apparently irrelevant genealogies. Yet the present text has been carefully shaped to highlight the importance of a family lineage that begins with Adam and is traced through to the sons of Jacob. To appreciate this we shall consider first the overall structure of the book and the function of the various genealogies found within it. Next, we shall briefly examine the concept of "seed" and observe how Genesis deliberately focuses on a single line of descendants. Finally, we shall draw some conclusions about the nature and significance of this special lineage.

The Structure of Genesis

A quick survey reveals that Genesis consists of narrative sections that are linked by genealogies. Many of these narrative sections and genealogies are

FIGURE 9.1.
A Linear Genealogy

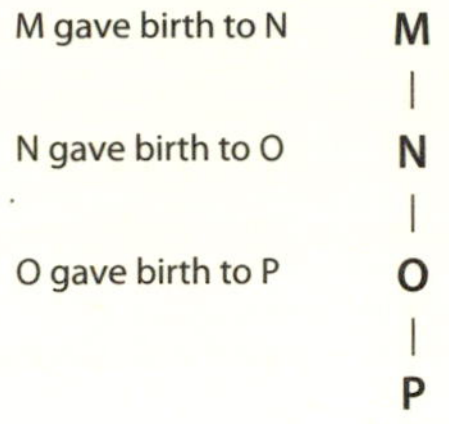

M gave birth to N	**M**
N gave birth to O	**N**
O gave birth to P	**O**
	P

introduced by similar headings; these occur in 2:4; 5:1; 6:9; 10:1; 11:10, 27; 25:12, 19; 36:1, 9; 37:2. The common element in all these headings is the Hebrew word *tôlĕdōt*, translated in the NIV as "account."[1] The word itself is associated with "giving birth"; when linked to a person or object, it refers to what that person or object produces. For example, the initial words of 11:27 could be translated, "And these were born of Terah"; the NIV has "This is the account of Terah's family line."

The *tôlĕdōt* headings serve two functions. First, they are like chapter or section headings in modern books. Some of them introduce major narrative sections, indicating a new stage in the development of the plot. These major sections deal mainly with the lives of Adam, Noah, Abraham, Jacob, and Joseph, and they are introduced by the headings in 2:4; 6:9; 11:27; 25:19; and 37:2 respectively. The other *tôlĕdōt* headings introduce either linear genealogies (see figure 9.1) listing descendants who belong to the central family line (5:1; 11:10), or segmented genealogies (see figure 9.2) providing details about family members of some of the minor participants in Genesis (10:1; 25:12; 36:1, 9). To ensure that the main line of descent is clearly established, segmented genealogies are never used; only linear genealogies are employed (5:1–32; 11:10–26).

FIGURE 9.2.
A Segmented Genealogy

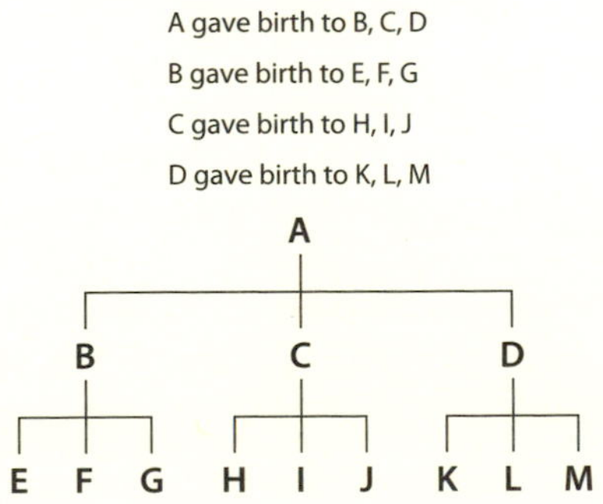

A gave birth to B, C, D

B gave birth to E, F, G

C gave birth to H, I, J

D gave birth to K, L, M

1. In Genesis the term *tôlĕdōt* is used elsewhere only in 10:32 and 25:13.

Second, the *tôlĕdōt* headings function like a zoom lens on a camera. They focus the reader's attention on a particular individual and his immediate children. This enables the author of Genesis to trace the fortunes of the main family line without needing to follow details of other relatives' lives. In this way Genesis highlights the importance of the lineage that, beginning with Adam, is traced through Adam's youngest son, Seth, to Noah, the father of Shem, Ham, and Japheth. The next stage of the line takes us from Shem to Terah, the father of Abraham, Nahor, and Haran. We then move from Abraham to Isaac, from Isaac to Jacob, and finally to Jacob's twelve sons.

The Chosen "Seed"

Closely linked to the genealogical structure of Genesis is the frequent use of the Hebrew word *zera'*, perhaps best translated as "seed." Unfortunately, the NIV translates *zera'* with a variety of terms—the most common being "descendants," "offspring," "seed." For this reason the importance of the concept of "seed" in Genesis is easily missed. *Zera'* is a keyword, however, occurring 59 times in Genesis compared to 170 times in the rest of the Old Testament.[2]

Several factors are worth noting briefly about the use of the term "seed" in Genesis. (1) The Hebrew word *zera'*, like the English word "sheep," can be either singular or plural; it may denote a single seed or many seeds. An example of the former comes in 21:13, where Ishmael is described as Abraham's "seed." However, in 28:14 *zera'* refers to the "seed" (descendants) of Jacob, "who will be like the dust of the earth." (2) "Seed" normally denotes an individual's natural child or children. When Eve gives birth to Seth, she comments, "God has granted me another child [seed] in place of Abel, since Cain killed him" (4:25). In 15:3 Abraham laments that his heir is Eliezer of Damascus and is not of his own seed; this reflects the fact that as yet Abraham and Sarah have no child of their own. (3) The Hebrew word *zera'* conveys the idea that there is a close resemblance between the "seed" and that which has produced it. We see this underlying the comment that plants and trees are to produce seeds "according to their various kinds" (1:11–12).

The Lineage of Adam

Viewing Genesis as a whole, it is apparent that the genealogical structure and the concept of "seed" are closely linked in order to highlight a single distinctive

2. These statistics exclude the one occurrence of the Aramaic word *zĕra'* in Dan. 2:43. In Genesis *zera'* comes in 1:11 (2x), 12 (2x), 29 (2x); 3:15 (2x); 4:25; 7:3; 8:22; 9:9; 12:7; 13:15, 16 (2x); 15:3, 5, 13, 18; 16:10; 17:7 (2x), 8, 9, 10, 12, 19; 19:32, 34; 21:12, 13; 22:17 (2x), 18; 24:7, 60; 26:3, 4 (3x), 24; 28:4, 13, 14 (2x); 32:12; 35:12; 38:8, 9 (2x); 46:6, 7; 47:19, 23, 24; 48:4, 11, 19.

family lineage (see figure 9.3). Moreover, although Genesis concludes by noting that the total seed of Jacob was reckoned as numbering seventy (46:6–27), within this group of seventy special attention is focused on the status given to the descendants of two of Jacob's sons, Joseph and Judah. As we shall observe

FIGURE 9.3. The Main Family Lineage in Genesis

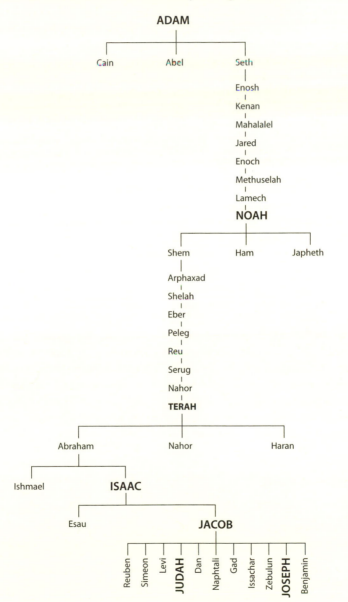

below, although Joseph's younger son, Ephraim, receives the blessing of the firstborn from his grandfather, Jacob (48:1–22), and is clearly viewed as the one through whom a royal line is anticipated, attention is also drawn to the future importance of Judah and his descendants (38:1–30; 49:8–12).

When we examine the nature and significance of the main family lineage in Genesis, various features are noteworthy. First, the lineage is always traced through male descendants, and all are clearly named.[3] Yet while it might be expected that the line of "seed" would always be traced through the eldest son, according to the concept of primogeniture, this is not so. In a number of instances a younger son is given priority over an older brother, and on each occasion the text of Genesis suggests why this occurs. For killing his brother Abel, Cain, the firstborn, is passed over in favor of Seth, the third-born (4:1–25). Although Ishmael is Abraham's firstborn son, he is excluded from the line of "seed" because he is the son of Sarah's Egyptian maidservant Hagar (16:1–16; 17:18–21; 21:9–21). As the God-given "seed" of Abraham, Isaac enjoys priority over Ishmael. Although Esau is born before Jacob, his secondary position to Jacob is divinely predicted before the birth of the twin boys (25:23). Furthermore, the narrator appears to justify this choice by highlighting Esau's dismissive attitude toward his birthright, which he sells to Jacob for a pot of red stew (25:29–34), and by the fact that he displeases his parents by marrying two Hittite women (26:34–35).

A more complex situation exists regarding the twelve sons of Jacob, where both Judah, the fourth-born son, and Joseph, the eleventh-born son, are privileged before older brothers. Once again the Genesis narrative reveals that the eldest brothers, Reuben, Simeon, and Levi, are excluded from enjoying their father's foremost blessing due to unseemly actions (see 35:22; 34:25–30). From the outset of Genesis 37, Joseph is clearly presented as the one who is privileged by his father as though the firstborn (cf. 1 Chron. 5:1–2). That he was Rachel's first child undoubtedly encouraged this. Later, Joseph's status as firstborn is confirmed when Jacob gives the blessing of the firstborn to Joseph's family by blessing his two sons, Manasseh and Ephraim (Gen. 48:1–22).[4] Remarkably, yet again in Genesis, a younger son, Ephraim, receives the superior blessing normally associated with the firstborn.

3. This does not necessarily imply that every generation is included in the record. R. R. Wilson, *Genealogy and History in the Biblical World*, YNER 7 (New Haven: Yale University Press, 1977), 133–34, notes that even in written genealogies there is a tendency to limit the maximum length of the lineage to ten generations, such as we have in Gen. 5 and 11. Consequently, it is not uncommon to find Near Eastern genealogies being modified by the addition and omission of names. Examples of this process of "telescoping" are also to be found in the biblical texts (e.g., cf. 1 Chron. 6:3–14 and Ezra 7:1–5; cf. W. H. Green, "Primeval Chronology," *BS* 47 [1890]: 285–303).

4. The status of Joseph as the firstborn of Jacob's twelve sons is probably also reflected in that "Joseph," through the tribes of Ephraim and Manasseh, received a double portion of the land of Canaan when it was distributed among the tribes of Israel.

While Joseph's position as the "firstborn" is assumed in the Genesis narrative, a subtle development occurs involving Judah. This centers chiefly on Genesis 38, which interrupts the report of Joseph's time in Egypt to focus attention on the "seed" of Judah. Given the special interest that Genesis displays in tracing a unique line of descendants, the events of this chapter are especially noteworthy.

Remarkably, the account of Judah's extraordinary relationship with Tamar concludes by describing the birth of twins, during which the younger boy, Perez, "breaks out" in front of the "firstborn," Zerah. The significance of this event should not be overlooked in the light of the larger story that unfolds in the books of Genesis to Kings. Whereas the tribe of Ephraim is initially presented as the one from which Israel's leader will come, as reflected in the important role played later by Joshua, the "firstborn" line of Ephraim is rejected in the time of Samuel and replaced by the line of David, from the tribe of Judah.[5]

Second, the central family line exists due to the gracious activity of God. At the outset Eve recognizes this following the birth of Seth: "She named him Seth, saying, 'God has granted me another child [seed] in place of Abel, since Cain killed him'" (Gen. 4:25). Yet it is in the lives of Abraham, Isaac, and Jacob that we most clearly see God's role in sustaining the family line. In the account of Abraham's life, one of the first details recorded is that "Sarai was childless because she was not able to conceive" (11:30). As the Abraham story unfolds, God on various occasions reiterates that Sarah will indeed give birth to a son (17:16–21; 18:10–14), even though both Abraham and Sarah are well beyond the natural age of having children; Abraham is one hundred years old (17:17; 21:5) and Sarah ninety (17:17). When at last Sarah gives birth to Isaac, the text specifically states that this is due to divine intervention: "Now the LORD was gracious to Sarah as he had said, and the LORD did for Sarah what he had promised" (21:1). A similar situation is recorded briefly in 25:21 regarding Isaac and Rebekah: "Isaac prayed to the LORD on behalf of his wife, because she was childless. The LORD answered his prayer, and his wife Rebekah became pregnant." Remarkably, history repeats itself yet again in the case of Jacob, for we learn that his wife, Rachel, was also childless (29:31). When Rachel eventually gives birth to a child of her own, the narrative affirms God's part in this: "Then God remembered Rachel; he listened to her and enabled her to conceive. She became pregnant and gave birth to a son and said, 'God has taken away my disgrace.' She named him Joseph, and said, 'May the LORD add to me another son'" (30:22–24). All these examples highlight that God is actively responsible for the continuation of the family line.

5. Apart from the evidence derived from the book of Genesis, Ps. 78:59–72 provides a strong case for believing that a royal line descended from Joseph was divinely rejected in favor of a lineage associated with Judah. Here, as in the books of Samuel, the rejection of Ephraim is linked to the demise of Shiloh as the central sanctuary, whereas the choice of David is associated with the divine decision to make Zion/Jerusalem the new location for God's sanctuary.

Third, the Genesis narrative emphasizes the existence of a special relationship between God and individual members of the main family line. We see this in a variety of ways. Sometimes it is highlighted in the briefest of comments. For example, we read that "Enoch walked faithfully with God; then he was no more, because God took him away" (5:24). The *tôlĕdōt* heading of Noah is immediately followed by the statement "Noah was a righteous man, blameless among the people of his time, and he walked faithfully with God" (6:9).[6] Elsewhere the presence of a special relationship is revealed in considerably more detail. This is so in the longer accounts concerning Noah, Abraham, Isaac, Jacob, and Joseph. In the cases of Noah and Abraham, God not only reveals future plans but also establishes eternal covenants through both of them. Isaac and Jacob also receive revelations from God confirming, in particular, promises that were previously made to Abraham. Although God never reveals himself directly to Joseph, he enables him to discern future events by interpreting dreams. Furthermore, the account of Joseph's time in Egypt highlights God's providential care of him.

While the members of the main family line enjoy God's favor and blessing, their faults and failures are never disguised. We read of Noah becoming drunk (Gen. 9:20–21), Abraham being less than fully truthful concerning his marriage to Sarah (12:10–13), and Jacob willfully deceiving his father (27:1–40), to mention some more obvious shortcomings. Nevertheless, in spite of such faults, the members of the family line are viewed as more righteous than others. This is perhaps most evident in the case of Noah, who is introduced as "a righteous man, blameless among the people of his time" (6:9), who with his family is not condemned to destruction by the flood like all other humans. Abraham's righteousness is highlighted in various ways. It is first mentioned specifically in 15:6, where the narrator comments that "Abram believed the LORD, and he credited it to him as righteousness." Later, the extent of Abraham's righteousness is revealed by his willingness to obey God and sacrifice his much-loved son, Isaac (22:1–19). Although in comparison to the other patriarchs relatively little information is given about Isaac, the fact that he clearly enjoyed God's favor suggests that he too was viewed as righteous (cf. 26:12–13, 23–24). Jacob's relationship with God develops over a long period of time, and while Genesis focuses initially on his deceptive behavior (27:1–29), we see him eventually taking active steps to rid his household of foreign gods (35:1–5). Like Abraham and Isaac, Jacob too knows God's blessing. Furthermore, all

---

6. The Hebrew original of the comments in Gen. 5:22, 24 and 6:9 that Enoch and Noah "walked faithfully with God" uses a distinctive form of the verb "to walk"—the *hitpa'el* form. The same form occurs elsewhere in Genesis in 3:8; 13:17; 17:1; 24:40; 48:15. Apart from 3:8, where God is the subject of the verb, and with the possible exception of 13:17, on all these occasions the verb "walk" denotes a special relationship with God. N. M. Sarna (*Genesis*, JPSTC [Philadelphia: Jewish Publication Society], 123) comments, "This expression seems originally to have been a technical term for absolute loyalty to a king."

three patriarchs actively worship God by building altars and offering sacrifices (12:7–8; 13:18; 22:9; 26:25; 35:1–7).

Fourth, as noted above, the concept of "seed" implies a resemblance between the "seed" and the one who has produced it. In the context of Genesis, this suggests that sons will resemble their fathers. The most obvious example of this comes in the record of Isaac's stay in the region of Gerar (26:1–33). Here Isaac's behavior mirrors closely that of his father. Like Abraham, he pretends that his wife is his sister (26:1–11; cf. 12:10–20; 20:1–18), is involved in a dispute with the inhabitants of Gerar over the ownership of certain wells (26:17–25; cf. 21:22–34), and enters into a covenant with Abimelech (26:26–31; cf. 21:22–34). In a different way Jacob's sons resemble him in that they too knowingly deceive their father (27:1–29; 37:12–35). Significantly, those elder sons who are overlooked in favor of younger brothers generally exhibit behavior that is not in keeping with that expected of the line of seed. For example, Reuben's affair with his father's concubine Bilhah (35:22; cf. 49:3–4) and the murderous actions of Simeon and Levi apparently exclude them from receiving the blessing of the firstborn from their father, Jacob (34:1–31; cf. 49:5–7).

Members of the main family line are not the only ones in Genesis to share common features; the same is true of others. Cain's descendant Lamech repeats his murderous actions (4:19–24). Similarly, among the descendants of Ham, who sinned against his father Noah, we find listed the Canaanites (who include the inhabitants of Sodom and Gomorrah) and the Amorites (10:15–19), all of whom are viewed as worthy of divine punishment (cf. 13:13; 15:16; 19:1–29).

Fifth, there are strong grounds for believing that the main line of descent in Genesis is viewed as a royal lineage. This possibility is implied by the divine promise made to Abraham that "kings will come from you" (17:6), echoed in a similar statement concerning Sarah, that "kings of peoples will come from her" (17:16). Moreover, although Abraham is never directly designated a king, he is sometimes portrayed as enjoying the status of a king. We see this in his defeat of the eastern kings in Genesis 14; in the desire of Abimelech, king of Gerar, to make a covenant with him (21:22–34); and finally in the title "mighty prince" (lit., "a prince of God") given to him by the Hittite inhabitants of Hebron (23:6).

While there are only a few allusions to kingship in Genesis 25–36, they are nevertheless noteworthy. Isaac's importance is reflected in Abimelech's wish to enter into a treaty with him (26:26–31), as he had previously done with Abraham. When Isaac blesses Jacob, his remarks clearly imply kingship, even though the term is not used: "May God give you heaven's dew and earth's richness—an abundance of grain and new wine. May nations serve you and peoples bow down to you. Be lord over your brothers, and may the sons of your mother bow down to you. May those who curse you be cursed and those who bless you be blessed" (27:28–29). In a divine promise that echoes Genesis 17, Jacob is promised that "kings will be among your descendants" (35:11).

141

Finally, the brief comment in 36:31, "These were the kings who reigned in Edom before any Israelite king reigned," indicates that whoever wrote this either anticipated or already knew of a royal dynasty within Israel.

The subject of kingship is prominent in the Joseph story. At the outset his brothers interpret Joseph's first dream as implying that he will be a king: "Do you intend to reign over us? Will you actually rule us?" (37:8). His second dream reinforces this idea (37:9–11), and later we witness the fulfillment when Joseph rises from the obscurity of an Egyptian prison to hold the office of governor of Egypt, second only to Pharaoh (41:39–43).

Although Joseph enjoys the spotlight in Genesis 37–50, of the other sons of Jacob most attention is focused on Judah.[7] This is particularly so in Genesis 38, where we have one of the more unusual episodes in the book. The inclusion of this story in Genesis can best be accounted for by noting that it focuses on Judah's reluctance, following the deaths of his sons Er and Onan, to allow Er's wife Tamar to marry Judah's third son, Shelah, in order to produce "seed" and so maintain the family line. When Tamar eventually becomes pregnant by deceiving Judah, he is forced to acknowledge the righteousness of her actions (38:26). The account concludes by recording the birth of Perez (and his twin brother, Zerah), from whom the royal line of David is descended.[8]

Judah's importance is further indicated by the special blessing he receives from his father in 49:8–12. Without considering every aspect of this blessing, the following points are worth noting. (1) When compared with the other blessings pronounced by Jacob on his sons, the length and content of Judah's blessing clearly suggest that he enjoys a special relationship with his father. Only Joseph receives a comparable blessing. (2) Jacob states that Judah and his descendants will exercise leadership over his other brothers and their descendants (49:8). We see this especially in the comment, "Your father's sons will bow down to you" (49:8) and in the reference to the scepter and ruler's staff not departing from Judah (49:10). (3) Jacob anticipates that eventually there shall come in the royal line of Judah one to whom the nations will submit in obedience (49:10) and whose reign will be marked by prosperity and abundance (49:11). Such comments would clearly have been very important for the royal line of David, justifying their claim to rule over the whole of Israel.[9]

---

7. See Gen. 43:8–9; 44:16, 18–34; 46:28; cf. B. Smith, "The Central Role of Judah in Genesis 37–50," *BS* 162 (2005): 158–74.

8. There are interesting parallels between Gen. 38 and the book of Ruth, which concludes by giving the genealogy of King David, beginning with Perez the son of Tamar (Ruth 4:18–22). Although Tamar and Ruth are non-Israelites, they both play an active role in continuing the royal line. David even names one of his daughters Tamar (2 Sam. 13:1). See T. D. Alexander, *The Servant King: The Bible's Portrait of the Messiah* (Leicester: Inter-Varsity, 1998), 49–54.

9. Gen. 1:28 indicates that humans were created by God to rule over the earth. This being so, Adam is to be viewed as the first member of this royal line. However, not only was Adam

Sixth, the "seed" of the main family lineage is frequently associated with the divine promises, which are an important feature of the patriarchal stories. Three aspects of these promises deserve special notice. (1) God promises the land of Canaan to the "seed" of Abraham. This is mentioned specifically when Abraham first arrives in Canaan—"To your offspring [seed] I will give this land" (Gen. 12:7)—and repeated on various occasions to Abraham, Isaac, and Jacob (13:15; 15:18; 17:8; 22:17; 26:3; 28:13; 35:12; cf. 24:7, 60; 28:4; 48:4). On the significance of these promises concerning land, see chapter 10. (2) It is frequently stressed that the "seed" of Abraham will be very numerous. Different images are used to highlight the extent of the "seed": the dust of the earth (13:16; 28:14), the stars of the heavens (15:5; 22:17; 26:4), and the sand of the seashore (22:17; 32:12). The fulfillment of the promise of numerous descendants, like that of land, clearly lies beyond the book of Genesis, indicating that it merely records the beginning of something that will be completed later. Taken together, these promises related to the creation of a "great nation" (12:2).[10] (3) It is emphasized that through Abraham's "seed" all nations on earth will be blessed (22:18; 26:4; 28:14). This will be discussed more fully in the next chapter, where we shall consider the theme of blessing in Genesis; yet here we should notice that in this context the expression "Abraham's seed" designates a single descendant. As we shall observe, Genesis anticipates that a royal descendant from Abraham will play an important role in bringing divine blessing to all the nations of the earth.

Seventh, given all that has been said about the unique line of seed traced throughout Genesis, it is surely highly significant that in the light of Adam and Eve's betrayal of God in the Garden of Eden, God states that the "seed of the woman" shall overcome the serpent (3:15).[11] While many scholars adopt a plural interpretation of "offspring [seed]" in Genesis 3:15, the syntax of the Hebrew favors a singular reading. The idea that this seed of the woman refers to an individual is supported by how the rest of Genesis is structured around a unique family line. Everything about this family line suggests that it is intimately linked to the fulfillment of God's promise regarding the defeat of the serpent.

---

a king, but he was also a priest (see chap. 8 above). In the light of this, the concept of priest-king takes on a special significance. In Gen. 14 we encounter this unusual status in the figure of Melchizedek. Clearly it is implied that anyone who enjoys this particular status resembles Adam before he was expelled from the Garden of Eden. Later the Israelites are called by the LORD to be a royal priesthood (Exod. 19:6).

10. The nature of this nation—holy and righteous—becomes a prominent theme in Exodus, Leviticus, and Deuteronomy.

11. For a fuller discussion of this passage, see T. D. Alexander, "Messianic Ideology in the Book of Genesis," in *The Lord's Anointed: Interpretation of Old Testament Messianic Texts*, ed. P. E. Satterthwaite, R. S. Hess, and G. J. Wenham (Grand Rapids: Baker; Carlisle: Paternoster, 1995), 27–32; M. A. Rydelnik, *The Messianic Hope: Is the Hebrew Bible Really Messianic?* NACSBT 9 (Nashville: B&H Academic, 2010), 129–45.

Old Testament Summary

The entire book of Genesis is clearly composed around the history of a unique family line that enjoys a special relationship with God. With Abraham we are informed on the one hand that the "seed" of this lineage will become very numerous and possess the land of Canaan, and on the other hand that one particular line of "seed" will establish a royal dynasty through which all the nations of the earth will be blessed. Though this royal line is clearly linked to Joseph and Ephraim, Genesis anticipates that the line of Judah through Perez will replace this "firstborn" lineage. In this way Genesis focuses on both the birth of the nation of Israel and the early ancestry of a future monarchy. Since the nation and the king are of the "seed" of Abraham, they share a common origin and, as recipients of the divine promises, a common destiny. To the promises of blessing others and receiving land we shall turn in chapters 10 and 11 respectively.

New Testament Connections

In the New Testament various passages relate directly or indirectly to the family lineage that we have identified in Genesis. By far the most important connection is that this special line of seed finds its fulfillment in Jesus Christ. Since Genesis anticipates a royal line of seed descended from Judah, it is easy to understand how Jesus, "the son of David" (cf. Rom. 1:3; 2 Tim. 2:8), is linked to the "seed" of Abraham. Paul explicitly states this in his Letter to the Galatians: "The promises were spoken to Abraham and to his seed. Scripture does not say 'and to seeds,' meaning many people, but 'and to your seed,' meaning one person, who is Christ" (Gal. 3:16). Paul correctly interprets the text of Genesis as anticipating a singular seed.[12] The same idea probably underlies other New Testament passages that associate Abraham with David. For example, Matthew's genealogy of Jesus begins with Abraham and is traced downward through David to Joseph (Matt. 1:1–17).[13] In Zechariah's song of praise, the arrival of a "savior" from the house of David is viewed as the fulfillment of the oath that God swore to Abraham (Luke 1:68–75 NRSV). In a slightly less obvious way, the same link is found in Peter's speech in Acts 3:12–26. Here Peter explains that Jesus as the suffering Messiah fulfills God's promise to Abraham that through his "seed" all peoples on earth will be blessed (Acts 3:25–26 KJV).

12. Cf. C. J. Collins, "Galatians 3:16: What Kind of an Exegete Was Paul?" *TynBul* 54 (2003): 75–86; J. S. DeRouchie and J. C. Meyer, "Christ or Family as the 'Seed' of Promise? An Evaluation of N. T. Wright on Galatians 3:16," *SBJT* 14 (2010): 36–48.
13. Although the genealogy ends with Joseph, Matthew nowhere claims that Joseph is the natural father of Jesus; he merely observes that Joseph is married to Mary, the mother of Jesus (Matt. 1:16). In keeping with this, the immediately following account is concerned to show that Joseph adopts Jesus as his son (Matt. 1:18–25).

Although the New Testament writers view Jesus as belonging to the line of Abraham/David, they reveal that he is much greater than either Abraham or David. John 8:52–58 and Matthew 22:41–46 record Jesus's own assessment that he is superior to Abraham and David respectively. A similar claim is also recorded regarding Jesus and Solomon in Matthew 12:42 (cf. Luke 11:31). Further links between Jesus and the "seed" of Abraham will be noted in chapters 10 and 12.

The special lineage in Genesis also appears in Paul's Letters to the Romans and Galatians. In Romans 9 and Galatians 4 he draws an important distinction between children by physical descent (Rom. 9:8 NIV 1984) and "children of promise" (Gal. 4:28). Using the Genesis stories concerning Ishmael/Isaac and Esau/Jacob, he argues that "not all who are descended from Israel are Israel. Nor because they are his descendants are they all Abraham's children" (Rom. 9:6–7). Paul is concerned to show that natural descent from Abraham is no guarantee of salvation. From Genesis he demonstrates that although Ishmael and Esau are both descendants of Abraham, they are not part of the chosen line of "seed."

Another element of Paul's discussion in Romans and Galatians is that the seed of Abraham should resemble him. We see this clearly in his comments in Galatians 3:6–7: "So also Abraham 'believed God, and it was credited to him as righteousness.' Understand, then, that those who have faith are children of Abraham." The same point underlies Paul's words in Romans 4:16–17: "Therefore, the promise comes by faith, so that it may be by grace and may be guaranteed to all Abraham's offspring—not only to those who are of the law but also to those who are of the faith of Abraham. He is the father of us all. As it is written: 'I have made you a father of many nations.' He is our father in the sight of God, in whom he believed—the God who gives life to the dead and calls things that were not." In both these passages Paul argues that the true children of Abraham are those who, like Abraham, exercise faith. Consequently, descent from Abraham counts for nothing unless his natural descendants resemble him by being made righteous through faith. On this we shall have more to say in chapter 12.

10

The Blessing of the Nations

Although the first chapter of Genesis affirms that humans were created in the divine image and blessed by God, the disobedience of Adam and Eve in the Garden of Eden resulted in a series of divine curses that radically affected human existence. The tragic events resulting from the broken relationship between God and humankind are highlighted in Genesis 4–11. After the division of humanity into different peoples and nations, Abraham is introduced as the one through whom God's blessing will once again extend to humans. Genesis looks forward to all families and nations being blessed through Abraham and his royal "seed."

Introduction

Blessing and cursing are important concepts in the book of Genesis, as reflected by the fact that the Hebrew verbs for "bless" (*bārak*) and "curse" (*'ārar*) occur seventy-three and nine times respectively. Normally in Genesis blessing is associated with God's favor and cursing with his disfavor. To be blessed, the recipient must be at harmony with the donor. Consequently, God's blessing extends only to those who seek to be righteous; the wicked are under his curse.

Genesis presents a picture of changing human fortunes. When God created the first generation of humans, they enjoyed his favor and were blessed by him (1:28). Soon this situation was disrupted by events that took place in the Garden of Eden. For disobeying God's command not to eat from the tree of the knowledge of good and evil, Adam and Eve were divinely punished through various curses. Some of the immediate consequences are described in Genesis 4–11. Here we observe the total destruction of the human race except for Noah and his family and the later division of humans into different nations. Although the accounts of the flood and of the tower of Babel highlight the disastrous consequences of evoking God's displeasure, with the call of Abraham in Genesis 12 the way begins to open for humans once more to enjoy God's favor. Significantly, as illustrated in the record of the lives of Isaac, Jacob, and Joseph, God's blessing is mediated through the "firstborn seed" descended from Abraham.

Creator and Creation in Harmony

The opening section of the book of Genesis describes how God created the heavens and the earth. It stresses the ease with which everything was made and that nothing happened by chance: everything was made according to design. By merely speaking, God created time in the form of "day" and "night" (1:3–5). Next he made three distinctive regions, the sky (1:6–8), the land, and the seas (1:9–11), and as appropriate placed in each plants (1:11–13), stars and planets (1:14–19), fish and birds (1:20–23), living creatures (1:24–26), and humans (1:27–31). God's final verdict that everything "was very good" (1:31) echoes a common refrain in the chapter, "God saw that (it) was good" (1:4, 10, 12, 18, 21, 25). With remarkable brevity and skill, the narrator conveys a picture of total harmony between God the Creator and the world, his creation.

The creation of human beings comes as the climax to God's creative activity: "So God created mankind in his own image, in the image of God he created him, male and female he created them" (1:27). This comment is immediately followed by the remark that "God blessed them and said to them, 'Be fruitful and increase in number; fill the earth and subdue it. Rule over the fish of the sea and the birds of the air and over every living creature that moves on the ground'" (1:28). Unlike all other creatures, humans alone enjoyed the privilege of being made in the divine image and having a special relationship with God. Moreover, blessed by God they were to increase numerically and rule over the earth as his representatives.

Although God's creative activity ends on the sixth day, the account of creation concludes by focusing on the seventh day, in which God rested from all work (2:1–3). Of significance is the comment, "God blessed the seventh day and made it holy, because on it he rested from all the work of creating that he had done" (2:3). The seventh day is set apart from all the other days of the week because rest is viewed as the climax of the work pattern established by God. As reflected in God's own experience, the opportunity to rest, having completed one's work, is a sacred blessing.

In the Garden of Eden

The account of creation in Genesis 1:1–2:3 is followed by a second in 2:4–25. While the first account gives a cosmic picture of God's activity, the second is much more down to earth, portraying God as the one who personally molds the man from clay and breathes life into him (2:7).[1] The narrative also reveals that God provides the right environment for the man (2:8–17) and a suitable companion (2:18–25). Although the two accounts of humanity's creation differ in style, they complement each other, both emphasizing the special relationship that existed between the LORD God and the first man and woman.

Unfortunately, the harmony of creation is soon broken by the serpent, who persuades the woman and, through her, the man to disobey God's command by eating "from the tree of the knowledge of good and evil" (2:17). Although few details are given, the narrative makes it clear that eating from this tree radically changes the man and the woman. Only at this stage do they become conscious of their own nakedness.

When the LORD God next visits the garden, the man and the woman are unable to hide what has taken place. Aware of their actions, God pronounces judgment on all the participants. No longer does God's blessing favor the man and the woman; now they must endure the consequences of his displeasure. As a result of their broken relationship with God, Adam and Eve are expelled from Eden.

The contents of God's pronouncements against the serpent, the woman, and the man are significant. Regarding the serpent he states:

> Because you have done this,
>> Cursed are you above all livestock
>> and all wild animals!
> You will crawl on your belly
>> and you will eat dust
>> all the days of your life.
> And I will put enmity
>> between you and the woman
>> and between your offspring [seed] and hers [her seed];
> he will crush your head,
>> and you will strike his heel.
>
> Gen. 3:14–15

Of particular interest here is the comment about the enmity that will exist between the "seed" of the serpent and the "seed" of the woman. Unfortunately, most commentators miss the obvious connection that exists between

---

1. By placing these two accounts side by side, the divine attributes of transcendence and immanence are given equal weight and presented in a manner that highlights their importance while avoiding confusion.

this reference to "seed" and the fact that Genesis highlights a particular line of "seed" (see chap. 9 above). The implication is surely that the divine pronouncement against the serpent will be fulfilled through the divinely chosen family lineage.[2]

God's judgment on the woman is directed against two important aspects of her life: her ability to produce children and her relationship to her husband:

> I will make your pains in childbearing very severe;
> > with painful labor you will give birth to children.
> Your desire will be for your husband,
> > and he will rule over you.
>
> > > > Gen. 3:16

Since in the future every birth will be accomplished only through pain, this pronouncement partly reverses God's initial blessing that humans should be fruitful and increase in number (1:28).

The man's punishment is also designed to cause him severe discomfort:

> Cursed is the ground because of you;
> > through painful toil you will eat from it
> > all the days of your life.
> It will produce thorns and thistles for you,
> > and you will eat the plants of the field.
> By the sweat of your brow
> > you will eat your food
> until you return to the ground,
> > since from it you were taken;
> for dust you are
> > and to dust you will return.
>
> > > > Gen. 3:17–19

God originally intended the man's work to be a responsibility undertaken with joy and satisfaction; now it becomes hard labor. On the basis of 2:7 it is obvious that the LORD God intended there to be a close and harmonious relationship between the man and the ground; this is evident in the Hebrew original, where the words for "man" and "ground," 'ādām and 'ādāmâ respectively, are very similar.[3] By disrupting the man's relationship with the ground, God ensures that humans are not able to enjoy, like their creator, rest from labor.

The story of the fall brings to a bitter end the harmony that was the hallmark of God's creative activity. In particular we witness a breakdown in relations between animals and humans, between men and women, and most important of all, between God and humanity. Genesis 3 describes dramatic changes to

2. See pages 138–45.
3. We shall have more to say about the theme of "land" in chap. 11 below.

the created world. People no longer know God's blessing but must now come to terms with his displeasure. The final act of judgment is the expulsion of the man and woman from Eden. Not only are they prevented from eating of the tree of life (3:22); they are also expelled from the place where they have enjoyed a close relationship with God. As we shall observe below, Genesis 4–11 focuses mainly on the terrible consequences of humanity's initial disobedience and provides a grim picture of what life is like without God's blessing. Only with the call of Abraham in 12:1–3 do we begin to see a brighter prospect, with some humans once again experiencing divine blessing in their lives.

Outside Eden

After the departure of Adam and Eve from the Garden of Eden, the next episode in Genesis focuses on the murder of Abel by his brother Cain. Because Abel enjoys God's favor, Cain becomes jealous and kills him. As punishment, Cain is cursed by God; the ground "will no longer yield its crops" for him, and he will become a "restless wanderer on the earth" (4:11–12). This marks an extension of the curse imposed on Cain's parents in Eden and highlights the fact that every unrighteous action alienates humankind further from the ground, making it even more difficult to cultivate food and so experience divinely intended rest.

The Genesis story reveals that God's curse on the ground has brought increased pain for humankind. Lamech particularly highlights this in a brief comment concerning his son Noah. He names him Noah because "he will comfort us in the labor and painful toil of our hands caused by the ground the LORD has cursed" (5:29). Thus when the earth is re-created after the flood, Noah is described as "a man of the soil [ground]" (9:20), implying that he enjoys greater harmony with the ground than did his immediate ancestors.

The concept of curse underlies the entire story of the flood. God's decision to wipe humankind from the face of the earth is motivated by the fact that he "saw how great the wickedness of the human race had become on the earth, and that every inclination of the thoughts of the human heart was only evil all the time" (6:5). However, Noah finds favor in God's eyes and, together with some of his family, is spared from destruction. When Noah disembarks from the ark and offers sacrifices to God, the LORD remarks, "Never again will I curse the ground because of humans, even though every inclination of the human heart is evil from childhood" (8:21). The curse mentioned here is not the one pronounced in the Garden of Eden. Rather, it refers to the flood. The continued existence of "thorns and thistles" and the necessity for humankind to toil with sweat indicate that the original divine curse on the ground has not been canceled. Here God promises that he will never again send another flood upon the earth.[4] Later this is confirmed in the covenant outlined in 9:8–17.

In passing we should note that the story of the flood exhibits close parallels with the initial account of creation. The rising of the waters marks a return to the chaos that existed at the beginning of creation (7:11–24; cf. 1:2). Later, the dry land emerges from the waters (8:1–14; cf. 1:9–10). Finally, God's blessing of Noah and his sons in 9:1 echoes closely 1:28: "Be fruitful and increase in number and fill the earth." Although these parallels suggest that the flood story should be understood as marking the re-creation of the earth, it is apparent that human nature is not renewed. We see this reflected in God's comments in 8:21 and 9:6, which draw attention respectively to the evil inclination of the human heart and the likelihood that murders will still occur.

The topic of blessing is prominent in 9:20–29. Here the narrative focuses on the contrasting actions of Ham and his brothers Shem and Japheth toward their father, Noah. Though Ham sees "his father naked," Shem and Japheth take great care to cover their father without seeing him naked. When Noah awakes, he pronounces a curse on Ham's son Canaan, but blesses Shem and Japheth. Of significance is the fact that this is the first occasion in Genesis when a human pronounces a blessing or a curse; previously it was always God who blessed or cursed. Yet in cursing Canaan and blessing Shem and Japheth, Noah's words obviously carry divine authority. For the first time we meet something that is repeated later in Genesis: those within the chosen line of "seed" are divinely empowered to bless or curse others.

Noah's speeches highlight another important motif in the book of Genesis, which concerns the descendants of Canaan and Shem. Although Canaan's descendants are destined to a future of servitude (9:25), Noah indicates that the line of Shem will enjoy a special relationship with God (9:26–27). Later, we see God promising to Abraham, a descendant of Shem, that he and his descendants will take possession of the land occupied by the descendants of Canaan (15:18–21).[5] Noah also predicts that Japheth will be blessed through having a close relationship with Shem.

Although blessing or cursing is not mentioned explicitly in the story of the tower of Babel, it is clear from the conclusion that the creation of different languages and the scattering of the peoples over the whole earth represent further divine curses on the human race. God's punishment is intended to prevent human beings from working together in harmony.

4. The syntax of the Hebrew original indicates that here God promises not to add to the curse pronounced against the ground in Gen. 3:17. Furthermore, the Hebrew word for "curse" in 8:21 comes from a different root than the one used in 3:17.

5. Among the various nations listed in Gen. 15:19–21, the following are named as descendants of Canaan in 10:15–18: Hittites, Amorites, Canaanites, Girgashites, and Jebusites. Furthermore, 10:19 draws attention to the fact that the borders of the Canaanite clans reached as far as Sodom and Gomorrah (cf. 14:1–24; 18:16–29).

The picture of human existence under God's curse, in Genesis 3–11, contrasts sharply with the initial account of the divine creation and blessing of humankind. The narrator, however, makes it very evident that God's displeasure is not arbitrary but is in proportion to the extent of human wickedness. Yet although Genesis 3–11 concentrates on the divine punishment of wicked humans, the narrative reveals here and there that God still displays mercy in the face of unrighteous behavior. We see this in the clothing of Adam and Eve (3:21), the placing of a mark on Cain (4:13–15), the saving of Noah and his family from the flood (6:8–8:19), and the making of an eternal covenant with every living creature (9:1–17). Significantly, the remaining chapters of Genesis develop further the possibility that humans may once again know God's blessing in their lives.

Abraham and the Blessing of the Nations

The *tôlĕdōt* heading in 11:27 introduces a new section in Genesis, which concludes in 25:11. The central character of these chapters is Abraham, and there is good reason to view him as the most important human participant in the whole of Genesis. After some brief preliminary details in 11:27–32, the account of his life begins with a short but highly significant divine speech that marks the beginning of a major new stage in God's relationship with humans. At the heart of this speech is God's desire to bless humanity and so reverse the negative effects of the divine curses under which they live. The LORD says to Abraham, "Leave your country, your people, and your father's household and go to the land I will show you, so that I may make you into a great nation and bless you and make your name great. Be a blessing, so that I may bless those who bless you, and curse the one who disdains you, and so that all the families of the ground may be blessed through you" (12:1–3, my trans.).[6] A number of points are noteworthy. First, the fulfillment of the promises listed here is conditional on Abraham's obedience. God commands him to leave the security of his own country, people, and family and "be a blessing." Since the divine curses are due to human disobedience, it is hardly surprising that God expects Abraham to be obedient before blessing him. Second, the promise that Abraham will become a great nation implies that he will have numerous descendants who will possess their own land. Although the fulfillment of this lies in the distant future, at the outset we need to observe that major barriers stand in the way: Abraham has

6. Two aspects of the translation adopted here require comment. First, the imperative form *wehyēh* (*vehyēh*), "be," in 12:2d is maintained; NIV reads, "and you will be a blessing." Second, special consideration has been given to the fact that the imperatives "go" and "be a blessing" are both followed by cohortatives. In such contexts the cohortative normally expresses purpose or result. To highlight this syntactic arrangement, the imperatives "go" and "be a blessing" are followed by "so that."

neither children nor land. Third, the reference to "a great name" alludes back to the story of the tower of Babel and possibly also to the "men of renown" mentioned in 6:4. The people of Babel tried to establish a "name" for themselves without God's help (11:4), but the LORD will make Abraham famous. Fourth, God promises that those who "disdain" Abraham will be divinely "cursed." Implicit in this is a guarantee of protection for Abraham and victory over his enemies. The wording of the Hebrew original possibly also indicates that whereas a few will disdain Abraham, a majority will bless him. Fifth, the climax of the passage comes in the concluding words that "all the families of the ground may be blessed through you." Here for the first time we meet an idea that is prominent in the rest of Genesis. Through Abraham and his "seed," as we shall observe below, God's blessing will be mediated to humanity. Sixth, underlying the fulfillment of all these promises is the establishment of a special relationship between God and Abraham, on account of which Abraham will be blessed.[7] The promises will be fulfilled as a result of divine blessing.

The theme of blessing is also prominent in the divine oath in 22:16–18, which marks the conclusion to the main part of the Abraham narrative.[8] Here the LORD declares to Abraham, "I swear by myself, declares the LORD, that because you have done this and have not withheld your son, your only son, I will surely bless you and make your descendants [seed] as numerous as the stars in the sky and as the sand on the seashore. Your descendant [seed] will take possession of the gate of his enemies, and through your descendant [seed] all nations of the earth will be blessed, because you have obeyed me" (22:16–18, my trans.). Although the wording here differs from that found in 12:1–3, the same basic ideas underlie both speeches. Yet 12:1–3 marks the beginning of the Abraham story, and the divine oath in 22:16–18 comes at the climax and looks beyond Abraham to his "seed." Unfortunately, the precise identity of this "seed" is not always clearly recognized. While the first mention of "seed" denotes "descendants" in the plural, the remaining references refer to a single descendant. The shift from many to one is favored by the syntax of the Hebrew text and is in keeping with the overall aim of Genesis to highlight a royal lineage.[9]

All the material in the Abraham story relates in one way or another to the promises highlighted in the opening verses of Genesis 12 and so to the theme

7. Abraham is later designated the friend of God, in 2 Chron. 20:7; Isa. 41:8.
8. The Abraham narrative falls into two sections, separated by a brief genealogy in 22:20–24. The main narrative is 11:27–22:19, with 23:1–25:11 forming an appendix. The divine speeches in 12:1–3 and 22:16–18, which come at the beginning and end of the main section, form what is known technically as an *inclusio*, marking the boundaries of the narrative. Although the promises in 12:1–3 are conditioned on Abraham's obeying God, the oath in 22:16–18 comes as a reward for Abraham's obedience, confirming the fulfillment of the earlier divine promises. For a fuller discussion, see chap. 12 below.
9. See T. D. Alexander, "Further Observations on the Term 'Seed' in Genesis," *TynBul* 48 (1997): 363–67.

of blessing. Some episodes focus on Abraham and his descendants' possessing the land of Canaan (e.g., 13:1–18; 15:7–21); others are concerned with Abraham's lack of a son and the establishment of Isaac as his legitimate heir (e.g., 15:1–6; 16:1–18:15; 20:1–21:21). Interlinked with these episodes are passages reflecting the fulfillment of God's promise that those who bless Abraham will know God's favor and those who act against Abraham will experience God's displeasure. On the one hand, Pharaoh and Abimelech are divinely punished for taking Sarah (12:17; 20:18), and the eastern kings are defeated when Abraham rescues Lot (14:1–16). On the other hand, Melchizedek blesses Abraham and receives in return a tenth of everything captured from the eastern kings (14:18–20). Much later we learn that Abimelech enters into a covenant with Abraham in order to ensure his own prosperity (21:22–34). Finally, to underline that the divine promises to Abraham have indeed been fulfilled, insofar as this is possible during his lifetime, Genesis 24 begins with the comment "The LORD had blessed him [Abraham] in every way" (24:1; cf. 24:35).

Blessing in the Remainder of Genesis

The theme of blessing, which is so important in the Abraham story, continues to play a major role in the remaining chapters of Genesis. Among the different aspects of blessing introduced in the Abraham narrative and then continued and developed, the following are the most important.

First, God's blessing is closely associated with prosperity. This figures prominently in a number of episodes in the Abraham narrative. When Abraham returns from Egypt, we read of a conflict between the servants of Abraham and Lot because both men have become very wealthy (13:2, 5; cf. 12:16). Later, after rescuing Lot from the eastern kings, Abraham refuses to take anything from the king of Sodom lest he should claim to have made Abraham rich (14:21–23; cf. 15:1, which attributes Abraham's reward to the LORD). In Genesis 24 Abraham's servant not only presents valuable gifts to Rebekah and her family (24:22, 53), but also directly associates his master's prosperity with the LORD's blessing: "The LORD has blessed my master abundantly, and he has become wealthy. He has given him sheep and cattle, silver and gold, male and female servants, and camels and donkeys" (24:35). In the same context we may observe that Laban likewise attributes wealth to divine blessing (24:29–31).

Prosperity is also linked to blessing in the accounts concerning Isaac, Jacob, and Joseph. Although it is only mentioned briefly, the narrator emphasizes that Isaac's great wealth is due to God's blessing (26:12–13). While Jacob flees to Paddan Aram with few possessions, as a result of God's blessing he returns to Canaan a very rich man (30:43; 32:3–21), and this in spite of attempts by his uncle Laban to limit his wealth (31:6–9). The story of Joseph also revolves around the idea that it is through God's blessing that he prospers in Egypt. Although he begins life there as a slave (39:1–6) and later is unjustly imprisoned (39:6–23), he eventually becomes governor of the country second only to Pharaoh (41:39–43). Throughout the patriarchal stories prosperity is closely tied to divine blessing.[10]

Second, God's blessing is also associated with fertility. We see this in Genesis 1, where the first reference to God's blessing the man and the woman is directly followed by the command "Be fruitful and increase in number" (1:28). This close association of blessing and fertility is echoed in 9:1: "Then God blessed Noah and his sons, saying to them, 'Be fruitful and increase in number and fill the earth.'" The same phrases are used when first Isaac and then God bless Jacob in 28:3 and 35:11 respectively (cf. 48:4). In the Abraham story the lack of fertility is the setting against which the LORD promises that Abraham will become a great nation. Thereafter we have frequent reminders that the "seed" of Abraham will be as numerous as the dust of the earth (13:16; 28:14), the stars of the heavens (15:5; 22:17; 26:4), and the sand of the seashore (22:17; 32:12). The topic of fertility is also prominent in the story of Jacob, where it dominates the competitive relationship between Leah and Rachel (29:31–30:24), and on a different level the relationship between Jacob and Laban (30:25–43). Here also fertility is linked to divine blessing (cf. 29:32–33; 30:6, 17–18, 20, 22–24, 27–30). Throughout Genesis the ability to reproduce is viewed as a sign of divine blessing.[11]

Third and most important, the power to mediate God's blessing to others is passed on through the chosen line of patriarchs. This is highlighted in Genesis in two ways: through God's renewing his special relationship with the head of each generation, and through a unique blessing that each father bestows on his "firstborn" son.

In the patriarchal stories the LORD renews his special relationship with the head of the chosen family in each generation. The promises associated with God's desire to bless Abraham in 12:1–3, and later confirmed by oath in 22:16–18, are passed on to his firstborn "seed." When Isaac is faced with a famine in the land of Canaan, the LORD appears to him and says,

> Do not go down to Egypt; live in the land where I tell you to live. Stay in this land for a while, and I will be with you and bless you. For to you and your descendants I will give all these lands and will confirm the oath I swore to your father Abraham. I will make your descendants [seed] as numerous as the stars in the sky and will give them [your seed] all these lands, and through your offspring [seed] all nations on earth will be blessed, because Abraham obeyed me

10. The idea that God blesses the righteous materially is important in the OT. Yet the OT counterbalances this belief by teaching that the righteous may suffer (e.g., the story of Job) and that the wicked may prosper (e.g., Ps. 49).

11. The reference to the rapid increase of the Israelites in Exod. 1:7 provides an important link between the books of Genesis and Exodus.

and did everything I required of him, keeping my commands, my decrees and my instructions. (26:2–5)

Much of this speech echoes 22:16–18, highlighting Abraham's willingness to obey God. In this way God encourages Isaac to obey him. As in 12:1–3, God's blessing through the fulfillment of the divine promises depends on Isaac's obeying him and remaining in Canaan. Genesis 26, the only chapter to focus exclusively on Isaac, contains three explicit references to God's blessing him (26:12, 24, 29).

The story of Jacob also includes a divine speech containing promises regarding numerous descendants, possession of the land, and the blessing of all peoples on earth. It occurs when Jacob is fleeing to Paddan Aram to escape from his brother Esau. God says,

I am the LORD, the God of your father Abraham and the God of Isaac. I will give you and your descendants [seed] the land on which you are lying. Your descendants [seed] will be like the dust of the earth, and you will spread out to the west and to the east, to the north and to the south. All peoples on earth will be blessed through you and your offspring [seed]. I am with you and will watch over you wherever you go, and I will bring you back to this land. I will not leave you until I have done what I have promised you. (28:13–15)

Although it is not specifically mentioned, the contents of the speech, which closely resemble earlier divine statements, clearly imply that God will bless Jacob. In response, Jacob vows that if God will indeed protect him and bring him back safely to his father's house, "then the LORD will be my God and this stone that I have set up as a pillar will be God's house, and of all that you give me I will give you a tenth" (28:21–22). Many years later when Jacob returns from Paddan Aram, God appears to him again, blesses him (35:9), and states,

I am God Almighty; be fruitful and increase in number. A nation and a community of nations will come from you, and kings will be among your descendants. The land I gave to Abraham and Isaac I also give to you, and I will give this land to your descendants after you. (35:11–12; cf. 48:3–4)

Here God confirms Jacob as the heir to the covenant earlier established with Abraham and Isaac.

In the light of these divine speeches, it is apparent that Abraham, Isaac, and Jacob all enjoy the same privileged relationship with the LORD. Though Abraham and Isaac have other children, they are not part of the chosen lineage and so do not have the same unique relationship with God.[12]

12. This is highlighted, for example, in Gen. 17, where God explicitly states that the covenant will be established through Isaac and not Ishmael (17:19–21). Although Ishmael is here blessed by God (17:20), he does not enjoy the same standing as Isaac.

As a result of this special relationship, the patriarchs are able to mediate God's blessing to others. This blessing, however, is in direct proportion to how the patriarchs and their "seed" are treated by others. Apart from the examples in the Abraham story considered above, the stories of Jacob and Joseph contain further illustrations. Laban learns by divination that the LORD has blessed him because of Jacob (30:27). Potiphar and his household prosper on account of Joseph (39:2–6), as does the prison warden (39:20–23). Later, following Joseph's appointment as governor over Egypt, not only is the entire nation able to survive a seven-year famine (47:13–26) but other nations also benefit from his wise leadership (41:56–57). Finally, when Pharaoh offers Joseph's relatives "the best part of the land" (47:6), Jacob blesses him (47:7–10).

The other way in which the Genesis narrative reveals that the power to bless others is granted to succeeding patriarchs is through the paternal blessing of the firstborn. Clearly it was the custom that the firstborn son should receive from his father a special blessing that gave him privileges not enjoyed by other sons. This idea lies at the heart of the account of Jacob's deceiving his father, Isaac, in order to obtain the blessing about to be given to Esau (27:1–40). So important is this blessing to Jacob that he is prepared to face both his father's displeasure, should he be found out (27:11–12), and his brother's anger at being deprived of what by custom was rightfully his (cf. 27:41). Although Isaac becomes fully aware that Jacob has deceived him, he subsequently blesses him again before sending him to find a wife in Paddan Aram.[13] This suggests that Isaac willingly accepts what has happened (28:1–5).

While some readers may feel that, by deceiving his father and stealing his brother's blessing, Jacob acts immorally, various details in the narrative suggest that Jacob's actions are excused, at least in part, by the narrator. First, it is emphasized that Rebekah instigates the deception (27:5–10); she also states that she will accept full responsibility if the deception is discovered (27:13). Second, on a prior occasion, Esau was persuaded by Jacob to sell his birthright for some stew (25:29–34). Although Jacob's exploitation of his hungry brother is less than commendable, the narrator underscores Esau's negative attitude toward his birthright: "So Esau despised his birthright" (25:34). This short episode reveals much about the aspirations of the two brothers. Esau has little regard for his privileged position as firstborn son and heir to the divinely promised royal line; Jacob desires to have this privilege more than anything else. The contrasting attitudes of the two brothers toward God's plans for Abraham's lineage set them apart. Although Jacob at this stage is a flawed character, he will later be transformed through a dramatic encounter with God (32:22–32) and subsequently renamed "Israel" (35:9–15). Third, the narrator appears to be critical of Isaac for allowing his appetite for wild

13. Interestingly, this blessing echoes Gen. 1:22, 28; 9:1, 7.

game to influence his attitude toward Esau (25:28). By favoring Esau, Isaac seemingly ignores the implications of the divine statement made before the birth of the twin boys that Esau will be subservient to Jacob (25:23). Fourth, the concluding comments of Genesis 26, that Esau's wives were a source of grief to Isaac and Rebekah (26:34–35), suggest that Esau is not worthy of the special paternal blessing. In the light of these factors, all the family members share responsibility for Jacob's deception. Finally, later in the story, when Jacob and Esau are reconciled after years of living apart, Jacob gives to his brother a "blessing/present" (33:11).[14] Though this is not the paternal blessing that was bestowed on Jacob by Isaac, Jacob seeks to partially compensate his brother, Esau, for having taken what rightfully belonged to him.

The subject of paternal blessing also figures prominently in Genesis 48 and 49. In the first of these we have the account of how Jacob blesses Joseph's two sons, Manasseh and Ephraim. Not only does Jacob deliberately give the younger son, Ephraim, the superior blessing (48:17–20), but also Ephraim receives the rights of the firstborn that should have gone to his father's oldest brother, Reuben (cf. 1 Chron. 5:1). This event established the tradition that through the tribe of Ephraim, God would create a royal dynasty. Undoubtedly this idea influenced later developments, especially the choice of Joshua as a leader and the importance of Shiloh, in the tribal region of Ephraim, as the location for the central sanctuary. All this changed, however, when God rejected the Ephraimites due to their wrongdoing and chose David as king and Jerusalem as his temple-city (Ps. 78:59–72).

In Genesis 49 we have a long list of pronouncements that Jacob makes regarding his twelve sons. The narrator's comment in 49:28 indicates that these are given in the context of Jacob's blessing his sons, with each one receiving "the blessing appropriate to him." Clearly the content of these blessings reflects Jacob's attitude toward each son. Without examining them in detail, it is significant that the pronouncements concerning the eldest brothers—Reuben, Simeon, and Levi—are all negative, whereas those given to Judah and Joseph are very favorable. In the light of the special interest that Genesis has in the theme of blessing, Jacob's comments about Joseph are noteworthy:

> Joseph is a fruitful vine,
>   a fruitful vine near a spring,
>   whose branches climb over a wall.
> With bitterness archers attacked him;
>   they shot at him with hostility.

---

14. M. A. Fishbane, "Composition and Structure in the Jacob Cycle (Gen. 25:19–35:22)," *JJS* 26 (1975): 15–38. Fishbane highlights how the story is enriched by a wordplay involving the key terms "birthright" (Hebrew *běkôrâ*; cf. Gen. 25:31–34; 27:36) and "blessing/gift" (*běrākâ*; cf. Gen. 27:12, 35–36, 38, 41; 28:4; 33:11).

> But his bow remained steady,
>> his strong arms stayed limber,
> because of the hand of the Mighty One of Jacob,
>> because of the Shepherd, the Rock of Israel,
> because of your father's God, who helps you,
>> because of the Almighty, who blesses you
> with blessings of the skies above,
>> blessings of the deep springs below,
>> blessings of the breast and womb.
> Your father's blessings are greater
>> than the blessings of the ancient mountains,
>> than the bounty of the age-old hills.
> Let all these rest on the head of Joseph,
>> on the brow of the prince among his brothers.
>
> Gen. 49:22–26

Here, as in Genesis 48, we encounter the idea of blessing coming through Joseph's descendants. Although Joseph is richly blessed, when Jacob blesses Judah, he declares that "the scepter will not depart from Judah" and that one of his descendants will enjoy "the obedience of the nations" (49:10). Although it is not explicitly stated that the nations will be blessed as a result, in the light of Genesis as a whole, this is possibly implied.

By highlighting the patriarchs' special relationship with God and their ability to impart a unique blessing to one of their sons, Genesis draws attention to the privileged position of the "seed" of the chosen lineage. As a result, the expectation is created that through a future royal descendant all the nations of the earth will be blessed.

Old Testament Summary

As a whole the book of Genesis records three important phases regarding the theme of divine blessing. At the outset all of creation, including especially humanity, experiences God's favor. However, as a result of the disobedience of Adam and Eve, a significant reversal occurs with human beings and the rest of creation coming under God's curse. The tragic consequences of this are reported throughout the rest of Genesis. However, at the beginning of the Abraham narrative, God promises not only to bless Abraham but also through him to bless all the families of the earth. The remaining episodes of the patriarchal narratives focus on this latter promise by linking it to the firstborn/royal "seed" of Abraham. Although none of them is biologically the firstborn, Isaac, Jacob, and Joseph are all treated as such, and through them blessing is imparted to others. While Joseph stands out in Genesis as the one who comes closest to fulfilling the divine promise of international blessing,

159

the ultimate fulfillment of God's promise to bless all the nations of the earth through the "seed" of Abraham still lies in the future. Genesis thus establishes the concept that through a (royal) "firstborn" descendant of Abraham, God's blessing will be imparted to the nations of the earth.

New Testament Connections

The most obvious allusions in the New Testament to the theme of blessing in Genesis come in Acts 3:25–26 and Galatians 3:14. In the first of these passages, Peter suggests that Jesus Christ is the one through whom God's blessing will come to others. "And you are heirs of the prophets and of the covenant God made with your fathers. He said to Abraham, 'Through your offspring all peoples on earth will be blessed.' When God raised up his servant, he sent him first to you to bless you by turning each of you from your wicked ways" (Acts 3:25–26). Paul makes the same point in Galatians: "He redeemed us in order that the blessing given to Abraham might come to the Gentiles through Christ Jesus" (Gal. 3:14). In both of these contexts, Jesus Christ, the "seed" of Abraham, is the one through whom the divine promise that all peoples of earth will be blessed is fulfilled. The same idea is also prominent in Romans 15:8–12, although the concept of blessing is not mentioned specifically. With these passages one might also include Romans 4:6–9. Though Paul does not specifically mention the text of Genesis in these verses, his brief comment regarding divine blessing, based on Psalm 32:1–2, comes in the context of his argument that Abraham is the father of those who have faith, both Jews and Gentiles.

Other passages that may allude indirectly to the concept of blessing highlighted in Genesis include Elizabeth's reaction to Mary in Luke 1:42–45 and the beatitudes of Jesus in Matthew 5:3–12 and Luke 6:20–26.

11

Paradise Lost

The motif of "land" is important in Genesis due to the special relationship that God establishes between the first man and the ground, a relationship reflected in their respective names *'ādām* and *'ādāmâ*. At harmony with God, each depends on the other. However, when the first human couple disobeyed the LORD God and ate of the forbidden fruit, two important consequences followed. First, their relationship with the ground was severely affected; no longer did the earth give willingly of its bounty to satisfy their needs. Second, they were expelled from Eden and so deprived of a unique environment in which to commune with God. With every subsequent unrighteous act, humankind was further alienated from the earth. The accounts of Cain's killing Abel, Noah and the flood, and the tower of Babel all reveal the increasing tension that existed between humanity and the earth. In each episode divine judgment comes in the form of exile and alienation. Against this background the divine gift of land to Abraham is significant. It is indicative of Abraham's positive relationship with the LORD and anticipates the divine presence in the midst of the nation of Israel.

Introduction

A careful reading of Genesis reveals that the concept of land figures prominently in the thinking of the author. From the initial creation of the dry land through to Joseph's desire that his bones be buried in the land promised by God to Abraham, Isaac, and Jacob, hardly an episode in the entire book does

161

not in one way or another mention land. Although not all references to land are to be viewed as equally important, it is clear that the relationship between humans and the earth is of major interest to the author.

Before looking at the theme of land in Genesis, it may be helpful to observe briefly that in the Hebrew text three terms are used for "land." By far the most common is the word 'ereṣ ('erets), which comes 312 times in Genesis. Usually 'ereṣ denotes either the earth as a whole (e.g., 1:1, 10, 26) or a particular country (e.g., 12:1, 5). The term 'ădāmâ occurs 43 times and normally means "ground" or "soil" (e.g., 2:5, 7, 19). The third term is śādeh, which comes approximately 50 times in Genesis and usually refers to wide-open spaces, it is often translated "field" (e.g., 2:19, 20). Although it is possible to view each term as having distinctive aspects, they may on occasions be used to denote the same thing.[1]

The Creation of the Earth

The opening chapter of Genesis establishes the nature of the earth's relationship to both God and humanity. Of fundamental importance is the belief that the earth is created by God; by merely speaking he both fills and brings order to that which is "formless and empty" (1:2). With the creation of the dry land, God establishes three distinct realms: "sky," "land," and "seas" (1:6–10). Of these the most important is the land. Unlike the sky and the seas, the land plays an active role in God's creative activity. It is divinely commanded to produce both vegetation (1:11–12) and living creatures (1:24). Having created the earth, God delegates authority to human beings to govern it and its creatures (cf. 1:28).

Complementing Genesis 1, the account in 2:4–25 develops more fully the close relationship that exists between the man and the ground. First, the man is actually made from the ground: "The LORD God formed a man from the dust of the ground and breathed into his nostrils the breath of life, and the man became a living being" (2:7). Second, in the Hebrew original the terms for "man" and "ground" are very similar; they are respectively 'ādām and 'ădāmâ.[2] This unique relationship between the first man and the ground is further emphasized when the LORD God places him in the Garden of Eden

---

1. An interesting example of this comes in the Abraham narrative. The expression "all peoples on earth" (lit., "families of the ground") in Gen. 12:3 is later replaced by the expression "all nations on earth" (18:18; 22:18). No essential difference in meaning is meant. However, in 12:3 the emphasis is on the oneness of all humans in that they have a common origin, the dust of the ground. The expression in 18:18 and 22:18 highlights the idea that the earth consists of different nations. The switch from the former expression to the latter suggests that the creation of Israel as a nation is linked to the fulfillment of the divine promise that the nations will be blessed.

2. In English we might capture the connection between the terms 'ādām and 'ădāmâ by translating them as "earthling" and "earth" respectively.

and permits him to enjoy freely, with one exception, all its produce (2:16–17). Thus Genesis 1–2 highlights the special relationship that exists among God, humanity, and the land/ground. Humans are charged by God to exercise authority over the earth, and the earth is divinely empowered to produce food in abundance for humankind. Dependent on each other, humanity and the earth are both accountable to God.

Expelled from Eden

The harmony of Eden ends when the man and the woman knowingly disobey God and eat from the tree of the knowledge of good and evil (3:1–13; cf. 2:16–17). Two consequences are significant regarding the subject of land. First, God curses the ground because of Adam's disobedience (3:17–19). No longer is the ground divinely empowered to produce food in abundance. Man must work by the sweat of his brow in order to eat. Furthermore, his task is made more difficult because the ground "will produce thorns and thistles" (3:18). No longer is the man at harmony with the ground from which he was taken and on which he depends for food.

Second, the man and the woman are banished from the Garden of Eden (3:23). Like a landlord expelling an unsatisfactory tenant, God ousts them from Eden. The reason for their expulsion is recorded by the narrator: "He must not be allowed to reach out his hand and take also from the tree of life and eat, and live forever" (3:22). Separated from the tree of life, each human will experience death, the divine punishment for eating from the tree of the knowledge of good and evil (2:17). To ensure that humans may not return to Eden, God places "cherubim and a flaming sword flashing back and forth to guard the way to the tree of life" (3:24). Expelled from Eden, Adam and Eve will no longer enjoy the intimacy of God's presence. Although this does not mark the end of God's relationship with humanity, it does indicate a dramatic change. The special relationship that was established at creation will exist only with those to whom God now makes himself known. No longer will humanity automatically have a personal knowledge of God. As a result of human disobedience, the initial harmony of creation between God, humanity, and the land is replaced by alienation.

Cain, a Restless Wanderer on the Earth

The relationship between humans and the ground is important in the story of Cain's killing of his brother Abel. Initially Cain is described as one who "worked the soil [ground]" (4:2). When, out of jealousy, he kills his brother, the LORD God confronts him regarding his crime. The relationship between Cain's action and the ground is highlighted in God's speech: "What have you done? Listen! Your brother's blood cries out to me from the ground. Now you are under a curse and driven from the ground, which opened its mouth to receive your brother's blood from your hand. When you work the ground, it will no longer yield its crop for you. You will be a restless wanderer on the earth" (4:10–12). Adam's punishment resulted in the ground being difficult to till; now Cain is actually "driven from the ground" and forced to become a restless wanderer. He must also go out from the LORD's presence (4:14, 16). Alienated from both God and the ground, Cain receives a punishment like that of his parents.

Two points are worth underlining from the story of Cain's killing of Abel. First, the narrative highlights the continuing relationship between humanity and the ground. Cain's actions have a direct bearing on the ground: it is stained by Abel's blood. Second, each unrighteous action increases humanity's alienation from the ground. The ground, which was to nourish humankind, is now the agent of divine punishment. The natural environment no longer automatically favors humanity as God intended; it is now hostile, and the degree of this hostility is determined in some measure by the extent of human unrighteousness.

The Flood Narrative

The subject of land is prominent in the account of Noah's rescue from the flood. It first appears in the naming of Noah by his father, Lamech: "When Lamech had lived 182 years, he had a son. He named him Noah and said, 'He will comfort us in the labor and painful toil of our hands caused by the ground the LORD has cursed'" (5:28–29).[3]

Here Noah is presented as the one who will bring relief to those already heavily burdened by the task of working the ground. Behind this comment is the hope that Noah will reverse the ever-worsening relationship between humanity and the ground.

God's decision to send a flood that will destroy all living creatures is clearly linked to the wickedness of humankind (cf. 6:5). "Now the earth was corrupt in God's sight and was full of violence. God saw how corrupt the earth had become, for all the people on earth had corrupted their ways. So God said to Noah, 'I am going to put an end to all people, for the earth is filled with violence because of them. I am surely going to destroy both them and the earth'" (6:11–13). Once again we see how the continual violence of humanity has a direct bearing on the earth. Through the shedding of innocent blood, the ground is polluted, reducing its fertility. Consequently the task of tilling the ground had become almost unbearable by the time of Noah.

3. Although the name Noah is probably linked etymologically to the Hebrew verb *nûaḥ* (*nûakh*), meaning "to rest," it also sounds like the Hebrew verb *niḥam* (*nikham*), "to comfort."

The flood narrative in 6:9–9:19 exhibits close parallels with Genesis 1. The description of the floodwaters gradually covering the entire earth, including the highest mountains, portrays a return to the earth's original state before the separation of the land and seas (cf. 1:9–10). With the retreat of the floodwaters and Noah's departure from the ark, we have the re-creation of the earth.[4] Consequently those who emerge from the ark now inhabit ground that has been cleansed from the pollution caused by unrighteous behavior. Although the earth has been re-created, the same is not true of human nature, for as God comments, "Every inclination of the human heart is evil from childhood" (8:21). Nevertheless, God promises that he will never again "curse the ground because of humans" (8:21) by sending another flood.[5] This is later confirmed in the covenant outlined in 9:8–17.

Before the flood the shedding of innocent blood polluted the ground, significantly decreasing its fertility. In 9:1–7 God issues instructions intended to prevent the earth from being contaminated in the future. These focus on the "lifeblood" of both animals and humans, which must be treated with due respect.

Noah, a Man of the Soil

The episode following the account of the flood begins by describing Noah as a "man of the soil [ground]" (9:20) and focuses briefly on his ability to cultivate a vineyard that produces an abundant crop. This part of the story is clearly intended to highlight the dramatic change that has occurred as a result of the

4. According to G. V. Smith, the flood narrative echoes the initial account of creation in the following ways:

> When Genesis 1 and 2 are compared with 8 and 9, one begins to perceive the extent to which the author uses repeated phrases and ideas to build the structural relationships within the units. The following relationships are found: (a) Since man could not live on the earth when it was covered with water in chaps. 1 and 8, a subsiding of the water and separation of the land from the water took place, allowing the dry land to appear (1:9–10; 8:1–13); (b) "birds and animals and every creeping thing that creeps on the earth" are brought forth to "swarm upon the earth" in 1:20–21, 24–25 and 8:17–19; (c) God establishes the days and seasons in 1:14–18 and 8:22; (d) God's blessing rests upon the animals as he commands them to "be fruitful and multiply on the earth" in both 1:22 and 8:17; (e) man is brought forth and he receives the blessing of God: "Be fruitful and multiply and fill the earth" in 1:28 and 9:1, 7; (f) Man is given dominion over the animal kingdom in 1:28 and 9:2; (g) God provides food for man in 1:29–30 and 9:3 (this latter regulation makes a direct reference back to the previous passage when it includes the statement, "As I have given the green plant"); and (h) in 9:6 the writer quotes from 1:26–27 concerning the image of God in man. The author repeatedly emphasizes the fact that the world is beginning again with a fresh start. But Noah does not return to the paradise of Adam, for the significant difference is that "the intent of man's heart is evil" (Gen. 8:21) ("Structure and Purpose in Genesis 1–11," *JETS* 20 [1977]: 310–11).

5. As we have noted in chap. 10, this refers to the flood.

flood. Though the ground's fertility was severely limited before the flood, now it produces abundantly. In this we see the fulfillment of Lamech's comments regarding Noah in 5:29.

The Table of Nations

The Table of Nations in Genesis 10 outlines where the descendants of Noah gradually settle.[6] Of particular note are the details concerning Canaan and his sons; 10:15–18 provides a detailed list of the various people descended from Canaan, and 10:19 describes the borders of the land of Canaan. These details are significant in the light of later events in Genesis, when God promises Abraham that his descendants will possess the land of Canaan (cf. 15:18–21). This development clearly builds on the blessing that Noah pronounces on Shem, which contrasts sharply with the curse upon Canaan (9:25–27).

The Abraham Narrative

The Abraham narrative marks an important turning point in the book of Genesis. This is certainly true regarding the subject of land. Whereas the early chapters of Genesis are dominated by accounts of human disobedience resulting in exile, one of the main themes of the story of Abraham is God's gift of land to Abraham and his descendants.

Several factors are significant regarding God's promise of the land of Canaan to Abraham. First, it is conditional on Abraham's obedience to God. At the very outset Abraham must obey the LORD's call to leave his own land and go to a new land (12:1). Implicit in this divine command, and in the associated promise that God will make Abraham "into a great nation" (12:2), is the idea that God will give Abraham a new land. The identity of this land is soon revealed as Canaan (12:5–7); even though it is already occupied by the Canaanites (12:6), the LORD confirms that Abraham's descendants will possess it. Later, in the account of the separation of Abraham and Lot, the promise of land is stated in more detail (cf. 13:14–17). These initial promises,

6. This genealogical-geographical passage describes a process that covered a long period of time, as family clans migrated to particular regions. The ancestor, after whom the clan or tribe is named, may not have lived in the region that later bears his name. Each of the three main parts of this section concludes with a reference to clans, languages, and nations (Gen. 10:5, 20, 31). Because this passage indicates that the descendants of Noah were divided into different clans and nations, each with its own language, the material in Gen. 10 ought chronologically to come after the account of the tower of Babel (11:1–9); 10:25 probably alludes to the creation of different nations, speaking different languages. The writer of Genesis may have felt it inappropriate to place the Table of Nations between 11:1–9 and 11:10–26, since this would bring into immediate proximity two quite different types of genealogy, both concerning the descendants of Shem.

however, are given added weight by the covenant that God makes with Abraham in 15:7–21.[7] This unconditional covenant is ratified by God in the light of Abraham's being credited as righteous on account of his faith (15:6). The early chapters of Genesis focus on the loss of land as a result of disobedience; now Abraham is portrayed as gaining the land due to obedience and trust in God.

Second, God informs Abraham that his descendants will occupy the land of Canaan only after a period of over four hundred years (15:13–14). The announcement of this delay has important implications for the rest of the Pentateuch. Although Genesis records that Abraham and Isaac live within the borders of Canaan, the concluding chapters describe how Jacob and his family leave Canaan to dwell in Egypt. The remaining books of the Pentateuch focus on the future exodus of the Israelites from Egypt and developments that occur before they take possession of the promised land.

Third, although Abraham is divinely promised the land of Canaan, various peoples already occupy the land. This naturally raises a question: How can God give to Abraham land that is already owned by others? The author of Genesis, however, answers this question indirectly by indicating that the inhabitants of Canaan are unworthy occupants of the land. We first encounter this idea prior to the Abraham narrative itself, in 9:20–29. Here attention is drawn to the unrighteous behavior of Ham and the resulting curse on his son Canaan. Implicit in this is the idea that the descendants of Canaan may behave like their forefather Ham. The identity of these descendants is provided in 10:15–18, along with details of the land occupied by them (10:19). "Canaan was the father of Sidon his firstborn, and of the Hittites, Jebusites, Amorites, Girgashites, Hivites, Arkites, Sinites, Arvadites, Zemarites and Hamathites. Later the Canaanite clans scattered and the borders of Canaan reached from Sidon toward Gerar as far as Gaza, and then toward Sodom, Gomorrah, Admah and Zeboiim, as far as Lasha" (10:15–19). Within the Abraham story itself, various passages draw attention to the unrighteous nature of the descendants of Ham. In 13:13 the narrator comments, "Now the people of Sodom were wicked and were sinning greatly against the LORD." This negative view of the Canaanite inhabitants of Sodom is reflected in Abraham's attitude toward the king of Sodom (14:21–24), especially when compared with his reaction to Melchizedek, king of Salem (14:18–20). In the light of these passages, the later account of the destruction of Sodom and Gomorrah in Genesis 19 is hardly surprising; indeed, it is anticipated in 13:10. God's comment in 18:20–21 about the sin of Sodom and Gomorrah is confirmed by the events surrounding the visit of the two angels in Genesis 19. Significantly, the sexual nature of the sin of the men of Sodom is reminiscent of the unrighteous action of their ancestor Ham. Another reference to the sin of Ham's descendants comes in

---

7. Although further references to the land occur in the Abraham narrative (e.g., 17:8; 22:17), the covenant in Gen. 15 marks a climax regarding land.

15:16. Here God indicates that Abraham's descendants will return to the land of Canaan in the fourth generation, "for the sin of the Amorites has not yet reached its full measure." Since the early chapters of Genesis have established the idea that unrighteous behavior results in exile from the land, there can be little doubt that the present inhabitants of Canaan will be dispossessed due to their sin. The later conquest of the land by the Israelites is thus understood to be an act of divine judgment on those already living there.[8]

Fourth, although Abraham is divinely promised that his descendants will not take possession of the land of Canaan until several centuries later, by allowing Abraham to buy the cave of Machpelah in Ephron's field the Hittites of Hebron acknowledge Abraham's right to be an inhabitant of Canaan (23:1–20). Moreover, because the land is bought for the purpose of being a burial place, this guarantees Abraham's descendants a permanent right of ownership. Although the divine promise of the land will not be fulfilled until the future, Abraham witnesses the beginning of the process.

The Jacob Story

The story of Jacob revolves around his temporary exile in the region of Paddan Aram, caused when he deceives his father into giving him the firstborn blessing. In spite of his deceitful behavior, Jacob receives various assurances regarding the land of Canaan. The first comes from his father in 28:4. Although Isaac encourages Jacob to leave Canaan in order to find a wife, he prays that God Almighty will bless him: "May he give you and your descendants the blessing given to Abraham, so that you may take possession of the land where you now reside as a foreigner, the land God gave to Abraham" (28:4).

Next, just as Jacob is about to depart from Canaan God reassures him regarding the land through a dream at Bethel:

> I am the LORD, the God of your father Abraham and the God of Isaac. I will give you and your descendants the land on which you are lying. Your descendants will be like the dust of the earth, and you will spread out to the west and to the east, to the north and to the south. All peoples on earth will be blessed through you and your offspring. I am with you and will watch over you wherever you go, and I will bring you back to this land. I will not leave you until I have done what I have promised you. (28:13–15)

Although Jacob must flee from Canaan on account of Esau, the narrative anticipates his future return. Much later the divine promise of land is again repeated to Jacob (35:11–12).

8. On different occasions the same principle of judgment and exile was later applied to the inhabitants of the northern kingdom of Israel and the southern kingdom of Judah.

The turning point in Jacob's exile in Paddan Aram comes when the LORD says to him, "Go back to the land of your fathers and to your relatives, and I will be with you" (31:3). With this assurance, Jacob prepares to return to Canaan. Though he has arrived in Paddan Aram alone, he leaves with a large family and numerous possessions. In spite of all that the LORD has done for him in Paddan Aram, Jacob is still very conscious of the reason for his exile there. Consequently, on returning to the borders of Canaan, he makes preparations for his encounter with Esau (32:1–21). Just as Jacob experienced the LORD's presence when he left Canaan (28:10–22), so once again he has a dramatic meeting with the LORD as he is about to reenter the land (32:22–32). By locating these theophanies on the border of Canaan, the narrative draws attention to the importance of the land.

The reconciliation between Jacob and Esau not only brings to an end the conflict that has separated them for years (33:1–16), but it also results in Jacob's settling in the land of Canaan (33:17–20). Esau, however, eventually settles outside Canaan, in the land of Seir (33:16; 36:6–8). Remarkably, this parting of the brothers echoes the earlier separation of Abraham and Lot; Jacob and Esau agree to dwell in different regions because the land is not able to support all their livestock (36:7–8; cf. 13:5–18). As a result Jacob is the one left dwelling in the land of Canaan.

The Joseph Story

The final quarter of Genesis revolves around the character of Joseph and tells of his role in bringing the descendants of Abraham out of Canaan and into Egypt. Given God's comments to Abraham, "that for four hundred years your descendants will be strangers in a country not their own and that they will be enslaved and mistreated there" (15:13), the Joseph story provides an essential link between the Abraham and Jacob narratives and the later account of the exodus from Egypt. The overall plot of the Pentateuch requires a transition from Canaan to Egypt.

Several features of the Joseph story invite further comments regarding the topic of land. First, it is a famine in Canaan that brings the brothers of Joseph back into contact with him in Egypt. Throughout Genesis, famines are associated with God's curse upon the earth; they reflect the absence of divine blessing and highlight the lack of harmony that ought to exist between humans and the ground. But for the preparations made by Joseph, the effects of this famine would have been much more terrible.

Second, given Jacob's own experience of having been exiled from Canaan in Paddan Aram, it is not surprising that he is somewhat reluctant to leave Canaan again. He goes only when the LORD intervenes and commands him to do so: "Do not be afraid to go down to Egypt, for I will make you into a great nation there. I will go down to Egypt with you, and I will surely bring you back again. And Joseph's own hand will close your eyes" (46:3–4). Jacob's reluctance to go to Egypt should be viewed against other episodes in Genesis. Earlier, during a famine in Canaan, Abraham had gone down to Egypt (12:10–20). However, his experience there had placed in jeopardy the fulfillment of the divine promises. Later, when another famine occurred in the land of Canaan, Isaac was specifically commanded by God not to go down into Egypt (26:1–2). In the light of these events, Jacob may have felt strongly inclined to remain in Canaan.

Third, although the movement in the Joseph story is from Canaan to Egypt, there are various indications that this is not to be a permanent move. This is reflected, for example, in God's words to Jacob: "I will surely bring you back again" (46:4). The Israelites' attachment to Canaan is also reflected in the events surrounding the death of Jacob. After his death, Jacob's embalmed body is transported back to Canaan to be buried in the cave at Machpelah alongside the bodies of Abraham and Isaac (49:29–50:14). Later, Joseph makes a similar request that his bones should be carried up from Egypt to Canaan (50:24–25). Significantly, Joseph does not expect this to happen immediately after his death, as with his father, but thinks in terms of this being done when God comes to the aid of the Israelites (cf. Exod. 13:19). Thus, although Genesis ends with the account of Joseph's death, there is an expectation of things yet to come; the Israelites shall one day return to the promised land.

Old Testament Summary

Throughout the book, Genesis emphasizes the close relationship that humans have with the ground. The basis for this interdependence is explained in the account of creation where the first man, Adam (*'ādām*), is created from the dust of the ground (*'ādāmâ*). Unfortunately, although God initially blesses the relationship between humanity and the earth, the disobedience of Adam and Eve in the Garden of Eden leads to a dramatic reversal of this situation. Moreover, Adam and Eve are exiled from Eden, ending the intimate relationship that they enjoyed there with the LORD. Later, through the promises given to Abraham, the restoration of divine blessing becomes a possibility. This, however, will be fully achieved only when all the families of the ground are blessed. In the meantime Abraham is assured that, as part of the process by which the nations shall be blessed, his descendants will possess the land of Canaan. For them Canaan will partly resemble the Garden of Eden: there the people will enjoy a special communion with God, surrounded by signs of God's blessing upon the land.[9]

9. For a fuller discussion of the implications of this, see T. D. Alexander, "Beyond Borders: The Wider Dimensions of Land," in *The Land of Promise: Biblical, Theological and Contemporary Perspectives*, ed. P. Johnston and P. Walker (Leicester: Apollos, 2000), 35–50.

New Testament Connections

The New Testament develops the concept of land in ways that are both similar and dissimilar to those found in Genesis. To appreciate the reason for this, it is important to observe that in Genesis the theme of land comes in two different contexts. First, it is used in the context of humanity as a whole. All humans must daily confront the reality that nature is under God's curse due to humanity's disobedience—from Adam and Eve onward. The New Testament makes it clear that nature, like all believers, awaits redemption from the bondage of decay (Rom. 8:19–25). For Paul, the reconciliation of all things to God is achieved by Jesus Christ "through his blood, shed on the cross" (Col. 1:20; cf. 2 Cor. 5:17–21; Eph. 1:7–10). Significantly, Paul views Christ not only as the one responsible for the restoration of harmony within the cosmos, but also as the creator of all things in the first instance (Col. 1:15–17; cf. 1 Cor. 8:6). Similar ideas are found elsewhere in the New Testament (e.g., John 1:3; Heb. 1:2).

The climax of the re-creation process is the appearance of a new heaven and a new earth, where God and humans live together in harmony (Rev. 21:1). Portrayed in Revelation 21:1–22:5 in terms of "the Holy City, the new Jerusalem, coming down out of heaven from God" (21:2), this city marks the completion of the building project that was first associated with the Garden of Eden. Various factors suggest this, the most significant being the reference to the "tree of life" (22:2; cf. Gen. 2:9; 3:22, 24) and the comment that "no longer will there be any curse" (Rev. 22:3). However, whereas Eden is presented as prime development land, the "new Jerusalem" is a fully constructed city.

For the author of Hebrews, the goal of God's redemptive activity for humanity is expressed in terms of rest (Heb. 4:1–11). Two related ideas are developed. First, this rest resembles that which God enjoyed following the creation of the heavens and the earth (Gen. 2:2–3) and which humanity lost as a result of the disruption of creation following the disobedience of Adam and Eve. Second, due to their disobedience the ancient Israelites failed to obtain such rest when they took possession of the land of Canaan. However, the opportunity to enter into God's rest still exists for those who believe the gospel.

The second context in which land is used in an important way in Genesis has to do with the establishment of Abraham's descendants as a nation in the land of Canaan. With the introduction of a new covenant embracing all nations, it is hardly surprising that the New Testament plays down the importance of Israel as a nation. Israel's role in God's purposes has now dramatically changed; as a consequence, it is no longer important that Israel should possess the land of Canaan. Though the Sinai covenant centered on one nation, the new covenant is international in its scope. Although the promise of land to Abraham in Genesis is generally stated in terms of the land of Canaan (12:7; 13:14–17; 15:18–21; 17:8), there are indications that for the nations to be blessed, Abraham's "seed" would exercise authority over the entire earth (49:10; cf. 22:17; Ps. 2:8; Mic. 5:2–5). In the light of this movement from one nation, Israel, to all nations, it is hardly surprising that there is a similar shift from thinking in terms of one land to the whole world. This, for example, is reflected in Paul's treatment of the fifth commandment, to honor one's father and mother, in Ephesians 6:2–3. In the original context of Exodus 20:12 and Deuteronomy 5:16, the commandment includes the promise of long life in possession of the land of Canaan; in Ephesians Paul expands this to include the whole earth.

12

By Faith Abraham . . .

The Abraham story (Gen. 11:27–25:11) forms the heart of the book of Genesis. At the outset Abraham is the recipient of major divine promises (12:1–3), with the fulfillment of these being linked to Abraham's obedience to God. As the narrative develops, special attention is drawn to how Abraham's faith in God is credited to him as righteousness (15:6). In response, God covenants unconditionally to give Abraham's descendants the land of Canaan (15:18–21). Later God initiates a second covenant, which differs from the first in two main ways: (1) it guarantees that Abraham will be the "father" of many nations who will be blessed through him and his "seed"; (2) in order for the covenant to be established, Abraham must remain loyal and obedient to God. This second covenant is later established by divine oath when Abraham displays total trust in God through his willingness to sacrifice his son Isaac (22:16–18). The entire narrative highlights Abraham's faith in God as he awaits the fulfillment of the initial divine promises.

Introduction

In terms of the number of chapters given over to him, Abraham is clearly the most important of all the human characters in Genesis. Moreover, his life marks an important watershed in God's relationship with human beings. Although Genesis 3–11 gives indications that divine mercy will triumph over the consequences of Adam and Eve's betrayal of God, it is with Abraham that a clearer picture begins to emerge. The divine promises associated with his call (12:1–3) reveal that he is to play a central role in restoring humanity's broken relationship with God.

Overview of the Abraham Narrative

The Abraham narrative falls into two sections, separated by a brief genealogy in 22:20–24; the main section consists of 11:27–22:19, with 23:1–25:11 forming an appendix. Running through the main section are the three closely intertwined themes of seed, land, and blessing.

Within the Abraham narrative the theme of seed centers on the divine assurance that Abraham will have many descendants. The initial promises that Abraham will become a "great nation" (12:2) and that his "seed" will possess the land of Canaan (12:7) are set against the background of Sarah's inability to have children (11:30). Later, after the LORD assures Abraham that he will have a son of his own and many descendants (15:1–5), Sarah persuades him to have a child by her maidservant Hagar (16:1–4).[1] By naming him, Abraham claims Ishmael as his own (16:15). Afterward, however, God on two separate occasions reveals that Sarah will indeed have a son who will be Abraham's true heir (17:15–21; 18:9–15). Eventually Sarah gives birth to Isaac (21:1–7), and he is established as Abraham's heir through the divinely approved departure of Hagar and Ishmael (21:8–21). Isaac's birth marks the first step toward the fulfillment of the divine promise that Abraham will become a "great nation" and have numerous descendants.

The second theme in the Abraham narrative concerns land. Initially God commands Abraham to leave his own land and "go . . . to the land I will show you" (12:1). Although it is not mentioned specifically that Abraham will possess this land, the promise that he will become a "great nation" (12:2) implies that his descendants will possess it; the Hebrew term *gôy*, "nation," denotes people inhabiting a specific geographical location and forming a political unit. Thus, when Abraham first arrives in Canaan, the LORD promises, "To your offspring [seed] I will give this land" (12:7). Later, following the separation of Lot from Abraham, God repeats this promise, emphasizing the extent of the land to be possessed by Abraham's descendants (13:14–17).[2] The topic of land reappears in 15:7–21, where the idea is introduced that Abraham's descendants will take possession of the land of Canaan only after a period of four hundred years, during which they will be slaves in another country (15:13–14). This revelation of a delay regarding the acquisition of the land probably explains why the promise of land, which is very prominent in Genesis 12–15, is mentioned

---

1. It was a custom in the ancient Near East that the maidservant of a barren wife might act as a surrogate mother.
2. Although Abraham is mentioned as possessing the land, there is no suggestion that the present inhabitants of the land will be dispossessed during Abraham's lifetime.

less frequently in the remaining chapters of the Abraham narrative (cf. 17:8; 22:17). Although later episodes highlight Abraham's acquisition of a well at Beersheba and a tomb at Hebron, these mark only the beginning of the process by which God will fulfill his promise to Abraham regarding nationhood.

The third main strand in the Abraham narrative is, as we have already noticed in chapter 10, the idea that Abraham and his "seed" will be a source of divine blessing, or possibly cursing, for others. This is highlighted in both the initial call of Abraham and the concluding oath in 22:16–18. Although various episodes partly reflect the divine blessing or cursing of others (e.g., the visit to Egypt [12:10–20], the abduction of Lot by the eastern kings [14:1–24], the rescue of Lot from Sodom [18:16–19:29], the abduction of Sarah by Abimelech [20:1–18], and the treaty between Abimelech and Abraham [21:22–34]), it is clear that, like the promise of nationhood, the promise of God's blessing on all the families of the earth will only be fulfilled in the future (cf. 22:18).

This brief survey of the themes of seed, land, and blessing establishes their presence within Genesis 12–25. To explore further how they are developed within the Abraham narrative, we shall examine in more detail the initial call of Abraham in 12:1–3, the covenants in Genesis 15 and 17, and the divine oath in 22:16–18. This will enable us to have a clearer picture of how the overall narrative is structured.

The Divine Call of Abraham in Genesis 12:1–3

Within the context of the book of Genesis, the divine speech in 12:1–3 is very important. It marks the beginning of a new stage in God's relationship with humanity, sets the agenda for the entire Abraham story and beyond, and introduces themes that will be developed in the following narrative. The LORD says to Abraham, "Leave your country, your people, and your father's household and go to the land I will show you, so that I may make you into a great nation and bless you and make your name great. Be a blessing, so that I may bless those who bless you, and curse the one who disdains you, and so that all the families of the ground may be blessed through you" (12:1–3, my trans.). Two features of this speech are noteworthy in the present context. First, the fulfillment of the divine promises is conditional on Abraham's obedience. By commanding him to leave his homeland and be a blessing, God places the onus on Abraham to obey in order that the promises concerning land, descendants, and the blessing of others may be fulfilled.[3] Second, the climax of the speech comes in the statement that "all the families of the ground may

3. As it stands, the divine speech to Abraham falls naturally into two halves, each introduced by an imperative. The first half focuses on the promise of nationhood (i.e., land and descendants); the second centers on the blessing of others. As we shall observe below, this twofold division is reflected in the two covenants found in Gen. 15 and 17.

be blessed through you." The primary motive behind the call of Abraham is God's desire to bring blessing, rather than cursing, on the nations of the earth. The promise that Abraham will become a great nation, implying both numerous seed and land, must be understood as being subservient to God's principal desire to bless all the families of the earth.[4]

Abraham's positive response to God's command is noted immediately, and his arrival in the land of Canaan is rewarded by the assurance that "to your offspring [seed] I will give this land" (12:7). The subject of land dominates Genesis 13: following the separation of Lot and Abraham, God confirms that Abraham's many descendants will take possession of the land of Canaan (cf. 13:14–17). The promise of land then comes to an important climax in Genesis 15, with God's covenanting to give Abraham's descendants the land "from the Wadi of Egypt to the great river, the Euphrates" (15:18).

The Unconditional Promissory Covenant of Genesis 15

Genesis 15 falls into two parts that have in common the subject of inheritance. Whereas verses 1–6 are concerned with Abraham's immediate and future heirs, verses 7–21 focus on what shall be inherited. God reassures Abraham that (1) he will have a son of his own from whom shall come numerous descendants, and (2) after several centuries these descendants will take possession of the land of Canaan. The two parts of the chapter parallel each other structurally. They both begin with a divine statement (15:1, 7), followed by a question from Abraham (15:2, 8). Next we have God's response involving an appropriate sign (15:4–5, 9–17),[5] and finally a concluding comment by the narrator (15:6, 18–21).

Two elements in the chapter deserve special attention. First, verse 6 contains the observation that "Abram believed the Lord, and he credited it to him as righteousness." The rarity in Genesis of such comments by the narrator makes them all the more important when they occur. Here Abraham is viewed as righteous in God's sight because he unreservedly believes that the Lord will fulfill his promise regarding a son and numerous descendants. Abraham is reckoned righteous on account of his faith in God's promise, rather than due to any deeds performed by him.

---

4. The importance of the theme of blessing is underlined by the fivefold repetition of the Hebrew root *brk*, "to bless," in 12:2–3.

5. The first sign, the stars in the heavens, conveys the vast number of Abraham's descendants. The second sign is more complex. Probably the sacrificial animals represent Abraham's descendants, the birds of prey are the Egyptians, and "the smoking brazier with a blazing torch" (my trans.) indicates God's presence. The sign thus looks forward to the release of the Israelites from slavery in Egypt and the subsequent presence of the Lord in their midst. After the exodus, God's presence is indicated by the pillar of cloud by day and the pillar of fire by night (Exod. 13:21; 19:18; 20:18).

Second, the LORD makes a covenant with Abraham and thereby affirms that his "seed" will possess the land of Canaan. This marks the climax of the earlier divine promises regarding land and descendants found in 12:7 and 13:14–17. Several features of the covenant are worth noting:

1. It unconditionally guarantees what the LORD has stated to Abraham. Nowhere is it indicated that the fulfillment of the covenant depends on the actions of either Abraham or his descendants; God unreservedly covenants to fulfill his promise that Abraham's descendants will possess the land of Canaan. For this reason it may be designated an unconditional promissory covenant.
2. The structure of the chapter suggests that there is a link between the making of the promissory covenant in verses 18–21 and the comment about Abraham's believing God in verse 6. Because of the righteousness attributed to Abraham, God blesses Abraham by guaranteeing that the divine promises regarding descendants and land will be fulfilled.
3. The terms of the covenant mention only descendants and possession of the land; there is no reference to blessing being mediated to others. This omission is significant and is one of the main ways in which this covenant differs from that outlined in Genesis 17. The covenant in Genesis 15 guarantees only some of the divine promises mentioned in 12:1–3. For the remainder we must look ahead to Genesis 17.

The Eternal Covenant of Circumcision

The introduction of a second covenant in Genesis 17 is somewhat surprising. Why should God make another covenant with Abraham? To answer this, it is necessary to observe that the covenant in Genesis 17 differs in a number of important ways from that given in Genesis 15. First, it is a conditional covenant. Whereas the promissory covenant of Genesis 15 is unconditional, the establishment or ratification of the covenant of circumcision depends on Abraham's continuing obedience to God. This is highlighted in the introduction to the covenant. After identifying himself as El Shaddai (God Almighty), the LORD says to Abraham, "Walk before me and be blameless so that I may confirm my covenant between me and you and increase you greatly" (17:1–2, my trans.; cf. ESV). Unfortunately, many English translations fail to appreciate the distinctive syntax of the Hebrew original and so miss the important link that exists between the initial imperatives, "Walk before me and be blameless," and the fact that these must be obeyed before the covenant will be established. The LORD will ratify the covenant only if Abraham walks before God and is blameless. For the actual establishment of the covenant, we must look to the divine oath that concludes the account of the testing of Abraham in Genesis 22.[6]

Second, the covenant of circumcision differs from the promissory covenant of Genesis 15 in that it is an eternal covenant. Whereas the covenant of Genesis 15 is a divine guarantee to Abraham that his descendants will possess the land of Canaan, the covenant of circumcision entails a continuing special relationship between God and Abraham's "seed."[7] Although the covenant will embrace those who are not Abraham's natural children—others within his household, including foreigners, may be circumcised (17:12)—God makes it clear that his covenant is intimately linked to the chosen family line; it will be established with the promised "seed" Isaac and not with Ishmael (17:19–21).

Third, whereas the emphasis in Genesis 15 is solely on descendants and land, the covenant in Genesis 17 focuses primarily on Abraham as the father of many nations. God states, "As for me, this is my covenant with you: You will be the father of many nations. No longer will you be called Abram; your name will be Abraham, for I have made you a father of many nations. I will make you very fruitful; I will make nations of you, and kings will come from you" (17:4–6). These words are briefly echoed regarding Sarah: "I will bless her so that she will be the mother of nations; kings of peoples will come from her" (17:16). The mention of nations coming from Abraham and Sarah presents a problem if this is interpreted as referring only to the nations directly descended from both of them; strictly speaking, only the Israelites and Edomites come within this category.[8] However, it is likely that the concept of "father" is not restricted here to actual physical descendants. Rather, Abraham is the "father" of all who are circumcised. God instructs Abraham to circumcise not merely his own family members but also every male "including those born in your household or bought with your money from a foreigner—those who are not your offspring [seed]. Whether born in your household or bought with your money, they must be circumcised" (17:12–13).[9]

6. Although the covenant of circumcision is initiated in Gen. 17, it is not finally established until Gen. 22. A period of time must elapse between the initiation and the establishment of the covenant due to its conditional nature. What establishes the covenant is not the act of circumcision itself, but obedience to God.

7. In Gen. 15:18 God "cuts a covenant" with Abraham (Hebrew *kārat běrît*); then in 17:7, 19, 21 God speaks of "establishing" an everlasting covenant (Hebrew *hēqîm běrît*) with Abraham and his "seed." This everlasting covenant will be established with Isaac, but not with Ishmael, even though he and other males in Abraham's household are circumcised (17:24–27). There is good reason to believe that the everlasting covenant is established with the members of the unique line of "seed" that is traced in Genesis from Abraham to Isaac and then Jacob, but not with all of Abraham's descendants.

8. The Israelites and Edomites are descended from Jacob and Esau respectively. The Ishmaelites and Midianites are probably not to be included here because they are not descended from Sarah.

9. Those who were circumcised enjoyed a special relationship with one another. We witness evidence of this in Gen. 34, where the sons of Jacob promise Shechem and his father Hamor that if they are circumcised, "Then we will give you our daughters and take your daughters

By changing Abram's name to Abraham, God underlines the importance of the fact that he will be the father of many nations. This occurs not because these nations are his natural descendants but because he is for them the channel of divine blessing. This understanding of "father" is probably reflected in the unusual comment that Joseph was "father to Pharaoh" (45:8). Furthermore, when God blesses Jacob in 35:11, echoing an earlier blessing by Isaac on Jacob (28:3), a distinction is drawn between "a nation" and "a community of nations" coming from him. The implication would seem to be that whereas many nations will be closely associated with him, only one nation will be directly descended from him.[10]

In the light of the divine promises given in 12:1–3, it is clear that the covenants in Genesis 15 and 17 complement each other. Whereas Genesis 15 focuses on descendants and land, the emphasis in Genesis 17 is on Abraham as the one who imparts God's blessing to others; in this capacity he is the father of many nations. This understanding of the covenant of circumcision is later reflected in the divine oath of Genesis 22, which establishes the covenant with Abraham.

The Divine Oath in Genesis 22:16–18

The divine speech in 22:16–18 forms a frame (*inclusio*) with Abraham's call in 12:1–3 and so brings to a conclusion the main section of the Abraham narrative. All that was promised conditionally in 12:1–3 is now guaranteed by divine oath: "I swear by myself, declares the LORD, that because you have done this and have not withheld your son, your only son, I will surely bless you and make your descendants [seed] as numerous as the stars in the sky and as the sand on the seashore. Your descendant [seed] will take possession of the gate of his enemies, and through your descendant [seed] all nations of the earth will be blessed, because you have obeyed me" (22:16–18, my trans.; cf. KJV, ESV). This oath not only signals the end of the main section of the Abraham narrative, but also establishes the covenant of circumcision promised in Genesis 17. By demonstrating his obedience to God, even to the point of being willing to sacrifice his son Isaac, Abraham fulfills the conditions laid down in 17:1; he shows beyond doubt his willingness to walk before God and be blameless.

---

for ourselves. We'll settle among you and become one people with you" (34:16). Against this background the killing by Simeon and Levi of all those who have just been circumcised is exceptionally repulsive to their father Jacob (34:24–31). What God has intended to be a symbol of family solidarity is misused for the destruction of others.

10. The same idea of blessing as being mediated to others may underlie Noah's comments regarding the relationship between Japheth and Shem: "May God extend Japheth's territory; may Japheth live in the tents of Shem" (9:27).

Evidence supporting the idea that Genesis 22 should be linked to the covenant of circumcision in Genesis 17 may be deduced by considering the account of the covenant with Noah in Genesis 6–9.[11] An analysis of this earlier covenant reveals that it has the following structure:

1. The promise of a covenant (6:18)
2. The obligations of the covenant (6:14–16, 19–21; 7:1–3)
3. The fulfillment of the obligations (6:22; 7:5)
4. The sacrifice of burnt offerings (8:20)
5. The establishment of the covenant (9:9–17)

Remarkably, the same structure emerges if Genesis 17 and 22 are taken together. Chapter 17 records the promise of a covenant with Abraham, accompanied by certain obligations: Abraham is to walk before God and be blameless. While these obligations are more general than those given to Noah, God later tests Abraham's obedience in a specific way; he demands that Abraham should offer up his "only son Isaac" as a burnt offering (22:2 NRSV). In spite of the terrible consequences of killing his heir, Abraham displays his willingness to fulfill even the most testing of divine commands. After God's intervention and the deliverance of Isaac, as a burnt offering Abraham offers up a ram that has been unexpectedly provided.[12] Finally, God establishes the covenant with Abraham by swearing an oath (22:16–18).

By linking Genesis 17 and 22, we may shed new light on a number of issues. First, it is possible to account for the divine testing of Abraham. Through his obedience in Genesis 22, Abraham demonstrates his willingness to keep the conditions of the covenant laid out in 17:1. Second, the fact that the events of Genesis 22 are part of a conditional covenant explains why Abraham by

11. Six important parallels can be observed between the two covenants: (1) Both covenants are described as eternal or everlasting covenants, $běrît$ $\,\hat{o}l\bar{a}m$ (Gen. 9:16; 17:7, 13, 19). (2) These covenants are accompanied by an appropriate sign. In the case of Noah it is the rainbow (9:12–14), and in the case of Abraham it is circumcision (17:11). The rainbow is related to rain, which in turn would remind the people of the flood. Circumcision relates to the procreation of descendants, which is a point of emphasis in the covenant of Gen. 17. (3) In both cases, the expressions used of forming the covenant are $h\bar{e}q\hat{i}m$ $běrît$ (9:9, 11, 17; 17:7, 19, 21) and $n\bar{a}tan$ $běrît$ (9:12; 17:2). (4) The covenants in Gen. 9 and 17 are spoken of by God as "between me and you" (9:12, 15; 17:2, 7). However, at the same time they also include the descendants of Noah and Abraham (9:9, 12; 17:7, 9). (5) The benefit that each covenant brings for those with whom it is established is that they shall not be cut off (9:11; 17:14). (6) The divine command in 17:1, "Walk before me faithfully and be blameless," resembles the description of Noah in 6:9, "blameless in his generation; Noah walked with God" (NRSV). The word "blameless," $t\bar{a}m\hat{i}m$, is found only on these two occasions in the whole of Genesis. This list of similarities highlights the close parallels that exist between the two covenants (T. D. Alexander, "Genesis 22 and the Covenant of Circumcision," *JSOT* 25 [1983]: 19–20).

12. In the whole of Genesis, only in this chapter and in 8:20 is the term "burnt offering" used to designate a sacrifice.

his obedience is considered in 22:16–18 and 26:2–5 to have merited the divine guarantee of the promises concerning seed, land, and the blessing of others. Third, the oath in 22:16–18 forms a very fitting conclusion to the main section of the Abraham narrative. Although many scholars view verses 15–18 as a later addition to the original account of the testing of Abraham, the structure of the covenant requiring the sacrifice of a burnt offering before God could confirm with an oath the earlier promises. Verses 15–18 are an integral and essential part not only of Genesis 22 but also of the entire Abraham narrative.[13]

The divine oath in 22:16–18 not only embraces the contents of the earlier promissory covenant regarding many descendants and land but also includes the additional aspect that all nations will be blessed through Abraham's "seed." The mention of "seed" is significant. Unfortunately, the identity of this "seed" is not easy to determine. While the first mention of "seed" denotes "descendants," in the plural, the remaining references refer to a single descendant (cf. ESV). This latter possibility deserves special consideration for four reasons. First, the syntax of the Hebrew strongly supports the idea that the "seed" mentioned in verses 17b–18 is singular.[14] Second, the book of Genesis as a whole devotes considerable attention to tracing a line of "seed" that, beginning with Adam and ending with Judah, forms the early ancestry of the Davidic dynasty. Unfortunately, scholars generally overlook the importance of this single line of descendants. Third, the Jacob and Joseph stories give prominence to the blessing that the patriarchs, as members of this family line, may bestow on others. Although Esau and Jacob are both the "seed" of Isaac, it is clear that the brother who receives the father's blessing is favored more than the other. It is Jacob who experiences God's blessing and is able to mediate it to others. Similarly, Joseph is undoubtedly favored by his father, Jacob, who eventually imparts the blessing of the firstborn to Joseph's son Ephraim (48:1–22). Significantly, Genesis focuses on the blessing that others receive through Jacob and Joseph. They alone are presented as the ones who may impart blessing to others. Although other brothers exist, the Genesis narrative associates the power to bless with those who receive the firstborn blessing. Fourth, in announcing the covenant of circumcision to Abraham, God emphasizes the unique role of Isaac; it is with Isaac that the covenant will be established and not with Ishmael (17:19, 21). Given the limited interest that Genesis displays in the descendants of Ishmael, it seems logical to conclude that the "seed" of Abraham mentioned in 22:18 does not include Ishmael and his descendants. For these reasons, this final reference to "seed" in this

13. Various commentators propose that originally in verses 1–14, the sparing of Isaac was the reward for Abraham's obedience: that proposal is surely inadequate. If Abraham had disobeyed the divine command and stayed at home, the life of Isaac would not have been placed in immediate danger. The sparing of Isaac is hardly a suitable reward for Abraham's obedience.

14. See T. D. Alexander, "Further Observations on the Term 'Seed' in Genesis," *TynBul* 48 (1997): 363–67.

chapter (in 22:18) denotes a single descendant, who is perceived as exercising authority by defeating his enemies.

The covenants in Genesis 15 and 17 differ markedly.[15] Whereas Genesis 15 records an unconditional promissory covenant that does not necessarily entail an ongoing relationship between God and the descendants of Abraham, the covenant of circumcision is both conditional and eternal. Furthermore, though Genesis 15 implies that Abraham's faith, credited as righteousness, is the catalyst for the making of the promissory covenant, the establishment of the covenant of circumcision rests on Abraham's obedience to God. As reflected in 26:2–5, Abraham's obedience is an important factor in the establishment of this eternal covenant.

Old Testament Summary

Viewed as a whole, the Abraham narrative provides an interesting picture of the interplay between divine word and human faith and obedience. Initially the LORD makes a series of promises, the fulfillment of which is conditional on Abraham's obedience (12:1–3). As Abraham in faith obeys and journeys to Canaan, God declares that he shall have both land and descendants (12:7; 13:14–17). In time these statements are confirmed in a promissory covenant (15:18–21), which is linked to Abraham's being credited as righteous on account of his faith (15:6). The narrative, however, does not conclude here; it goes on to highlight Abraham's continuing faith in and obedience to God, as revealed in the establishment of the eternal covenant of circumcision (17:1–27; 22:1–19), a covenant that focuses on the divine blessing that will come through Abraham and his "seed" to all nations. From beginning to end, faith expressed through obedience is the hallmark of Abraham's relationship with the LORD.

Abraham's faith, however, is all the more remarkable when the following factors are also taken into account. First, it is clear that the divine promises concerning nationhood (i.e., seed and land) and the blessing of all the families of the earth will never be fulfilled in Abraham's lifetime; at the very most Abraham will experience only the firstfruits of their fulfillment. Second, circumstances exist or develop that militate against the fulfillment of these promises. Sarah's barrenness is a major obstacle for much of the narrative, and even when all seems assured with the birth of Isaac, God himself places the future fulfillment of the promises in jeopardy by demanding that Abraham sacrifice Isaac. Yet in spite of these factors, Abraham displays a faith in God that in the book of Genesis is matched only by that of Noah.

15. A full discussion of the relationship between Gen. 15 and 17 is provided by P. R. Williamson in *Abraham, Israel and the Nations: The Patriarchal Promise and Its Covenantal Development in Genesis*, JSOTSup 315 (Sheffield: Sheffield Academic Press, 2000).

New Testament Connections

There is little doubt that within the New Testament Epistles the most note-worthy aspect of Abraham's life is his faith. We see this clearly in Hebrews 11, which provides a detailed list of "ancients" who were commended for having faith. Approximately one-third of the chapter is devoted to Abraham (11:8–19), making him by far the most important person listed.[16] Fittingly, the author of Hebrews highlights Abraham's faith as an example of "confidence in what we hope for and assurance about what we do not see" (11:1).

Regarding Paul's understanding of Abraham, in Romans 4 and Galatians 3 the emphasis is clearly on the fact that, according to Genesis 15:6, Abraham was justified or made righteous by his faith and not by being circumcised and keeping the law.[17] For Paul, the sequence of events in the Abraham story is all-important. Since Abraham is credited as righteous before being circumcised, circumcision is not necessary in order for an individual to be reckoned righteous in God's eyes. He writes,

> We have been saying that Abraham's faith was credited to him as righteousness. Under what circumstances was it credited? Was it after he was circumcised, or before? It was not after, but before! And he received the sign of circumcision, a seal of the righteousness that he had by faith while he was still uncircumcised. So then, he is the father of all who believe but have not been circumcised, in order that righteousness might be credited to them. And he is then also the father of the circumcised who not only are circumcised but who also walk in the footsteps of the faith that our father Abraham had before he was circumcised. (Rom. 4:9–12)

Here Paul stresses that Abraham is the father of those who have faith, whether they are his natural descendants or not (cf. Rom. 9:6–8). Thus he concludes that Jews and Gentiles can be justified only by faith.

A similar, but not identical, argument is advanced in Galatians 2:5–3:29 as Paul responds to those who emphasize the necessity of circumcision in order to be children of Abraham and hence recipients of the promises made to him. He writes: "So also Abraham 'believed God, and it was credited to him as righteousness.' Understand, then, that those who have faith are children of Abraham" (Gal. 3:6–7). By stressing the importance of faith over against circumcision, Paul concludes that it is not necessary for an individual to be circumcised in order to be a child of Abraham.

Paul, however, does not conclude his argument in Galatians at this point. He focuses on three further aspects of the Abraham narrative in order to drive home his case that the Gentiles are now the recipients of God's blessing.

---

16. Moses, who is next in importance, receives about half the space given to Abraham (cf. Heb. 11:23–28).

17. Gen. 15:6 is quoted in Rom. 4:3 and Gal. 3:6.

First, in the justification of the Gentiles he sees the fulfillment of the divine promise to Abraham that all nations would be blessed through him. "The Scripture foresaw that God would justify the Gentiles by faith, and announced the gospel in advance to Abraham: 'All nations will be blessed through you.' So those who have faith are blessed along with Abraham, the man of faith" (Gal. 3:8–9). By highlighting the importance that the Genesis narrative places on all nations' being blessed through Abraham, Paul challenges the view of his opponents that God's blessing is only intended for the actual (biological) descendants of Abraham.

Second, Paul argues that the divine promises made to Abraham find their ultimate fulfillment in Jesus Christ. To arrive at this conclusion, Paul focuses on the concept of "seed" (Greek *sperma*, Gal. 3:16). He argues that the promises were given to Abraham and to his "seed," implying one person, and that this "seed" is Jesus Christ. Some biblical scholars conclude that here Paul adopts a form of rabbinic exegesis that might have been practiced by his Jewish contemporaries, but that his approach is clearly not in keeping with modern critical methods of exegesis. Unfortunately, these scholars have perhaps too readily dismissed Paul's interpretation without examining in detail how the term "seed" is used in Genesis. As noted in chapter 9 (above), the Hebrew word *zera'*, "seed," is clearly a keyword in Genesis; while it sometimes denotes a group, it may also refer to a single individual (as in KJV: Gen. 4:25; 21:13). This latter possibility is significant, especially when we observe that the entire book of Genesis focuses on a particular line of seed that enjoys a special relationship with God. Genesis devotes considerable attention, especially in the patriarchal stories, to identifying the seed of this special line. Furthermore, it gives clear indications that this line of seed formed the early ancestry of the royal line of David. Apart from the reference to kings being descended from Abraham (17:6), Jacob's blessing of Judah in 49:8–12 indicates that royalty will come from the line of Judah. Since Genesis as a whole focuses on a royal line of seed through which God will fulfill his promises to Abraham, then Paul's interpretation of the term *zera'* as referring to Jesus Christ is in keeping with the common New Testament understanding of Jesus as the Davidic Messiah. Paul affirms that it is only through faith in Jesus Christ, the "seed" of Abraham, that Jews and Gentiles may now receive the blessing given to Abraham and become God's children.

Finally, Paul in Galatians also argues that the divine covenant made with Abraham takes precedence over the law given several centuries later at Mount Sinai. His opponents are advocating that believers must keep the law in order to be righteous; Paul responds by declaring that the law, given later to fulfill a temporary role until Christ came, could never make anyone righteous since it merely indicated the righteousness required by God, not the means of achieving such righteousness. As such it underlined the necessity of becoming righteous through faith.

Paul uses the Abraham narrative in four distinctive ways in Galatians to challenge the view of his opponents that Gentile believers must be circumcised and obey the law of Moses in order to know God's salvation. Thus it is apparent that his understanding of the gospel was heavily influenced by his reading of Genesis 12–25.

Abraham's faith is also discussed in James 2:20–24. Here, however, the context differs from that found in Romans and Galatians. Paul seeks to demonstrate the priority of faith over circumcision; James is concerned to clarify the nature of saving faith: "What good is it, my brothers and sisters, if someone claims to have faith but has no deeds? Can such faith save them?" (2:14). At the heart of James's discussion is the desire to show that true faith in God will exhibit itself in righteous actions. Thus he focuses on Abraham and in particular the offering of Isaac on the altar. "Was not our father Abraham considered righteous for what he did when he offered his son Isaac on the altar? You see that his faith and his actions were working together, and his faith was made complete by what he did. And the scripture was fulfilled that says, 'Abraham believed God, and it was credited to him as righteousness,' and he was called God's friend. You see that a person is considered righteous by what they do and not by faith alone" (2:21–24). Here James reveals how faith in and obedience to God cannot be separated. Although James accepts that Abraham was considered righteous by faith, as stated in Genesis 15:6, he views the later actions of Abraham as visible expressions of his inner faith. Undoubtedly he focuses on Genesis 22 because of the way in which Abraham is rewarded for his willingness to sacrifice Isaac. For James, there can be no separation of faith and deeds. He views Abraham's actions in Genesis 22 as the fulfillment or culmination of what was stated in Genesis 15:6.

Although James writes, "A person is considered righteous by what they do and not by faith alone" (2:24), it is clear from the context that he does not actually contradict what Paul has to say in Romans and Galatians. The two men are addressing different situations and therefore highlight different aspects of Abraham's faith. On the one hand, Paul concentrates on Genesis 15:6 because he is responding either directly or indirectly to those who emphasize the necessity of circumcision for salvation. On the other hand, James is concerned to show that Abraham's faith, by which he was considered righteous, produced righteous actions. Thus he writes, "Faith without deeds is dead" (2:26). Undoubtedly Paul and James would have agreed wholeheartedly with what the other had to say, given the different problems that confronted them.

The final New Testament passage to be briefly considered is Hebrews 6:13–18. It is included here not because it focuses on Abraham's faith, but because it draws attention to the oath that God made to Abraham in order to guarantee beyond doubt the fulfillment of the divine promise made to Abraham: "Because God wanted to make the unchanging nature of his purpose very clear to the heirs of what was promised, he confirmed it with an oath. God did this so that, by two unchangeable things in which it is impossible for God to lie, we who have fled to take hold of the hope set before us may be greatly encouraged" (Heb. 6:17–18). The oath mentioned here clearly refers to Genesis 22:16–18. By anticipating the coming of a royal descendant of Abraham who will impart God's blessing to the nations, this oath is an important part of the New Testament understanding of Jesus Christ's mission.

13

Who Is the LORD?

Exodus is essentially a book about knowing God through personal experience. The plot centers on the relationship that develops between the LORD God and the Israelites, from the dramatic meeting with Moses at the burning bush (3:1–4:17) to the glory of the LORD filling the tabernacle (40:34–38). Throughout Exodus, God always takes the initiative, revealing himself not only through words but also through signs and wonders. In differing ways he reveals his most significant attributes: his sovereign majesty, his holiness, his power to perform signs and wonders, his awesome glory, his righteousness, his compassion.

An Overview of Exodus

The book of Exodus continues the story of Genesis by tracing the destiny of Jacob's children. Although Exodus itself forms a continuous account, it may be divided into two parts, both focusing on the theme of knowing God. The first half of the book is dominated by the theme of coming to a personal knowledge of God. At the outset Moses encounters God at the burning bush and in the ensuing conversation discovers much about God's nature, including his divine name, Yahweh (= "the LORD," 3:1–4:17).[1] The theme reappears when Pharaoh expresses his ignorance about the LORD: "Who is Yahweh, that I should obey him and let Israel go? I do not know Yahweh and I will not let Israel go" (5:2). As the

1. In most English translations the divine name Yahweh is rendered "the LORD." See footnote 5 below. In this chapter I quote NIV but sometimes replace "the LORD" with "Yahweh."

various signs and wonders unfold, the Egyptians gradually come to acknowledge Yahweh's sovereign power. When God finally lures Pharaoh and his army to their death in the Lake of Reeds,[2] it is with the expressed purpose that "the Egyptians will know that I am Yahweh" (14:4, 18). In celebration of their deliverance from Egypt, the Israelites worship God in a dynamic song of praise that highlights their knowledge of him: "Who among the gods is like you, [O] Yahweh? Who is like you—majestic in holiness, awesome in glory, working wonders?" (15:11).

The second half of Exodus further develops the theme of knowing God by focusing on the establishment of a special relationship between Yahweh and the Israelites. To this end the narrative concentrates on two topics that receive extensive coverage: the making of a covenant and the construction of the tabernacle.[3] The former of these, like signing a contract or making marriage vows, sets out the conditions under which the Israelites must live in order to enjoy an ongoing relationship with God; these conditions are recorded in the Decalogue (20:3–17) and the Book of the Covenant (20:22–23:33). If the people wish to experience God's continued blessing and presence, they must reflect his righteous and compassionate nature. Exodus records not only the establishment of the initial covenant agreement (Exod. 19–24) but also the making of the golden calf, an event that almost brings the covenant relationship to an early and abrupt conclusion (Exod. 32–34). The construction of the tabernacle forms a natural sequel to the making of the divine covenant. Built according to divine instruction, the tabernacle becomes the focal point of the LORD's presence in the midst of the people; through its materials and structure, it reminds them of God's sovereign, holy nature. Following the erection of the tabernacle, the LORD takes up residence amid his people (40:34–38), bringing the book of Exodus to a fitting conclusion.

The Israelites in Egypt

The initial two chapters of Exodus record events that span a period of several centuries and form a bridge between the detailed account of the life of

2. The Hebrew expression *yam-sûp* means "sea/lake of reeds" or "reed sea/lake" (cf. "Sea of Reeds," NJPS, NIV mg., NRSV mg.: 10:19; 13:18; 15:4, 22; 23:31). Various factors need to be taken into account when trying to identify this body of water. First, the Hebrew term *yām* and its Greek equivalent θάλασσα (*thalassa*) may denote a lake. The OT Hebrew has no alternative word for lake (cf. Deut. 33:23 [*yām* translated as "west" in NJPS, NRSV]; Job 14:11). The Lake of Galilee (Sea of Kinnereth) is designated a *yām* in Num. 34:11 and Josh. 13:27 (with *yām* translated by θάλασσα in the LXX). Second, the earliest Greek translation of Exodus rendered *yam-sûp* as "Red Sea," and this tradition is reflected in most English versions (cf. KJV, RSV, NIV, ESV, NET). However, *yam-sûp* probably refers to the region of the el-Ballah Lakes and not the Red Sea as known today (J. K. Hoffmeier, *Ancient Israel in Sinai: The Evidence for the Authenticity of the Wilderness Tradition* [Oxford and New York: Oxford University Press, 2005], 75–109; idem, "Out of Egypt: The Archaeological Context of the Exodus," *BAR* 33 [2007]: 30–41, 77).
3. For a fuller discussion of these topics, see chaps. 15 and 16 below.

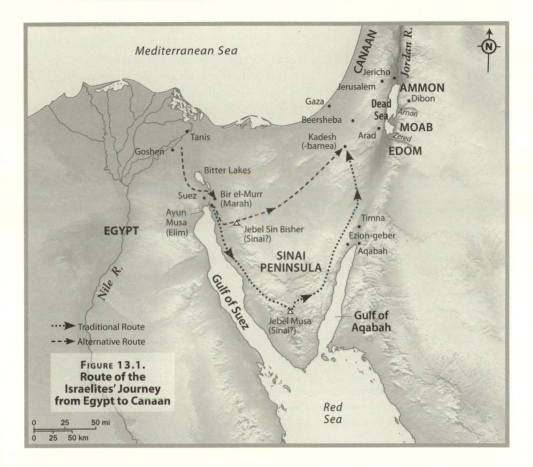

FIGURE 13.1.
Route of the Israelites' Journey from Egypt to Canaan

Joseph in Genesis 37–50 and the report of the Israelites' release from Egypt in Exodus 3–15. Not only do chapters 1–2 presuppose that the reader is already familiar with the book of Genesis; they also continue an important trend in Genesis regarding how God is portrayed. Though Genesis begins with God as the central participant in the story, a change occurs throughout the book as God gradually retreats from the center of the stage and adopts the role of an offstage director. We see this most clearly with Joseph; unlike his immediate ancestors, he has no direct encounter with the LORD. Rather, God controls the destiny of both Joseph and his wider family without revealing himself directly.

The opening two chapters of Exodus also convey the impression that God no longer reveals himself in person. The narrative highlights only his providential care as reflected in the case of the two midwives and inferred in the remarkable increase of the Israelites. Against this background the narrator's comments in 2:23–25 are significant. Although the Israelites may have felt that God was no longer concerned about them, such was not the case. God was well aware of their situation, and when the time was right, he would act in a dramatic way to free them from oppression.

The opening verses of Exodus contain an important allusion back to Genesis 1. The description of the Israelites as being fruitful and multiplying and filling the land echoes God's mandate to humanity in Genesis 1:28, later repeated to Noah (Gen. 9:1). Although Exodus portrays Abraham's descendants as fulfilling this creation mandate, almost immediately they encounter opposition in the form of the Egyptian king, who subjects them, among other things, to building store-cities for his benefit. This city-building stands in contrast to the temple-city that God desires to establish on earth. Later, freed from Pharaoh's control, the Israelites devote themselves to constructing the tabernacle, a portable residence for God that marks the first stage toward the establishment of the temple-city. Pharaoh's treatment of the Israelites underscores his opposition to the fulfillment of God's plans for creation. This sets the scene for the confrontation between Pharaoh and Yahweh that dominates Exodus 1–15.

Exodus 2 also gives special attention to the events surrounding the early life of Moses and his later exile in Midian. By highlighting his remarkable deliverance from death at birth and the irony of his growing up within the household of Pharaoh, the narrative anticipates the important role that Moses will play within the rest of the book. Furthermore, the nature of this role is hinted at by his actions on behalf of those who are oppressed by others (i.e., his concern for oppressed Israelite slaves; his intervention on behalf of Jethro's daughters). With Moses's flight to Midian, the scene is set for God to reveal himself in a most remarkable way.

The LORD Reveals Himself to Moses

Although the reader is partially prepared for the encounter between God and Moses, it must have come as a surprise to Moses. Several elements of the meeting are worth noticing briefly. First, Moses encounters God in a burning bush. Throughout Exodus the divine presence is frequently symbolized by fire, smoke, and cloud (13:21–22; 14:24; 19:18; 24:17; 40:38; cf. Lev. 9:24; 10:2; Num. 9:15–16; 11:1–3; 14:14; Deut. 1:33; 4:11–12, 15, 24, 33, 36; 5:4–5, 22–26; 9:3, 10, 15; 10:4; 18:16). Second, Moses acknowledges God's holiness by removing his sandals; God must be approached with caution. The concept of divine holiness reappears in Exodus (and especially Leviticus) as a major theme.[4] Third, having led his father-in-law's flock through the desert to Horeb (v. 1), Moses will later lead the Israelites to the same location (cf. 3:12; 19:1–2), where they also will witness God's holy presence revealed through fire.

4. See chap. 17 below.

190

Although God initially introduces himself to Moses as "the God of your father, the God of Abraham, the God of Isaac and the God of Jacob" (3:6), the issue of his identity reappears in verses 13–15, when Moses inquires about his name. This request is important because the Israelites believed that an individual's nature was reflected in one's name. In Genesis different aspects of God's nature are highlighted by the names used to designate him: *El Elyon* ("God Most High," Gen. 14:18–20), *El Roi* ("God who sees me," Gen. 16:13), *El Shaddai* ("God Almighty," Gen. 17:1), *El Olam* ("God Everlasting," Gen. 21:33). Here God introduces himself by using the personal name "Yahweh," translated in most English versions as "the LORD" (Exod. 3:15).[5]

The Hebrew name "Yahweh" is derived from the verb "to be" and means "he is" or "he will be." The personal name "Yahweh" is closely related to the phrase in verse 14 that is perhaps best translated: "I AM WHO I AM." An abbreviated form of this phrase comes in the statement, "I AM has sent me to you" (3:14). "I AM" translates the Hebrew word *'ehyeh*, which could also be translated "I will be." However, when *'ehyeh* is used by God to refer to himself, it must mean "I AM," for God already exists and is the actual speaker on this occasion. If God refers to himself as "I AM," others speaking of him will express this as "HE IS." This may explain the origin of the divine name Yahweh, which appears to be derived from the verb "to be." Although Yahweh could mean "HE WILL BE," like *'ehyeh* it must be understood as referring to the present time rather than the future.

Unlike previous designations, the name Yahweh does not restrict God's nature to any particular characteristic: HE IS WHO HE IS. Furthermore, his nature does not change. He is the God worshiped by earlier generations ("the God of Abraham, the God of Isaac and the God of Jacob") and generations yet to come: "This is my name forever, the name you shall call me from generation to generation" (3:15).

God instructs Moses to return to Egypt and assemble the elders of Israel. With his brother, Aaron, they will petition Pharaoh to take the Israelites on a short three-day journey into the desert so that they may serve their God (3:18). Pharaoh's reaction to this relatively minor demand will underscore his strong antagonism toward the Israelites. He will refuse to accommodate them, not because their request is excessive, but because of his own hatred of them. Exodus 7–15 reinforces this initial observation. Pharaoh will not change his mind "unless a mighty hand compels him" (3:19). Eventually the influence of

---

5. The English translation "LORD" fails to convey the idea that the Hebrew word *yhwh* is a personal name. Due to the veneration of God's name, it became the practice of Jews to substitute the Hebrew word *'ădônāy*, "Lord," for *yhwh* when they were reading the Bible. English translations in the main have retained this tradition. When vowels were eventually added to the consonantal text of the Hebrew Bible in the medieval period, the vowels of *'ădônāy* were used in conjunction with the consonants *yhwh*. This in turn led to the name "Yahweh" being wrongly read as "Jehovah."

God's hand on the Egyptians will be such that they will readily give of their possessions in order to see the Israelites leave Egypt (11:1–3; 12:35–36). These gifts will compensate the Israelites for the suffering they have already endured.

In spite of the assurance of God's presence, Moses raises a problem. What if the Israelites do not believe him? How will he convince them that God has indeed appeared to him? In response God provides three signs that involve miraculous transformations: Moses's staff will become a snake (4:2–4); his hand will become leprous (4:6–7); Nile water will become blood (4:9). Moses witnesses for himself the first two of these signs. The third, at this stage, must be accepted by faith. Soon afterward, when all three are later shown to the Israelites, they are convinced that God has indeed sent Moses (4:30–31).

When Moses first encounters Pharaoh, the Egyptian king displays his contempt toward Moses, Aaron, and especially the LORD: "Who is the LORD, that I should obey him and let Israel go? I do not know the LORD and I will not let Israel go" (5:2).[6] Although Pharaoh has no knowledge of the LORD, this will soon change dramatically. The motif of knowing the LORD recurs frequently throughout the following chapters (cf. 6:7; 7:5, 17; 8:10, 22; 9:14, 16, 29; 10:2; 14:4, 18). Having already revealed himself to Moses, Aaron, and the Israelite elders, God will now reveal himself powerfully to Pharaoh and the Egyptians.

A further divine speech to Moses in 6:28–7:7 anticipates the "miraculous signs and wonders" (7:3 NIV 1984) that are to dominate Exodus 7–14. Attention is drawn to the strengthening of Pharaoh's heart and to the "mighty acts of judgment" (7:4) by which God will lead Israel out of Egypt. God declares that as a result "the Egyptians will know that I am the LORD" (7:5). This sets the scene for the cycle of episodes that comprise 7:8–14:31.

Signs and Wonders in Egypt

The Exodus narrative devotes considerable space to the account of the signs and wonders performed in Egypt. While they are often described as "the ten plagues," this is not an entirely satisfactory designation. First, although the biblical text refers to a few of them individually as "plagues"[7] (9:3, 14, 15; 11:1; cf. 8:2), as a whole they are more frequently designated "signs" (7:3; 8:23; 10:1, 2) or "wonders" (4:21; 7:3; 11:9, 10; cf. "miracle" in 7:9). Second, there are actually eleven miraculous signs recorded in Exodus 7–12. The first of these, when the staff becomes a "snake" or more likely a "crocodile" (7:8–13), is

6. The personal name of Pharaoh is never given. For the reader, *he* is the unknown one.
7. In the NIV the term "plague" translates different Hebrew words, some of which would be more accurately rendered "strike" or "blow." In Jewish tradition the miraculous events in Egypt are called the "ten strikes."

generally not included in the list of "plagues."[8] This was also the first sign that God gave Moses in order to convince the Israelites that the LORD had indeed appeared to him (4:2–5). The next sign that Moses performs before Pharaoh, turning water into blood (7:14–25), was also earlier used to demonstrate Moses's divine calling to the Israelites (4:8–9). Even though the Israelites believed Moses on account of these signs (4:28–31), Pharaoh pays no attention to them (7:13, 22); his own magicians are able to perform the same wonders (7:11, 22).

The individual accounts of the miraculous signs follow the same pattern, but with some variation to avoid monotony.[9] Certain features are common to all eleven episodes. The report of each miraculous sign begins with the phrase, "the LORD said to Moses" (7:8, 14; 8:1, 16, 20; 9:1, 8, 13; 10:1, 21; 11:1). The initiative for each sign rests with God, with every stage in the encounter between Moses and Pharaoh being divinely controlled. Each episode, echoing the predictions given in 4:21 and 7:3–4, concludes with an explicit reference to the "hardening"—or better, "strengthening"—of Pharaoh's heart (7:13, 22; 8:15, 19, 32; 9:7, 12, 35; 10:20, 27; 11:10). The numerous references to the strengthening of Pharaoh's heart underline the importance of this motif, which is described in two ways. In the initial stages it is reported that Pharaoh strengthens his own heart (7:13, 14, 22; 8:15, 19, 32; 9:34, 35); in the latter stages the narrative states that the LORD strengthened Pharaoh's heart (9:12; 10:20, 27; 11:10; 14:4, 8, 17).

Unfortunately, the concept of God's "hardening" Pharaoh's heart is generally misunderstood, with many readers assuming that God caused Pharaoh to act against his own will. It is often suggested that although Pharaoh wanted to release the Israelites, God prevented him from doing this. However, a careful reading of the text reveals that by strengthening Pharaoh's heart, God actually enables him to remain true to his inner convictions. To this end, it is important to observe that the strengthening of Pharaoh's heart always comes after a hardship is removed and Pharaoh is no longer being pressured into releasing the Israelites. The motif of Pharaoh's heart being strengthened

8. In Exod. 4:3 Moses's staff becomes a *nāḥāš*, "snake"; in Exod. 7:9–10 it becomes a *tannîn*, which in this context probably refers to a crocodile.

9. It has been suggested that the plagues described in Exodus can be related to a series of natural phenomena that may have occurred in ancient Egypt. For example, the turning of the Nile waters to blood was due to an unusually high inundation of the river during the months of July and August. The river became bloodlike due to the presence of red earth carried in suspension from the basins of the Blue Nile and Atbara rivers. Such an explanation, however, does not account for the presence of such "blood" in wooden buckets and stone jars everywhere in Egypt (Exod. 7:19). Nor does it explain either the earlier signs that Moses performed before the Israelites (4:30), or the activities of the Egyptian magicians (7:22). The text consistently emphasizes the divine source of these events. This is indicated, e.g., by the many references to Moses or Aaron as stretching out their hands or a staff in order to bring about the different signs or wonders. Although some of these may be associated with natural phenomena, their occurrence is clearly attributed to divine intervention.

reveals that God wants the Egyptian king to release the Israelites willingly and not while under duress.

The strengthening of Pharaoh's heart stands in sharp contrast to other developments that occur in the narrative. Although the Egyptian magicians can initially duplicate the miraculous signs of Moses and Aaron, they soon reach the limit of their power and affirm to Pharaoh, "This is the finger of God" (8:19). Later, it is specifically stated that they "could not stand before Moses because of the boils that were on them" (9:11). Similarly, Pharaoh's own officials are gradually persuaded of the LORD's power. When Moses predicts "the worst hailstorm that has ever fallen on Egypt" (9:18), some of them take precautions against this threat (9:20). When Moses next warns of a plague of locusts, the officials urge Pharaoh to let the Israelites go (10:7; cf. 11:3).

Although those around him gradually concede to the LORD's power, Pharaoh remains stubbornly resistant. Nevertheless, even he is forced to make concessions as a result of the divine signs and wonders. Initially he is willing to let the people go on the condition that Moses prays for the removal of the frogs (8:8). Next, though he desires that the Israelites should stay within Egypt, he is persuaded to let them go a little way into the desert (8:25–28). Although after the hail he actually states that the people may go (9:28), this does not happen then. When Moses threatens an invasion of locusts, Pharaoh is prepared to allow the Israelite men, but not the women and children, to go and offer sacrifices to the LORD (10:8–11). Finally he concedes that men, women, and children may go, but not their flocks and herds (10:24). However, in spite of his apparent willingness to give way to Moses and Aaron in the face of divine signs and wonders, Pharaoh persistently refuses to let the people go.

The final demonstration of God's power to Pharaoh and the Egyptians involves the death of the male firstborn. At this point the narrative expands to give a detailed account of the events surrounding the night on which the Israelites are delivered from Egypt. The Passover not only marks the deliverance of the Israelites from bondage to Pharaoh; it also involves the consecration of the Israelite firstborn males as holy to the LORD.[10] As a result of the death of all the male firstborn in Egypt, Pharaoh recognizes and concedes to the power of the LORD. No longer can he deny any knowledge of the God who has demonstrated his existence by signs and wonders that have surpassed anything the Egyptians have previously witnessed.

Although Pharaoh permits the Israelites to leave Egypt after the death of the firstborn, there is to be one further demonstration of the LORD's power. To achieve this, God delays the Israelites' departure for Canaan, and they remain in Egypt on the western side of the Lake of Reeds (cf. 13:18; 15:4). When Pharaoh and his army pursue their former slaves, the Israelites believe themselves trapped and are terrified (14:10–12). However, when Moses stretches

10. See chap. 14 below.

194

out his staff God provides a safe escape route for the people through the divided waters of the sea. When the Egyptians follow, Moses stretches out his hand over the sea, this time with tragic consequences for Pharaoh's soldiers: "Not one of them survived" (14:28). Through repetition, verses 4 and 18 draw attention to the LORD's prime motive in destroying the Egyptian army: "The Egyptians will know that I am the LORD." Earlier Pharaoh rejected Moses's request to let the people go by stating, "Who is the LORD, that I should obey him and let Israel go?" (5:2). Pharaoh eventually discovers why the LORD should be obeyed. This episode also highlights the changing attitude of the Israelites from unbelief and fear in the face of the Egyptian threat (14:10–12) to faith and trust in the light of the LORD's deliverance (14:31).

As a fitting conclusion to the account of the divine deliverance of the enslaved Israelites from Egyptian control, the exodus narrative records how Moses and the people celebrate in song the majesty and power of the LORD (15:1–18).[11] Here the narrative switches from prose to poetry. The exalted language of the poetry conveys better than prose the thoughts and feelings of the Israelites as they worship the one who has taken pity on them and rescued them from the tyrant's power. By rehearsing what has already been recorded in prose, the reader too is encouraged to participate in the celebrations of the Israelites.

As the people respond in adoration and praise for what God has already done, they look forward with confidence to the future. Their song concludes by focusing on what God has yet to accomplish on their behalf, with particular emphasis being given to the people's dwelling with God on his sacred mountain (15:17–18). In the light of past events and future expectation, it is hardly surprising that at the end of this section we read of Miriam and all the women playing tambourines and dancing with joy.

The Sinai Covenant

Following their divine rescue from Egypt, the Israelites gradually proceed to Mount Sinai in fulfillment of what God has earlier told Moses (cf. 3:12). Once there, they experience further developments in their relationship with God. A special agreement, or covenant, is established between God and the Israelites, based on the principle that if the people obey God, then they will be his treasured possession. Instructions are given for the construction of a suitable dwelling place for the LORD, to be located in the middle of the Israelite camp. This would enable God to be visibly present among his people. As a result of these developments, the people will have a more intimate knowledge of their God. No longer will he only live in heaven and at a distance from the

---

11. The initial Hebrew verb in Exod. 15:1 indicates that this song is sung on a regular basis by Moses and the Israelites and not just on one occasion.

Israelites. God comes to dwell on the earth in anticipation of the temple-city that has yet to be established.

At Sinai, God reveals himself in a new way to the Israelites. Three aspects of this revelation are significant. First, attention is drawn to the holiness of God's nature. We see this in the instructions given to Moses. The people must consecrate themselves, wash their clothes, and abstain from sexual relations for three days (19:14–15). Furthermore, Moses must establish a boundary around the mountain in order to prevent the people from coming into direct contact with God; even the priests are subject to this constraint. As the ground near the burning bush was made holy by God's presence (3:5), so too is Mount Sinai (19:23). Second, God's presence—accompanied by thunder and lightning, fire and smoke, and the violent trembling of the mountain (19:16–19)—is seen, heard, and felt by all the people. This theophany marks the arrival of God at the mountain. Contrary to what some scholars claim, God was not perceived as dwelling on Mount Sinai. Third, God speaks directly to all those gathered at the foot of the mountain and declares the principal obligations to which they must adhere in order for the covenant relationship to be established (20:1–17). The effect of all this on the people is such that they ask Moses to mediate with God on their behalf. Moses subsequently receives further obligations concerning the covenant (20:22–23:33). Both sets of obligations reflect God's nature, especially his divine attributes of righteousness and compassion.[12]

Following the ratification of the Sinai covenant (24:3–8), Moses is summoned into God's presence to receive instructions for building a tent, or tabernacle, that will be God's dwelling place on earth. The special nature of this tent reflects certain aspects of God's character, in particular his sovereignty and holiness. The precious metals and bluish fabrics used in its construction are indicative of royalty, and the appointment of priests and the consecration of all the furnishings underline the holiness of God.[13]

While Moses is receiving God's instructions for constructing the tabernacle, the people who remain at the foot of Sinai desire to have a symbol of the LORD's presence. This ironically results in the making of a golden calf. The tabernacle, with its golden furnishings, will portray the LORD as a royal personage, but the golden calf, in marked contrast, represents him as a mere beast. Although the people offer sacrifices, their worship of the calf degrades the one who has delivered them from slavery in Egypt. Worship, to be true, must be based on a right perception of God. The book of Exodus emphasizes the importance of knowing God as he truly is, and not as we imagine him to be.

Following the golden calf incident, Moses asks to see God's glory (33:18). From the LORD's response, it is clear that he equates his glory with "all my goodness" (33:19). To assure Moses of his identity, God proclaims his personal

---

12. For a fuller discussion of the Sinai covenant, see chap. 15 below.
13. For a fuller discussion of the tabernacle, see chap. 16 below.

name, the LORD (Yahweh). Interestingly, when God previously revealed his name to Moses, "Moses hid his face, because he was afraid to look at God" (3:6). Now he displays a greater confidence. Though Moses was granted the opportunity to see God as no one else had done, even he cannot look on the divine face with immunity (33:20).

When God reveals himself to Moses on top of the mountain, he stresses not only his mercy and compassion, "forgiving wickedness, rebellion and sin" (34:7; cf. 33:19), but also his justice: "He does not leave the guilty unpunished" (34:7; cf. 32:34). The revelation of these divine characteristics to Moses is so significant that this passage is echoed on many occasions in the Old Testament (e.g., Num. 14:18; Neh. 9:17; Pss. 86:15; 103:8; 145:8; Joel 2:13; Jon. 4:2). In this dramatic setting, we have, verbally stated, two of the most important characteristics of God's nature—mercy and justice—qualities that have already been revealed through his deliverance of the Israelites from Egypt.

Apart from this unique encounter with God on the mountain, Moses also communes with God regularly by entering a tent that is pitched at some distance from the main encampment.[14] Given its specific function, this tent is known as the "tent of meeting" (33:7).[15] Here Moses enjoys a unique and personal relationship with God: "The LORD would speak to Moses face to face, as one speaks to a friend" (33:11). Although they are in close proximity to each other, even Moses the faithful servant is not permitted to look directly on God; 33:9 implies that the tent curtain shields Moses, who is within, from the LORD, who is without. Remarkably, every time Moses meets with God, his face becomes radiant and remains so afterward (34:29–35).[16]

When the tabernacle is finally erected, a cloud covers it and the glory of the LORD fills it (40:34). God now dwells in the midst of the people. The tabernacle becomes the "tent of meeting" (40:35), replacing the tent previously used by Moses (cf. 33:7–11). Moses went inside the earlier tent and God remained outside (33:9); now God dwells within the tent and Moses stays outside (40:35). God's presence is visible to everyone through the cloud and fire that settle upon the tabernacle. From here he guides them on their journeys (40:36–38). Appropriately, Exodus comes to a dramatic conclusion by recording the arrival of the glorious presence of the sovereign God as he comes to dwell in the midst of his people Israel.

14. The tenses of the Hebrew verbs in 33:7–11 and 34:34–35 indicate that these passages describe events that occur regularly.

15. This tent of meeting should not be confused with the tabernacle, also known as the "tent of meeting" (e.g., 40:2, 6), which was constructed only later (36:8–38) and was pitched in the midst of the Israelite encampment (Num. 1:53; 2:2, 17). See chap. 16 below.

16. Moses's radiant face sets him apart from the rest of the people as God's messenger. When he communicates God's words to the people, he speaks with his face uncovered. At all other times he covers his face with a veil. In this way the Israelites are able to know when Moses speaks with divine authority and when he speaks on his own behalf.

Old Testament Summary

There can be little doubt that the most important theme running through the book of Exodus is that of knowing God. The text highlights the different ways in which God may reveal himself, focusing on attributes that lie at the very heart of his nature: his sovereign majesty, his holiness, his awesome glory, his power to perform wonders, his righteousness, and his compassion. Not only does God make himself known to others through actions and words; significantly, Exodus also describes how he comes to reside as divine king in the very heart of the Israelite camp. As a result, the Israelites have an opportunity to know God in a unique way.

New Testament Connections

Many of the theological ideas highlighted in the book of Exodus reappear in the New Testament. Those associated with the Passover, the Sinai covenant, and the tabernacle will be considered in the next three chapters respectively. The themes of testing in the wilderness and God's remarkable provision for the people are dealt with in chapter 21 below. Here we shall focus briefly on a number of other ways in which the exodus story is echoed in the New Testament.

The New Testament writers generally picture God in the same way as he is revealed in Exodus. Paul highlights the sovereign majesty of God when he refers to him as "the King eternal" (1 Tim. 1:17) and "the blessed and only Ruler, the King of kings and Lord of lords, who alone is immortal and who lives in unapproachable light, whom no one has seen or can see" (1 Tim. 6:15–16). Similarly, the author of Hebrews, quoting Deuteronomy 4:24, speaks of worshiping God "with reverence and awe, for our 'God is a consuming fire'" (12:28–29).

Of all the New Testament writings, John's Gospel probably contains the broadest range of allusions to the exodus story. The following are the more obvious. First, the early chapters of Exodus and John's Gospel share a similar interest in "signs."[17] Apart from the resurrection, seven signs in John's Gospel draw attention to the uniqueness of Jesus:

water to wine (2:2–11)
healing of an official's son (4:46–54)
healing of paralyzed man (5:1–15)
feeding of 5,000 (6:1–14)
walking on water (6:16–21)

17. The Greek word *sēmeion*, "sign," is sometimes translated into English as "miracle."

healing of blind man (9:1–41)

raising of Lazarus (11:1–44)

For the author of the Gospel, these signs witness to Jesus's divine nature. "Jesus performed many other signs in the presence of his disciples, which are not recorded in this book. But these are written that you may believe that Jesus is the Messiah, the Son of God, and that by believing you may have life in his name" (20:30–31). While the "signs" performed by Jesus are all positive in nature, in marked contrast to the signs of "judgment" in Exodus, it is surely noteworthy that the signs in both books have something in common. The water into blood and the death of the firstborn in Exodus are replaced in John's Gospel with "signs" of hope: water turned into wine and a firstborn raised from death.

Second, in marked contrast to the Synoptic Gospels, the Gospel of John focuses particular attention on various visits undertaken by Jesus to Jerusalem. Indeed, if we only had John's record, we would be inclined to place most of Jesus's ministry in Jerusalem. Jesus's visits to Jerusalem coincide with major Jewish festivals that celebrate the exodus from Egypt: Passover (2:13; 11:55); Tabernacles (7:2); a feast (5:1). Furthermore, in John's Gospel John the Baptist describes Jesus as "the Lamb of God" (1:29, 36); perhaps most significant of all, the crucifixion of Jesus occurs at the time of the Passover.[18]

Third, another very distinctive and unique feature of John's Gospel is the series of "I am" sayings of Jesus:

I am the bread of life. (6:35)

I am the light of the world. (8:12)

I am the gate. (10:7, 9; "door," NIV 1984)

I am the good shepherd. (10:11)

I am the resurrection and the life. (11:25)

I am the way and the truth and the life. (14:6)

I am the true vine. (15:1)

Additionally, Jesus uses "I am" without completing the predicate with a complement on a number of other occasions (Greek: 8:24, 28, 58; 13:19). While the precise link between these "I am" saying and the book of Exodus is open to discussion,[19] it seems highly likely that the author of John's Gospel sees in

---

18. For further comments on the links between John's Gospel and the Passover, see chap. 14 below.

19. Although some writers have connected Jesus's special use of the expression "I am" with God's use of the same words in Exod. 3:14, the "I am" expressions in John's Gospel possibly echo similar expressions in the book of Isaiah (esp. 41:4; 43:10, 13, 25; 46:4; 48:12 [NIV: "I am he"]). Given that the phrase "I am" in Isaiah probably alludes back to Exod. 3:14, it is surely

them an allusion to Exodus 3:14: "God said to Moses, 'I AM WHO I AM. This is what you are to say to the Israelites: "I AM has sent me to you."'"

In the light of the other features that link John's Gospel with Exodus, we are probably intended to see in Jesus's statement "I am the light of the world. Whoever follows me will never walk in darkness, but will have the light of life" (John 8:12) a reference to the cloud and fire that guided the Israelites in the wilderness (Exod. 13:21–22; 14:19; 40:38). Jesus also clearly alludes to the manna that Israel ate in the wilderness when he comments, "I am the bread that came down from heaven" (John 6:41). Indeed, as we shall observe in chapter 22 (below), John 6 is especially rich in allusions to the exodus experience of the Israelites.

Turning from John's Gospel, we find other New Testament links with Exodus. In his Letter to the Romans, Paul refers briefly to God's remark in Exodus 9:16 that he has raised up Pharaoh in order to display his power (Rom. 9:17). Focusing throughout Romans 9 on the sovereignty of God, Paul draws on various examples to highlight God's freedom to use individuals in a variety of ways for the outworking of his purposes.

With vivid imagery the author of Hebrews contrasts Mount Sinai with Mount Zion, the heavenly Jerusalem (cf. Heb. 12:22).

> You have not come to a mountain that can be touched and that is burning with fire; to darkness, gloom and storm; to a trumpet blast or to such a voice speaking words that those who heard it begged that no further word be spoken to them, because they could not bear what was commanded: "If even an animal touches the mountain, it must be stoned." The sight was so terrifying that Moses said, "I am trembling with fear." But you have come to Mount Zion, to the city of the living God, the heavenly Jerusalem. You have come to thousands upon thousands of angels in joyful assembly, to the church of the firstborn, whose names are written in heaven. You have come to God, the Judge of all, to the spirits of the righteous made perfect, to Jesus the mediator of a new covenant, and to the sprinkled blood that speaks a better word than the blood of Abel. (Heb. 12:18–24)

The ancient Israelites encountered God at an earthly mountain; now those embraced by the new covenant "are receiving a kingdom that cannot be shaken" (Heb. 12:28).

---

appropriate to observe a link between Jesus's use of "I am" in John's Gospel and its use as a divine designation in Exod. 3:14.

14

The Passover

The Passover is at the heart of God's rescuing the Israelites from slavery in Egypt. To distinguish them from the Egyptians, God instructs the Israelites to undertake a special ritual involving a distinctive sacrificial meal. As a result the LORD promises to "pass over" their houses when he strikes down all the firstborn males in Egypt (Exod. 12:13, 27). Such is the importance of the occasion that later generations of Israelites were not to forget what the LORD had done in delivering their ancestors from slavery in Egypt. For the Israelites, the Passover was the most significant redemptive event in their history. It was both their divine deliverance from harsh oppression in Egypt and their first step toward becoming a holy nation.

Introduction

The account of the Passover in Exodus 12–13 forms the conclusion to the cycle of episodes that have demonstrated God's power to Pharaoh and the Egyptians (7:8–11:10). In the light of the divine pronouncement that "every firstborn son in Egypt will die" (11:5), 12:1–13:16 recounts ensuing developments. The unique way in which the Israelite firstborn are protected from death furnishes the designation for this remarkable occasion: "the Passover" (cf. 12:11, 13, 23, 27).

The narrator not only recounts the main events of the first Passover through a skillful use of dialogue, but by the same technique he also highlights how the Passover should be remembered by generations of Israelites. For seven days each year they will celebrate the Feast of Unleavened Bread (12:14–20; 13:3–10). Several other references underline the close association between unleavened bread and the Passover (12:34, 39). Given their swift departure from Egypt, it was not possible for the Israelites to observe this feast until the first anniversary of the exodus (cf. Num. 9:1–14). In conjunction with the Feast of Unleavened Bread, the Israelites were to commemorate the Passover through the eating of a year-old lamb or kid (12:24–27, 42–50).[1] Celebrated on the evening of the fourteenth day of the first month, the Passover preceded the start of the Feast of Unleavened Bread, which began on the fifteenth day and continued until the twenty-first day of the month (cf. 12:18). Additionally, to commemorate the survival of their firstborn sons, the Israelites were commanded to give the LORD all future firstborn sons and male animals (13:11–16). They belonged to God in a unique way because they had been delivered from death. These various activities were an ongoing testimony to how the LORD had not only brought them out of Egypt with his mighty hand (cf. 13:3, 9, 16), but had also taken the first step toward bestowing on them the special status of holy nation.

The Account of the Passover

Exodus 12:1–28 is composed of two speeches containing instructions for the activities associated with the Passover. Although placed side by side, the speeches are possibly given days apart. The first speech (12:1–20) is delivered by God to Moses some days before the first Passover night; verse 3 records instructions concerning the selection of the Passover lamb or kid four days before the Passover is observed. In the second speech (12:21–27) Moses addresses the elders of Israel, directing them how to observe the Passover. The second speech complements the first, providing additional information on various aspects of the Passover celebration. Through these two speeches the narrator highlights the events leading to the striking down of the Egyptian firstborn at midnight on the fourteenth day of the month (12:29). The two speeches parallel each other, both concluding with detailed guidance for future commemorations of the Passover (12:14–20, 24–27). Since the reader is able to reconstruct a picture of the events that take place from the content of the two speeches, the author refrains from describing the fulfillment of the instructions; he merely comments, "The Israelites did just what the LORD commanded Moses and Aaron" (12:28).

Various predictions made in 11:1–10 are fulfilled in 12:29–36. At midnight the LORD strikes down all the Egyptian firstborn, causing the people to wail

---

1. The Hebrew word *śeh* (Exod. 12:3–5) denotes either a lamb or a goat. The NIV translation "Passover lamb" in 1 Cor. 5:7 is unfortunate. A more accurate rendering of the verses is "For Christ, our Passover, has been sacrificed."

loudly (12:29–30; cf. 11:4–6).[2] After summoning Moses and Aaron for the final time, Pharaoh eventually permits the Israelites to leave unconditionally (12:31–32; cf. 11:1). As instructed in 11:2, the Israelites ask for and receive from the Egyptians "articles of silver and gold" and "clothing" (12:35). These are freely given because "the LORD had made the Egyptians favorably disposed toward the people" (3:21–22; 12:36; cf. 11:3). These gifts are a form of partial reparation for the way in which the Egyptians had treated the Israelites as slaves (cf. Gen. 15:14).

With Pharaoh's permission the Israelites begin their journey to freedom by traveling from Rameses to Sukkoth (12:37–41). At last, after 430 years, the people are able to leave Egypt as a result of the mighty wonders performed by the LORD.[3]

The account of the Israelites' departure is interrupted by 12:42–50, which records "regulations for the Passover." These regulations apply to both the first Passover and later commemorations (cf. 12:42). The section ends by mentioning the obedience of the Israelites, with verse 50 corresponding closely to 12:28, possibly indicating that the instructions belong there chronologically. By ordering the material as he does, the narrator brings together in 12:42–13:16 the three ways in which the Israelites' deliverance from Egypt is to be celebrated: by reenacting the Passover (12:43–49), by keeping the Feast of Unleavened Bread (13:3–10), and by consecrating as holy to God every firstborn male (13:11–16).

In 12:51 the narrative picks up where it left off in verse 41 by repeating various details (e.g., "on that very day," "divisions"; the NIV somewhat obscures how similar the two verses are in the Hebrew text). On the day following the destruction of the Egyptian firstborn males, God announces to Moses that the Israelites must set apart as special "the first offspring of every womb, . . . whether human or animal" (13:2). Moses in turn expands on this directive as he conveys it to the people (13:11–16). It is preceded, however, by instructions regarding the celebration of the Feast of Unleavened Bread (13:3–10). Although Moses and Aaron were divinely instructed about this feast earlier (12:14–20), it is only now that the people learn of it. Moses's speech to the people in 13:3–16 falls neatly into two halves, which parallel each other closely.

---

2. The precise identity of "the destroyer" (12:23) is not revealed in Exodus. A better translation of v. 23b is "he will not permit destruction to enter your houses."

3. Exod. 12:40–41 states that the Israelites lived in Egypt for 430 years (cf. Gal. 3:17); Gen. 15:13 implies that the descendants of Abraham were oppressed for 400 years (cf. Acts 7:6). Though the larger figure of 430 years could be interpreted as including the period of peace that they enjoyed after first arriving in Egypt during the time of Joseph, this is at odds with the fact that Joseph is said to have lived for 71 years after his family joined him in Egypt. On the basis of this latter figure, the period of oppression could not have lasted more than 359 years at the maximum (i.e., 430 − 71 = 359). Perhaps the simplest way to reconcile these various time periods is to interpret the reference to 400 years in Gen. 15:13 as a round number referring back to the initial phrase, "your seed will be sojourners in a land that is not theirs" (my trans.), and not simply the period of oppression.

Both begin with references to the people's taking possession of the land of Canaan in fulfillment of God's oath to their ancestors (13:5, 11). Next come instructions regarding the commemoration of the Israelites' deliverance from Egypt (13:6–7, 12–13), and the explanation of these activities to the children (13:8, 14–15). Finally, both halves are marked by similar endings, concluding with the comment that "the LORD brought you out of Egypt with his mighty hand" (13:9; cf. v. 16).

The Purpose of the Passover Ritual

At the heart of the Passover ritual is the slaying of a lamb or kid, the smearing of its blood on the doorposts, and the eating of its meat (12:6–11, 21–22). The details of the ritual closely parallel those relating to sacrifices, and this is confirmed by the comment in 12:27, "It is the Passover sacrifice to the LORD." Although resembling other sacrificial offerings, the Passover ceremony is unique, reflecting its peculiar historical setting. Coming before the establishment of the Aaronic priesthood (Lev. 8:1–9:24), Moses commands "all the elders of Israel" to slaughter the Passover victims (12:21). In keeping with its historical context, there is no reference to the central sanctuary, which is first instituted at Sinai, after the exodus (20:24–26; 24:4; 27:1–8). Although other sacrifices are normally offered up during daylight, the Passover is sacrificed at "twilight" since this is probably the most convenient time due to the exploitation of the Israelites by the Egyptians. Finally, the timing of the Passover to the fourteenth day of the month places it close to the full moon, the most suitable period in the month for undertaking the activities associated with the exodus from Egypt.

Special attention is focused on the use made of the animal's blood: it is smeared on the sides and top of the doorframe of the house (12:7, 22). Although some scholars emphasize the apotropaic purpose of this action, designed to protect those within from hostile powers without (cf. 12:13, 23), others suggest that the blood was used to purify the Israelite houses. This latter proposal is supported by the mention of hyssop (12:22), which is elsewhere associated with ritual purification (e.g., Lev. 14:4, 6, 49, 51, 52; Num. 19:6, 18).

An equally important part of the Passover rite is the eating of the sacrificial animal's flesh. Everyone in the Israelite community is to participate (12:47), and for each animal slaughtered there must be an adequate number of people to eat all the meat. Special instructions are given concerning the cooking of the meat: the entire animal is roasted, not boiled (12:9); the meat must be eaten indoors; and the animal's bones must not be broken (12:46). Any meat that remains must be burned in the morning (12:10).

Various factors suggest that the Passover is very significant theologically. Why did God on this occasion require a special ritual in order to distinguish the Israelites from the Egyptians? With previous afflictions, God ensured, without any ritual being used, that the Israelites were not affected. On this occasion, why must the houses of the Israelites be marked with blood? In addition, if the death of the Egyptian firstborn males is taken to be a punishment for their treatment of the Israelites, why should the Israelites also be threatened with death? This latter consideration suggests that the death of the firstborn sons involves more than the punishment of the Egyptians. In terms of the death threat, no distinction is made between the Israelites and the Egyptians: all their firstborn sons face death. What saves the Israelites is the Passover. Central to the Israelite understanding of Passover is the idea that its ritual delivers from death.

Taking into account that all firstborn sons and male animals will be struck dead, it is important to observe that the description of the Passover meal closely parallels procedures for consecrating the Aaronic priests in Exodus 29 and Leviticus 8. Various elements comprise the ritual by which Aaron and his sons are set apart from all other Israelites in order to serve as priests within the soon-to-be constructed tabernacle.[4] Of these elements, a number closely parallel features of the Passover. First, a ram is sacrificed to atone for their sin. Second, some of the animal's blood is sprinkled on the extremities of their bodies to cleanse them from all defilement caused by sin. Third, they eat portions of the sacrificial animal's meat. By consuming "holy" meat, they themselves are made holy, a necessary requirement before they can serve within the holy confines of the tabernacle. Fourth, unleavened bread is also eaten as part of the sacrificial meal. Together these four elements enable Aaron and his sons to be consecrated or sanctified as priests.

Although there are differences of detail, similar elements underlie the Passover, suggesting that it too functions as a consecration ritual. The sacrifice of the animal atones for the sin of the people, the blood smeared on the doorposts purifies those within, and the eating of the sacrificial meat and unleavened bread sanctifies those who consume it. By participating in the Passover ritual, the Israelites are endowed with a holy status (cf. 19:6), making it possible for God, the Holy One, to come and dwell in their midst.

Though every Israelite who participates in the Passover is endowed with a holy status, it is especially noteworthy that the firstborn males are perceived as having an even holier status. Since they alone have been delivered from death, they now belong to God, their redeemer, in a unique way. Attention is drawn to this in 13:11–16, where God gives instructions to Moses relating to the future ransom of firstborn sons and male animals. Later, in Numbers 3, additional instructions are given whereby every firstborn Israelite male is replaced by the male members of the tribe of Levi. The LORD says: "I have taken the Levites from among the Israelites in place of the first male offspring

4. For more on the consecration of the Aaronic priests, see chap. 16 below.

of every Israelite woman. The Levites are mine, for all the firstborn are mine" (Num. 3:12–13a; cf. 18:15–17). Affirming that the firstborn belong to him in a special way, the LORD immediately goes on to say: "When I struck down all the firstborn in Egypt, I sanctified for myself every firstborn in Israel, whether man or animal. They are to be mine. I am the LORD" (Num. 3:13, alt.). As these remarks make clear, not only do the firstborn Israelite males belong to God in an exceptional way, but they have also been sanctified or made holy by him. For this reason, as substitutes for the firstborn males, the Levites are viewed as having a holy status that exceeds that of other Israelites. Consequently, they are distinguished from all the other tribes and given special responsibilities relating to the tabernacle, God's holy dwelling place (cf. Num. 3:40–51; 8:5–26).

The special status of the firstborn males appears to derive from the fact that God has ransomed them from death. Though the text of Exodus itself does not explicitly mention ransoming from death, this seems to be implied by what is said in 13:11–16. Every firstborn male, both human and animal, belongs to God in a unique way because he has saved them from death. In the light of this, it is worth recalling that in Genesis 3, the expulsion of Adam and Eve from the Garden of Eden is linked to both punishment involving "death" and the loss of royal and priestly status. As a result of the Passover, "death" is overcome, and holiness is bestowed on the Israelites.

Old Testament Summary

The divine deliverance of the Israelites from Egypt comes to a dramatic climax in the events associated with the Passover. Later generations are never to forget this unique event, which signals the beginning of the process by which the LORD establishes Israel as his holy people. For later generations, the events and ideas associated with the Passover become a paradigm of God's saving activity, involving the defeat of a tyrannical oppressor, ransom from death, and restoration to a holy status.

New Testament Connections

The crucifixion of Jesus, the central redemptive event in the New Testament, is in various ways linked to the Passover, the paradigmatic saving event of the Old Testament period. First, the Gospels all highlight how the death of Jesus took place in Jerusalem when the Jews were commemorating the Passover by keeping the Feast of Unleavened Bread. Second, the Synoptic Gospels (Matthew, Mark, and Luke) present the Last Supper as a Passover meal (Matt. 26:17; Mark 14:12; Luke 22:7–8), emphasizing its importance and the special significance of Jesus's words and actions. This final meal of Jesus and his closest disciples is later commemorated in the Lord's Supper (1 Cor. 11:23–33).

Third, the actual death of Jesus is linked to the offering up of the Passover sacrifice. John's Gospel alludes to this by observing that, because Jesus's bones are not broken, his death resembles that of the Passover sacrifice (John 19:36; cf. Exod. 12:46). This connection is made even more explicit in 1 Corinthians 5:7: "For Christ, our Passover lamb, has been sacrificed." Fourth, the concepts of atonement, purification (or cleansing), and sanctification are all associated in John's Gospel with Jesus's sacrificial death as the "Lamb of God, who takes away the sin of the world!" (John 1:29; cf. 1:36). Additionally, John draws attention to the themes of deliverance from death and redemption from slavery to sin and the devil. All these reflect a strong Passover typology, associated with a new exodus, centered on Jesus Christ.[5] Finally, although other interpretations are possible, 1 Peter 1:18–19 probably also associates the death of Jesus with the Passover sacrifice.

One particular difficulty must be recognized regarding the New Testament association of the death of Jesus with the Passover. In the Old Testament the Passover sacrifice is always offered up before the eating of the Passover meal. However, this pattern is reversed in the New Testament; the Passover meal is eaten on the evening before the crucifixion of Jesus. One solution has been to argue that the Last Supper was only a preparatory meal, which took place on the evening before the real Passover celebration. Although this is a convenient explanation, taking into account how the Synoptic Gospels emphasize the preparations for this meal, it is difficult to imagine that it could be anything other than the Passover meal itself.

An alternative solution may lie in the observation that John does not explicitly say that Jesus was crucified at the very time when the Passover victims were being slaughtered at the temple. Perhaps John encountered no difficulty in the fact that Jesus was crucified a day after the other Passover sacrifices. What mattered to John was the manner and purpose of his death, not the timing.[6]

5. Cf. P. M. Hoskins, "Deliverance from Death by the True Passover Lamb: A Significant Aspect of the Fulfillment of the Passover in the Gospel of John," *JETS* 52 (2009): 285–99; idem, "Freedom from Slavery to Sin and the Devil: John 8:31–47 and the Passover Theme of the Gospel of John," *TJ* 31 (2010): 47–63.

6. John may have believed that the timing of Jesus's death accurately fulfilled the OT regulations regarding the Passover sacrifice. This observation is based on the premise that the timing of the Passover celebration in the NT period differed from that intended in the original OT instructions due to an important change concerning the way in which the start of the day was reckoned. Although the original OT Passover regulations presuppose that the day begins at *sunrise*, from the sixth century BC onward the Jews followed the Babylonian system of reckoning the day as beginning at *sunset*. This change has important implications for the timing of the Passover sacrifice.

John observes that the crucifixion took place on "the day of Preparation of the Passover" (19:14; cf. 19:31) and that the next day was to be a "special Sabbath" (19:31). This special Sabbath clearly refers to the first day of the Feast of Unleavened Bread. If we assume that this special Sabbath coincided with a normal Sabbath (i.e., it fell on a Saturday), then we may conclude that Jesus was crucified on the Friday immediately preceding the beginning of the Feast

By linking the crucifixion of Jesus to the Passover, the New Testament church drew attention to the redemptive nature of Jesus's death. Like the original Passover sacrifice, his death atoned for the sin of the people, his blood purified and cleansed believers, and his body sanctified those who ate it at the Lord's Supper. Paul alludes to this in 1 Corinthians 10:14–22, where he emphasizes how believers, by eating bread and drinking wine that represent respectively the body and blood of Jesus Christ, participate in his sacrificial death (cf. John 6:53–56). As a result of Christ's atoning death, individuals are made holy and perfect (cf. Heb. 10:1, 10, 14; 13:12).

---

of Unleavened Bread. Since in NT times the day was reckoned as beginning at sunset, sunset on Friday marked the beginning of the first day of the Feast of Unleavened Bread (that is, the fifteenth day of the month). If the Passover meal was eaten on the evening of the fourteenth day of the month, this would have been the Thursday evening (as implied in the Synoptic Gospels). We may assume that Jesus and his disciples followed the custom of their day and ate the Passover on the Thursday evening.

If the timings of the Passover had been reckoned on the basis of the earliest OT regulations, when the day was viewed as starting with sunrise, the following scenario would have occurred. Assuming that the day began at sunrise, the first day of Unleavened Bread (the fifteenth day of the month) would have commenced on the Saturday morning, not the Friday evening. The Passover sacrifice would have been offered up on Friday afternoon, with the meal being eaten on the Friday evening, the evening of the fourteenth day of the month. Possibly John saw in the death of Jesus on the Friday an exact fulfillment of the Exodus instructions for keeping the Passover.

15

The Covenant at Sinai

After their divine rescue from Egypt, the Israelites' relationship with God is formalized through a special agreement, which soon follows. This agreement, or covenant, sets out how the people must live in order to be a holy nation. Two sets of obligations are placed before the people. The Ten Commandments, which make up the principal obligations of the covenant, emphasize the importance of loving God and one's neighbor. A further document, the Book of the Covenant, contains more detailed obligations, which take a number of forms: some are model laws that can be enforced by human courts; others are moral rules that emphasize exemplary behavior, especially toward the weaker members of society; a further group of obligations focuses on religious duties. The principal and detailed obligations complement each other, setting out how God expects his people to live. Obedience will ensure God's blessing; disobedience will lead to punishment.

Introduction

At the heart of the book of Exodus is the establishment of a special covenant relationship between God and the Israelites. The basic form of this agreement is found in 19:4–6. If Israel, in the light of its divine deliverance from Egypt, will obey the LORD, then it will be his "treasured possession, . . . a kingdom of priests and a holy nation." Four factors are worth noting about this covenant.

First, from beginning to end God takes the initiative in making the covenant. He is the one who rescues the Israelites from Egypt and leads them to Mount Sinai (cf. 19:4; 20:2). There he instructs Moses on how the people must prepare themselves (19:10–13, 21–22). Following his dramatic arrival on Mount Sinai, God announces directly to the people the main conditions of the covenant; the Israelites do not negotiate. Throughout the scenes, God acts first, and the people are invited to respond. God does not compel them to enter into this covenant relationship but graciously offers them the opportunity to become his chosen people.

Second, God highlights Israel's special status: "Out of all nations you will be my treasured possession" (19:5). Furthermore, they will be "a kingdom of priests and a holy nation" (19:6). The expression "a kingdom of priests" can also be translated "priestly kings" or "royal priests," suggesting that the Israelites are to enjoy the privilege of being both priests and royalty. Everything points toward this being a restoration of the status that humanity lost through Adam and Eve's betrayal of God in the Garden of Eden (Gen. 3). As a "kingdom of priests," the Israelites will soon be involved in the construction of a dwelling place for God, in partial fulfillment of God's creation plans for the earth.[1] They are also to be a holy nation, something that will occur as the Holy One comes to reside in their midst.[2] This will have important implications regarding how the Israelites are to live their daily lives. The obligations that God places before the people require them to reflect his righteous and loving nature in everything they do.

Third, the establishment of the covenant relationship is conditional on Israel's obedience to God. After throwing off the yoke of Egyptian slavery, the Israelites must now obey a new sovereign. Obedience to God lies at the heart of the covenant relationship (cf. 19:8; 24:3, 7). However, obedience by itself does not create the special covenant relationship. Rather, it is a loving response to what God in his grace does first (cf. 20:6, "those who love me and keep my commandments").

Fourth, two sets of obligations are placed before the Israelites. The first set, the Ten Commandments (20:3–17), are announced directly to all the people by God. These are the main covenant obligations that the people must accept. Later through Moses, God gives further obligations that are recorded in a document known as the Book of the Covenant (20:22–23:33). The material in this document falls into different categories and consists of more specific obligations than those listed in the Ten Commandments. Both sets of obligations reveal how the Israelites must live in order to maintain their covenant relationship with God.

The Principal Covenant Obligations: The Ten Commandments (Exod. 20:1–17)

As the people stand in awe before Mount Sinai, they hear the very voice of God introducing himself to them: "I am the LORD your God, who brought you out

---

1. See chap. 8 above.
2. For a fuller treatment of the concept of holiness, see chap. 17 below.

210

of Egypt, out of the land of slavery" (20:2; cf. Deut. 4:12–13; 5:4). There then follows a list of stipulations that form the basis of Israel's covenant relationship with God (20:3–17). These are later termed "the Ten Words" (Exod. 34:28; Deut. 4:13; 10:4), from which we derive the designation Decalogue, or Ten Commandments. Their importance is further emphasized when God eventually inscribes them on two stone tablets (24:12; 31:18; 34:1, 28).

Strictly speaking, the Decalogue is not a collection of laws. Various factors set it apart from other legal collections of the Pentateuch. First, God speaks it directly to the people; at this stage Moses does not act as an intermediary (20:1, 19; cf. Deut. 4:12–13; 5:4–5, 22–27). Second, the Decalogue alone is inscribed on stone tablets by the "finger of God" (31:18; cf. 24:12; 32:15–16; 34:1, 28b; Deut. 5:22). Moses writes down all the other regulations and instructions (24:4; 34:27). Third, the Ten Commandments are not laws, since no punishments are listed. Although the second and fifth commandments appear to contain penalties, these are really motivational clauses designed to promote the observance of the divine instructions. Fourth, the language used in the Decalogue generally denotes broad concepts and lacks the kind of precision that one might expect from a legal document.[3] Finally, what human lawcourt could begin to enforce the prohibition against coveting described in the tenth commandment?

The stipulations outlined by the LORD are to govern Israel's relationship with its God. These represent the principal requirements that God places on the people of Israel for the establishment and maintenance of the divine/human covenant relationship. The covenant stipulations in Exodus 20 are listed in order of descending priority and focus on the Israelites' relationships first with the LORD and then with other people. The people are to be single-minded in their devotion to the one who has delivered them from Egypt; they are to worship only Yahweh (20:3). Furthermore, their social behavior is to follow a pattern that places a high priority on the rights of the individual with regard to life, marriage, and possessions. They are to obey these commands out of love for God, being people "who love me and keep my commands" (20:6).

First Commandment (20:3)

You shall have no other gods before me. Sole allegiance to the LORD lies at the very heart of the covenant relationship. It is the foundation upon which everything else rests. In practice the people are to be monotheistic, serving or worshiping only the LORD. As is made clear elsewhere in the Pentateuch, the worship of other deities is punishable by death (Num. 25:1–18; Deut. 13:1–18).

---

3. For this reason, attempts to carefully define the legal boundaries established by the Decalogue are fraught with problems. Anyone trying to decide precisely what is included and excluded by, e.g., "honoring parents" will never arrive at a satisfactory conclusion on the basis of the terminology used in the Decalogue. What we have here are broad principles, not laws designed for judicial use.

Second Commandment (20:4–6)

You shall not make for yourself an image. Unlike contemporary peoples, the Israelites are not to make or worship visual representations of their God. In both Egypt and Canaan, human and animal forms played an important function in depicting the attributes of a deity. Any attempt on the part of the Israelites to represent the LORD by using such images would produce a distorted picture of his true nature. However, in the ancient world the image played a more important role than merely being a representation of the deity. The image was understood to be the place where the deity would manifest itself. The book of Exodus, however, emphasizes the LORD's self-disclosure through "signs and wonders," theophanies, and verbal communications, occasionally in combination. Furthermore, God's presence among the Israelites is to be linked to the tabernacle or divine tent. Here the LORD will manifest himself to the people through theophany and speech. Given these alternative modes of divine manifestation, images are both unnecessary and inappropriate. The incident of the golden calf in Exodus 32 reveals both the necessity of this prohibition, in the light of the people's desire to have some visual image of the LORD, and the serious consequences of disregarding it.

Third Commandment (20:7)

You shall not misuse the name of the LORD your God. Whereas the second commandment prohibits visual representations of God, the third focuses on verbal representations. As a sign of their respect for God, the people are to exercise the greatest caution when talking about God or invoking his name. They are to say nothing that might detract from a true appreciation of his nature and character.

Fourth Commandment (20:8–11)

Remember the Sabbath day by keeping it holy. The people are to refrain from work on the seventh day, the Sabbath. According to 31:12–18, the Sabbath is the sign of the covenant relationship inaugurated at Sinai; as such it functions like the earlier covenant sign of circumcision (Gen. 17:9–14). Anyone failing to observe the Sabbath shows their disdain for the special relationship established between the LORD and Israel. With its emphasis on rest, this commandment anticipates the establishment of God's sovereign reign over all the earth, when he will "rest" in his temple-city (cf. Gen. 2:1–3).

Fifth Commandment (20:12)

Honor your father and your mother. The concept of honoring is usually associated with God or his representatives, prophets and kings. In all likelihood parents are envisaged as representing God to their children, the family unit being a miniature of the nation. Furthermore, in ancient Israel the extended family was important, and family heads played a significant role in communal matters. Any attempt to undermine the authority of parents was an attack on the basic authority structure within the local community. The seriousness of this commandment is reflected in the fact that the death penalty is required for children who willfully disrespect their parents (Exod. 21:15, 17). If children respect parents as authority figures within the family, then respect for authority figures within society at large will also follow.

Sixth Commandment (20:13)

You shall not murder. This commandment, by prohibiting murder or manslaughter,[4] demonstrates the high priority that God places on human life. No human has the right to take another's life, because each person is made in God's image (cf. Gen. 1:27; 9:6). In the Pentateuch the punishment for taking another's life is normally death, although different factors may be taken into account when determining the precise penalty. The Old Testament laws draw a careful distinction between premeditated and accidental deaths (see "The Sanctity of Life," below). Although the commandment prohibits individual Israelites from taking the life of another, it does not necessarily proscribe judicial executions for capital offenses or deaths resulting from war sanctioned by God himself.

Seventh Commandment (20:14)

You shall not commit adultery. In God's order of priority, the sanctity of human life is followed by the importance of the marriage relationship. Adultery here means sexual relations between a married person and someone who is not the spouse. Those caught in adultery could be executed (Lev. 20:10; Deut. 22:22). Divorce was permitted, but not encouraged (cf. Deut. 24:1). As a whole the Bible reveals that God desires the establishment of harmonious marital relationships, with neither partner doing anything to undermine this.

Eighth Commandment (20:15)

You shall not steal. The next principle to govern the Israelites' relationship with God was respect for the property of others. Any individual found guilty of dispossessing another was punished in accordance with the value of what was stolen, and the injured party was suitably compensated. While other ancient Near Eastern cultures sometimes invoked the death penalty for theft,

---

4. The Hebrew term used, *rāṣaḥ* (*rātsakh*), refers to the killing of a person (but not animals). Given its use elsewhere in the OT, it is not possible to restrict its meaning to "murder" (as does NIV).

the Old Testament consistently rejects such a position, indicating clearly that God values human life and the marital relationship above property.

Ninth Commandment (20:16)

You shall not give false testimony against your neighbor. In the final two commandments we proceed from prohibitions involving actions to prohibitions involving words and thoughts respectively. This concludes the downward progression of priorities that we have observed. The ninth commandment emphasizes the importance of truthfulness. While the prohibition against false testimony is primarily intended for a court of law, it may be extended to include any situation in which untrue words are used to harm another individual.

Tenth Commandment (20:17)

You shall not covet your neighbor's house. The final commandment forbids an individual to covet what belongs to another. Unlike all the other commands, it addresses specifically inner feelings and thoughts, such as envy or greed. If the Israelites are to enjoy a harmonious covenant relationship with God, every aspect of their lives must conform to his will. Outward adherence is insufficient; their inner selves need to be patterned according to the divine principles of morality found in the Ten Commandments.

The Detailed Covenant Obligations

Alongside the principal obligations of the Decalogue, God through Moses also gives other obligations that must be observed. Later Moses records everything that the LORD has said in a document known appropriately as the Book of the Covenant (24:7; cf. 24:4). Possibly most, if not all, of this document is preserved in 20:23–23:33. As it stands, it falls into five sections. The opening part focuses on issues regarding the divine presence and how the Israelites are to encounter God (20:23–26). Second, there is a long list of laws dealing with various aspects of social life (21:1–22:20). The next part consists of moral rules or requirements that highlight the exemplary behavior that God expects of his people, especially toward the underprivileged (22:21–23:9). Then follow instructions regarding the observance of the Sabbath and religious festivals (23:10–19). The final section outlines how God will act on behalf of the Israelites, enabling them to take possession of the land of Canaan (23:20–33).

In a book that underlines God's passionate concern for justice through his rescue of the Israelites from Egypt, it is hardly surprising that a similar concern for justice should dominate the covenant that he has established with the Israelites. This is most apparent in the legal material and moral rules that form the second and third sections of the Book of the Covenant.

The Legal Material of the Book of the Covenant (Exod. 21:1–22:20)

The material that comprises this section probably represents only some of the statutes that formed part of ancient Israel's law. Those listed are probably intended to be illustrations, offering guidance as to how various wrongdoings should be punished. In all likelihood some of those included here have been selected because they parallel God's actions in rescuing the Israelites from slavery in Egypt. At the very outset the principle is established that slaves have the right to be set free after a fixed period of time (21:1–4); this implies that the Egyptians acted illegally in holding the Israelites as slaves for a long period of time. In contrast, the inclusion of the statutes concerning a slave who loves his master (21:5–6) and a female servant (21:7–11) is intended to highlight various aspects of Israel's covenant relationship with the LORD: the Israelites will serve the LORD because they love him; having chosen Israel, God will remain faithful to them. A further group of laws draws attention to the necessity of compensation for those who have been physically injured (21:18–27). In particular, any slave who suffers serious injury at the hand of the master is to be released immediately (21:26–27). In the light of Israel's harsh treatment in Egypt (cf. 2:11; 5:14–16), these laws indirectly justify the LORD's action in freeing the Israelites. Another set of laws focuses on the concept of restitution (22:1–15). Here also it is possible to see a connection with earlier comments about how the Israelites demanded articles of silver and gold and clothing from the Egyptians (3:21–22; 11:2; 12:35–36). These items partially compensated the Israelites for the way in which they had been exploited in Egypt.

Apart from their relevance in justifying prior events in the book of Exodus, the laws in this section are also significant because of the ideals and values that permeate them. In all likelihood they are given as model laws, providing guidance for situations not directly covered by them.[5] The following concepts are the most noteworthy.

Moral Symmetry

The biblical laws are based on the principle that the punishment should match the crime. This is stated most clearly in the well-known but generally misunderstood "law of talion": "life for life, eye for eye, tooth for tooth, hand for hand, foot for foot, burn for burn, wound for wound, bruise for bruise" (21:23–25; cf. Lev. 24:17–21; Deut. 19:21). At first sight, the law of talion appears to be a rather barbaric way of ensuring justice. Yet within the development of law in the ancient Near East, it represents an important advance. In the earliest known collections of laws, monetary fines were

---

5. This possibility is highlighted by the detailed study of J. M. Sprinkle, *"The Book of the Covenant": A Literary Approach*, JSOTSup 174 (Sheffield: JSOT Press, 1994).

imposed in cases of assault and bodily injury. The weakness of such fines was that they failed to take into account an individual's ability to pay. (For an unemployed laborer, a fine of a thousand dollars imposes great hardship; to a millionaire it is a trifle.) The law of talion removes all such discrepancies by ensuring that the punishment should be no less, or no more, than the crime demands.

The law of talion, however, was not necessarily applied literally. In the Book of the Covenant it is preceded by a case of wounding, the punishment for which is the cost of medical expenses and compensation for lost wages (21:18–19). Similarly, it is followed immediately by a law in which a servant is granted release as compensation for the loss of an eye or a tooth (21:26–27). Clearly, there was no literal application of the law of talion in these instances.

The Sanctity of Life

Many modern readers of the biblical laws are likely to be disturbed by the use of capital punishment for a variety of crimes, including murder, kidnapping, physical or verbal assaults against parents, sorcery, bestiality, and idolatry (21:12–17; 22:18–20).[6] Against modern standards of justice, this punishment appears to be extremely harsh. Nevertheless, it reflects the value that God expected the Israelites to place on individual human life, the hierarchical structure within the family, and the purity of worship. In the case of murder the death penalty is invoked, not out of indifference for human life, but rather because each human life is of tremendous value (cf. Gen. 9:6). A life for a life does not express vengefulness, but rather the idea that the only payment that can be made for the taking of a human life is a human life itself. This even applies to animals responsible for human deaths (21:28).[7]

The distinctiveness of the biblical laws is apparent when one compares the other ancient Near Eastern laws. In the earlier Laws of Hammurabi (ca. 1750 BC), a murderer is required only to make financial compensation to the

6. Stoning was used as a common means of execution because it underlined that the whole community, without exception, was responsible for the judicial death of the criminal. Because of the serious consequences of their testimony in capital cases, the prosecution witnesses had to throw the first stones (Deut. 17:7).

7. In the light of these observations, it might appear that Christians ought to support the death penalty for crimes like murder. However, other factors must be considered. First, the ancient Israelites did not have the option of sentencing a murderer to life imprisonment; there were no facilities to imprison someone for a long period of time. Remarkably, imprisonment was rarely used as a means of punishment for any crime. Obviously this greatly restricted their choice of punishment. Second, it is likely that the death penalty was rarely utilized. This probably ensured that its use did not have the effect of devaluing human life. To make frequent recourse to capital punishment might suggest that human life is of little esteem, thus negating the very reason for adopting it. Whatever form of punishment we endorse, as Christians we must always ensure that it does not undermine the sanctity of human life.

victim's family. This contrasts sharply with the biblical insistence of a life for a life. However, the nonbiblical laws apply the death penalty to breaking and entering, looting at a fire, and theft. These examples reveal that in other cultures financial loss was sometimes treated more seriously than loss of life. The biblical laws consistently emphasize that human life is of greater value than material possessions.

Moral Imperatives (Exod. 22:21–23:9)

The material in this passage is generally taken to be detailed statutes. However, a number of factors suggest that it should be distinguished from the model laws found in 21:1–22:20:

1. The section is marked off from the surrounding material by the frame (*inclusio*) formed by 22:21 and 23:9. Both verses not only prohibit the mistreatment of aliens; they also underline this by reminding the Israelites that they were once aliens in Egypt.
2. The way in which the material is presented does not conform to the two distinctive forms used in 21:1–22:20;[8] rather, it is reminiscent of the form adopted in the Decalogue.
3. Apart from the general comment in 22:24, "I will kill you with the sword," no penalties enforceable by a human court are stipulated for breaking the rules outlined here.
4. The subject matter of this section is distinctive. It encourages both a caring attitude toward the weak and vulnerable members of society (aliens, widows, orphans, the needy, the poor) and a concern that the legal system be totally impartial. Those involved in disputes are to favor neither the rich, by accepting a bribe (23:8), nor the poor (23:3). Everyone, regardless of their class, is to be treated equally (23:6, 9). A witness must not be swayed by social pressure (23:2) and should ensure that their testimony is truthful (23:1, 7).

The commands found here seek to inculcate a standard of behavior that goes beyond the letter of the law. A human court is unlikely to prosecute someone for failing to return his enemy's straying animal; nevertheless, God demands that his people should overcome evil with good (23:4–5; cf. Matt. 5:43–48; Rom. 12:19–21). In the light of the special relationship being established between God and the people, it is surely significant that at the middle of this section is the command "You are to be my holy people" (22:31). Here we see how God's holy people should live.

8. It is not in the common forms of case law: "If . . . , then . . ."; "You shall surely . . ."

Instructions for the Sabbath and Religious Festivals (Exod. 23:10–19)

In the fourth section of the Book of the Covenant, the Israelites are reminded of their obligation to worship the LORD alone: "Do not invoke the names of other gods; do not let them be heard on your lips" (23:13).[9] Such worship lies at the heart of the three annual festivals, which celebrate the LORD's benevolence toward Israel and the Sabbath. The observance of the Sabbath is exceptionally important because it is the sign of the covenant that is being established between God and Israel (31:12–17). Anyone desecrating the Sabbath is guilty of renouncing this special relationship with God; the consequence is death (31:14–15).

The Reciprocal Nature of the Covenant (Exod. 23:20–33)

The final part of the Book of the Covenant (23:20–33) highlights the reciprocal nature of the covenant being established between God and Israel. If the Israelites obey the LORD their God, then they will take possession of the land of Canaan (23:22–23). Furthermore, God's blessing will ensure their future comfort (23:25–26) and security (23:27–28). As a consequence of their relationship with the LORD, the Israelites must distance themselves from the worship of other gods by destroying all pagan images and places of worship (23:24). For similar reasons, they are not to enter into any treaty with the inhabitants of Canaan lest this cause them to compromise their exclusive allegiance to the LORD (23:32–33). Such a warning is necessary. Although God promises to remove from the land the nations already living there, they will be expelled only gradually lest the land become desolate (23:29–30).

The Ratification of the Covenant

After descending from the mountain, Moses relays to the people God's words. Once more they express their willingness to do all that God commands (24:3; cf. 19:8). There follows a brief account of the ceremony by which the covenant between the LORD and Israel is ratified (24:4–11). The activities outlined here reflect the three main sections of the LORD's speech to Moses (20:24–24:2). The building of an altar and the offering of sacrifices parallel the instructions given in 20:24–26. Moses then reads to the people "the Book of the Covenant"

---

9. The material in Exod. 23:10–19 is carefully structured, falling into two halves, centered on v. 13, with each half subdivided into two parts. The first half deals with the seventh year (vv. 10–11) and the seventh day (v. 12). Verses 14–19 are concerned with the three main festivals that the Israelites celebrate annually: Unleavened Bread, Harvest, Ingathering. The instructions in vv. 17–19 correspond with the three feasts outlined in vv. 14–16; note in particular how v. 17 parallels v. 14.

(24:7), the middle section of the divine speech (21:1–23:33). After the Israelites again acknowledge their willingness to obey God (24:7), the covenant is sealed through the sprinkling of blood on the people (24:8). Finally, God's invitation to Moses and the elders to come up the mountain (24:9–11) corresponds to the third section of the divine speech (24:1–2).

Rebellion in the Camp

After having the covenant successfully ratified, Moses ascends Mount Sinai in order to receive instructions for building the tabernacle (25:1–31:18). However, his long absence of "forty days and forty nights" (24:18) creates an atmosphere of uncertainty in the Israelite camp. Perhaps fearful of what God may have done to Moses (cf. 20:19), the Israelites seek reassurance through the construction of an image that will represent the LORD's presence in their midst. Turning to Aaron, the people ask him to make "gods," or better, "a god" (so NIV mg.), to go before them (32:1).[10] Although the Israelites do not consciously reject the LORD as their God, their attempt to portray him as a golden calf is a major breach of the covenant stipulations that they have earlier accepted (cf. 20:4–6; 20:23).[11] Such an obvious violation of the LORD's instructions invites fierce condemnation (cf. 32:7–10).

Horrified by what has taken place, the LORD orders Moses to return to the camp (32:7). God's anger is roused by how the Israelites have so quickly turned away from his commands, and this in spite of their repeated affirmations that they will do everything that the LORD has said (19:8; 24:3, 7). Such disrespect for God merits the harshest of punishments: death. God assures Moses that he, in contrast to the people, will become "a great nation," echoing God's earlier promise to Abraham (Gen. 12:3). Perhaps surprisingly, Moses intervenes and pleads on behalf of the people for mercy, recalling God's marvelous deliverance of them from Egypt and his much earlier covenant with Abraham, Isaac, and Jacob (32:11–13). His petition throughout is based on the character and honor of God. Moreover, he makes no attempt to excuse the people's sinful behavior. So compelling is his intercession that God relents from the immediate destruction of the people (32:14). Nevertheless, as the narrative later reveals, the people do not go unpunished (32:28, 35).

10. Several factors indicate that the image of the golden calf is meant to represent the LORD. According to the latter part of Exod. 32:4, the calf represents the god who has delivered the people from Egypt; it is no new deity. Second, the festival, enthusiastically celebrated by the people (32:6), is described by Aaron as "to the LORD" (32:5). Moreover, the festal activities resemble those recorded in Exod. 24 regarding the ratification of the covenant between the LORD and the Israelites.

11. The narrator hints at this indirectly through his use of the Hebrew term 'ĕlōhîm, "god/gods," in Exod. 32:1, 4, 8; when used with plural verbs, 'ĕlōhîm normally refers to pagan gods; when used with singular verbs, as in these verses, it normally refers to the LORD.

When Moses eventually sees what has been happening in the camp, he too becomes enraged. By deliberately breaking the divinely inscribed stone tablets, containing the terms of agreement, Moses indicates that the covenant relationship between God and the Israelites is now ended.

In Exodus 32 the account is dominated by the rebellion of the Israelites and God's punishment of the people; but in Exodus 33 attention switches to Moses, the faithful servant, and his remarkable friendship with the LORD. Moses's unique relationship with God provides the opportunity for him to intercede on behalf of the people; as a result, the covenant is renewed. This is attributed not to some dramatic change of heart on the part of the people, but to the LORD's compassion and mercy. Consequently, Moses is instructed to bring up the mountain two stone tablets to replace those previously broken (34:1). Once more Moses writes down the detailed covenant obligations (34:27; cf. 24:4),[12] and God inscribes on the new stone tablets the "Ten Words," or Decalogue (34:28; cf. 20:3–17).[13]

Old Testament Summary

The covenant at Sinai marked an important stage in God's relationship with the Israelites. At the center of God's plans for his people was the hope that they would reflect his holy nature by being perfect in all they do, say, and think. Unfortunately, the people soon displayed, through building the golden calf, their inability to keep the obligations set before them. As a result the covenant relationship with God, which promised to be a source of great blessing, became for them, due to their disobedience, a source of divine cursing.

New Testament Connections

For religious Jews of the New Testament period, it was exceptionally important to keep the Mosaic law; it was considered to be the essence of God's requirements for holy living. Not surprisingly, much discussion and debate took place to determine the precise requirements of the law, and different schools of thought adopted differing views on how the Mosaic law should be interpreted and related to contemporary situations. Against this background it is no surprise that the law figured prominently both in the teaching of Jesus and in various issues addressed by the early church.

12. The terms of the covenant, outlined in Exod. 34:11–26 (land, festivals), closely parallel those found in the last two sections of the Book of the Covenant (23:14–33; festivals, land), except that their order is here reversed.

13. Although the subject of the verb in 34:28b is not clearly stated, it may be deduced from 34:1 that the tablets were again inscribed by the Lord (cf. 32:16). It is not unusual in Hebrew narrative for the subject of the verb to change without this being clearly indicated.

Jesus and the Law

The four Gospels all indicate that Jesus frequently came into conflict with the religious leaders of his day concerning his attitude toward the law. This is most apparent regarding the keeping of the Sabbath; the Gospels convey the impression that the Pharisees and teachers of the law regularly condemned Jesus's actions on the Sabbath, especially his willingness to heal then (Matt. 12:9–14; Mark 3:1–6; Luke 6:6–11; 13:10–17; 14:1–6; John 5:1–15; 7:21–24). Tension also existed regarding Jesus's attitude toward the laws on ritual cleanliness (Matt. 15:10–20; Mark 7:1–8), and the Pharisees were quick to condemn Jesus's willingness to eat with "sinners" (Matt. 9:10–11; 11:19; Mark 2:15–16; Luke 5:29–30; 7:34; 15:2). How then did Jesus view the Old Testament law?

Two observations may be made. First, Jesus held the law in high regard. Although he did not conform to all the ways in which his contemporaries kept the Mosaic law, he constantly affirmed the importance of the law.

> Truly I tell you, until heaven and earth disappear, not the smallest letter, not the least stroke of a pen, will by any means disappear from the Law until everything is accomplished. Therefore anyone who sets aside one of the least of these commands and teaches others accordingly will be called least in the kingdom of heaven, but whoever practices and teaches these commands will be called great in the kingdom of heaven. For I tell you that unless your righteousness surpasses that of the Pharisees and the teachers of the law, you will certainly not enter the kingdom of heaven. (Matt. 5:18–20)

Moreover, when asked, "Which is the greatest commandment in the Law?" Jesus answered by stressing the need to love God and love one's neighbor (Matt. 22:37–39; Mark 12:29–31). His answer summarizes the twofold division found in the Ten Commandments. Love for God must come first, but it must never be divorced from love for one's neighbor; the former leads automatically to the latter.

Second, Jesus emphasized the true intention of the law. Jesus parted company from most other religious leaders of his day on the fundamental issue of the law's nature and function. Many of his contemporaries viewed it as a line separating right and wrong behavior. In the light of this, they sought to determine which actions were within the law and which were outside the law; that is, an individual was righteous as long as he or she did not go beyond the boundary established by the law. This approach, however, encouraged individuals to focus on the minimum requirements of the law and fostered a very legalistic attitude toward human behavior. Furthermore, as Jesus pointed out, it created all kinds of anomalies and resulted in the law being used for unrighteous ends.[14] In marked contrast, Jesus viewed the law as a sign pointing

14. We see this in his comments about making oaths (Matt. 5:33–37) and the law of Corban (Matt. 15:3–9; Mark 7:9–13).

to the type of behavior that God desired. Jesus maintained that to keep the law fully one had to be perfect as God is perfect (cf. Matt. 5:48). Hence he called on his disciples to display a righteousness that surpassed that of the Pharisees and the teachers of the law (cf. Matt. 5:20). He reminded his followers that to interpret the commandments as requiring only outward obedience was to misunderstand their purpose (Matt. 5:17–48). His approach is clearly seen in his understanding of the commandments "Do not murder" and "Do not commit adultery." These he interpreted respectively to mean "Do not do, say, or think anything that might lead to murder or adultery." Furthermore, he indicated that the Old Testament law occasionally permitted certain actions (e.g., divorce) not because it reflected God's perfect will but because God sought to accommodate the hardness of human hearts (Matt. 19:3–9). While the Pharisees and the teachers of the law exploited such divine accommodations, Jesus emphasized that each individual should seek to fulfill in his or her life God's original design for human existence.

Paul and the Law

Much has been written about Paul's view of the Old Testament law. It is possible here to make only a few brief observations. Like Jesus, Paul condemned a legalistic understanding of the law that undermined its true purpose. In Galatians 3:15–25 he argues that the divine covenant made with Abraham takes precedence over the law given several centuries later at Mount Sinai. While his opponents were advocating that believers must keep the law in order to be righteous, Paul responded by noting that the law, given later to fulfill a temporary role until Christ came, could never make anyone righteous; it merely indicated the righteousness required by God, not the means of achieving such righteousness. For this reason, Paul underlined the necessity of becoming righteous through faith.

The New Covenant

An important conviction among the early Christians was the belief that through Jesus Christ, God had established a new covenant that superseded the covenant inaugurated centuries earlier at Sinai. Not surprisingly, such a view provoked considerable hostility from Jews whose religious outlook was centered on the Sinai covenant. This new covenant was introduced by Jesus at the Last Supper (Matt. 26:28; Mark 14:24; Luke 22:20; 1 Cor. 11:25) and sealed by his sacrificial death (Heb. 9:11–28). Regarding its superiority over the older Sinai covenant, the author of Hebrews, quoting Jeremiah 31:31–34, makes a number of important points. The new covenant is unlike the one made at Sinai (Heb. 8:9). Although the Sinai covenant was intended to secure a lasting relationship between God and the Israelites, it did not succeed because the people failed to keep the divine obligations that were placed on them; their faithlessness caused God to turn away from them (8:9). The success of the new covenant is guaranteed by God's ability to do for the people what they themselves could not achieve. The laws of the old covenant were inscribed on stone tablets; under the new covenant, God puts his laws in the hearts and minds of believers (cf. 2 Cor. 3:6). Through an inner transformation, accomplished by the indwelling of the Holy Spirit, God enables his people to live as he had originally intended. A further consequence of the new covenant is a better knowledge of God: "No longer will they teach their neighbor, or say to one another, 'Know the Lord,' because they will all know me, from the least of them to the greatest" (Heb. 8:11). Finally, the new covenant brings divine forgiveness for human sin and wickedness (8:12). Under the old covenant, God's forgiveness was linked to the atoning duties carried out by the high priest on the Day of Atonement. Because this was repeated annually, it guaranteed only limited forgiveness for the people. Since Christ's mediatorial role as a high priest far exceeds that of the Aaronic high priest, the new covenant provides a greater assurance of forgiveness.[15] Those who are justified by faith in Christ are divinely pardoned for all their sins, past, present, and future.

The inauguration of a new covenant by Christ influenced the early church in another way. Those bound by the old covenant were expected to demonstrate their allegiance by keeping holy the seventh day of the week; the Sabbath was the sign of the Sinai covenant (Exod. 31:13–17). With the arrival of a new covenant, the strict observance of the Sabbath, like circumcision, was no longer binding on Christians. Rather, to commemorate Christ's resurrection the early church met for worship on the first day of the week (cf. Acts 20:7; 1 Cor. 16:2). The Sabbath was replaced by the Lord's Day.

At the heart of the Sinai covenant was God's desire that Israel would be "a kingdom of priests and a holy nation" (Exod. 19:6). This thought is echoed in 1 Peter 2:9–10: "You are a chosen people, a royal priesthood, a holy nation, God's special possession, that you may declare the praises of him who called you out of darkness into his wonderful light. Once you were not a people, but now you are the people of God; once you had not received mercy, but now you have received mercy" (cf. Rev. 1:6; 5:10; 20:6). All that the Sinai covenant failed to achieve due to human disobedience is now fulfilled through the new covenant inaugurated by Jesus Christ's death, resurrection, and ascension.

15. This is discussed more fully in chap. 18 below.

16

The Tabernacle

The final third of the book of Exodus focuses almost exclusively on the construction and erection of the tabernacle. The extent of the material highlights the importance of the tabernacle as God's dwelling place. Although it takes the form of a rectangular tent, the extensive use of gold and blue fabrics indicates that the tabernacle is a royal residence. Its portable nature ensures that the divine king will be with his people wherever they go. A further aspect that plays an important part in the design of the tabernacle and its furnishings is the holy nature of God's being. The outer curtain fence separates sinful people from a holy God, and the bronze altar stands as a vivid reminder that only those who have made atonement for their sin and uncleanness may approach God. Finally, the tabernacle is designated "the tent of meeting," indicating that it is the place where divinity and humanity commune together.

Introduction

The importance of the tabernacle is highlighted by the attention given to recording both God's description of how the tent and its furnishing should be manufactured (Exod. 25:1–31:11), and then the construction (35:1–40:33). Altogether, including the details relating to the consecration of the priests, approximately one-quarter of Exodus is given to describing the making of the tabernacle. Chapters 25–31 consist of a very long divine speech, outlining the preparations necessary for the construction of a special tent and the appointment of priests. Much of this material is repeated in 36:8–39:31, where we have an almost word-for-word record of the fulfillment of the instructions

Table 16.1
Instructions and Fulfillment in Exodus 25–30 and 36–39

Object	Instructions	Fulfillment
Tabernacle	26:1–11, 14–29, 31–32, 36–37	36:8–38
Ark	25:10–14, 17–20	37:1–9
Table	25:23–29	37:10–16
Lampstand	25:31–39	37:17–24
Incense altar	30:1–5	37:25–28
Anointing oil	30:25	37:29
Bronze altar	27:1–8	38:1–7
Bronze basin	30:18	38:8
Courtyard	27:9–19	38:9–20
Ephod	28:6–12	39:2–7
Breastpiece	28:15–28	39:8–21
Robe	28:31–34	39:22–26
Tunic, turban, sash	28:39	39:27–29
Gold plate	28:36–37	39:30–31

the LORD has given to Moses (see table 16.1). Such repetition is the original author's way of underlining the importance of the tabernacle.[1]

The initial divine instructions list the more important objects first; the account of their construction reflects the order in which the items are assembled when the tabernacle is erected (cf. 40:2–8, 12–14; 40:17–33) and conforms to the pattern found in other summaries of the tabernacle equipment (cf. 31:7–9; 35:11–18; 39:33–40; see table 16.2). Occasionally the divine instructions, but rarely the fulfillment, contain additional material relating to the use of a particular object (e.g., 30:6–10; 30:18–21). The similarity between the instructions and their fulfillment indicates that the people obey the LORD "to the letter." Everything is made just as Moses has been instructed. Exodus ends in dramatic fashion by describing how God's glory fills the tabernacle "on the first day of the first month in the second year" (40:17), just in time for the people to celebrate the first anniversary of their deliverance from Egypt (cf. Num. 9:1–5).

A Royal Tent

An important theme in the final part of Exodus is God's intention to dwell among the people (25:8; cf. 29:45–46). Having rescued them from the control of

---

1. Remarkably, in spite of the space devoted to recording the making of the tabernacle, the present account does not provide all the information necessary to fully reconstruct the original tent.

Table 16.2
Order of Presentation in Exodus 25–30 and 36–39

Instructions		Fulfillment	
Ark	25:10–22	Tabernacle	36:8–38
Table	25:23–30	Ark	37:1–9
Lampstand	25:31–39	Table	37:10–16
Tabernacle	26:1–37	Lampstand	37:17–24
Bronze altar	27:1–8	Incense altar	37:25–28
Courtyard	27:9–19	Anointing oil	37:29
Ephod	28:6–14	Incense	37:29
Breastpiece	28:15–30	Bronze altar	38:1–7
Robe	28:31–35	Bronze basin	38:8
Gold plate	28:36–38	Courtyard	38:9–20
Tunic, turban, sash	28:39	Ephod	39:2–7
Incense altar	30:1–10	Breastpiece	39:8–21
Bronze basin	30:18–21	Robe	39:22–26
Anointing oil	30:23–25	Tunic, turban, sash	39:27–29
Incense	30:34–36	Gold plate	39:30–31

Pharaoh and established a special covenant relationship with them, the LORD desires to accompany them into the promised land. Consequently, he commands Moses to construct a portable dwelling. Like his people, the sovereign LORD will dwell in a tent. However, his dwelling differs in the nature of the materials used in its construction. From the inventory of precious metals and bluish colored fabrics (25:3–7; cf. 35:5–9, 22–27), it is apparent that this is no common tent; it is for royal use. This is emphasized not only by the kinds of material used ("gold, silver, and bronze; blue, purple and scarlet yarn and fine linen") but also by their quantity. According to 38:21–31 approximately one ton of gold, four tons of silver, and two-and-a-half tons of bronze are used to make the tabernacle and its furnishings.[2]

Initially Moses is instructed to make three items of furniture for inside the tent. The first of these is a rectangular wooden chest or box, covered "with pure gold, both inside and out" (25:10–11). For ease of transportation the chest, or "ark," as it is traditionally known, is to be constructed with gold rings and poles (25:12–15). Inside this container Moses will later place the stone tablets, recording the "Testimony," or "terms of agreement," for the covenant between God and Israel (Exod. 25:16, 21; Deut. 10:8 refers to the chest as the "ark of the covenant of the LORD"). The lid of the ark, made of pure

2. Although the quantities involved appear large, they are by no means unusual when compared with contemporary practices in the ancient world.

gold, is designated an "atonement cover" (Exod. 25:17; cf. Heb. 9:5). Leviticus 16:1–34 (esp. vv. 11–17) describes the annual ritual, which takes place when the high priest sprinkles blood on the ark's lid to make atonement for "the uncleanness and rebellion of the Israelites, whatever their sins have been" (Lev. 16:16).[3] Two golden cherubim (or cherubs) are attached to the ends of the lid, facing each other with outspread wings.[4] Here, between the cherubim, God will later meet with Moses to communicate his instructions to the people (Exod. 25:22; 30:36; cf. Lev. 16:2). Apart from being a container, the ark also functions as the footstool of a throne protected by guardian cherubim (cf. 1 Sam. 4:4; 2 Sam. 6:2; 2 Kings 19:15; 1 Chron. 28:2; Pss. 80:1 [2]; 99:1, 5; 132:7; Isa. 37:16). Because of its importance as part of the LORD's throne, the manufacture of the ark is outlined first.

The second piece of furniture is a wooden table, overlaid with gold and fitted with rings and poles (Exod. 25:23–28). Plates, dishes, and other utensils, all of gold, are to be provided, and the "bread of the Presence" is to be placed on the table "at all times" (25:29–30).

The third main fixture to be constructed is a gold lampstand with seven lamps (25:31–40). The lampstand is to be made in the pattern of a growing tree, decorated with "flowerlike cups, buds and blossoms" (25:31). Three branches extend to either side of the central stem; the tops of the stem and branches are designed to hold lamps. No explanation is given as to why the lampstand should resemble a tree. Possibly it is meant to look like the tree of life in Genesis 3:22, symbolizing the life-giving power of God.

The table and lampstand, together with the chest/footstool, comprise the main items of furniture in an ancient home. As such they indicate that God lives within the tent. The abundant use of gold emphasizes the importance of the occupant. The provision of bread (Exod. 25:30) and light (27:21) are symbolic reminders that God is there at all times, both day and night.

Next, detailed instructions are provided for the construction of the actual tent or tabernacle (26:1–37). Some uncertainty exists over how the various curtains and wooden frames fit together. Since the entire structure is designed to be portable, its construction is probably similar to that used for other tents. The bluish fabrics and gold fittings are indicative of royalty. The rectangular structure is divided into two rooms by a curtain, one room probably being twice the size of the other (26:31–33). The "ark of the covenant law" ("ark of the Testimony," NIV 1984) is to be placed in the smaller of these rooms, in the western half of the tabernacle. Because the LORD is seated there, enthroned between the cherubim, this part is called the "Most Holy Place," or Holy of Holies (26:34). The larger room, to the east, is designated the "Holy Place" and is to be

---

3. The Day of Atonement ritual is discussed more fully in chap. 18 below.

4. Cherubim were the traditional guardians of holy places in the ancient Near East. Apart from the two described here, others are woven into the curtains that surround the tabernacle and those that separate the Holy of Holies from the Holy Place (Exod. 26:1, 31).

furnished with the golden table and lampstand (26:35). The curtain separating the two rooms contains woven figures of cherubim as a reminder that the way into the immediate presence of God is barred to sinful humans (cf. Gen. 3:24).[5]

FIGURE 16.1. Schematic Floor Plan of the Tabernacle

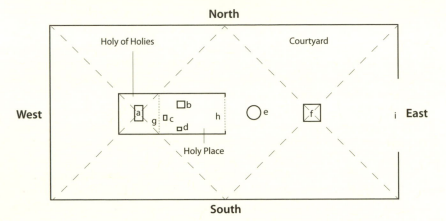

a. Ark of the Covenant   **b.** Table for the loaves   **c.** Altar for incense   **d.** Lampstand
e. Basin   **f.** Altar for offerings   **g.** Curtain   **h.** Screen   **i.** Entrance

One further item of furniture is to be made for inside the royal tent: an incense altar (Exod. 30:1–10). It is to be made of acacia wood and plated with pure gold, and placed in the Holy Place alongside the golden table and lampstand. Twice daily Aaron is to burn fragrant incense upon it (30:7–8), and once a year, probably on the Day of Atonement (cf. Lev. 16:15–19), he is to make atonement on its horns (Exod. 30:10).[6]

A Holy Tent

Around the tabernacle or royal tent, Moses is to construct a courtyard by erecting a curtain fence. The courtyard, a rectangular shape twice as long as it is broad, measures approximately fifty meters by twenty-five meters and is surrounded by a curtain about two-and-a-half meters high. The shorter sides are to the east and west. The only entrance is on the eastern side.[7] On passing through this gateway, a worshiper first encounters a large bronze altar before approaching the tabernacle, which stands in the western part of the courtyard.

---

5. For a fuller discussion of the problems involved in reconstructing the tabernacle, see "Tabernacle," *IBD*, 1506–11.

6. The altar had four horns, one at each of its top corners.

7. For a diagram of the tabernacle, see next page.

FIGURE 16.2. Cut-Away Diagram of the Tabernacle

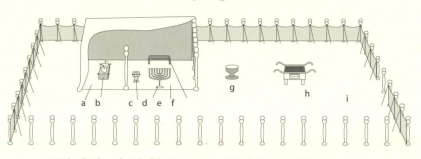

a. Holy of Holies   **b.** Ark of the Covenant   **c.** Altar for incense   **d.** Lampstand
e. Holy Place   **f.** Table for the loaves   **g.** Basin   **h.** Altar for offerings   **i.** Courtyard

The fence that surrounds the courtyard, along with the curtain that hangs across the entrance, prevents those outside from looking into the courtyard. Separated from the rest of the Israelite encampment, the courtyard is set apart as a holy area; only the tabernacle, in which God dwells, is considered to be more sacred.[8] This distinction between the holiness of the courtyard and that of the tabernacle is reflected in the value of the materials used in their construction. Whereas gold is regularly used within the tabernacle, the main metals utilized in the construction of the courtyard are silver and bronze. Just as Moses set a boundary around Mount Sinai to prevent the people from coming into the divine presence (Exod. 19:12–13, 21–24), so the courtyard fence prevents them from approaching God inadvertently. As Exodus regularly emphasizes, only those who are holy can come into the divine presence; to approach God otherwise has fatal consequences. Without the courtyard functioning as a buffer zone, it would be impossible for the Israelites to dwell in safety close to the LORD.

Since the area within the courtyard is holy ground, the priests—Aaron and his sons—assigned to serve there also must be holy. To indicate this, they are provided with "sacred garments." The materials used in their production, "gold, and blue, purple and scarlet yarn, and fine linen" (28:5), not only highlight the dignity and honor bestowed on Aaron and his sons, but also clearly associate them with the tabernacle, which is made of similar materials. As high priest Aaron is to wear "a breastpiece, an ephod, a robe, a woven tunic, a turban, and a sash" (28:4); his sons are to be given "tunics, sashes and caps" (28:40).[9] Most attention is focused on the special items worn by the high priest, especially the "ephod" (28:6–14) and "breastpiece" (28:15–30).

8. The two rooms of the tabernacle also differed in their degree of holiness. The Holy of Holies, which contains God's throne, may be entered by the high priest only on the Day of Atonement. The Holy Place, however, is entered daily by some of the priests who minister there.

9. The lack of reference to footwear may indicate that the priests serve barefooted; when God appeared in the burning bush, Moses was commanded to remove his sandals because the ground was holy (Exod. 3:5).

The first item mentioned in the list of high-priestly clothes is the ephod. Scholars refer to it by its Hebrew name *'ēpôd* (*'ēphôd*) because the biblical text does not provide sufficient information to reconstruct it exactly. Special reference is made to the two precious stones engraved with the names of the twelve tribes of Israel. They are mounted "in gold filigree settings" (Exod. 28:11), and are fastened "on the shoulder pieces of the ephod as memorial stones for the sons of Israel" (28:12). They are a reminder that Aaron serves God as high priest, not for his own benefit, but on behalf of all the Israelites.

The next item, designated a "breastpiece," appears from its description to be a square pouch that the high priest wears over his chest. The pouch is made of similar materials to the ephod and is attached to it. On the outside of the pouch are four rows of precious stones, with three stones in each row; each stone is to be inscribed with the name of an Israelite tribe. Although Aaron comes from the tribe of Levi, as high priest, wearing the names of the tribes on his chest, he ministers on behalf of all the people. The use of precious stones symbolizes the value that God places on his people Israel. Finally, instructions are given that "the Urim and the Thummim" should be placed in the pouch (28:30). The precise form of the Urim and Thummim remains uncertain. However, they are probably used as a means to determine God's judgment (cf. 22:8, 9).[10]

Other items of clothing worn by the high priest are mentioned in Exodus 28:31–43. A blue robe, adorned with embroidered pomegranates and golden bells, is presumably worn under the ephod and breastpiece. The tinkling of the bells serves to identify the one entering or leaving the Holy of Holies, enabling the high priest to come close to God in safety; anyone else venturing into the LORD's presence will die (cf. 19:12–13, 21–22, 24). As a further reminder of the sacred nature of priestly service, the front of Aaron's turban has a gold plate with the words "HOLY TO THE LORD" (28:36). Because he is set apart as holy, Aaron as high priest is able to mediate on behalf of the Israelites, ensuring that their sacrifices are acceptable to the LORD (28:38). Apart from the items already mentioned, Aaron is also to wear a tunic, turban, and sash (28:39); the tunic appears to be worn under the robe of the ephod (cf. 29:5). Since they do not relate directly to the "dignity and honor" of the priests (28:2), the instructions concerning underwear are given separately. The priests are to wear "linen undergarments" to prevent them from inadvertently exposing their genitalia in the Holy Place (cf. 20:26). Such nakedness is clearly inappropriate in the presence of the LORD (cf. Gen. 3:7, 10, 21). Moreover, since only the priests can enter the tabernacle, the command that they should wear undergarments will reassure those outside that nothing unseemly is occurring within the tabernacle.

To minister in God's holy presence the priests need to be holy. The instructions in 29:1–46 reflect the various stages (mentioned briefly in 28:41)

10. For a brief description and picture of a modern reconstruction of the breastpiece, see "Breastpiece of the High Priest," *IBD*, 207.

necessary for their consecration: clothe, anoint, "fill the hands,"[11] consecrate. After assembling the appropriate items (29:1–3), Moses is to wash[12] and clothe Aaron and his sons in their priestly garments (29:4–9). Then he is to anoint them with oil.[13] Next he is to offer up three different sacrifices, involving a bull and two rams. The first (29:10–14), best understood as a purification offering, involves the bull, and closely follows the instructions given later, in Leviticus 4:3–12, relating to the unintentional sin of an anointed priest. In this instance, however, the blood is probably placed on the horns of the large bronze altar in the courtyard and not on the gold incense altar within the tabernacle (Exod. 29:12; cf. Lev. 4:7). The blood purifies the altar, which has become defiled through contact with individuals who are considered unclean. The next sacrifice, a whole-burnt offering (29:15–18), follows exactly the instructions given later, in Leviticus 1:10–13, for the offering of a ram. The whole-burnt offering atones for the sins of Aaron and his sons. The total destruction of the animal is a vivid reminder that sinful humans cannot approach a holy God and live. The animal dies as a substitute for those who are identified with it by laying their hands on its head. The third sacrifice (29:19–34) closely resembles a fellowship or peace offering made as an expression of thankfulness (cf. Lev. 3:6–11; 7:12–15). However, the ritual described here has distinctive features, appropriate for this unique occasion. First, Aaron, his sons, and their garments are to be purified by sacrificial blood (29:19–21); whatever the blood touched is cleansed of defilement caused by human wrongdoing. By the anointing of the extremities, the entire body is made ritually clean. Second, verses 22–35 focus on the remuneration that Aaron and his sons are to receive as priests. The NIV wrongly refers to this as "the ram for the ordination" (29:22; cf. 29:26, 27, 31, 34); it is literally "the ram of [the] filling." This "filling" refers to the portion that is to be given to the priests after they offer up different sacrifices (cf. Lev. 6:14–18, 25–29; 7:1–38). The ritual that Moses will later perform consecrates the right thigh and breast for priestly consumption. A distinction is drawn between the "breast," which is "waved," and the "thigh," which is "presented" (29:27). On this occasion the breast will be given to Moses as his reward for offering the sacrifice (29:26), and the thigh will be burned on the altar, along with some bread (29:25). On future occasions, after the priests are consecrated, the breast of the fellowship sacrifice will be presented to all the priests, and the thigh given to the priest who officiates (Lev. 7:28–36). Apart from the breast, thigh, and various fatty portions, the rest of the ram of (the) filling is to be cooked and eaten, together with the remaining bread, at the entrance to the

11. Here NIV's "ordain" does not accurately translate the Hebrew original of Exod. 29:9.
12. Purity and cleanliness are closely associated with being holy (cf. Exod. 19:10, 14).
13. Special oil is to be manufactured to anoint the tabernacle, its furnishings, and the priests who serve there (Exod. 30:22–30). Since everything touched by this particular oil becomes holy, restrictions are placed on its production and use (30:31–33). Similar instructions are given for making and using the incense that is to be burned within the tabernacle (30:34–38).

tabernacle. By eating the sacrificial meat, the priests are sanctified or made holy. For this reason only the priests are to eat this holy food.

The ritual outlined in Exodus 29:1–34 is essential for the consecration of the priests. On the basis of verse 35, most commentators believe that this ritual is repeated every day for seven days. Alternatively, the sacrifices outlined in verses 36–41 are perhaps offered during the next six days, with Aaron and his sons under strict instructions to remain within the courtyard of the tabernacle (cf. Lev. 8:33–35). In either case the process of consecration or sanctification requires time. The fulfillment of the instructions regarding the consecration of Aaron and his sons is recorded in Leviticus 8:1–36.

Concerning the priests, Moses is also told to make a bronze basin (Exod. 30:17–21). This is to be placed between the tabernacle and the bronze altar so that Aaron and his sons can wash their hands and feet when serving within the tabernacle and courtyard (30:17–21). The requirement that the priests should wash symbolizes their need to remain holy and pure (cf. 19:14; 29:4).

Thus the Exodus narrative in a special way highlights the holy nature of the tabernacle and of those who minister within it.

A Tent of Meeting

The tabernacle is not only a royal and holy tent but also a tent of meeting. This is highlighted in God's comments in Exodus 29:43: "There . . . I will meet with the Israelites, and the place will be consecrated by my glory" (29:43). Like the Garden of Eden, the tabernacle is the place where divinity and humanity can commune together. However, to enable sinful people to meet a holy God, it is necessary for them to be sanctified from their sin and uncleanness. To this end God instructs Moses to construct a portable bronze-plated altar, which is to be situated in the courtyard, near the entrance to the tabernacle (27:1–8). From its dimensions, we can tell that this altar dominates the area in front of the tabernacle; it is 2.5 meters wide (half the width of the tabernacle) and 1.5 meters high. It consists of a square hollow framework made of acacia wood and overlaid with bronze. To create a draft for the incineration of the animal sacrifices, the lower part of each side is comprised of a grating of bronze network. The altar's position between the courtyard entrance and the tabernacle indicates that a worshiper can approach God only after offering a sacrifice to atone for sin.[14]

Following the erection of the tabernacle, a cloud covers it, and the glory of the LORD fills it (40:34). God now dwells in the midst of the people, and the tabernacle is designated "the tent of meeting" (40:35; cf. 27:21), replacing the tent used earlier by Moses (cf. 33:7–11).[15] It differs from this other tent, however,

---

14. Instructions for consecrating the altar are given in Exod. 29:36–37. Leviticus 1:1–7:38 details the various sacrifices that individuals are expected to offer.

15. Exod. 33:7–11 records how Moses, before the erection of the tabernacle, is in the custom of pitching a tent at some distance from the main encampment in order to meet with God. Given

in that God dwells within the tabernacle and Moses stays outside (40:35); with the earlier tent, Moses went inside and God remained outside (33:9). God's presence is visible to everyone through the cloud and fire that settle upon the tabernacle. From there he guides them on their journeys (40:36–38). Exodus concludes by recognizing the glorious presence of the sovereign God in the midst of his people Israel.[16]

The Provision of Materials and Skilled Craftsmen

The account of the making of the tabernacle also focuses on two practical matters regarding its construction. First, Moses is instructed to ask the people to make an offering to the LORD in order to provide the materials required for the construction of the tabernacle and related items (25:1–7). When Moses addresses the people (35:4–9), they respond generously (35:20–27). Indeed, such is their generosity that later they need to be restrained from giving too much (36:3–7). Their freewill gifts reflect their deep gratitude to God for delivering them from Egypt.

Second, God informs Moses that he has chosen and equipped certain men with the skills necessary to produce the tabernacle and its furnishings (31:1–11). Singled out for particular mention are Bezalel and Oholiab, whose special ability is attributed to the fact that they have been filled with "the Spirit of God" (31:3). Later, when placed in charge of the work (35:30–36:2), they also display their aptitude to teach others (35:34). Elsewhere attention is drawn to the women who devote their natural abilities and skills to the LORD by spinning yarn (35:25–26).

Various scholars have drawn attention to how Bezalel, who oversees the construction of the tabernacle, is portrayed by using terminology associated with the creation of the earth.

---

its specific function, this tent is known as the "tent of meeting" (33:7). Here Moses enjoys a unique and personal relationship with God: "The LORD would speak to Moses face to face, as one speaks to a friend" (33:11). Although they are in close proximity to each other, even Moses the faithful servant is not permitted to look directly on God; 33:9 implies that the tent curtain shields Moses, who is within, from the Lord, who is without. This tent of meeting should not be confused with the tabernacle, also known as the tent of meeting (e.g., 40:2, 6), which is constructed only later (36:8–38) and is pitched in the midst of the Israelite encampment (Num. 1:53; 2:2, 17), not "outside the camp some distance away" (33:7).

16. Although the Exodus narrative portrays the LORD as coming to dwell within the tabernacle, there are indications that the tabernacle is not viewed as his main residence. As Jacob Milgrom observes: "From the fact that Moses is commanded to build the Tabernacle and its appurtenances according to the pattern that was shown to him on Mount Sinai (Exod 26:30; cf. Exod 25:9, 40; 27:8; Num 8:4), it is possible that he was shown the earthly sanctuary's heavenly counterpart." See J. Milgrom, *Leviticus 1–16: A New Translation with Introduction and Commentary*, AB 3 (New York: Doubleday, 1991), 141. Compare Moses's comment in Deut. 26:15: "Look down from heaven, your holy dwelling place, and bless your people Israel."

> The LORD said to Moses, "See, I have called by name Bezalel the son of Uri, son of Hur, of the tribe of Judah, and I have filled him with the Spirit of God, with wisdom and intelligence, with knowledge and all craftsmanship." (Exod. 31:1–3, my trans.)

Highlighting verbal links between these verses and several other biblical passages involving the creation of the earth, J. R. Middleton writes:

> As overseer of tabernacle construction, Bezalel is filled (Exodus 31:3) with "wisdom" (*ḥokmâ*), "understanding" (*tĕbûnâ*), and "knowledge" (*da'at*), precisely the same triad by which God is said to have created the world in Proverbs 3:19–20. To this is added that Bezalel is filled with "all crafts" or "all works" (*kol-mĕlā'kâ*), the very phrase used in Genesis 2:2–3 for "all the works" that God completed in creation. Therefore, not only does the tabernacle replicate in microcosm the macrocosmic sanctuary of the entire created order, but these verbal resonances [also] suggest that Bezalel's discerning artistry in tabernacle-building images God's own construction of the cosmos.[17]

To the features noted by Middleton we could also highlight the reference to "the Spirit of God," which is mentioned at the start of Genesis (1:2).

These links between the account of constructing the tabernacle in Exodus and passages about the creation of the world are probably intended to convey the idea that the tabernacle itself is viewed as a model of the world. As such, it anticipates a time when the whole world will be filled with God's glorious presence.[18]

Old Testament Summary

Exodus 25–30 emphasizes three aspects of the tabernacle: it is (1) a royal tent, (2) a holy tent, and (3) a "tent of meeting." The first two of these are clearly linked to God's nature; he is a sovereign and holy God. The third aspect focuses on the special relationship that God has established with the people of Israel through the covenant at Sinai. The construction of the tabernacle enables the people to commune more directly with their God and reassures them of his presence in their midst. Furthermore, by coming to dwell among the Israelites, God moves his creation plan one step closer to completion. By

17. J. R. Middleton, *The Liberating Image: The Imago Dei in Genesis 1* (Grand Rapids: Brazos, 2005), 87. Similar links may be found in Exod. 39 regarding the completion of the tabernacle and Gen. 2:1–3; see R. P. Gordon, "The Week That Made the World: Reflections on the First Pages of the Bible," in *Reading the Law: Studies in Honour of Gordon J. Wenham*, ed. J. G. McConville and K. Möller, LHB/OTS 461 (Edinburgh: T&T Clark, 2007), 234–37.

18. The concept of the world as being created to become God's dwelling place is discussed in chap. 8 above.

residing in a tent, God is able to go with the Israelites as they journey toward the promised land, with the expectation that a more permanent sanctuary will be established there.[19]

New Testament Connections

The tabernacle was eventually replaced by a temple, modeled on it and constructed first by Solomon and later rebuilt at the end of the sixth century BC, after its destruction by the Babylonians. Yet the tabernacle is discussed in a number of New Testament passages.

The New Testament draws a close parallel between Jesus and the tabernacle/temple. In Jesus, God is viewed as inhabiting human flesh, just as he previously inhabited first the tabernacle and then the temple. John alludes to this when he writes, "The Word became flesh and made his dwelling [lit., 'tabernacled'] among us. We have seen his glory . . ." (John 1:14). The same idea clearly underlies Jesus's own comment in John 2:19: "Destroy this temple, and I will raise it again in three days." John clarifies the meaning of this statement by observing, "The temple he had spoken of was his body" (John 2:21; cf. Mark 14:58).

As God incarnate, Jesus prepares the way for an important new development that occurs in the New Testament. A significant transition takes place as God moves from dwelling within the Jerusalem temple to living within the post-Pentecost followers of Jesus. According to Paul, believers have the indwelling of the Holy Spirit and thus become the new temple of God:

> Consequently, you are no longer foreigners and aliens, but fellow citizens with God's people and members of God's household, built on the foundation of the apostles and prophets, with Christ Jesus himself as the chief cornerstone. In him the whole building is joined together and rises to become a holy temple in the Lord. And in him you too are being built together to become a dwelling in which God lives by his Spirit. (Eph. 2:19–22; cf. 1 Cor. 3:16–17; 6:19; 2 Cor. 6:16)

In line with this, the Spirit's presence causes God's glory to be reflected in the lives of those who are Christ's followers: "We all, who with unveiled faces contemplate the Lord's glory, are being transformed into his image with ever-increasing glory, which comes from the Lord, who is the Spirit" (2 Cor. 3:18). The image of the church as the new temple of God is also reflected in Paul's comment regarding his role in the early church. He understands his own

19. For a discussion of historical issues involving the tabernacle, see K. A. Kitchen, "The Tabernacle—A Bronze Age Artefact," *ErIsr* 24 (1993): 119–29; R. E. Averbeck, "Tabernacle," in *Dictionary of the Old Testament: Pentateuch*, ed. T. D. Alexander and D. W. Baker (Downers Grove, IL: InterVarsity; Leicester: Inter-Varsity, 2003), 818–19.

apostleship in terms of being a "skilled master builder" (1 Cor. 3:10 NRSV), fulfilling a task parallel to that of Bezalel in the book of Exodus.

This emphasis on the church as God's sanctuary, rather than the temple in Jerusalem, is also reflected in Jesus's comments to a Samaritan woman concerning the right place to worship God:

> Woman, . . . believe me, a time is coming when you will worship the Father neither on this mountain nor in Jerusalem. You Samaritans worship what you do not know; we worship what we do know, for salvation is from the Jews. Yet a time is coming and has now come when the true worshipers will worship the Father in the Spirit and in truth, for they are the kind of worshipers the Father seeks. God is spirit, and his worshipers must worship in spirit and in truth. (John 4:21–24)

Here Jesus anticipates a time when worship will not be restricted to any particular earthly location.

From another perspective, the early Christians emphasized the secondary nature of the earthly tabernacle/temple. It was merely a "copy and shadow of what is in heaven" (Heb. 8:5; cf. 9:11, 24). Consequently, the New Testament plays down the importance of the temple in Jerusalem, even to the extent of anticipating its destruction (Mark 13:1–2), and instead focuses attention on the heavenly tabernacle. The demise of the Jerusalem temple is clearly linked to how the early church understood the death and resurrection of Jesus Christ. First, Matthew 27:51 records that when Jesus died, the curtain in the temple, separating "the Most Holy Place" (Holy of Holies) from the Holy Place, was torn from top to bottom. The tearing of this curtain revealed that, by his sacrificial death, Christ removed the barrier that existed between God and humankind (cf. Heb. 9:1–8). Second, Jesus was viewed as entering the heavenly sanctuary, rather than the earthly sanctuary, to serve as a high priest: "For Christ did not enter a sanctuary made with human hands that was only a copy of the true one; he entered heaven itself, now to appear for us in God's presence" (Heb. 9:24; cf. 9:11–28).[20]

While the New Testament witnesses to the church's replacing the Jerusalem temple as God's dwelling place on the earth, this is but the next major stage in the outworking of God's purposes. Eventually, following the return of Jesus, there will be the creation of the new Jerusalem. John's vision of a new heaven and a new earth in Revelation 21–22 brings to culmination God's plans for humanity. As a gigantic golden cube, the new Jerusalem in its entirety is the reality toward which the Holy of Holies in the tabernacle/temple points. Most important, within the city there is no temple "because the Lord God Almighty and the Lamb are its temple" (Rev. 21:22).

---

20. On Christ's role as a high priest within the heavenly tabernacle, see chap. 18 below.

17

Be Holy

Leviticus is dominated by the topic of holiness. Its prominence derives from the fact that God is holy. Although Leviticus emphasizes God's power to sanctify, or make holy, other people or objects, it also highlights the danger posed by the moral and ritual uncleanness associated with human behavior. Holiness and uncleanness are presented as mutually exclusive. Consequently, for the Israelites to enjoy a close and meaningful relationship with God, they must reflect his holiness in their daily lives. Since differing degrees of holiness and uncleanness exist, the Israelites are divinely exhorted, "Be holy because I, the LORD your God, am holy" (19:2; cf. 11:44–45; 20:26).

Introduction

The book of Leviticus continues the story of Exodus by describing what takes place in the thirteenth month after the Israelites' divine deliverance from Egypt (cf. Exod. 40:17; Num. 1:1). As a result, the books of Exodus and Leviticus and, as we shall later observe, also Numbers are closely connected. Leviticus both assumes the erection of the tabernacle, which forms the climax of the book of Exodus (40:1–38), and records the consecration of Aaron and his sons as priests, fulfilling the instructions given to Moses by the LORD in Exodus 29:1–46. Leviticus must therefore be read in conjunction with Exodus, both books forming part of the continuous and carefully composed narrative that comprises the Pentateuch.

Although Leviticus continues the story of the Israelites' journey from Egypt to Canaan, almost 90 percent of the book consists of divine speeches on a

237

variety of topics. As a result, apart from numerous short introductions to these discourses (cf. 1:1; 4:1; 5:14; 6:1; 6:8; etc.), there are only two sections in which the narrator describes events rather than reports God's words. The first of these focuses on the consecration of the priests and the subsequent sin of Nadab and Abihu (8:1–10:20); the second passage is much briefer and deals with a man who blasphemes by cursing God (24:10–23). Even in this short episode more than half the verses record what the LORD says to Moses (24:13–22). Leviticus is thus composed almost entirely of divine speeches. In this regard it closely resembles Exodus 20:22–24:2 and 25:1–31:17.

In Leviticus, Moses continues his role of mediator between God and the Israelites. While the LORD nearly always speaks directly to Moses alone—on a few occasions Aaron is also included (11:1; 13:1; 14:33; 15:1)—his words are usually intended for either the Israelites (e.g., 1:2; 4:2; 7:23, 29; 11:2) or the priests (6:9, 20, 25; 21:1; 22:2). This distinction between the majority of Israelites and the selected few who are divinely appointed as priests is a significant feature in Leviticus. Not only is it reflected in many of the divine speeches, but also, more important, it lies at the very heart of the account of the consecration of Aaron and his sons as priests in Leviticus 8–9. Here the narrative highlights the three stages by which Aaron and his sons are set apart from the rest of the Israelites. First, they are brought out from the midst of the community (8:6) to be consecrated as priests. The special ritual—involving washing, clothing, and anointing—endows them with a degree of holiness that surpasses that of other Israelites (8:6–30).[1] Moreover, because Aaron is treated differently from his sons, he is recognized as being ever holier. Second, the priests are to stay at the entrance to the tabernacle for seven days (8:31–36). Not only does this further emphasize their separation from the people but it also confirms their holy status; unlike the rest of the population, they remain in close proximity to God. Third, on the eighth day there is a rite of incorporation by which the priests are once again brought into contact with the rest of the community (9:1–24). Although Moses provides instructions, the newly appointed priests offer up the sacrifices on behalf of the community, with Aaron, as high priest, performing the main tasks. By recording that "fire came out from the presence of the LORD and consumed the burnt offering and the fat portions on the altar" (9:24), the account of the consecration of the priests concludes by highlighting God's acceptance of Aaron and his sons as the community's cultic representatives.[2] Leviticus thus emphasizes the important distinction that God institutes between the priests and all other Israelites.

---

1. For a fuller discussion of the different elements that comprise the ritual for consecrating the priests, see chap. 16 above.
2. In Lev. 9:23 the appearance of the glory of the LORD to all the people parallels what occurs immediately after the erection of the tabernacle (Exod. 40:34–35). On both occasions God expresses his approval and acceptance of what has just taken place by displaying his presence to the people.

As well as stressing the differing degrees of holiness that exist between the priests and other Israelites, the book of Leviticus, especially in chapters 11–15, also draws attention to how ordinary Israelites belong to one of two categories: clean or unclean. Various factors—including eating particular foods, suffering from certain types of skin disease,[3] or experiencing particular bodily discharges—cause individuals, and sometimes even those who come into contact with them, to become unclean. Anyone designated as unclean must undergo a process of purification before they can fully participate in the religious life of the community.

Holy, Clean, and Unclean

The features noted briefly in the preceding paragraphs draw attention to three related categories that permeate almost all of the material in Leviticus; these are holy, clean/pure, and unclean/impure. The importance of these three categories is underlined by the frequent occurrence of these and associated words throughout Leviticus. Terms based on the Hebrew root *qādaš* (*qādash*) (e.g., "holy," "holiness," "sanctify") appear 152 times in Leviticus, representing about one-fifth of all occurrences in the Old Testament. The adjective *ṭāhôr*, "clean," and associated words occur 74 times, representing more than one-third of all Old Testament occurrences. The adjective *ṭāmēʾ*, "unclean," and cognate terms appear 132 times, representing more than half the total occurrences in the Old Testament. These statistics highlight the importance of the categories holy, clean/pure, and unclean/impure in Leviticus.

The existence of these three categories is reflected in the layout of the Israelite camp. At the heart of the camp stands the tabernacle courtyard, a holy area; the rest of the camp has the status of a clean area; and everywhere outside the camp is unclean.[4] This same threefold division is also found among the people; the priests are considered to be holy, the Israelites clean, and non-Israelites unclean. Moreover, the places and people correspond directly: the priests are associated with the tabernacle, the Israelites with the camp, and the non-Israelites with those outside the camp (see figure 17.1).

Within these main categories, subdivisions also exist. Regarding holiness, this is evident in a number of different spheres. First, differing degrees of holiness exist within the priesthood and laity. The high priest is distinguished from the other priests in a number of ways. Not only is the ritual for his consecration distinctive, as are his clothes, but he alone enjoys the title of "high" priest. At

---

3. Although these skin diseases have in the past been understood to be a form of leprosy (i.e., Hansen's disease), that is most unlikely.

4. While the entire area outside the camp is considered unclean, selected places are set apart as clean for the disposal of the ashes from the altar in the tabernacle courtyard (Lev. 4:12, 21; 6:11; cf. the burning of the bull of the purification offering [16:27]).

Figure 17.1. Holiness and Cleanness in the Layout of the Israelite Camp

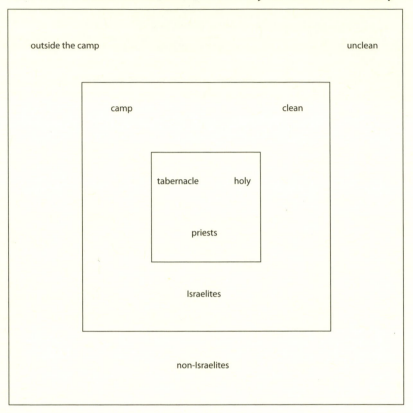

any time there can be only one high priest, and each new appointee needs to undergo a special consecration ritual. Of all the priests, the high priest alone is permitted to enter the Holy of Holies, the holiest room of the tabernacle. The high priest is also required to adhere to much stricter rules regarding marriage, purity, and mourning.

A lesser category of priests consists of those who suffer from some form of physical defect. Although they are prohibited from offering sacrifices, they are allowed to eat from the portions of sacrifices allocated to the priests. Next to the priests in holiness are the Levites. Though they are not permitted to offer sacrifices, they assist the priests with other duties concerning the tabernacle, especially its transportation and erection (Num. 4:1–49).[5] Although the priests and Levites enjoy a special status of holiness arising from their ancestry and

5. Although the Levites and the priests are all descended from Levi, the third oldest son of Jacob, only Aaron and his sons are designated priests. See chap. 20 below for a fuller discussion of the relationship between the priests and Levites.

divine appointment, nonpriestly Israelites are given the opportunity to have a higher degree of holiness by becoming Nazirites. To attain this holier status, one takes "a vow of dedication to the LORD," which entails (1) abstaining from the produce of the vine and (2) not cutting one's hair (Num. 6:1–21). These subdivisions of people surface in different contexts within Leviticus. For example, whereas ordinary Israelites could touch any corpse, regular priests are permitted to touch the corpse of only a close relative (Lev. 21:1–4), and the high priest is prohibited from having contact with any corpse (10:1–7).

Second, the tabernacle is divided into at least three distinct areas, each with a different degree of holiness. The tent itself consists of two rooms, the Most Holy Place (Holy of Holies) and the Holy Place. The former of these, containing the ark of the covenant, is considered to be much holier than the adjacent room, the Holy Place, which contains the lampstand, the table for the "bread of the Presence," and the incense altar.[6] The tabernacle courtyard is less holy than the tent itself, although holier than the camp, from which it is separated by a curtain fence. These different degrees of holiness within the tabernacle are also reflected in the access that people have. Only the high priest may enter the Holy of Holies, and even he is limited to one day in the year, the Day of Atonement (Lev. 16). Although any priest may enter the Holy Place, ordinary Israelites are barred; they have access only to the courtyard.

Third, the tabernacle furnishings also reflect the threefold pattern of holiness found within the different areas of the tabernacle. They do so in a number of ways, depending on (1) their location, (2) the materials used in their manufacture, (3) their accessibility to humans, and (4) their use in religious rituals. The holiest furniture, made of pure gold, is placed within the tent; the altar and basin, made of bronze, are located in the courtyard. Although ordinary Israelites are permitted to view the bronze altar and basin, only priests may look on the gold furnishings in the Holy Place with immunity (Num. 4:18–20). Within the tent, the ark of the covenant is set apart from the other items of furniture by being placed in the Holy of Holies. It is so holy that only the high priest may approach it, and even then he possibly uses smoke from incense to conceal the top of the ark from view (Lev. 16:12–13).[7]

Fourth, particular days of the week and year exhibit differing degrees of holiness. The weekly Sabbath and the annual Day of Atonement are marked as especially holy by the prohibition of all work (Lev. 23:3, 28). The pilgrimage festivals of Unleavened Bread, Weeks, and Tabernacles and certain other days are considered less holy and therefore require abstinence only from regular work (23:7, 21, 25, 35). Finally, while the Israelites are expected to make special

---

6. For a detailed discussion of the layout of the tabernacle, see chap. 16 above.

7. These distinctions between the items of furniture are also reflected in the instructions given in Num. 4:5–33 regarding the activities of the Kohathites, Gershonites, and Merarites in helping the priests transport the tabernacle.

offerings on the first day of each month, they are permitted to work on these days, indicating that they are the least holy of all special days.

In the light of these four factors, it is apparent that the book of Leviticus envisages a world in which people, places, objects, and even periods of time have differing degrees of holiness.

Just as there are varying degrees of holiness, so too with uncleanness.

1. The strength or weakness of an impurity is judged by its ability to communicate impurity to other objects or persons. Only more serious forms of impurity can pollute other people or objects. For example, if a man lies with a woman during her monthly period, she causes him to become unclean for seven days, and, in turn, any bed upon which he lies also becomes unclean (15:24). Furthermore, anyone who touches this bed becomes unclean; however, this latter uncleanness lasts for only one day and cannot be transferred to other people or objects.

2. Differing degrees of impurity are reflected by the way in which they pollute the sanctuary. The location of the pollution is indicated by where the blood of the purification offering is placed. Deliberate or intentional sins pollute the ark of the covenant in the Holy of Holies (cf. 16:16); unintentional or inadvertent sins by the high priest or the community pollute the incense altar in the Holy Place (4:2–21); lesser sins or impurities pollute the bronze altar in the courtyard (4:22–35).

3. Leviticus distinguishes between impurities that can be rectified and those that cannot. Regarding the former, considerable attention is given in chapters 12–15 to the rectification of uncleanness arising from skin diseases and various bodily discharges. In marked contrast, among impurities that cannot be rectified are sexual sins (18:20, 23–25, 27–30), idolatry (20:2–5), murder (Num. 35:16–21, 31), and profaning the sacred (e.g., Lev. 7:19–21; 22:3, 9). In these cases only the death of the guilty party can remove the pollution caused by the sin.

When rectification is possible, the process by which any uncleanness is to be purified varies, depending on its seriousness. Normally a person or object is purified by (1) the passage of time and (2) washing and/or laundering; objects that cannot be washed are disposed of by burial, burning, or some other method. For minor impurities, the length of time required for purification is one day (e.g., for touching the carcass of an animal; Lev. 11:39). More serious impurities require the passing of seven days (e.g., touching a human corpse; Num. 19:11). Longer periods of forty and eighty days are necessary for a woman who has given birth to a son or daughter respectively (Lev. 12:2–5). Regarding the washing of the body and the laundering of clothes, requirements again differ depending on the degree of impurity. For example, whoever *touches* an animal carcass is unclean for a day; whoever *carries* an animal carcass sustains greater impurity and is required to wash their clothes (11:24–25, 27–28).[8]

From these observations concerning holiness and uncleanness/impurity, it is apparent that they form a spectrum of closely associated categories. On the one side is holiness, in the middle is cleanness, and on the other side is uncleanness/impurity (see figure 17.2). The further one moves from the middle of this spectrum, the greater the intensity of either holiness or uncleanness. For the ancient Israelites every person, object, place, and period of time can be located somewhere on this spectrum.

Figure 17.2. Spectrum of Holiness, Cleanness, and Uncleanness

Increasing Holiness ◄———— Cleanness ————► Increasing Uncleanness

So far we have discussed the concepts of holiness and uncleanness without trying to define them. Hence it is necessary to clarify what is meant by these terms within the context of Leviticus. What is holiness? What is uncleanness?

Holiness

In Leviticus, holiness is always associated with God. Four aspects of this are very significant:

1. God is innately holy; he is the supreme manifestation of holiness. To be holy is to be God-like.
2. Holiness emanates from God; he is the sole source of holiness. He alone endows other objects, places, or people with holiness. Everything that is given to God or belongs to him is holy. Since God radiates holiness to all that is close to him, the ark of the covenant, which functions as the footstool of his throne, is the most holy item of furniture in the tabernacle. For the same reason the Holy of Holies is the holiest part of the tabernacle; indeed, God's presence makes it the holiest location on the entire earth.

8. According to J. Milgrom, *Cult and Conscience: The Asham and the Priestly Doctrine of Repentance* (Leiden: Brill, 1976), 108–21, when an individual expresses remorse regarding a deliberate sin, this has the effect of lessening the resulting pollution and thereby reduces the amount of rectification required.

3. Holiness describes the moral perfection and purity of God's nature. For this reason God's command to the Israelites, "Be holy because I, the LORD your God, am holy" (Lev. 19:2), comes in the context of imperatives governing the people's behavior. Their actions and attitudes are to reflect God's perfect nature.

4. Sanctification, the process by which someone or something becomes holy, is the result of divine activity. It is God who sanctifies. This is reflected in the refrain "I am the LORD, who makes you holy ["I sanctify you," NRSV]" (20:8; 21:8, 15, 23; 22:9, 16, 32). Though Leviticus presents the divine side of sanctification, it also emphasizes the human side. Those made holy by God are expected to remain holy by doing nothing that would compromise their special status (cf. 11:44). The Israelites are also to keep holy anything sanctified by God. This applies, for example, to the Sabbath day. Because God has sanctified it, the Israelites are commanded to maintain its sanctity by refraining from all work (Exod. 20:8–11).

A natural extension of the belief that God is holy is the idea that holiness means wholeness or perfection. To be holy is to be unblemished or unmarred. It is to experience life in all its fullness as God has originally intended it to be. This is reflected on one level in the divine requirements regarding both priests and sacrifices. Priests with physical defects are not permitted to offer sacrifices (Lev. 21:17–23). Similarly, it is regularly stated that the sacrificial offerings must be without defect (1:3, 10; 3:1, 6; 4:3, 23, 28, 32; 5:15, 18; 6:6; 9:2–3; 14:10; 22:19–25; 23:12, 18; cf. Exod. 12:5); only in the case of a freewill offering is an exception made (Lev. 22:23).[9] On another level, holiness is associated with perfect moral behavior (cf. 20:7; 22:32–33). This is especially revealed in chapter 19 (but cf. also Lev. 18 and 20), which contains a long list of commands governing personal behavior. The material in this chapter closely echoes the Decalogue, or Ten Commandments (Exod. 20:2–17), and the collection of moral instructions found in the Book of the Covenant (Exod. 22:21–23:9). To be holy is to live in a way that reflects the moral perfection of God; it is to live a life marked by love, purity, and righteousness, which are the three most important hallmarks of perfect behavior.

Uncleanness

In simple terms, uncleanness is the opposite of holiness. It represents all that is less than God-like. Although Leviticus never identifies the original source of uncleanness, we may surmise that it is believed to emanate from

9. The defects that disqualify priests and sacrificial animals correspond closely (cf. Lev. 21:18–20; 22:22–24).

that which opposes God. Uncleanness is associated with humans in two ways. First, certain forms of uncleanness or impurity arise as a natural consequence of being human. These include suffering from specific skin diseases and experiencing bodily discharges. These and related forms of uncleanness all appear to be linked in one way or another to death. By associating some bodily diseases and conditions with death, the regulations of Leviticus indicate that death dominates human existence. Only by becoming holy can a human escape the domain of death and experience the life-giving power of God.

Second, there are other forms of uncleanness that humans have the power to control. These occur when individuals by their actions transgress any boundary established by God. People who willfully ignore God's commands, decrees, or laws are a source of uncleanness and defile all that they touch. Their actions both distance them from God and bring them further under the domain of death.

The Relationship between Holiness and Uncleanness

Leviticus highlights two important factors regarding the relationship between holiness and uncleanness. First, holiness and uncleanness are totally incompatible. Not only is it impossible for anyone or anything to be holy and unclean at the same time; more important, no holy object or person is normally permitted to come into contact with anything unclean.[10] This incompatibility between holiness and uncleanness accounts for the existence of many of the regulations found in Leviticus. It explains the necessity of the complex sacrificial system, outlined in chapters 1–7, that enables those who are unclean to become pure and holy. Without the offering of sacrifices, it is impossible for the Israelites to live in close contact with the LORD their God.[11]

Second, both holiness and uncleanness were perceived by the ancient Israelites as being dynamic in nature: they have the ability to transmit their nature to other people or objects. In this regard they differ significantly from the state of cleanness/purity, which is merely neutral and unable to make anything else clean or pure. Consequently, any clean person or thing is constantly in the middle of a struggle between the powers of holiness and uncleanness.[12] Since the status of an individual can change, Leviticus consistently underlines the danger posed by uncleanness to those who are holy or pure. This danger is greatest for the priests, who work within the tabernacle, a holy area, and handle the tabernacle furniture, holy objects. For a priest to serve in the tabernacle, it

---

10. When such contact occurs, it either has a purifying or defiling effect, depending on the specific circumstances.

11. For a fuller treatment of sacrifice, see chap. 18 below.

12. Elsewhere in the OT this conflict is presented in terms of Yahweh's conflict with death.

is essential that he remain holy. If he becomes unclean, he can no longer carry out his duties; to do so would mean death.[13]

Old Testament Summary

Since the narrative in Genesis and Exodus moves toward the creation of Israel as a "holy nation," it is hardly surprising that Leviticus should define in more detail what it means for the Israelites to be holy. This increased interest in holiness follows naturally from the creation of the tabernacle and God's occupation of it. Although in Genesis the concept of holiness is barely mentioned because God does not dwell on earth, with the construction of the tabernacle, everything is transformed. Given that holiness emanates from God, the Holy One, his presence amid the people brings into their daily lives an important new dynamic. Because their God is holy, the people themselves must be holy. This, however, will be a constant struggle for them due to internal and external powers that oppose God. By dominating the book of Leviticus, the concept of holiness lies at the heart of the Pentateuch.

New Testament Connections

The concepts of holiness and uncleanness are frequently mentioned in the New Testament and closely reflect what we observe in Leviticus. Regarding uncleanness, Jesus focuses attention on actions or attitudes that make a person unclean: "What comes out of a person is what defiles them. For it is from within, out of a person's heart, that evil thoughts come—sexual immorality, theft, murder, adultery, greed, malice, deceit, lewdness, envy, slander, arrogance and folly. All these evils come from inside and defile a person" (Mark 7:20–23; cf. Matt. 15:17–20). In doing so, he is highly critical of the Pharisees and teachers of the law who have neglected these causes of uncleanness while concentrating on relatively minor aspects of ritual purity (cf. Matt. 23:23–28; Luke 11:37–41). Paul likewise associates impurity with wickedness and immorality (e.g., Rom. 1:24; 6:19; 2 Cor. 12:21; Eph. 4:19; 5:3, 5). According to Paul, such sinful behavior is to be shunned by believers, "for God did not call us to be impure, but to live a holy life" (1 Thess. 4:7; cf. 1 Cor. 1:2; 1 Tim. 2:8). Holiness is clearly linked to behavior that is morally exemplary. This explains why Jesus instructs his followers: "For I tell you that unless your righteousness surpasses that of the Pharisees and the teachers of the law, you will certainly

13. The danger that the holy furnishings of the tabernacle pose to an unclean person is also reflected in the regulations concerning an individual who unintentionally kills another person. They are instructed to cling to the horns of the altar. Only one who is morally clean can expect to touch the altar with immunity.

not enter the kingdom of heaven. . . . Be perfect, therefore, as your heavenly Father is perfect" (Matt. 5:20, 48).

The New Testament references to purification highlight two complementary aspects. On the one hand, they underline that God is the one who purifies those who are unclean (cf. Acts 15:9). More specifically, they emphasize that purification is achieved through the sacrificial death of Jesus Christ: "But if we walk in the light, as he is in the light, we have fellowship with one another, and the blood of Jesus, his Son, purifies us from all sin" (1 John 1:7; cf. John 15:3; Titus 2:14; Heb. 1:3; 1 John 1:9). On the other hand, believers are exhorted to purify themselves: "Since we have these promises, dear friends, let us purify ourselves from everything that contaminates body and spirit, perfecting holiness out of reverence for God" (2 Cor. 7:1; cf. James 4:8). Significantly, there are thirty-three occasions in the New Testament (excluding Revelation) when believers are designated as "saints" or "holy ones" (e.g., Acts 9:13, 32; 26:10; Rom. 1:7; 8:27; 15:25, 26, 31; 16:2, 15).

The concept of holiness figures prominently in all the New Testament Epistles. Holiness of life is to be the ambition of every believer. Peter expresses this most clearly and quotes Leviticus: "But just as he who called you is holy, so be holy in all you do; for it is written: 'Be holy, because I am holy'" (1 Pet. 1:15–16; cf. Rom. 6:19, 22; 2 Cor. 1:12; Eph. 4:24; Col. 3:12; 1 Thess. 2:10; 3:13; 1 Tim. 2:15; Titus 1:8; Heb. 12:14; 2 Pet. 3:11). The author of Hebrews underlines the importance of holiness: "Make every effort to live in peace with everyone and to be holy; without holiness no one will see the Lord" (Heb. 12:14).

Although believers are constantly exhorted to be holy, God's role in the process of sanctification is also recognized (1 Thess. 5:23). Hebrews pictures God as a father disciplining his children in order to produce holiness of character: "God disciplines us for our good, that we may share in his holiness" (Heb. 12:10). Most attention, however, tends to be focused on the role played by Jesus Christ and the Holy Spirit. On three occasions the two are mentioned together in connection with the sanctification of believers (1 Cor. 6:11; Heb. 10:29; 1 Pet. 1:2). Second Thessalonians 2:13 refers specifically to "the sanctifying work of the Spirit" (cf. Rom. 15:16). This is obviously linked to the belief that the Holy Spirit dwells within believers: "Do you not know that your bodies are temples of the Holy Spirit, who is in you, whom you have received from God?" (1 Cor. 6:19). As God's presence made the tabernacle holy, so too the presence of the Holy Spirit sanctifies believers. Elsewhere the sanctifying work of Jesus Christ is highlighted; he is "the one who makes people holy" (Heb. 2:11; cf. Acts 26:18; 1 Cor. 1:2). This is all-importantly linked to Christ's death: "We have been made holy through the sacrifice of the body of Jesus Christ once for all" (Heb. 10:10; cf. Col. 1:22; Heb. 10:14; 13:12).[14]

14. The concept of consecration lies at the heart of the Passover. See chap. 14 above.

A number of incidents recorded in the Gospels focus on the relationship between the holy and the unclean. When Jesus touches those who are unclean with skin diseases, he displays his power both to heal and to purify (Matt. 8:1–4; Mark 1:40–44; Luke 5:12–14). The same is true when the woman who has been suffering from bleeding for twelve years touches Jesus (Matt. 9:20–22; Mark 5:24–34; Luke 8:42–48). Similarly, when Jesus restores the dead to life, he reveals his power over death, a primary source of uncleanness (Matt. 9:18–26; Mark 5:35–43; Luke 7:11–17; 8:49–56). Jesus's holy nature is also recognized by his disciples (John 6:69; cf. Acts 3:14; 4:27, 30; Heb. 7:26) and by the unclean spirits or demons who refer to him as "the Holy One of God" (Mark 1:24; Luke 4:34).

18

The Sacrificial System

When Moses and the Israelites complete the building of the tabernacle, it becomes possible for God to dwell in their midst. However, to enable the people to live in close proximity to the Holy One of Israel, God through Moses institutes a sacrificial system by which the people can atone for their sins. At the heart of this system lie a number of different sacrifices that complement one another by addressing differing facets of human wrongdoing. For example, the purification offering cleanses the tabernacle of pollution caused by sin. Of all the sacrifices offered throughout the year, those presented on the Day of Atonement are the most important. Annually the high priest enters the Holy of Holies to atone for the sin of the whole nation and to purify the most sacred part of the tabernacle. Without this and other rituals, it would have been impossible for the people to live in harmony with the LORD their God.

Introduction

The first seven chapters of Leviticus consist of regulations governing the offering of sacrifices. These come between the account of erecting the tabernacle in Exodus 40 and the account of the consecration of the priests in Leviticus 8–9. Since the instructions for erecting the tabernacle and consecrating the priests are given together in Exodus 25:1–31:17, we might have expected the description of their fulfillment to be placed side by side. They are separated, however, by the sacrifice regulations. Nevertheless, the present location of the sacrifice instructions is very apt. First, their place at the beginning of Leviticus emphasizes their importance: they are central to Israel's relationship with God. Second, overseeing the offering of sacrifices is the foremost duty of the priests. It therefore is quite appropriate that these instructions should be placed immediately before the account of consecrating the priests in Leviticus 8–9.

Several features of the material in Leviticus 1–7 are noteworthy. First, the information provided about the sacrifices is in the form of instructions or regulations. These fall into two sections. The instructions in 1:2–6:7 and 7:22–34 are addressed to the Israelite laity; those in 6:8–7:21 are for the priests. Two sets of instructions are provided because the ordinary Israelites and the priests perform different functions when sacrifices are offered.

Second, the instructions cover five types of sacrifices. In the NIV these sacrifices are termed burnt offering, grain offering, fellowship offering, sin offering, and guilt offering. Some scholars, however, prefer the designations purification and reparation for the sin and guilt offerings respectively. As we shall see below, these alternative titles more accurately reflect the distinctive functions of these offerings. The differences between the various types of sacrifices will be discussed later.

Third, these sacrifices, involving ordinary people and priests respectively, are presented in slightly different orders in the two sections. This is due to the location of the peace offering (see table 18.1). Although it comes in the middle of the list of regulations addressed to the laity, it is at the end of the rules for the priests. In the first list the peace offering is grouped with the burnt and grain offerings because all three are "food offerings," which produce "an aroma pleasing to the LORD" (Lev. 1:9). The purification and reparation offerings are discussed separately due to their distinctive functions. In the second section the order is determined by the holiness of the meat associated with each sacrifice. The peace offering is placed last in the list because ordinary Israelites may eat this meat. In both sections the burnt offering comes first because it is viewed as the most important of all the sacrifices.

Table 18.1
Instructions for Sacrifices in Leviticus

Regulations for laity	Regulations for priests
Burnt offering 1:2–17	Burnt offering 6:8–13
Grain offering 2:1–16	Grain offering 6:14–23
Peace offering 3:1–17	Purification offering 6:24–30
Purification offering 4:1–5:13	Reparation offering 7:1–10
Reparation offering 5:14–6:7	Peace offering 7:11–21

Fourth, for both sections the order of the sacrifices does not reflect the sequence in which they are normally offered. Although the burnt offering, as the most important sacrifice, is mentioned first, it is often presented only after a purification offering has been made. This is evident in the case of the sacrifices offered by a Nazirite at the end of his period of separation. Although the burnt offering is mentioned first in Numbers 6:14–15, in practice it is presented after a purification offering (6:16–17). A similar situation can be observed regarding the purification ritual for someone suffering from a skin disease. The purification offering is made first (Lev. 14:19–20), although in the list of offerings it comes after the burnt offering (14:10; the ewe lamb for the purification offering is mentioned after the male lamb for the burnt offering).[1] The presentation of a purification offering before other sacrifices appears to have been a common pattern in the sacrificial rituals of other ancient Near Eastern societies.

The General Pattern for Animal Sacrifices

Of the five main types of sacrifices listed in the early chapters of Leviticus, all but one involve offering up an animal. Although there are important differences in detail regarding the procedure for these animal sacrifices, which will be considered below, a common pattern was adopted for each offering. This falls into two parts: the first involves the actions of the Israelite worshiper; the second concerns the duties of the priest. An individual wishing to make a sacrifice brings an animal to the tabernacle courtyard (1:3; 4:4, 14). There the worshiper lays a hand on the animal's head (e.g., 1:4; 3:2, 8, 13) before slaughtering it (e.g., 1:5, 11; 3:2, 8, 13). The blood from the animal is collected by the priest and usually sprinkled against the sides of the bronze altar (1:5, 11, 15; 3:2, 8, 13); in the case of the purification offering, some of the blood is put to special use (4:7–8, 16–18, 25, 30, 34). Next the whole animal, or selected parts, is placed on the altar to be consumed by fire (e.g., 1:6–9, 12–13, 16–17; 3:3–5, 9–11, 14–16; 4:8–10, 19–20, 26, 31, 35). Finally, the priests or Israelites usually consume any meat that is not burned up upon the altar (e.g., 6:26–29; 7:6, 15–21).

Two aspects of this pattern require further consideration:

1. Laying a hand upon the animal's head has been understood in a variety of ways. Probably it at least indicates ownership of the animal. By leaning on the animal, the worshiper signals that this is his or her sacrifice to God. An extension of this idea is that of association. The worshiper associates him- or herself with what happens to the animal. Since the death of the animal is meant to atone for the sin of the worshiper, by touching the animal the worshiper acknowledges that in reality he or she should be put to death. This understanding may even have extended

1. In this case a reparation offering (Lev. 14:12–18) precedes both the purification offering and burnt offering.

to the belief that the animal is a substitute for the worshiper.[2] Some scholars have argued that the laying of a hand on the animal symbolizes the transference of sin from the worshiper to the animal. However, a clear distinction may need to be drawn between placing one hand on the animal's head and placing two hands. With two hands it undoubtedly is a case of transference. This is clearly illustrated in the ritual of the scapegoat that is sent off into the wilderness on the Day of Atonement (16:20–22). The high priest is instructed "to lay both hands on the head of the live goat and confess over it all the wickedness and rebellion of the Israelites" (16:21). The text then specifically states, "The goat will carry on itself all their sins to a remote place" (16:22). In the case of laying a single hand on the head of an animal, no passage clearly states that the transference of sin takes place.

2. For all animal sacrifices, special instructions are given regarding the use or disposal of the animal's blood. As we shall see in more detail below, with the purification offering the sacrificial blood is used to cleanse sacred objects within the sanctuary that are defiled or polluted due to human sin or impurity. With the other types of sacrifices, the blood is collected and sprinkled against the sides of the bronze altar (1:5, 11, 15; 3:2, 8, 13; 7:2). These ritual actions reflect the importance with which the ancient Israelites viewed blood; it symbolized life. For this reason sacrificial blood was a powerful antidote to the deathly consequences of sin and impurity.[3]

The Five Types of Sacrifices

The early chapters of Leviticus provide instructions for five main types of sacrifices. Although they share common features, each type has its own distinctive elements. Naturally, the existence of five types of sacrifices suggests that each type has its own function. For the purification and reparation offerings, it is possible to be reasonably certain about their differing purposes. Regarding the other sacrifices, we can make only tentative suggestions.

The Burnt Offering (Lev. 1:2–17; 6:8–13)

The burnt offering was easily distinguished from all the other sacrifices by the fact that the entire animal was burned upon the altar. For all other sacrifices, only selected portions of the offering are placed on the altar, with the

---

2. Against the idea of substitution, however, is the fact that the meat of some sacrifices is consumed by the priests or even by the worshiper.

3. The special importance of blood is also highlighted in the food regulations; see chap. 19 below.

remainder of the offering being eaten by the priests and/or other worshipers.[4]
Of the different sacrifices, the burnt offering is viewed as the most important.
It comes first in both sets of instructions, and worshipers are clearly expected
to present their best animals; this is implied by the brief comment that the
offering is to be "a male without defect" (1:3, 10). Although the burnt offering
is intended to be costly, allowance is made for those who are poor and able to
bring only "a dove or a young pigeon" (1:14).

Few details are given regarding the specific function of the burnt offering.
The repetition of the phrase "an aroma pleasing to the LORD" (1:9, 13, 17)
suggests that it is intended to gain divine favor (cf. Gen. 8:20–21). This understanding of the sacrifice is probably to be linked to the comment in 1:4,
"It will be accepted on your behalf to make atonement for you." The Hebrew
verb *kipper*, often translated "to atone," conveys two distinctive meanings:
"to pay a ransom" and "to cleanse/purify."[5]

Within the judicial systems of ancient Israel and its neighbors, it was sometimes possible for a guilty party to substitute a ransom in place of the death
penalty (cf. Exod. 21:30). The animal offered as a burnt offering is presented as
an alternative to the death penalty imposed by God for human sin. By paying
this "ransom," the worshiper appeases God's righteous anger against his or
her own sin and uncleanness. God's justice demands the death of an animal
as a substitute for the judicial death of the worshiper. Given that burnt offerings are used to restore broken relationships between God and humans, it is
hardly surprising that such offerings figure prominently in the ratification of
divine-human covenants (e.g., Gen. 8:20–9:17; 22:1–19; Exod. 24:3–11).

The Grain Offering (Lev. 2:1–16; 6:14–23)

The grain offering is unique in that, of the five main types of sacrifices, it
is the only one not involving animals. It consists of an offering made of fine
flour, which can be presented either "baked" (2:4–7) or unbaked (2:1–2). After
the worshiper presents the offering, part of it is burned upon the bronze altar;
the rest is allocated to the priests, who depend on it for their daily food.

Like the burnt offering, the grain offering is clearly intended to evoke a
pleasing response from God (cf. 2:2, 9). However, whereas the whole of the
burnt offering is consumed by fire, only a portion of the grain offering is burned
on the altar. Most of it is handed over as a gift to the priests in recognition
of their unique service for the people (cf. 8:22–31). The Hebrew term for a
"grain offering" (*minḥâ, minkhâ*) is translated in other contexts as "gift" or
"tribute." Sometimes it has the idea of a gift intended to ingratiate the giver

4. For this reason the burnt offering is sometimes described as the whole-burnt offering
or holocaust.
5. J. Sklar, *Sin, Impurity, Sacrifice, Atonement: The Priestly Conceptions*, HBM 2 (Sheffield:
Sheffield Phoenix Press, 2005).

253

to someone else (e.g., Gen. 32:13–21; 2 Kings 8:7–8). Elsewhere it can refer to the money given by a lesser king to a greater king to guarantee a peaceful relationship (e.g., Judg. 3:15–18; 1 Kings 4:21; 10:23–25; 2 Kings 17:3–4). This suggests that the grain offering is possibly viewed as a gift or tribute paid to God in recognition of his divine sovereignty. In this case the priests receive it as God's representatives.

The Peace Offering (Lev. 3:1–17; 7:11–21)

The peace offering is distinguished from the other offerings by the fact that most of the meat from the sacrificial animal is retained by the worshiper for a festive meal. Certain portions, however, are set apart for God and the priests: the fat associated with the kidneys and liver is burned on the altar to produce "an aroma pleasing to the LORD" (3:5, 16); the right thigh is given to the officiating priest, and the breast is shared among the other priests (7:28–34). The burnt offering requires that the larger sacrificial animals be male, but for the peace offering females could also be offered. Since a meal is an important aspect of the sacrifice, doves and pigeons are excluded as suitable offerings. Under the general heading of peace offerings, further divisions exist. According to Leviticus 7, the peace offering can express thankfulness (vv. 12–15), fulfill a vow, or serve as a freewill offering (vv. 16–21). For the first of these, the meat of the animals must be consumed on the day it is offered. In the second and third cases, the meat may also be eaten on the second day, but if any remains until the third day, it must be burned up.

Due to the festive nature of the peace offering, it is sometimes referred to as the "fellowship offering" (3:1, 3, 6). The Hebrew name for the sacrifice, šĕlāmîm (shĕlāmîm), has traditionally been linked to the concept of peace (cf. Hebrew šālôm [shālôm]). Since "peace" in Hebrew thought implies well-being in general, it is likely that an important element of the peace offering is the acknowledgment of God as the source of true peace (cf. "sacrifice of well-being" NRSV).

The Purification Offering (Lev. 4:1–5:13; 6:24–30)

The distinctive nature of the purification offering is highlighted by the special use made of the animal's blood to cleanse sacred items within the tabernacle. Although Leviticus 4 focuses on different types of purification offerings, on each occasion attention is drawn to how the priest places or sprinkles the sacrificial blood on particular items within the tabernacle. The examples in Leviticus 4 are given in descending order, with the most serious offenses listed first. If the anointed priest or whole community of Israel has sinned, the blood is placed on the horns of the golden incense altar, which stands within the Holy Place (4:7, 18). If a leader has committed the sin, the blood is put on the horns of the bronze altar, which is located in the tabernacle courtyard (4:30, 34).

Traditionally the purification offering has been known as the "sin offering," because the Hebrew word used to designate the sacrifice, *ḥaṭṭā't* (*khaṭṭā't*), frequently means "sin." However, the title "purification offering" is preferable because it indicates more precisely the purpose or function of the sacrifice. As we have already noted in chapter 17 (above), sin and uncleanness have the power to defile or pollute sacred objects; the more serious the sin, the greater the pollution. Consequently, if the anointed (or high) priest,[6] who is expected to be especially holy and blameless, has sinned unintentionally, this pollutes the golden incense altar in the Holy Place. In contrast, a tribal leader's sin defiles the bronze altar. For the purification offerings outlined in Leviticus 4:1–5:13, the blood is placed on the sacred furnishings and not on the people responsible for the sin, indicating that the pollution caused by the sinner is being cleansed rather than the actual sinner. On other occasions, however, blood is applied to people in order to cleanse and sanctify them (e.g., in making the covenant at Sinai and in consecrating the priests).

The Reparation Offering (Lev. 5:14–6:7; 7:1–10)

Few details are given concerning the ritual of the reparation offering. Most attention is focused on the circumstances requiring such a sacrifice. Regarding the sacrifice itself, special emphasis is placed on the bringing of a "ram from the flock, one without defect and of the proper value in silver, according to the sanctuary shekel" (5:15; cf. 5:18; 6:6). The animal is slaughtered, its blood is sprinkled against the altar, and the fatty portions associated with the kidneys and liver are burned upon the altar (7:2–5). The rest of the animal is given to the priests, who alone are permitted to eat the meat (7:6).

Some English translations refer to this sacrifice as the "guilt offering." The Hebrew word *'āšām* (*'āshām*) can mean "guilt." However, it can also mean "reparation" or "compensation." This latter understanding seems to be more appropriate given the function of this sacrifice. The emphasis placed on the value of the ram and the references to adding "a fifth of the value" to make restitution suggest that the sacrifice is intended to compensate God for wrongs committed against him (cf. 5:16; 6:5). In this regard the reparation sacrifice partly resembles the practice of redemption outlined in Leviticus 27.

From the preceding survey of the five main types of sacrifices mentioned in Leviticus 1–7, it is clear that each sacrifice has a distinctive function. These functions reflect the different ways in which the divine/human relationship is affected by human sin and uncleanness. Together these different sacrifices seek to restore humans to a harmonious relationship with God.

---

6. The title "anointed priest" is used only in Lev. 4:3, 5, 16; 6:22. Although all priests are anointed, most commentators accept that this designation must be a reference to the high priest, who is viewed as having received a special anointing (cf. Num. 35:25).

The Day of Atonement (Lev. 16:1–34)

The ritual associated with the Day of Atonement was also important for maintaining a harmonious relationship between God and the people of Israel. This ritual falls into three main parts: (1) the purification of the sanctuary, (2) the sending away of the scapegoat, and (3) the presentation of two burnt offerings. The first part closely parallels the ritual outlined above for a purification offering. The second part is unique to the Day of Atonement. The final part is mentioned only briefly, fuller details being unnecessary in the light of those already given in 1:2–17 and 6:8–13. An important aspect of the ritual on the Day of Atonement is that it centers on the high priest, named here as Aaron. He alone bears responsibility for what takes place, and the onus is on him to ensure that atonement is achieved for all the people.

The Purification of the Sanctuary

Annually on the Day of Atonement the high priest, wearing his special priestly clothing (16:4), passes through the curtain that separates the Holy of Holies from the Holy Place. Inside the Holy of Holies he sprinkles blood on and before the cover of the ark of the covenant, cleansing it and the Holy of Holies from pollution caused by sin. This process is repeated twice. On the first occasion a bull is sacrificed as a purification offering; its blood atones for the sins of the high priest and his family. Afterward one of two male goats is sacrificed and its blood brought into the Holy of Holies by the high priest to atone for the sins of the whole community of Israel (16:15–16). The high priest enters the Holy of Holies a second time and places some of the goat's blood on the cover of the ark of the covenant before sprinkling more blood seven times before the ark of the covenant. He then performs a similar ritual in the Holy Place before the golden altar of incense.[7] The high priest next puts some of the blood from the bull and the goat on the horns of the bronze altar in the courtyard (16:18). Finally, he sprinkles more of this blood seven times on the altar to cleanse it (16:19). Later, the remains of the bull and the goat are taken outside the camp and burned (16:27). The man designated to perform this task must wash himself before returning to the camp (16:28).

The Scapegoat

At a preliminary stage in the Day of Atonement ritual, two goats are brought before the high priest. Lots are cast to determine which of the two will be sacrificed as a purification offering. After the high priest has purified the tabernacle with the blood of the first goat, he takes the second goat and, placing both hands upon it, confesses over it "all the wickedness and rebellion of the

---

7. This is implied in Lev. 16:16–17.

Israelites—all their sins" (16:21). This "scapegoat" is then led to an uninhabited place in the desert and released (16:8–10). Finally, the man responsible for taking the goat into the wilderness washes himself and his clothes before coming back into the camp (16:26).

The Burnt Offerings

Apart from the animals listed as purification offerings, two rams are sacrificed as burnt offerings. The first is provided by the high priest (16:3), the second by the Israelites (16:5). Following the purification of the sanctuary and the sending away of the scapegoat, the high priest takes off his special garments and washes himself. He then offers up both rams in order to atone for himself and the people (16:23–24).

The Day of Atonement was probably the most important occasion in the cultic calendar of ancient Israel, designed to atone for sins not covered by sacrifices offered throughout the rest of the year. The seriousness of the pollution caused by these sins is indicated by the fact that the high priest, with the blood of the purification offering, had to cleanse the most sacred part of the tabernacle, the Holy of Holies. The expulsion of the scapegoat that removed the people's sin from the camp was a visible sign of the special cleansing achieved on this important occasion.

Old Testament Summary

The detailed attention given to the sacrificial system in the opening chapters of Leviticus underlines its importance. In the light of humanity's disposition to sin against God, the provision of means by which atonement may be made represents a gracious and unmerited response from God. By instituting the sacrifices and associated rituals outlined in Leviticus, the LORD places at the disposal of the Israelites a way of restoring and maintaining a harmonious relationship with their God.

New Testament Connections

The concepts associated with the Old Testament sacrificial rituals strongly influenced the way in which New Testament writers viewed the death of Jesus Christ. In particular, they believed that through the offering of a unique sacrifice by a unique high priest, it was possible for the divine-human relationship to be restored to complete harmony. Though this was central to the faith of the early Christians, we should not overlook the brief observation by the author of Hebrews that it was never God's desire that sacrifices should be offered. Their existence was due to human failure to keep God's commands (Heb. 10:5–9).

Jesus Christ as a Sacrifice

The New Testament writers frequently understand the death of Jesus Christ in sacrificial terms. This is highlighted, for example, by the description of Jesus as "the Lamb of God, who takes away the sin of the world!" (John 1:29; cf. 1 Pet. 1:19) and various references to the "blood" of Jesus Christ (e.g., Acts 20:28; Rom. 5:9; Eph. 2:13; Col. 1:20; 1 Pet. 1:2; Rev. 7:14; 12:11). Similarly, Paul refers to the death of Jesus as a "sacrifice of atonement" (Rom. 3:25), and it is recorded in Hebrews 9:26 that Christ "appeared once for all at the culmination of the ages to do away with sin by the sacrifice of himself."

For the author of Hebrews, Christ's death was the ultimate sacrifice, of which the Old Testament sacrifices were merely an illustration (9:9–10; 10:1). The inadequacy of the Old Testament sacrifices is highlighted by the fact that they had to be repeated; they could never make perfect for all time those who offered them (10:1). Christ, however, constituted the perfect offering. Consequently his sacrificial death was all-sufficient, and further animal sacrifices became unnecessary. For this reason the early church dismissed as irrelevant and superfluous the temple sacrifices in Jerusalem. Nevertheless, the Old Testament regulations about sacrifices had continuing significance because they shed light on the nature of the atonement achieved through Christ's death.

Special attention is drawn to the cleansing associated with Christ's sacrificial blood. Whereas the blood of animals was able to cleanse objects and people who outwardly were ceremonially unclean, the blood of Christ is viewed as superior in that it can cleanse or purify inner, human consciences (Heb. 9:14; cf. Titus 2:14). Since the forgiveness of sins comes through the shedding of blood (Heb. 9:22; cf. Matt. 26:28; Eph. 1:7), those cleansed by the blood of Christ need no longer feel guilty (Heb. 10:2; cf. 1 John 1:7).

Jesus Christ as High Priest

Closely associated with the description of Christ's death in sacrificial terms is his portrayal as a high priest. To this end the author of Hebrews argues that although Jesus did not belong to the family of Aaron, he was divinely appointed to be "a high priest in the order of Melchizedek" (Heb. 5:10; 7:11–22).[8] Furthermore, he differs from all previous high priests in that he alone is "holy, blameless, pure, set apart from sinners, exalted above the heavens" (7:26). Also, the Aaronic priests served in the earthly tabernacle, "a copy and shadow of what is in heaven" (8:5; cf. 9:24), but Christ serves in the heavenly "sanctuary" (8:1–5). The Aaronic high priest of necessity had to purify the earthly tabernacle each year on the Day of Atonement, but Christ,

8. By associating Jesus with Melchizedek, the author of Hebrews presents Jesus as both a priest and a king. A further dimension to this may be noted. In Gen. 1–3 Adam is presented as a priest-king. Not surprisingly, therefore, Jesus is viewed as the Second Adam (Rom. 5:12–21; cf. Luke 3:38; 4:3).

by offering himself, has purified the heavenly temple once and for all (9:23; 13:11–12). Moreover, because his priestly mediation was completely acceptable to God, having entered the heavenly temple, there is no need for him to leave. Consequently he is able continually to represent others before God (7:25); because God accepts Christ's high-priestly mediation, believers may have confidence that God also accepts them.[9] Finally, with the establishment of a new priesthood, the regulations associated with the Levitical priesthood become redundant (cf. 7:12, 18).

By emphasizing that Jesus Christ, as God's unique Son, has provided the sacrifice necessary to completely atone for human sin, the New Testament highlights two important aspects of God's character: his justice and his love. Motivated by love, God provides the sacrifice necessary to meet the demands of his own justice. It is God, in the person of his own Son, who pays the price of forgiveness for human sin.

9. Another OT idea that may be linked to the death of Jesus Christ as a high priest is the belief that a high priest's death purges pollution.

19

The Clean and the Unclean Foods

The food regulations contained in the book of Leviticus highlight two important theological principles. The distinction between clean and unclean foods emphasizes the divine calling of Israel to be a holy nation, different from the other nations of the earth; the clean and unclean animals symbolize Israelites and non-Israelites respectively. The law prohibiting the eating of blood derives from the idea that all life, both human and animal, is sacred. Although God sanctions the eating of meat, due respect must be shown for the life of any animal slaughtered for food; blood, as the symbol of life, must not be consumed by humans.

Introduction

As we have already noticed, most of Leviticus consists of divine speeches mediated through Moses to the Israelites. Although these speeches cover various topics, a major unifying theme is God's concern that the people should be a holy nation. To this end Leviticus contains regulations governing the offering of sacrifices (chaps. 1–7) and the procedures for being purified from various forms of uncleanness (chaps. 12–15). This latter block of material is immediately preceded by rules concerning the animals that the Israelites may and may not eat (11:1–47). These regulations divide all living creatures on the basis of specific criteria into two groups: clean and unclean. Only the animals that belong to the clean category may be eaten by the Israelites. These regulations are repeated later, in Deuteronomy 14:3–20.

At first sight it is difficult to see any connection between these food regulations and the divine desire that Israel should be a holy nation. In what way does the eating of particular animals fulfill Israel's calling to be a holy people?

The Food Regulations Summarized

The regulations defining clean and unclean animals are divided into three sections, which correspond with their three main regions of habitation: land (11:1–8), sea (11:9–12), and air (11:13–23). All animals are categorized as clean or unclean on the basis of a single principle governing each location:

1. Only cloven-hoofed, cud-chewing land animals are clean; all other mammals are unclean.
2. Only fish with fins and scales are clean; all other fish are unclean.
3. Birds of prey and flying insects that walk rather than hop are unclean; all other birds and insects are clean.

Leviticus 11 clearly states the general principles for land animals, fish, and flying insects, but in the case of birds, principles need to be deduced from the different types listed. Even when a principle is given, further details are usually added to clarify particular cases. Regarding land animals, for example, special attention is given to the camel, the hyrax ("coney," NIV 1984; "rock badger," NRSV), the rabbit, and the pig; they are all declared unclean even though they meet one of the two criteria for clean animals given in the general principle (11:4–8).[1]

The Function of the Food Regulations

Various explanations have been offered to account for the dietary rules in Leviticus 11 and Deuteronomy 14. Some commentators have suggested that the classification of the animals into two types symbolizes people and their behavior. An animal that chews its cud resembles a human who meditates on the divine law. The sheep is designated clean because the ancient Israelites view God as their heavenly shepherd. The pig is unclean because of its dirty habits, which are reminiscent of a sinner's behavior. Although the arbitrary nature of such explanations has led contemporary scholars to reject them, the basic idea that the two types of animal are symbolic of people is probably correct.

1. Three basic ideas underlie Jewish dietary laws: (1) it is forbidden to consume blood (Deut. 12:23); (2) meat and dairy produce must not be eaten together (Exod. 23:19); (3) certain types of animals, birds, and fish are classified as unclean and should not be consumed (Lev. 11:1–47; Deut. 14:3–21). Food that meets these requirements is described in Hebrew as *kāšēr* (*kāshēr*; cf. "kosher"), "ritually fit," "wholesome."

Other writers have proposed that these ancient food regulations anticipate the findings of modern science regarding hygiene. The clean animals were safe for human consumption, the unclean animals were not. Two factors argue against this proposal. First, while pork is often cited as an example of an unclean meat that is dangerous to human health, this is true only when the meat is not properly cooked. Thoroughly cooked pork is as safe to consume as any of the meats classified as clean. Similarly, camel meat poses little danger to health; indeed, Arabs view it as a delicacy. Second, if a danger to health was the reason behind the food regulations, it is strange that this motive is never mentioned in the Bible. Might we not have expected that the Israelites would have been warned of this danger in order to encourage them not to eat the unclean meats? In the light of these factors, the hygiene explanation is unconvincing.[2]

Some commentators suggest that the Israelites were instructed to avoid the unclean animals because of their close association with non-Israelite religions. For example, archaeological evidence suggests that the pig was eaten in Canaanite rituals. Yet while some unclean animals were clearly used in the cultic activities of ancient Israel's neighbors, it is not possible to demonstrate this for all the animals designated unclean. Furthermore, if this is the rationale behind the classification of the animals, it is surprising that the bull, which was prominent in both Egyptian and Canaanite religious rituals, was not included among the unclean animals. Although the rationale of religious associations might account for certain cases, it fails to explain all the distinctions made between clean and unclean animals.

The most satisfactory explanation of the food regulations rests on the observation that for the Israelites the animal world was structured in the same way as the human world. The clean and unclean animals parallel clean and unclean people (i.e., Israelites and non-Israelites). Within the category of clean animals, two further classes may be observed, sacrificial and nonsacrificial; these correspond with the human classes of priestly and nonpriestly.[3] By restricting their diet to clean animals, the Israelites were reminded of their obligation to be a clean people, distinct from others.[4] Consequently, each meal at which meat was served had religious implications for the Israelites; it spoke of their divine calling to be a holy nation. This link between the food

2. From a Christian perspective, a further reason can be added. How could Jesus Christ have abolished rules that were supposed to protect the health of those who abided by them?

3. We have already noticed the importance of the three categories of holy, clean, and unclean (in chap. 17 above). It therefore is not surprising that they should reappear in the context of the food regulations. In the correspondence between priests and sacrificial animals, Lev. 21 and 22 parallel each other: Lev. 21 deals with blemished priests and Lev. 22 with blemished sacrificial animals.

4. The dietary rules are placed immediately after material dealing with the separation of the priests from the rest of the Israelites. As the priests are set apart as holy from the rest of the Israelites, so is Israel set apart as holy from the rest of the nations.

regulations and Israel's divine election is clearly reflected in Leviticus 20:24–26: "I am the LORD your God, who has set you apart from the nations. You must therefore make a distinction between clean and unclean animals and between clean and unclean birds. Do not defile yourselves by any animal or bird or anything that moves along the ground—those that I have set apart as unclean for you. You are to be holy to me because I, the LORD, am holy, and I have set you apart from the nations to be my own."

Moreover, the food regulations made it difficult for an Israelite to participate in meals provided by non-Israelites. They not only symbolized that Israel was to be a clean nation in contrast to other nations; they also had the practical effect of limiting contact with other people, which might compromise Israel's special status.

The Rationale behind the Clean/Unclean Classification

While the distinction between clean and unclean peoples accounts for the purpose of the food regulations, it is still necessary to explain why some animals were considered clean and others unclean. Why, for example, was a sheep categorized as clean, but a pig unclean? Was this classification merely arbitrary, or were there particular reasons for designating some animals clean and others unclean? Although most scholars accept that some rationale must have governed the categorization of the animals as clean and unclean, no explanation commands unanimous support. One factor, however, deserves special consideration.

A common factor among many of the unclean animals is that they depend on the death of other creatures in order to survive.[5] A survey of animals that are declared unclean reveals one feature that is common to most of them: they eat meat. All the birds listed as unclean in verses 13–19 are birds of prey; their diet consists of the meat of other animals. The same is true regarding the land animals; those designated unclean have claws (e.g., cats and dogs), and such animals are carnivorous. In marked contrast, cloven-hoofed animals do not eat meat. This distinction between carnivores and noncarnivores (or ruminants) is emphasized by including the criterion of chewing the cud. The idea that animals associated with death should be viewed as unclean is in keeping with what we have observed in chapter 17; in Leviticus, death and uncleanness are generally linked, being the opposites of life and holiness. By eating clean animals, the Israelites distanced themselves from death, which was perceived as the source of uncleanness.

5. As if to highlight this association with death, much of Lev. 11 focuses on the uncleanness that occurs through touching or carrying the carcasses of unclean animals (cf. vv. 24–38). Even the carcasses of clean animals—those that die by some means other than ritual slaughtering—communicate uncleanness to humans (vv. 39–40).

The Blood Prohibition

Before concluding our discussion of the food regulations in Leviticus 11, it is important to say something about the prohibition against eating (or drinking) blood, which is highlighted in 17:1–16 (cf. 3:17; 7:26–27; Deut. 12:16, 23–25). This prohibition is so serious that anyone who eats blood is to "be cut off" (17:14).

To understand the reason for this, we need to refer back to the book of Genesis. Although God initially created human beings to be vegetarian (Gen. 1:29), one result of Adam and Eve's rebellion in the Garden of Eden was that humanity thereafter desired to eat meat. As a result, humans killed animals for food, apparently adding to the general violence of humankind that ultimately caused God to send the flood (6:11–13). After the flood, God appears to make a concession to Noah and his descendants regarding the eating of meat. They are permitted to do so, on the condition that they "must not eat meat that has its lifeblood still in it" (9:4). Although God allows the taking of an animal's life, the prohibition against eating blood draws attention to the importance that he places on all life. The Israelites' attitude to the killing of animals, even for food, is required to differ from that of their neighbors. They are to behave in a way that reflects their belief that God is the source of all life. Since God is the giver and sustainer of life, he alone has the right to sanction the taking of a life.[6]

In passing, we need to recognize that meat did not form part of the regular diet of the Israelites, especially during the wilderness wanderings. The absence of meat was a recurring reason for complaints against God. When meat was eaten, it often appears to have been within the context of religious celebrations.

Old Testament Summary

From the preceding discussion it is clear that the food regulations contained in Leviticus reflect important theological ideas. On the one hand, the distinctions between clean and unclean animals emphasize the special calling of Israel to be a holy nation. On the other hand, the prohibition against eating blood underlines the value that God places on all life, animal as well as human. In a remarkable way religious truths are reflected in the daily routine associated with eating.

New Testament Connections

The concept of clean and unclean foods appears in a number of New Testament passages. In the Gospels, the parallel passages in Matthew 15:1–20 and Mark

6. On the significance of blood within the sacrificial system, see chap. 18 above.

7:1–23 focus on Jesus's attitude toward eating something that is unclean. In these passages it is not specifically stated that the meat is unclean; rather, the issue centers on how the disciples are "eating food with hands that were defiled, that is, unwashed" (Mark 7:2). In response, Jesus comments to the people: "Nothing outside a person can defile them by going into them. Rather, it is what comes out of a person that defiles them" (Mark 7:15; cf. Matt. 15:11).

Later, Jesus explains the saying to his disciples: "Don't you see that nothing that enters a person from the outside can defile them? For it doesn't go into their heart but into their stomach, and then out of the body. . . . What comes out of a person is what defiles them. For it is from within, out of a person's heart, that evil thoughts come—sexual immorality, theft, murder, adultery, greed, malice, deceit, lewdness, envy, slander, arrogance, and folly. All these evils come from inside and defile a person" (Mark 7:18–23; cf. Matt. 15:17–20). Mark adds the brief but significant observation: "In saying this, Jesus declared all foods clean" (7:19).

The topic of clean and unclean foods also arises in the account of Peter's visit to Cornelius, a God-fearing Gentile (Acts 10:1–11:18). This is an important incident within the book of Acts because it marks the first significant occasion on which the gospel is proclaimed to Gentiles. Before being asked to visit Cornelius, in a vision Peter is commanded by God to kill and eat animals that are unclean. Although Peter strongly objects, God warns him not to "call anything impure that God has made clean" (Acts 10:15). Later, when he visits Cornelius, Peter comments on the significance of the vision: "You are well aware that it is against our law for a Jew to associate with or visit a Gentile. But God has shown me that I should not call anyone impure or unclean" (Acts 10:28).

Previously God had introduced the concept of clean and unclean foods in order to separate the Israelites from other nations; now in the New Testament period the distinction between clean and unclean foods is abandoned in order to show that God no longer distinguishes between "clean" Jews and "unclean" Gentiles. With the death, resurrection, and ascension of Jesus Christ, the Gentiles are now recipients of God's grace and mercy. In the light of this, it is only natural that the divinely instituted regulations concerning clean and unclean foods should be abandoned; they no longer serve any meaningful purpose. So significant is Peter's vision in shaping the outlook of the early church that it is recorded twice in Acts (10:9–16; 11:5–10). Later, at the Jerusalem Council, Peter defends his action in taking the gospel to the Gentiles by commenting that God no longer makes a distinction between Jews and Gentiles (Acts 15:7–9).

Although the early church abandoned the distinction between clean and unclean foods on theological grounds, they still insisted that Gentiles should adhere to the principle of not eating blood. This is seen in the conclusion reached by the Jerusalem Council, which was called to clarify the position of Gentiles regarding circumcision and the law of Moses. James summarizes the

265

council's findings by declaring that Gentile believers should be instructed "to abstain from food polluted by idols, from sexual immorality, from the meat of strangled animals and from blood" (Acts 15:20; cf. 15:29). Although the Old Testament regulations concerning clean/unclean foods are no longer relevant under the new covenant established by Jesus Christ, the theological basis for the Old Testament prohibition against the eating of blood remains unchanged as a result of the new covenant (cf. Gen. 9:4–6). Thus there is good reason for insisting that both Jewish and Gentile believers should adhere to it.

Remarkably, although the early church insisted on maintaining the Old Testament regulation concerning the eating of the blood of animals, several New Testament passages contain startling statements about eating the blood of Christ. The most striking of these is John 6:53–56: "Jesus said to them, 'Very truly I tell you, unless you eat the flesh of the Son of Man and drink his blood, you have no life in you. Whoever eats my flesh and drinks my blood has eternal life, and I will raise him up at the last day. For my flesh is real food and my blood is real drink. Whoever eats my flesh and drinks my blood remains in me, and I in him.'" These comments, which highlight a special relationship between Jesus and those who eat his flesh and drink his blood, are clearly related to the celebration of the Lord's Supper, or Eucharist.[7] In commemorating the new covenant, believers are to eat bread and drink wine, representing the body and blood of Jesus Christ (Matt. 26:27–28; Mark 14:23–24). By doing so, they acknowledge their association with Jesus and participate in the benefits derived from his death (1 Cor. 10:16–21; 11:23–26). At the very heart of the meal instituted by Jesus Christ is communion with God.

7. Cf. P. M. Hoskins, *That Scripture Might Be Fulfilled: Typology and the Death of Christ* (LaVergne, TN: Xulon, 2009), 103–9.

20

Toward the Promised Land

A lthough the Israelites' encounter with the LORD at Sinai lies at the heart of the Pentateuch, Sinai is not their final destination. Consequently the initial chapters of Numbers focus on the people's preparations before leaving Sinai for the land of Canaan. These preparations show that the Israelites will be required to militarily defeat the nations that already occupy the land. However, the middle chapters of Numbers reveal, as we shall examine in more detail in the next chapter, that the people's trust in God wavers in the face of opposition, and as a result they fail to take possession of what God has promised them. Of all those who have left Egypt as adults, only Joshua and Caleb will enter the promised land. Nevertheless, in spite of this initial failure, the final chapters of Numbers reveal that the promise of land is renewed with the next generation of adults. God's promise to Abraham will not be thwarted by human disobedience.

Introduction

Whereas the book of Leviticus is dominated by divine speeches outlining regulations and laws for the people of Israel, with few descriptions of events, the reverse occurs in Numbers. Most of the book records events that take place in the forty-year period beginning shortly after the making of the covenant at Sinai and ending with the Israelites camped on the plains of Moab, ready to enter the land of Canaan. Interspersed among these narrative passages are a number of sections that record further regulations and laws (e.g., chaps. 5–6, 15, 18–19, 28–30).

1. Although the book of Numbers spans a forty-year period, the coverage is uneven: Numbers 1–10 records events that fall within a two-month period; Numbers 11–24 focuses on selected experiences scattered throughout the next forty years; Numbers 25–36 concentrates on developments that take place in the fortieth year. Though the opening and closing chapters are generally favorable in their portrayal of the Israelites, the middle section presents a series of incidents that highlight the failure of the people to trust and obey the LORD. These observations suggest that the book falls into three major parts, and several other features further support this division.

2. The first and third sections begin with censuses of all the men who are twenty years old or older (1:1–54; 26:1–65). The account of the second census specifically mentions that of all those included in the first census, only Caleb and Joshua remain alive (26:64–65). This second census marks a new stage in the narrative and highlights an important difference between the second and third sections of the book: chapters 11–25 record various events that describe the death of large numbers of Israelites; chapters 26–36 mention no deaths; even during a battle with the Midianites, no Israelite soldier is killed (31:49).

3. All the material in Numbers 27–36 relates directly in one way or another to the occupation of the land of Canaan. This is highlighted by the fact that the final section of Numbers is framed by two episodes that focus on problems concerning the inheritance of land by the daughters of Zelophehad (27:1–11; 36:1–12).

In this chapter we shall concentrate on the first and last sections of Numbers. The middle section of the book shall be considered in the next chapter.

Preparations for the Journey

The events recorded in the initial chapters of Numbers all take place close to Mount Sinai. Although the material in these chapters appears somewhat diverse, a common theme ties much of it together: Numbers 1–10 describes how the Israelites prepare to leave Sinai, to occupy the land of Canaan.[1] The following features of these preparations are noteworthy.

First, the Israelites are to prepare for war against the inhabitants of Canaan. This is highlighted in the first chapter of the book, which records a census of

1. Observe that the material in Num. 1–10 is not in strict chronological order.

the people that takes place "on the first day of the second month of the second year after the Israelites came out of Egypt" (1:1). The census was intended to "count . . . all the men in Israel who are twenty years old or more and able to serve in the army" (1:3; cf. 1:45). This emphasizes an idea, alluded to elsewhere (cf. Exod. 23:31), that the Israelites are expected to fight for the land that God has promised them. The Levites, however, are excluded from this census due to their special association with the tabernacle. Because of their responsibility for its care and transportation, the Levites are not to be involved directly in any killing that might occur during the taking of the land.[2]

Second, linked to the preparations for conflict is the requirement that those living in the camp must be pure. Anything that might defile the camp is a potential danger to the success of the Israelites' occupation of the land of Canaan. Thus anyone, male or female, who is unclean—as a result of a skin disease, a bodily discharge, or contact with the dead—is to be sent outside the camp (5:1–4). For the same reason, instructions regarding restitution for wrongs (5:5–10) and suspected adultery (5:11–31) are included here. Nothing is to be allowed to defile the camp.[3]

Third, instructions are given regarding the layout of the camp (2:1–34). Though these specify the location of the tribes around the tabernacle or tent of meeting in terms of north, south, east, and west,[4] they also indicate the order in which the tribes are to set out when they journey from one location to another (cf. 2:9, 16, 24, 31). The travel aspect of these arrangements is especially emphasized in the comments regarding the tabernacle and the tribe of Levi (2:17).

Fourth, apart from specifying the arrangement of the tribes when they journey, various other practical details are mentioned. In outlining the duties of the Levitical clans, the LORD draws special attention to the transportation of the tabernacle and its furnishings (4:5, 10, 12, 15, 19, 24, 25, 27, 31, 32). The account of the census of all the Levites ends by noting, "At the LORD's command through Moses, each was assigned his work and told what to carry" (4:49). Later the tribal leaders present to the LORD "six covered carts and twelve oxen" (7:3), which Moses hands over to the Levites to assist them with transporting some of the tabernacle furnishings. However, the holiest items of the tabernacle are to be carried on human shoulders rather than transported by animals (7:9). The LORD commands Moses to make two silver trumpets that are to be used, among other purposes, "for calling the community together and for having the camps set out" (10:2; cf. 10:5–6).

2. A further reference to battle comes in Num. 10:8–9 as the priests sound a blast on the silver trumpets.

3. Uncleanness also figures in Num. 9 regarding the celebration of the Passover in the second month. For a fuller discussion of the topic of cleanness/uncleanness, see chap. 17 above.

4. The east side of the tabernacle is viewed as the most important since the entrance to the tent of meeting is located there.

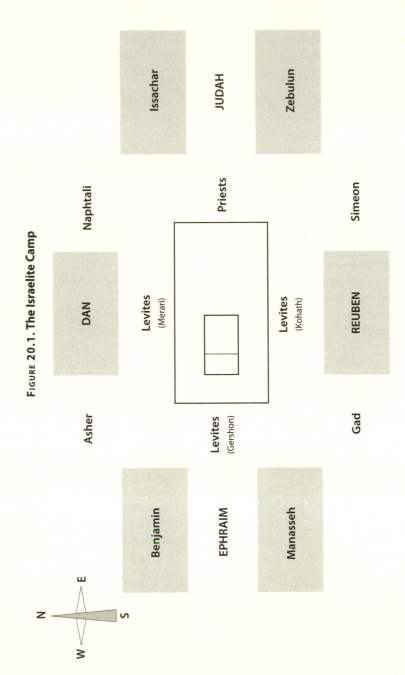

FIGURE 20.1. The Israelite Camp

Fifth, the concept of travel is prominent in remarks about the cloud that covers the tabernacle in 9:15–23. This passage explains, even before the Israelites leave Sinai, how God will lead them during the journey from Sinai to Canaan. Attention is repeatedly drawn to the way in which the movement of the cloud determines whether the Israelite camp moves or remains where it is.

The Role of the Levites

Apart from highlighting the preparations necessary for the Israelites' journey to Canaan, the early chapters of Numbers also give prominence to setting the Levites apart. This is evident in a number of ways. At the outset the tribe of Levi is excluded from the census because they are appointed to be in charge of the tabernacle and its furnishings (1:47–53; cf. 2:33). Later Moses is instructed by God to present the Levites to Aaron the high priest as special assistants (3:6–9). Immediately next is a lengthy passage that associates the setting apart of the Levites with the sparing of the Israelite firstborn in Egypt (3:11–51; cf. Exod. 13:1–16). This passage also reports how God assigns different responsibilities regarding the tabernacle and its furnishings to the main Levite clans. More detailed instructions, which relate primarily to the transportation of the tabernacle by the three main branches of the Levites, are given to Moses in 4:1–49. Later the LORD instructs Moses regarding the process by which the Levites are to be set apart (8:5–19). These instructions underline that the Levites are to purify themselves in order to "do the work at the tent of meeting on behalf of the Israelites and to make atonement for them so that no plague will strike the Israelites when they go near the sanctuary" (8:19).[5] The actual setting apart of the Levites is recorded briefly in 8:20–22. This is followed by further instructions regarding the age of Levitical service at the tabernacle (8:23–26). In a variety of ways the opening chapters of Numbers highlight the special role of the Levites.

In some respects the setting apart of the Levites resembles the appointment of Aaron and his sons as priests (cf. Exod. 29:1–46; Lev. 8:1–36). However, it is clear that the Levites are not granted the same holy status as the priests. Although, like the priests, they serve within the tabernacle, they are not permitted to directly touch the holiest of the tabernacle furnishings or to perform the duties assigned to the priests regarding the offering of sacrifices.

This distinction between the priests and the Levites is significant. Before the book of Numbers, the Pentateuch makes few references to Levites. Their loyalty to God is noted in Exodus 32:26–28; apart from a brief mention in Exodus 38:21, there is only one other minor reference to them (Lev. 25:32–33). In the light of this, the detailed attention given to them in the early chapters

---

5. In the light of this, the rebellious actions of Korah, a Levite, take on added significance (Num. 16).

of Numbers is striking. Their prominence at this stage is probably tied to later developments within the book. As we shall observe in more detail in the next chapter, the account of the rebellion of Korah in 16:1–50 centers on the relationship between the priests and the Levites. As a leading Levite, Korah is found guilty and punished for trying to usurp the position of the divinely appointed priests.

Closely associated with the appointment of the Levites are the instructions in 6:1–21 for setting apart ordinary Israelites as Nazirites. The inclusion of this material in the early chapters of Numbers reveals that the taking of a special holy status was freely available to all Israelites. Although non-Levites are prohibited from serving in the tabernacle, they are not excluded from adopting a special degree of holiness.

Further Preparations to Enter the Land of Canaan

The final part of the book of Numbers (26:1–36:13), like the first, begins with a census of "all those twenty years old or more who are able to serve in the army of Israel" (26:2; cf. 1:3). The significance of this second census lies in the fact that of all those included in the previous census, forty years earlier, only Caleb and Joshua remain alive (26:64–65; cf. 32:11–12). This fact is clearly linked to the earlier account of the rebellion led by ten Israelite spies following their reconnaissance of the land (13:1–14:45) and the LORD's prediction that "not one of you will enter the land I swore with uplifted hand to make your home, except Caleb son of Jephunneh and Joshua son of Nun" (14:30). Even Moses, as recorded later in Deuteronomy 34:1–8, dies outside the promised land due to his failure to honor God in the sight of the Israelites at the waters of Meribah (Num. 20:9–13; cf. 27:13–14).

Numbers 11–25 catalogs a series of events that result in the death of the entire adult generation that was delivered from Egypt; Numbers 26–36 records no comparable events; no Israelite deaths are mentioned in the final section of the book. Even when the narrative recounts a major battle against the Midianites (31:1–24), it is specifically noted that not one soldier fails to return alive from the conflict (31:49). This contrast between the second and third sections of the book is particularly striking and highlights the fact that the death of the exodus generation is due to their failure to trust God. As we shall observe in the next chapter, the middle section of Numbers highlights various occasions on which large numbers of Israelites perish as a result of disobeying God.

All the material coming after the census in Numbers 26 focuses in one way or another on the future occupation of the land of Canaan. With the death of all those who have failed to enter the promised land on the first occasion, the narrative now focuses on the preparations for the second generation to possess Canaan. These preparations are framed by two accounts that involve the daughters of Zelophehad (27:1–11; 36:1–12). Significantly, both episodes address the topic of land inheritance. In the first instance, Zelophehad's daughters are guaranteed that they shall have "property as an inheritance among their father's relatives" (27:7). On the second occasion they are required to marry within their own tribe so that their inheritance will not pass to another tribe. In both episodes questions concerning inheritance are resolved before the Israelites enter the promised land.

Of the other episodes in the final section of Numbers, the land of Canaan figures prominently in Numbers 32 and 34–35. The first of these chapters focuses on the request of the tribes of Reuben and Gad to settle on the east side of the Jordan in the "lands of Jazer and Gilead" (32:1). Their wish is granted only when it is made clear that they are prepared to assist the other tribes in obtaining their inheritance on the west side of the Jordan. Moses is deeply concerned that the desire of the tribes of Reuben and Gad to stay on the east side of the Jordan does not arise from wrong motives; they are not to follow the rebellious example of their fathers, who refused to enter the promised land. Toward its conclusion Numbers 32 also reports that "the descendants of Makir son of Manasseh went to Gilead, captured it and drove out the Amorites who were there" (32:39). As a result, half the tribe of Manasseh is permitted to settle on the eastern side of the Jordan.

Numbers 34 falls into two parts, each focusing on the land of Canaan. The first half delineates the boundaries of the land to be possessed by the Israelites. The rest of the chapter lists the names of the leaders appointed from each tribe to assist Eleazar the priest and Joshua in assigning the land between the nine and a half tribes (34:17). Because of their separation from the other tribes to serve in the tabernacle, the Levites are not allocated a specific region of the land of Canaan. Rather, they are given forty-eight towns, each with some pastureland surrounding it, distributed throughout the twelve tribal regions. Six of these towns are designated "cities of refuge, to which a person who has killed someone may flee" (35:6). Further details are added to explain how these cities should function as places of refuge for those who unintentionally kill another person (35:9–28). The chapter concludes by highlighting yet again the theme of land: the Israelites must not defile the land because the LORD will be dwelling in their midst (35:34).

Old Testament Summary

The opening and final sections of the book of Numbers are clearly linked to the overall development of the narrative plot in the Pentateuch. Chapters 1–10 describe the final preparations of the people before they leave Sinai to enter the promised land; chapters 25–36 anticipate the next major development in the narrative, the possession of the land. However, as we shall observe in detail in the next chapter, Numbers 11–24 records a series of events that result in the death of the generation that has left Egypt to go to the promised land. An entirely new generation of adults prepares to occupy the land of Canaan.

New Testament Connections

Most of the main links with the New Testament will be considered at the end of the next chapter, where we consider the central section of Numbers. Regarding the theme of land, we have already discussed the relevant New Testament material in chapter 11 (above).

21

Murmurings

The opening and concluding chapters of Numbers describe the preparations that the Israelites make before entering the promised land; the middle chapters provide a contrasting picture. Here various incidents portray the true nature of the exodus generation of adult Israelites. In spite of all that they have witnessed in Egypt and at Sinai, they display a remarkable lack of faith in the LORD's ability (1) to provide for their daily needs, and (2) to ensure their safety in the land of Canaan. In these chapters their complaints against the LORD form a recurring pattern. Furthermore, there are frequent challenges to the hierarchical structures that God has introduced for the well-being of all the people. As a consequence of their rebellious actions, the entire adult generation, with the exception of Caleb and Joshua, is consigned to remain in the wilderness until they are all dead by the end of forty years.

Introduction

After highlighting certain preparations for the next stage of the journey from Egypt to Canaan, the early chapters of Numbers reach a climax in 10:11 with the departure of the Israelites from Sinai. The narrative now focuses on their progress. At the outset a very positive picture is presented, with the tribes setting out just as the LORD has commanded them (10:11–28). To underline this, the narrator includes material that displays Moses's optimism regarding the future. When Hobab, his brother-in-law, talks of returning to his own land and people, Moses responds by commenting: "If you come with us, we will share with you whatever good things the LORD gives us" (10:32). A similar confidence underlies Moses's words each time the ark sets out and comes to rest. "Rise up, O LORD! May your enemies be scattered; may your foes flee before you" (10:35). "Return, LORD, to the countless thousands of Israel" (10:36). In these ways the second half of Numbers 10 conveys a sense of confidence that the LORD will successfully bring the Israelites into the promised land of Canaan.

Against this brief optimistic introduction, the events of Numbers 11–25 contrast markedly. God's anger turns against the Israelites, eventually causing the death of the entire generation of adults who left Egypt. As we shall explore in more detail below, a number of themes are prominent. We frequently encounter the people complaining about the conditions under which they must now live during their journey to the promised land. These complaints reflect a deep-seated failure to trust the LORD. A second related theme is that of rebellion against those exercising authority. Associated with both of these are two other motifs: (1) the divine punishment of those at fault and (2) the role of Moses and the Aaronic priests as mediators on behalf of the people. Also, various episodes in Numbers closely parallel Exodus 15:22–17:16, where the theme of "testing" is prominent.

Murmurings against the LORD

As soon as the journey from Sinai to Canaan begins, we encounter the first of a number of incidents in which the Israelites express their dissatisfaction with the LORD (11:1–3). Though this brief account does not specify the reason for the people's unrest, it sets the tone for much that follows in Numbers 11–25. Various elements in this episode will reappear later:

1. God's anger is roused against the people because of their complaints (11:1; cf. 11:10, 33; 12:9; 21:5).
2. As a result they are divinely punished (11:1; cf. 11:33; 12:10; 21:6).
3. Moses prays to the LORD on behalf of the people (11:2; cf. 12:13; 14:13–19; 21:7).
4. The punishment is limited (11:2; cf. 12:13–15; 21:8–9).
5. A particular name, reflecting some aspect of what has occurred, is given to the location of the event. On this occasion the place is called Taberah, which means "burning," on account of the punishment by fire that comes upon the people (11:3; cf. 11:34; 20:13).

The incident at Taberah is immediately followed by another, which is recorded in much more detail (11:4–34). As is often the case, the reason for the people's dissatisfaction with God is linked to their craving for food. Even though the LORD has provided them with manna, the Israelites yearn to return to Egypt.

276

The narrative conveys well this sense of longing: "If only we had meat to eat! We remember the fish we ate in Egypt at no cost—also the cucumbers, melons, leeks, onions and garlic" (11:4–5). Their complaint is full of irony. On the one hand they forget the terrible conditions under which they labored as slaves in Egypt, and on the other hand they ignore the fact that they are journeying toward a land "flowing with milk and honey."[1] The former reflects their lack of gratitude for all that God has done for them in the past, and the latter displays their lack of faith regarding all that God will do for them in the future. Not surprisingly, the LORD interprets their complaint as a personal rejection of him (11:20). Although the LORD provides quails in abundance, at the same time he sends a severe plague, killing some of the people. Thereafter the place is called Kibroth Hattaavah (Graves of Craving, 11:34).[2]

The next occasion on which the people murmur against the LORD occurs following the return of the twelve spies from the land of Canaan. Sent to discover the nature of the promised land, the spies report back that the land "does flow with milk and honey" (13:27). As evidence of this, they display a single cluster of grapes needing two men to carry. However, they also describe the inhabitants of the land as powerful, living in large, fortified cities (13:28). While Caleb and later Joshua speak up in favor of entering the land (13:30; 14:6–9), the rest of the spies discourage the people from doing so. As a result, the Israelites grumble against Moses and Aaron, indicating their desire to return to Egypt (14:1–4). Joshua and Caleb outline the implications of this: not only will the people miss out on the opportunity to possess a land that is "exceedingly good," but they are also rebelling against the LORD (14:7–9). This is confirmed by the LORD's comments to Moses: "How long will these people treat me with contempt? How long will they refuse to believe in me, in spite of all the signs I have performed among them?" (14:11). In the light of this, the LORD states that he will destroy the Israelites with a plague and create a new nation through Moses. Moses, however, argues against the destruction of the people on the grounds that it will cause other nations to doubt the LORD's ability to bring his own people into the promised land.[3] Though the LORD relents from wiping out the entire nation, he makes it abundantly clear that not one of the adults who witnessed his glory and miraculous power, both in Egypt and in the desert, will enter the promised land; the only exceptions

1. The Hebrew term translated as "honey" probably refers here to "sweet syrup" derived from grapes, dates, and figs rather than "honey" produced by bees.

2. The dissatisfaction of the people at Kibroth Hattaavah provides the setting and also frames the account of God's appointing seventy of Israel's elders to assist Moses in leading the people (Num. 11).

3. Here one sees various echoes of the golden calf incident at Sinai, when God similarly proposed to make a new nation (Exod. 32:9–10). On this latter occasion (Num. 14), Moses intercedes for the people by quoting the LORD's earlier comment about being "slow to anger, abounding in love and forgiving sin and rebellion" (14:18). This statement was first made in the context of the people's rebellion at Sinai (Exod. 34:6–7).

will be Joshua and Caleb. Consequently, on account of the unfaithfulness of their parents, the children are subjected to forty years in the desert—one year for each of the forty days that the spies spent in the land.

Regarding the story of the spies, two further points are noteworthy. First, the spies who speak out against entering the land are immediately punished: a plague strikes them dead (14:36–38). Second, the people belatedly try to enter the land of Canaan. This, however, is viewed as a further act of disobedience: the LORD has just stated that they shall remain in the desert forty years. Consequently the Amalekites and Canaanites defeat them (14:39–45).

A further report of the people's grumbling against Moses and Aaron comes in Numbers 16 in response to the divine execution of Korah and his followers. This time criticism is leveled at Moses and Aaron because they "have killed the LORD's people" (16:41). This remark is a further indication of the distorted outlook of the people. Even in the dramatic and terrible death of Korah and his followers, they fail to recognize the hand of God. Once more the LORD threatens to kill the whole assembly. Before Aaron, at Moses's command, can atone for them, 14,700 are struck dead by a plague.

Another incident involving grumbling is recorded in 20:1–13. On this occasion a lack of water prompts the people's complaint. Apart from wishing to return to Egypt, the Israelites state that it would have been better for them, like their brothers, to be struck dead by God (20:3). Once again the narrative highlights the rebellious nature of their comments (cf. 20:10). This time, however, the actions of Moses and Aaron come in for the LORD's severest criticism. By striking the rock twice and saying, "Must we bring you water out of this rock?" Moses and Aaron dishonor God (20:10). As a result, the LORD announces that they shall not enter the promised land (20:12).[4]

Numbers records one further occasion when the people speak against God and Moses: "Why have you brought us up out of Egypt to die in the desert? There is no bread! There is no water! And we detest this miserable food!" (21:5). Yet again their criticisms focus on food and water. When the LORD sends venomous snakes to attack the people, they soon acknowledge their sin and seek help from Moses. Remarkably, this is the first occasion when the people themselves acknowledge their sin. As a result, the LORD commands Moses to place a bronze snake on the top of a pole. When those bitten by the venomous snakes look to this bronze snake, they do not die (21:6–9).

All the episodes considered so far are linked by the common motif of the people's lack of trust in the LORD. Their complaints about food and water echo earlier incidents in Exodus 15:22–17:7. In the light of this, it is no surprise that Numbers 14:22 picks up the idea that through their disobedience

---

4. Although the narrative does not make it explicitly clear, it seems likely that this episode occurs in the fortieth year (cf. 20:1 with 33:36–38). If so, this incident reveals that the next generation of adult Israelites is in danger of copying the rebellious behavior of their parents.

the Israelites tested God. Although the concept of testing is mentioned only once in Numbers, it is clear from the material in Exodus that, although God intended the desert experience to test the faith and obedience of the Israelites (cf. Exod. 15:25–26; 16:4; cf. 20:20), it was they who tested God (Exod. 17:2, 7; Num. 14:22). Furthermore, Exodus 15:26 emphasizes that if the people obey him, God will not bring on them any of the diseases which came on the Egyptians. In the light of this, it is interesting to observe the frequent references to "strikes" in Numbers 11–25.[5] Ironically, by longing to be back in Egypt, the Israelites bring on themselves the same suffering that earlier afflicted the Egyptians when God struck them with signs and wonders (cf. Exod. 7:25; 9:15; 12:12–13).

Challenges against Those in Authority

Interspersed between the episodes about the murmurings of the Israelites are others that focus on various challenges to those appointed by God to positions of authority. The first such challenge comes from the least likely source. Miriam and Aaron, Moses's own sister and brother, contest the uniqueness of his claim to speak on the LORD's behalf (Num. 12:1–2). No doubt their challenge is prompted by the authority that they already have, Aaron as the high priest and Miriam as a prophetess (Exod. 15:20). The LORD, however, soon responds and confirms Moses's special status: whereas the LORD speaks to prophets in visions and dreams, he speaks to Moses "face to face, clearly and not in riddles" (12:8). Consequently the LORD's anger burns against Aaron and Miriam, with the result that Miriam is afflicted with a skin disease. Although her punishment is reduced due to the intercession of Moses, she is still required to remain outside the Israelite camp for seven days (12:15).

The sinful nature of the challenge by Miriam and Aaron is highlighted by the comment, "Moses was a very humble man, more humble than anyone else on the face of the earth" (12:3). This clearly indicates that Moses himself does not unduly emphasize his own importance. In the light of Moses's attitude toward his own position, the challenge of Miriam and Aaron is all the more serious. Furthermore, because Moses does not relish the idea of having absolute authority over the nation, he involves seventy of the elders in the task of leading the people (11:24–30).

The next challenge to authority comes in Numbers 16 and centers on an attempt by Korah and certain Reubenites—Dathan and Abiram—to usurp the unique position of Moses and Aaron. Once again the challenge comes from those who already enjoy a special standing within the nation: Korah as a Levite has been previously set apart to assist in the work of the tabernacle;

5. Different terms used in Exodus for the "strikes" or "blows" inflicted by God upon the Egyptians reappear in Numbers. See chap. 13 above.

his supporters are described as "well-known community leaders who had been appointed members of the council" (16:2). Their challenge is against the hierarchical structure introduced by God, whereby Aaron and his sons, as priests, have a holier status than that of the Levites and other Israelites (cf. 8:5–26). In the light of the early chapters of Numbers, there can be little doubt that Korah's actions run counter to God's instructions for the people.[6] Furthermore, Korah's sin is all the greater because he himself enjoys a more privileged status than that of the majority of Israelites. Though he should have been grateful for the opportunity to serve in the tabernacle, he uses this as a springboard to aspire to priestly status (see the comments of Moses in 16:8–11). As the basis for his challenge to Moses and Aaron, Korah claims that "the whole community is holy, every one of them, and the LORD is with them" (16:3). Implicit in this is the idea that there is no reason for Moses and Aaron to restrict others from approaching the LORD.[7] The attitude of Dathan and Abiram to Moses is highlighted in 16:12–14. As far as they are concerned, Egypt, not Canaan, is the "land flowing with milk and honey" (16:13). Not only has Moses led them away from all that is best materially but he has also failed to provide them with anything better; his motive throughout has been to lord it over the people and kill them in the desert. The response of God to both these challenges is dramatic. The earth opens its mouth and swallows the families of Korah, Dathan, and Abiram (16:31–34), and a further group of 250 supporters are consumed by fire (16:35). Once again Moses is portrayed as interceding on behalf of the whole community (16:20–22).

In the light of Korah's challenge to the authority of Aaron, Numbers 17–19 takes on a special significance. In the first of these chapters, Moses demonstrates the unique standing of the tribe of Levi by having twelve staffs, one for each ancestral tribe, placed in the tent of meeting.[8] When these are removed on the next day, the staff of Aaron has "budded, blossomed and produced almonds" (17:8), indicating the unique and life-giving status of the tribe to which Aaron belongs. Moses then commands that the staff be kept as a sign to "the rebellious" that they must end their "grumbling" against the LORD (17:10). To further emphasize the uniqueness of Aaron's position as high priest, Numbers 18 records divine instructions regarding the relationship between the priests and Levites. Here it is stated that the Levites are a "gift" to Aaron "to do the work at the tent of meeting" (18:6). Furthermore, the "service of the priesthood" is also a divine gift (18:7). Since the priests and the Levites are divinely appointed to fulfill specific roles, it is wrong for others to usurp their positions. Numbers 19 also alludes back to the rebellion of Korah by focusing

6. On the role of the Levites, see chap. 20 above.

7. In believing that all the Israelites are holy and can draw near to the LORD, Korah fails to appreciate one of the distinctive roles given to the Levites: they are to act as a barrier between the LORD and the other tribes (1:53; cf. 8:19).

8. The Hebrew word for "staff" can also mean "branch" or "tribe."

on the ritual involving the water of cleansing. First, it highlights the special mediatorial role of the divinely appointed priests. Second, it emphasizes that anyone who sins becomes unclean and of necessity must undergo a process of purification. Korah's claim in 16:3 that the whole community is holy is clearly presumptuous.

Alongside these challenges to those in authority, we may also include the reaction of Moses and Aaron to the people's demand for water in 20:2–13. In their impatience with the people, they claim responsibility for the miraculous appearance of the water, thus failing to acknowledge the LORD as the one who provides it from the rock.

Religious Apostasy

The long line of episodes in which the exodus generation of Israelites exhibits their lack of trust in the LORD comes to a conclusion in Numbers 25. On this occasion they are guilty of both religious apostasy, worshiping the Baal of Peor, and sexual immorality, having relationships with Moabite women. Once more the LORD's anger burns against the people, with the result that 24,000 of them are killed by a plague. Three factors stand out in the story as significant:

1. After the LORD's condemnation of their activity, the Israelites display a spirit of repentance, "weeping at the entrance to the tent of meeting" (25:6).
2. Phinehas, the grandson of Aaron, is commended for his willingness to kill a fellow Israelite who blatantly ignores the LORD's condemnation of idolatrous and immoral behavior. The execution of the guilty party is presented as an act of atonement, with the result that the plague against the Israelites stops. Afterward Phinehas is rewarded through being divinely granted "a covenant of a lasting priesthood, because he was zealous for the honor of his God and made atonement for the Israelites" (25:13).
3. As confirmed by the census of Numbers 26 (cf. 26:63–65), this incident marks the death of the last of the Israelites who left Egypt as adults. The forty-year period in the desert is almost complete.

Destination—the Promised Land

In spite of the people's rebellion and the death of the entire exodus generation of adult Israelites, the central chapters of Numbers contain clear indications that the occupation of the land of Canaan is still a priority in God's dealings with the Israelites. This is reflected in several ways. First, instructions given by the LORD in Numbers 15 begin with the words "After you enter the land

I am giving you as a home" (15:2). This introduction is significant in that it immediately follows the account of the people's failure to enter the land of Canaan. Furthermore, the instructions in Numbers 15 presuppose a situation in which the people are able to grow crops of grain and grapes. Second, Numbers 21 records the defeats of the Canaanite king of Arad (21:1–3), Sihon king of the Amorites (21:21–31), and Og king of Bashan (21:33–35). These victories contrast with the defeat recorded earlier, in 14:44–45,[9] and the backing away from battle with the Edomites, in 20:14–21; they are a first step toward the possession of the promised land (cf. 31:1–24). Third, the lengthy account of the activities of Balaam son of Beor in Numbers 22–24 reveals God's desire to bless rather than curse Israel. Although Balaam is hired by Balak king of Moab to curse the Israelites, he blesses them on four occasions (23:7–10, 18–24; 24:3–9, 15–19; cf. 22:12). In doing so, he briefly echoes the promises made earlier to the patriarchs: "Who can count the dust of Jacob?" (Num. 23:10; cf. Gen. 13:16; 28:14); "The LORD their God is with them" (Num. 23:21; cf. Gen. 17:8); "May those who bless you be blessed and those who curse you be cursed!" (Num. 24:9; cf. 23:8, 20; Gen. 12:3); "A star will come out of Jacob; a scepter will rise out of Israel" (Num. 24:17; cf. Gen. 17:6, 16; 49:10).[10] In the light of these factors, it is apparent that, in spite of the death of the exodus generation, God still intends to bring his people into the promised land. This is further emphasized by the fact that almost all the material in Numbers 26–36, as noted in the previous chapter, anticipates in various ways the possession of the land.

Old Testament Summary

The central chapters of Numbers provide a very negative portrait of the Israelites. This is highlighted in a number of ways. In spite of their remarkable deliverance from slavery in Egypt, they are unwilling to enter the promised land. Contemptuous of all that God has already done for them, they constantly complain and desire to return to Egypt. Furthermore, they challenge those whom God has placed in authority over them; in the divine punishment of others, they fail to see God's power at work, believing that those struck dead are the LORD's people (16:41). Finally, they commit idolatry, the ultimate rejection of and rebellion against the LORD. In the light of all these shortcomings, it is hardly surprising that (except for Joshua and Caleb) the entire adult generation of those who came out of Egypt die in the desert, outside the promised land.

Whereas the exodus generation of Israelites shows no sign of learning from its experience in the desert, their children, while initially revealing similar

9. Note the mentions of Hormah in 14:45 and 21:3.
10. Although the Balaam story (Num. 22–24; cf. 31:8, 16) shows signs of being a once-independent unit, it picks up a number of important themes found in Genesis. As it stands, it has been carefully integrated into the Pentateuch as a whole.

characteristics of unbelief and rebellion, demonstrate a greater capacity to trust the LORD. They, at least, willingly acknowledge their own sin (Num. 21:7; 25:6). For this reason, the book of Numbers portrays them as making progress toward inheriting the land promised to the patriarchs.

New Testament Connections

The account of the Israelites' time in the wilderness is picked up in a number of ways in the New Testament. One of the most striking uses comes in the account of the temptation of Jesus (Matt. 4:1–11; Luke 4:1–13). Indeed, it is impossible to fully understand the story of Jesus's temptation without appreciating how he is contrasted with the Israelites who came out of Egypt. Whereas the ancient Israelites were tested in the wilderness and failed, Jesus, as the new Israel, succeeds. This theme is reflected in all three temptations. In the first, Jesus is hungry after fasting for forty days and is asked to turn stones into bread. But if, like the ancient Israelites, he would give priority to his own physical appetite, he would imply dissatisfaction with God's provision for him. The second temptation, following Matthew's order, focuses on God's ability to save. Here Jesus is challenged to follow the example of the earlier Israelites and test, rather than trust, God's might to protect him. The third temptation focuses on God's capacity to give to Jesus the kingdoms that are under the control of another. Whereas the Israelites doubted God's strength to give them the land of Canaan, Jesus expresses complete confidence in God. Thus in various ways, Jesus's faith in God contrasts sharply with that of the Israelites who came out of Egypt.

Several passages in John's Gospel refer directly to the Old Testament account of the Israelites' sojourn in the wilderness. In his conversation with Nicodemus, Jesus briefly mentions the incident of the bronze snake in Numbers 21:4–9: "Just as Moses lifted up the snake in the wilderness, so the Son of Man must be lifted up, that everyone who believes may have eternal life in him" (John 3:14–15). Here Jesus draws an important parallel between himself and the bronze snake. While the ancient Israelites received life by trusting in the bronze snake, those who trust in Jesus will receive eternal life.

Later in John's Gospel, in a discussion that takes place shortly after the feeding of the five thousand, Jesus compares himself to the manna provided in the wilderness (John 6:25–59). Like the manna, he has been sent from heaven to give life to those who feed upon him (6:33, 35–40, 50–51, 54–58). However, the life that Jesus offers, in contrast to that given by the manna, is eternal (6:47–51, 58). John observes that many of the Jews respond to Jesus's words by grumbling (6:41, 43). Like their unbelieving ancestors, they fail to appreciate what has happened in their midst. For them, the miraculous feeding of the five thousand, which should have been seen as a sign of Jesus's divine origin, conveys nothing of significance.[11]

The experience of the Israelites in the wilderness is also used by Paul to warn the Corinthian Christians against pursuing various unrighteous practices: "Now these things occurred as examples to keep us from setting our hearts on evil things as they did. Do not be idolaters, as some of them were; as it is written: 'The people sat down to eat and drink and got up to indulge in revelry.' We should not commit sexual immorality, as some of them did—and in one day twenty-three thousand of them died. We should not test Christ, as some of them did—and were killed by snakes. And do not grumble, as some of them did—and were killed by the destroying angel" (1 Cor. 10:6–10).[12] Because Paul views the wilderness experience as a time of testing, he concludes by exhorting his readers to resist temptation: "No temptation has overtaken you except what is common to mankind. And God is faithful; he will not let you be tempted beyond what you can bear. But when you are tempted, he will also provide a way out so that you can endure it" (1 Cor. 10:13). Here Paul shares an understanding of the Numbers material similar to that found in the Gospel account of Jesus's temptation.

Before we leave Paul's comments in 1 Corinthians 10, one other issue deserves mention. This concerns his comment that the ancient Israelites "drank from the spiritual rock that accompanied them, and that rock was Christ" (1 Cor. 10:4). At first sight it seems remarkable that Paul should associate Jesus with an inanimate object. However, an alternative reading is possible. In 1 Corinthians 10 Paul seeks to draw a parallel between the wilderness experience of the Israelites and that of the Corinthian believers. He argues that because the ancient Israelites perished on account of eating food associated with idols, the Corinthian believers should not indulge in such activities. As part of this argument, Paul compares the food and drink that the ancient Israelites received from God (1 Cor. 10:3–4) with the food and drink that the Corinthians eat at the Lord's Supper (1 Cor. 10:16–17). To strengthen the parallels between the two situations, Paul associates the food and drink of the wilderness with a "spiritual rock" and says that rock is Christ (1 Cor. 10:4). Undoubtedly Paul's reference to Christ is influenced by the designation of God as a Rock in the Old Testament. In this regard, the Song of Moses in Deuteronomy 32 is significant, given that it is presented as having been composed at the end of the Israelites' period in the wilderness. On five separate occasions God is designated "the Rock" (Deut. 32:4, 15, 18, 30, 31; cf. 32:37), making this one

11. Apart from the obvious parallels with Exodus already noted, we observe that John 6 briefly refers to the "Jewish Passover Festival" as near (v. 4) and says that Jesus asks a question to "test" Philip (v. 6). The latter is particularly noteworthy because it is absent from the Synoptic versions of the feeding of the five thousand.

12. The reference to 23,000 dying probably relates to the events of Exod. 32 and not Num. 25:9, where 24,000 are reported as dying from the plague.

of the main divine titles in the entire song. Paul does not think of Christ as a physical rock; rather, he is a "spiritual rock." By presenting Christ as the source of the drink that the ancient Israelites received, Paul (1) affirms Christ's divine status and oneness with the God of Israel and (2) reinforces the parallel that he wishes to demonstrate between the situation of the Corinthians and that of the ancient Israelites.

The author of Hebrews also highlights the failure of the wilderness generation and uses this as a warning to his readers (3:7–19). Quoting Psalm 95:7–11, one of a number of psalms to recount the Israelites' experience in the wilderness, he observes that they did not enter the promised land "because of their unbelief" (Heb. 3:19; cf. 8:9).

22

Love and Loyalty

The book of Deuteronomy brings the Pentateuch to a significant climax. As the Israelites stand on the verge of entering the promised land, Moses outlines God's agenda for the future. This centers on the special covenant relationship that exists between the LORD and Israel. At the heart of this covenant is a commitment by both parties to love the other wholeheartedly and faithfully. For the Israelites, this commitment will require them to be completely obedient to all the obligations placed on them by God. Obedience will ensure blessing in terms of material prosperity and national security; disobedience will have the opposite consequence, resulting in the Israelites' being expelled from the promised land. As Moses invites the people to renew their covenant relationship with the LORD, he sets before them an important choice, a choice between "life and death, blessings and curses" (30:19).

Introduction

The setting of the events described in Deuteronomy is introduced in the opening verses of the book. It is the end of the fortieth year since the Israelites left Egypt, and the people are camped to the east of the river Jordan. At last they are on the brink of entering the land that God promised to their ancestors, Abraham, Isaac, and Jacob. Following the death of the first generation of adults who came out of Egypt, the next generation of Israelites is at a decisive point in its relationship with God. Will they, like their parents, fall at the

286

hurdle before them? Or through faith in the LORD, will they cross the Jordan and possess the promised land?

Given the importance of the setting, it is hardly surprising that Moses addresses the people at length. Having led their parents out of Egypt, he reminds a new generation of adult Israelites of all that has happened in the preceding years and challenges them to affirm their personal commitment to the special covenant relationship with the LORD, initiated at Mount Sinai. At the heart of Deuteronomy is the future of the relationship between Israel and its God.

Only in Deuteronomy does Moses address the people at length by using his own words. Elsewhere he usually repeats what the LORD has told him. Here he speaks on his own behalf, persuading the Israelites to follow the LORD. As a result, Deuteronomy often reads like a sermon, with frequent exhortations and much repetition. This gives the book a character not found elsewhere in the Pentateuch.

Moses's speeches take on added significance in that they are given shortly before his death, which is recounted in the final verses of the book (34:1–12). They are the final words of an elder statesman to his people, a father to his children, encouraging them to proceed in the right direction for the future.

Apart from brief comments by the book's narrator, the bulk of Deuteronomy consists of the words of Moses. Two main speeches dominate the book, the first coming in 1:6–4:40 and the second in 5:1–26:19. The former speech begins with a survey of Israel's relationship with the LORD since leaving Mount Sinai nearly forty years earlier and concludes with exhortations to obey the LORD in the future. This provides a suitable introduction for the second speech, which begins in 5:1 and continues unbroken until 26:19, constituting approximately two-thirds of the book of Deuteronomy. The narrator's introduction to this second speech (4:44–49) indicates that it forms the "law" (Hebrew *tôrâ*) that "Moses set before the Israelites" (4:44). This understanding of the speech is confirmed as Moses (1) calls for "all the words of this law [*tôrâ*]" to be inscribed on stones coated with plaster (27:2–8) and (2) finishes "writing in a book the words of this law [*tôrâ*] from beginning to end" (31:24). The "Book of the Law" (*tôrâ*) is then to be placed "beside the ark of the covenant of the LORD" (31:26). Moses also instructs the priests and elders to read this law (*tôrâ*) to the people every seventh year (31:9–13). We shall say more on the Book of the Law below.

The concluding chapters of Deuteronomy consist mainly of a number of shorter addresses, not all by Moses, introduced by brief narrative comments. The first of these speeches is comprised of instructions for the inscribing of the Book of the Law (*tôrâ*) on plaster-coated stones once the people have crossed the Jordan and entered the land of Canaan (27:1–8). The next speech, which also looks to the future occupation of the land, begins with instructions to the tribes of Israel for the pronouncement of blessings from Mount Gerizim and curses from Mount Ebal (27:11–13; cf. 11:26–32), followed by the recital

287

of a list of curses by the Levites (27:14–26). To these instructions Moses adds a further exhortation, encouraging the people to obey the LORD (28:1–68). Moses's exhortation mirrors the previous instructions by highlighting the blessings that will flow from obedience (28:2–14) and the curses that will come as a result of disobedience (28:15–68). Though we might anticipate that equal weight would be given to blessings and curses, this is not the case; in both parts of Moses's speech, greater prominence is given to the curses (27:15–26; 28:15–68). Following the blessings and curses, Moses once more exhorts the people to keep the terms of the covenant by highlighting that the choice before them is one of life or death (29:2–30:20). Next there is a brief passage on Joshua's appointment as Moses's successor (31:1–8). After this, Moses commands the priests and elders regarding the reading of the law (*tôrâ*) every seven years (31:9–13). Significantly, the LORD then predicts that after entering the promised land, Israel will soon forsake him and break the covenant (31:16–18). Consequently, Moses is instructed to teach them a song "so that it may be a witness" for the LORD against them (31:19–22). Before reciting this song to the people (31:30–32:43), Moses tells the Levites to place the Book of the Law (*tôrâ*) beside the ark of the covenant so that it also may witness to the waywardness of the people (31:24–29). The remaining sections of Deuteronomy focus on the death of Moses. The LORD instructs Moses to go up Mount Nebo so that he may see the promised land before dying (32:48–52). Next, Moses pronounces a series of blessing on the Israelites (33:1–29). Finally, Moses's death is recorded, and the book ends with a brief epitaph concerning his greatness as a prophet (34:1–12).

Deuteronomy and Ancient Near Eastern Treaties

As we have already noticed, Deuteronomy is concerned with the renewing of the special covenant relationship between the LORD and the Israelites. Since the mid-1950s biblical scholars have in some detail discussed the similarities that exist among the covenant in Deuteronomy and other ancient documents, in particular political treaties and law codes. While some scholars have argued that the book of Deuteronomy as a whole conforms to the pattern of certain second-millennium-BC treaties, others have challenged this by observing either that the parallels are not particularly close or that those parallels that do exist may be accounted for on the basis of mid-first-millennium-BC treaties. Without wishing to enter into this debate in detail, I will give a few needed comments.

The closest parallels to the covenant found in the book of Deuteronomy appear to come in ancient treaties made between kings of powerful nations and the rulers of weaker, vassal states. These treaties have a formal structure that may be outlined as follows:

1. A preamble introduces the treaty and those participating in it.
2. A historical prologue describes earlier relationships between the parties.
3. Stipulations set out the obligations placed on the weaker party to the covenant. They fall into two parts: (a) general and (b) detailed.
4. Document clause (regulations about preserving and reading the treaty).
5. Witnesses, listing the gods who witness the making of the treaty.
6. Curses and blessings, declaring the consequences of either keeping or breaking the covenant stipulations.

According to some scholars this very treaty form is reflected in the text of Deuteronomy as it stands. Consequently, attempts are made to assign the material in Deuteronomy among the various elements of the treaty form. This can result in a proposal such as follows:

1. preamble: 1:1–5
2. historical prologue: 1:6–3:29
3a. general stipulations: 4:1–40; 5:1–11:32
3b. detailed stipulations: 12:1–26:19
4. document clause: 27:1–26
5. witnesses: not applicable due to the monotheistic outlook of Deuteronomy
6. curses and blessings: 28:1–68

Other scholars, however, adopt a more cautious approach, suggesting that it is mistaken to find the treaty form replicated in the book of Deuteronomy as it stands. Though the essential elements of the treaty form are reflected in the present narrative form of the text, the book itself is not an actual treaty document. There is much to commend this view, especially since Deuteronomy in its entirety does not claim to be a self-contained covenant document. At the most only 5:1–26:19, and possibly 28:1–68, are presented as an independent document within the present text.[1]

Although formal correspondence between the whole of Deuteronomy and ancient Near Eastern vassal treaties is lacking, the process by which the covenant was ratified between the Israelites and the LORD does bear a striking resemblance to that found in vassal treaties. In each we have the formalizing of a special relationship between two parties, one strong and one weak, with the listing of extensive obligations and the pronouncement of blessings and curses. While scholars will undoubtedly continue to debate the precise nature of this correspondence, there can be little doubt that an awareness of it enables us to appreciate better the main characteristics of the covenant in Deuteronomy.

1. Two references suggest that Deut. 28 and perhaps other material should be included in the Book of the Law (see 28:58, 61).

Love the LORD

Although the book of Deuteronomy focuses on a formal renewal of the relationship between the LORD and the Israelites, considerable attention is given to the fact that the formal act of renewal by itself does not constitute the relationship. Rather, the relationship between the LORD and his people is to be based on the twin pillars of love and loyalty. To appreciate this better, it may be helpful to consider a modern analogy. The relationship between God and Israel can be partly compared to that between husband and wife. In many societies the relationship between husband and wife is formally instituted by their making marriage vows. Though the wedding ceremony formalizes the relationship of husband and wife, it cannot of itself sustain the relationship. For the marriage relationship to exist and develop in a meaningful way, it is essential that there be mutual love and loyalty. If love and/or loyalty disappear from the relationship between a husband and wife, their being formally united will mean little. Indeed, both partners may seek to have this formal bond removed by instituting another formal procedure: divorce. The making of the treaty between God and Israel resembles a marriage ceremony. While both parties promise allegiance to each other, the strength of the relationship between them depends not on the covenant ceremony itself, but on the love and loyalty that each has for the other. For this reason, Moses emphasizes that the Israelites are to love the LORD with their whole being. He expresses it thus: "Love the LORD your God with all your heart and with all your soul and with all your strength" (6:5; cf. 11:13; 13:3; 30:6). Without such love the covenant relationship will be meaningless.

Moses's frequent exhortations to love the LORD suggest that this is likely to prove difficult for the Israelites. Their ability to love stands in marked contrast to that of the LORD. Nowhere is there any suggestion that his love might cease toward Israel. On the contrary, Moses highlights God's lasting faithfulness toward his people. From the outset he was the one who initiated the relationship. Motivated by love he chose Israel and delivered the people from slavery in Egypt (4:37; 7:8; cf. 10:15). For the same reason, he did not allow Balaam to curse his chosen people (23:5). Elsewhere Moses expresses confidence regarding God's love for the future: his love will continue for a thousand generations (5:10; 7:9).

Although Moses is absolutely certain that the LORD loves Israel and that he will be completely faithful to Israel, this is no open-ended guarantee of divine blessing and favor. On the contrary, the covenant relationship involves a commitment from each Israelite to love the LORD. If they fail to love the LORD, the consequences are clearly set out: they will experience God's disfavor in the form of various curses that are listed at length in 27:15–26 and 28:15–68.

In the light of this, love in Deuteronomy is never presented as something emotional; it is not just a matter of feelings. Loving God has very practical implications for the people. They must fulfill the obligations placed on them by the covenant. Thus Moses repeatedly draws attention to the link between loving the LORD and keeping "his requirements, his decrees, his laws and his commands always" (11:1; cf. 5:10; 7:9; 10:12; 11:13, 22; 19:9; 30:16). On the one hand, true love will demonstrate itself in perfect obedience. On the other hand, disobedience indicates a failure to love God (cf. 13:3).

Given this link between love and obedience—if you love me, you will obey me—it is no surprise that the central core of Deuteronomy consists of a long list of obligations that the Israelites are expected to keep. These obligations constitute the Book of the Law (*tôrâ*), a designation used in 28:61; 29:21; and 31:26. Although the Hebrew word *tôrâ* has traditionally been translated as "law," this is partially misleading. While it includes laws that might be enforced by a legal court, it also embraces commands or stipulations that by their nature are not "laws"; for example, it would be wrong to categorize the divine commands in 6:6–9—to teach *tôrâ* to one's children—as "law." For this reason, some scholars prefer to translate *tôrâ* as "instruction." Although this avoids the legal connotations of the term "law," it fails to adequately convey the judicial aspect of *tôrâ*. As 17:8–13 reveals, *tôrâ* includes legal decisions taught by Levitical priests. Since in English it is difficult to find a single word that accurately reflects the full meaning of the term *tôrâ*, it is perhaps best to retain the Hebrew term and understand it in terms of all the material found in 5:1–26:19.

The importance of *tôrâ* is underlined throughout Deuteronomy. At the very beginning of the book, reference is made to it in the brief comment, "East of the Jordan in the territory of Moab, Moses began to expound this law [*tôrâ*]" (1:5). According to the narrator's remark in 4:44, the Book of the Law (*tôrâ*) begins in 5:1. Later Moses instructs the people to have the Book of the Law (*tôrâ*) inscribed on plaster-coated stones on Mount Ebal (27:1–8), with a further copy being placed beside the ark of the covenant (31:24–26). Elsewhere attention is drawn to the importance of the Book of the Law (*tôrâ*) in that future kings are to make a copy of it for their own use and are expected to read it all the days of their lives (17:18–20). It is also mentioned in the last of the curses recited by the Levites: "Cursed is anyone who does not uphold the words of this law [*tôrâ*] by carrying them out" (27:26).

Since Israel's obedience to the *tôrâ* demonstrates the people's love for the LORD, Moses underlines the importance of being familiar with all that it demands. Consequently, he instructs the Israelites not only to meditate on all that he commands them, but also to teach it to their children:[2] "These commandments that I give you today are to be upon your hearts. Impress them on your children. Talk about them when you sit at home and when you walk along the

---

2. The noun *tôrâ* is closely related to the Hebrew verb "to teach" (cf. 17:11). *Tôrâ* is that which is taught (by God).

road, when you lie down and when you get up. Tie them as symbols on your hands and bind them on your foreheads. Write them on the doorframes of your houses and on your gates" (6:6–9; cf. 4:4; 11:18–21; 31:9–13). For Moses, the stipulations of the covenant are to be a vital part of everyday life for all God's people, both young and old. Familiarity with them is essential to maintain a harmonious relationship with the LORD; to ignore them will bring disaster.

Conscious of the Israelites' strong tendency toward disobedience (see chap. 23, below), Moses within his exhortations incorporates various comments to encourage obedience. These motivation statements are found throughout Deuteronomy. Apart from the longer section of curses in Deuteronomy 28, Moses generally motivates the people by highlighting the positive aspects of obedience. Only rarely does he mention the consequences of disobedience (e.g., 8:19–20). The most common motive is the promise of divine blessing, mentioned on a number of occasions within the Book of the Law. When, for example, in 15:7–10 Moses encourages the Israelites to be generous toward the poor, he adds the comment: "then because of this the LORD your God will bless you in all your work and in everything you put your hand to" (15:10). Similar remarks are found in 7:12–15; 14:29; 15:4, 18; 23:20. The promise of blessing, however, is developed most fully in Deuteronomy 28, where Moses lists not only the blessing that will flow from obedience (28:3–14), but also the curses that will result from disobedience (28:16–68). Here in detail Moses spells out the practical consequences of experiencing divine blessing or cursing. Since a detailed examination of this chapter lies beyond the scope of this work, some general observations must suffice.

First, there is an emphasis on fruitfulness and prosperity. Blessed by God, the people will increase numerically, as will their livestock. Moreover, the land will produce abundant harvests, enabling the people to prosper richly, so much so that other nations will come to borrow from them. Under God's curse, however, the reverse will occur. Diseases will strike down the people, as well as their animals and crops.[3] Such will be the decline in their fortunes that the Israelites will be forced to borrow from the alien living in their midst.

Second, under God's blessing the Israelites as a nation will enjoy security from their enemies, who will be easily defeated. Implicit in this promise, and in the references to the fruitfulness of the land, is the assurance that the Israelites will occupy the promised land. This picture of national security is reversed, however, if the people come under God's curse. Not only will they be defeated by their enemies, but significantly, they will also be led out of the promised land into captivity elsewhere.[4] These two aspects of blessing and

---

3. The description of what will happen to the Israelites echoes the punishments that fell on the Egyptians at the time of the exodus.

4. We shall have more to say on this in the next chapter. The promise of blessing was both national and personal. This is reflected in comments concerning the future king who is promised a long reign for obeying the law (17:18–20).

cursing—prosperity and security—occur frequently in the briefer motivation statements made by Moses. References to life and prosperity come in the following passages: 4:1, 40; 5:29, 33; 6:2–3, 18, 24; 7:13–15; 8:1; 11:9, 14–15; 12:25, 28; 16:20; 29:9; 30:16, 20; 32:47. The land is mentioned in 4:1, 40; 5:33; 6:3, 18; 7:13; 8:1, 6–9; 11:8–9, 14–15, 23; 16:20; 17:20; 23:20; 30:16, 20; 32:47.[5] Stated briefly, Moses constantly reminds the Israelites that obedience brings life, but that disobedience brings death. This choice between life and death, prosperity or destruction, comes at the climax of Moses's final speech to the Israelites:

> See, I set before you today life and prosperity, death and destruction. For I command you today to love the LORD your God, to walk in obedience to him, and to keep his commands, decrees and laws; then you will live and increase, and the LORD your God will bless you in the land you are entering to possess. But if your heart turns away and you are not obedient, and if you are drawn away to bow down to other gods and worship them, I declare to you this day that you will certainly be destroyed. You will not live long in the land you are crossing the Jordan to enter and possess. (30:15–18)[6]

Be Loyal to the LORD

While Moses stresses the importance of love for a secure relationship between the Israelites and God, he also equally emphasizes the necessity of loyalty. The Israelites must be faithful in loving only the LORD. In religious terms this means that they are not to practice idolatry; they must worship the LORD alone. This aspect of the covenant relationship heads the list of obligations found in the Decalogue: "You shall have no other gods before [besides] me" (5:7; cf. Exod. 20:3).

In the book of Deuteronomy, a number of important ideas are associated with idolatry. Though most of these are found in the Exodus account of the Sinai covenant, they are developed in greater detail at this stage. First, Moses commands the people, "Do not follow other gods" (6:14; 8:19; 11:28; 28:14; cf. 13:2). They are to neither "serve" or "worship"[7] these gods (7:4, 16; 8:19; 11:16; 17:3; 28:14, 36, 64; 29:18; 30:17; cf. 13:2, 6, 13; 29:26), nor "bow down" to them (8:19; 11:16; 17:3; 30:17; cf. 4:19; 29:26). Underlying this terminology is the idea that the relationship between worshiper and deity resembles that between slave and master. Since for the Israelites true worship

---

5. Deut. 8:7–9 provides a vivid picture of the "good land": "For the LORD your God is bringing you into a good land—a land with brooks, streams, and deep springs gushing out into the valleys and hills; a land with wheat and barley, vines and fig trees, pomegranates, olive oil and honey; a land where bread will not be scarce and you will lack nothing; a land where the rocks are iron and you can dig copper out of the hills."

6. Deuteronomy and Genesis display close links regarding the concepts of blessing and cursing.

7. The same Hebrew verb may be translated by the English words "serve" or "worship."

involves total obedience to all that the LORD demands, it is not possible for them to give allegiance to any other deity. Ironically, by being restricted to worship only the LORD, the Israelites are freed from the difficulty of trying to meet the sometimes conflicting demands of different deities. Not only are the Israelites prohibited from worshiping other gods; they are also prohibited from worshiping anything that God has made, in particular the sun, moon, or stars (4:19; 17:3).

Second, Moses highlights the danger posed by the religious beliefs of the nations living in the land of Canaan: the Israelites will be enticed to worship their gods. In an attempt to prevent this from occurring, Moses commands them not to copy Canaanite religious practices (16:21–22; 18:14); such practices are described as "detestable" to the LORD (12:31; 13:14; 17:4; 18:9, 12; 20:18).[8] The Israelites are also to destroy everything associated with the worship of other gods in the land of Canaan: "Break down their altars, smash their sacred stones, cut down their Asherah poles and burn their idols in the fire" (7:5; cf. 7:25; 12:2–3). Most significant because the Canaanites will encourage the Israelites to worship their gods, the nations of Canaan are to be completely destroyed (7:16; 20:17–18).

Third, picking up another of the obligations found in the Decalogue (5:8–10; cf. Exod. 20:4–6), Moses warns the people against making idols (Deut. 4:15–31). Since the LORD did not reveal his form at Sinai, the Israelites must not try to depict him by using human or animal forms (4:15–18). Elsewhere in Deuteronomy, it is made very clear that all idols are "detestable" to the LORD (7:25–26; 27:15; 29:17; 32:16; cf. 32:21).

Fourth, those who engage in idolatrous activities are guilty of "doing evil in the eyes of the LORD" (4:25; 9:18; 17:2; 31:29; cf. 13:5, 11; 17:5, 7). One consequence of this is that they provoke him to anger (4:25; 6:15; 7:4; 11:17; 29:24–29; cf. 9:7–8, 18–20; 13:5, 11; 17:5, 7). Consequently, those guilty of idolatry should be put to death (6:14–15; 7:4; 13:15; cf. 9:8, 14, 19–20, 25–26). Furthermore, the regulations within the Book of the Law (tôrâ) make it clear that anyone who entices others to worship foreign gods must be put to death. The Israelites are to execute those who, possibly claiming to be prophets either of the LORD or some other deity, entice others to worship gods they have not previously known (13:1–5; cf. 18:20). This rule applies even to the closest of relatives or friends (13:6–11). Moreover, entire Israelite communities are to be wiped out if they commit idolatry (13:12–16).[9] If the nation as a whole becomes guilty of idolatry, the punishment will be destruction and exile (4:26–28; 29:24–28). As part of this punishment, ironically, the people

8. Deuteronomy 25:16 includes dealing "dishonestly" among various things the LORD "detests."

9. Regarding idolatry, the LORD intends to treat the Israelites in the same way as the nations already living in the land of Canaan; the same punishment would be applied to Israel as to these other nations.

"will worship man-made gods of wood and stone, which cannot see or hear or eat or smell" (4:28; 28:36, 64).

These regulations against idolatry emphasize that the Israelites are expected to remain completely loyal to the LORD their God.

Old Testament Summary

In the book of Deuteronomy the story of the LORD's relationship with Israel reaches an important landmark. As they stand poised to take possession of the land of Canaan, Moses sets before a new generation of adult Israelites the obligations that they must fulfill in order to enjoy God's blessing in the land of Canaan. At the heart of these obligations is the requirement to love the LORD wholeheartedly. Israel's future in the promised land is tied directly to their willingness and ability to fulfill their covenantal duties. While Deuteronomy holds out the prospect of divine blessing in the promised land, as we shall examine in more detail in the next chapter, it also envisages a future in which Israel, through failure to fulfill the covenant obligations, will come under God's curse.

New Testament Connections

The book of Deuteronomy is one of the most frequently quoted books in the New Testament.[10] Since of all the Old Testament books it sets out most fully the essential requirements for a harmonious relationship with God, this is hardly surprising. It is often quoted as stating what the Old Testament law requires (e.g., Matt. 5:31, 38; 15:4; 18:16; 19:18–19; Mark 7:10; 10:19; Luke 18:20; 1 Cor. 5:13; 9:9; 2 Cor. 13:1; Eph. 6:2–3; 1 Tim. 5:18).

Deuteronomy's influence pervades the teaching of Jesus. When asked by "an expert in the law," "Which is the greatest commandment?" (Matt. 22:35–37), Jesus responds by quoting first Deuteronomy 6:5: "Love the Lord your God with all your heart and with all your soul and with all your mind."[11] Elsewhere his commitment to the agenda set by Deuteronomy is clearly seen in the parallel accounts of his temptation (Matt. 4:1–11; Luke 4:1–13). On each occasion that he is tested by the devil, Jesus replies by quoting from

10. The NT quotes Deuteronomy some eighty-three times. The only other OT books to be referred to as often in the NT are Genesis, Psalms, and Isaiah. Two factors, however, should be borne in mind in considering the number of times Deuteronomy is quoted in the NT. First, many of the quotations come in parallel accounts recorded in the Synoptic Gospels. Second, on a few occasions part of the Decalogue is quoted; in such instances it is possible to see the source of the quotations as either Exod. 20 or Deut. 5 (e.g., Rom. 7:7; 13:9; James 2:11).

11. Parallel accounts come in Mark 12:28–34; Luke 10:25–28. To emphasize an important consequence of loving God, Jesus also quotes Lev. 19:18: "Love your neighbor as yourself."

Deuteronomy.[12] In doing so, he highlights one of the principal tenets of the book: "Worship the LORD your God, and serve him only" (Deut. 6:13, quoted in Matt. 4:10; Luke 4:8).

Even when the text of Deuteronomy is not quoted directly, its influence is still apparent. We see this in Jesus's insistence that his followers must be single-minded in their commitment to God: "No one can serve two masters. Either you will hate the one and love the other, or you will be devoted to the one and despise the other. You cannot serve both God and money" (Matt. 6:24).

Later this principle is highlighted in the story of the rich young man (Matt. 19:16–30; Luke 18:18–30). By insisting that he give his wealth to the poor, Jesus reveals that the man has divided allegiances. The idea of wholehearted commitment to God also appears in the parables of Jesus, especially those that involve a master-servant relationship (Matt. 18:23–35; 24:45–51; 25:14–30; Luke 12:42–48; 19:12–27); these parables commonly emphasize the importance of loyalty and faithfulness.

Another aspect of Deuteronomy that is developed briefly in the New Testament is that of cursing. Paul picks this up in his Letter to the Galatians, where he declares, "all who rely on the works of the law are under a curse, as it is written: 'Cursed is everyone who does not continue to do everything written in the Book of the Law'" (Gal. 3:10, quoting Deut. 27:26). Since, according to Paul, no one can keep the law fully, all are cursed. However, this for Paul is not the end of the matter. He then confidently affirms that Christ has "redeemed us from the curse of the law by becoming a curse for us, for it is written: 'Cursed is everyone who is hung on a pole'" (Gal. 3:13, quoting Deut. 21:23).

12. He quotes Deut. 8:3; 6:16; 6:13.

23

Why Israel?

By establishing a special covenant relationship with the Israelites, the LORD set them apart from all other nations as his people. God's choice of Israel is not linked to any special quality that they possess; it is not due to their righteousness or size. When the LORD promised them the land of Canaan, this was because by their wickedness the nations living there had forfeited their right to the land. Yet, even though the Israelites are commanded to completely destroy the nations living in Canaan, it is God's intention that they should be a light to other nations, reflecting the righteousness that he expects of all people. Although the Israelites stand to benefit greatly from the privilege of being God's holy nation, their calling also carries with it important responsibilities. Failure to fulfill these will bring upon them God's disfavor.

Introduction

The book of Deuteronomy, as we have already recognized in the previous chapter, revolves around the covenant that is renewed between the LORD and Israel. As a consequence of this, Israel enjoys a relationship with the LORD that differs markedly from that experienced by other nations. Various passages within Deuteronomy focus on the nature and purpose of this special relationship and indirectly address a number of important theological issues. Why did the LORD choose Israel and deliver its people from Egypt? Did the LORD display favoritism in wiping out the nations of Canaan in order to give their land to the Israelites? Did Israel, as a result of its special relationship with God, have an unfair advantage over all the other nations of the earth? The answers to these questions permeate the book of Deuteronomy.

The Election of Israel

Throughout Deuteronomy it is made clear that Israel as a nation has a unique relationship with the LORD. Moses summarizes this as follows: "For you are a people holy to the LORD your God. The LORD your God has chosen you out of all the peoples on the face of the earth to be his people, his treasured possession" (7:6; cf. 14:2).[1]

Here we encounter several distinctive ideas that occur elsewhere in Deuteronomy and point to God's setting Israel apart as his own special nation. First, on a number of occasions it is stated that God has chosen Israel "out of all the peoples on the face of the earth" (14:2; cf. 4:37; 7:6–7; 10:15). The emphasis rests on how it was the LORD who chose Israel, not Israel who chose the LORD. Second, the Israelites are to be *his* people (4:20; 7:6; 26:18; 27:9; 28:9–10; 29:13; cf. 9:26, 29; 21:8; 26:15). Israel alone is the LORD's people; no other nation can claim this. The uniqueness of this relationship is underlined by the comment that Israel is God's "treasured possession" (7:6; 14:2; 26:18). The Hebrew term *sĕgullâ*, "treasured possession," is used elsewhere in the Old Testament to describe the jewels and valuable objects in a king's treasury (1 Chron. 29:3; Eccles. 2:8); Israel is precious to the LORD. Elsewhere the closeness of this bond is presented in terms of a parent-child relationship (32:18–20). Third, the distinctive relationship between Israel and the LORD is reflected in the designation "holy nation" (Exod. 19:6; cf. Deut. 7:6; 14:2, 21; 26:19; 28:9). Of all the nations on earth, Israel alone is under a special obligation to exhibit the holiness of God's nature. This is necessary because God has committed himself to live in a unique way among the Israelites.

Further evidence pointing to the LORD's choice of Israel comes in the many references to what he has already done for them in the past. Some of these focus on the special promises, chiefly concerning the possession of the land of Canaan, that God made to the patriarchs (Deut. 4:31; 6:18, 23; 7:8; 8:1; 9:5; 13:17; 19:8; 26:15; 31:20; 34:4). Others deal with their divine redemption from Egypt (5:6; 6:12; 7:8; 8:14; 9:26; 13:5; 15:15; 21:8; 24:18) and the defeat of their enemies (2:24–3:11). Deuteronomy frequently highlights how the LORD has acted uniquely and decisively on the people's behalf. One passage that is particularly vivid in this regard is the poetic description in 32:8–15:

> When the Most High gave the nations their inheritance,
> when he divided all mankind,

1. A similar description of Israel's unique status among the nations of the earth comes in Exod. 19:4–6.

he set up boundaries for the peoples
    according to the number of the sons of Israel.
For the Lord's portion is his people,
    Jacob his allotted inheritance.
In a desert land he found him,
    in a barren and howling waste.
He shielded him and cared for him;
    he guarded him as the apple of his eye,
like an eagle that stirs up its nest
    and hovers over its young,
that spreads its wings to catch them
    and carries them aloft.
The LORD alone led him;
    no foreign god was with him.
He made him ride on the heights of the land
    and fed him with the fruit of the fields.
He nourished him with honey from the rock,
    and with oil from the flinty crag,
with curds and milk from herd and flock
    and with fattened lambs and goats,
with choice rams of Bashan
    and the finest kernels of wheat.
You drank the foaming blood of the grape.
Jeshurun grew fat and kicked;
    filled with food, they became heavy and sleek.

To highlight Israel's relationship with the LORD, however, Deuteronomy looks not only to the past but also to the future. The concluding words of Moses's second speech emphasize in a special way one important aspect of the LORD's future for Israel: "He [the LORD] has declared that he will set you in praise, fame and honor high above all the nations he has made and that you will be a people holy to the LORD your God, as he promised" (26:19). Elsewhere the future benefits of Israel's election are highlighted indirectly through the sections of the legal material that presuppose the occupation of the land of Canaan. Although the Israelites have yet to cross the river Jordan and take possession of the promised land, many of the regulations outlined by Moses to the people anticipate their settlement in the land. Thus some rules are given regarding the eating of animals away from the tabernacle (12:15–25),[2] pilgrimage festivals (16:1–17), and the giving of tithes (14:22–27). All these presuppose that the Israelites will occupy a large territory, with many of them living at a considerable distance from

2. In Deuteronomy, the place where the tabernacle is to be located in the promised land is referred to by using either the phrase "the place the LORD (your God) will choose" (12:5, 11, 14, 18, 21, 26; 14:23–25; 15:20; 16:2, 6, 7, 11, 15, 16; 17:8, 10; 18:6; 26:2; 31:11) or the phrase "to put his Name there for his dwelling" (12:5, 11; 14:23; 16:2, 6, 11; 26:2; cf. 12:21, 14:24).

the tabernacle. Similarly, the giving of instructions to establish cities of refuge (19:1–9) also implies that the Israelites will be dispersed throughout the whole of Canaan.

Apart from providing evidence that Israel is set apart by God from all other nations, the book of Deuteronomy also sheds light on the reason for Israel's divine election. What has caused the LORD to choose Israel rather than some other nation? In Deuteronomy this question is answered mainly by excluding certain possibilities. First, Israel's election is not due to its righteousness. This is clearly stated in 9:4–6:

> After the LORD your God has driven them out before you, do not say to yourself, "The LORD has brought me here to take possession of this land because of my righteousness." No, it is on account of the wickedness of these nations that the LORD is going to drive them out before you. It is not because of your righteousness or your integrity that you are going in to take possession of their land; but on account of the wickedness of these nations, the LORD your God will drive them out before you, to accomplish what he swore to your fathers, to Abraham, Isaac and Jacob. Understand, then, that it is not because of your righteousness that the LORD your God is giving you this good land to possess, for you are a stiff-necked people.

This passage is not alone in emphasizing Israel's lack of righteousness: there are frequent references to the nation's waywardness. Moses reminds the people that when God tested their obedience through the wilderness experience (Deut. 8:2–5), they rebelled and were punished (1:26–46; 9:7–24), and but for the intercession of Moses, the LORD would have rejected them completely (9:18–20, 25–29; 10:10). Not only are they occasionally described as a "stiff-necked people" (9:4–6, 13; 10:16; 31:27), but also Moses comments, "You have been rebellious against the LORD ever since I have known you" (9:24; cf. 31:27). In these and other ways, Israel is consistently portrayed as failing to achieve the high standard of righteousness demanded by the LORD. Even regarding the future, Deuteronomy highlights the Israelites' inability to fulfill the obligations placed on them (e.g., 31:16–18; 32:15–35).[3] Clearly God's election of Israel is not determined because they are morally superior to others.

Another factor that is briefly mentioned regarding the election of Israel is that of size. According to Moses, "The LORD did not set his affection on you and choose you because you were more numerous than other peoples, for you were the fewest of all peoples" (7:7). It was not because of Israel's superiority in numbers and strength that God choose Israel; on the contrary, when God initiated his dealings with Israel, he started with one individual, Abraham.

3. This failure is discussed more fully below.

If Deuteronomy dismisses Israel's righteousness and size as reasons for its divine election, is any other explanation provided? The only other factor mentioned is God's oath with the "ancestors" (7:8; 9:5; cf. 4:31; 6:18, 23; 8:1; 13:17; 19:8; 26:15; 31:20; 34:4). Yet even here the emphasis rests on God's love and faithfulness to the oath that he swore (7:8–9). The part played by the patriarchs in the process of election is secondary to that of the LORD. Deuteronomy is consistent in emphasizing that the LORD's election of Israel was not due to some inherent quality found in the people; rather, it resulted from the LORD's unmerited love for them.

Having observed how Deuteronomy emphasizes the divine election of Israel, what can be said about the purpose underlying this? What did the LORD hope to achieve through choosing the Israelites to be his own people? The clearest answer to this question comes in 4:6–8:

> Observe them [God's decrees and laws] carefully, for this will show your wisdom and understanding to the nations, who will hear about all these decrees and say, "Surely this great nation is a wise and understanding people." What other nation is so great as to have their gods near them the way the LORD our God is near us whenever we pray to him? And what other nation is so great as to have such righteous decrees and laws as this body of laws I am setting before you today?

Underlying this passage is the idea that Israel is divinely chosen to be an example for others to emulate. Two aspects of this are highlighted here. First, the nearness of the LORD's presence is emphasized. Israel will enjoy an intimate relationship with God, which will be seen in the LORD's willingness to hear the people's prayers. Second, others will praise the *tôrâ* ("body of laws," 4:8), by which the nation shall regulate its affairs, because of the inherent righteousness of its decrees and laws.

Naturally, this requires that the Israelites be consistent in keeping all the demands of the *tôrâ*. Israel's election is linked to its obligation to be a holy nation (cf. 7:7–11). Because the LORD has chosen Israel and promised to bless its people abundantly, they have the responsibility of living up to their divine calling. Moses expresses this link between election, obedience to the LORD, and other nations as follows: "The LORD will establish you as his holy people, as he promised you on oath, if you keep the commands of the LORD your God and walk in obedience to him. Then all the peoples on earth will see that you are called by the name of the LORD, and they will fear you" (28:9–10). Given the importance that is placed on Israel's being a light to the nations, it is not surprising that much of Deuteronomy is devoted to outlining the regulations and laws that are intended to make Israel more righteous than other nations, to lead them to obey God. Though it is not possible here to provide a detailed survey of all the material in the Book of the Law (*tôrâ*), a number of general observations can be made. At the outset we should notice that the regulations in Deuteronomy seek to promote a sense of "community" (17:15 NRSV). An example of this comes in the regulations concerning kingship (17:14–20). Not only is it stated that the king "must be from among your fellow Israelites" (17:15), but later it is added that he "must not consider himself better than his fellow Israelites" (17:20). The law (*tôrâ*) requires that the king not use his special status to promote his own interests above those of others. Linked to the concept of community is a concern for the weaker members of society. Throughout the Book of the Law (*tôrâ*) special mention is made of the fatherless, the widow, the slave, the poor, and the alien.[4] Because of their vulnerability, they must not be mistreated or exploited; all are to be shown dignity and respect. Furthermore, the law (*tôrâ*) is also concerned to promote a generous spirit (e.g., 10:18–19; 15:12–14). In their dealings with others the Israelites must reflect the LORD's generosity toward them.[5]

Deuteronomy throughout also emphasizes the importance of Israel's being a righteous nation. We see this highlighted, for example, in the refrain that occurs often in the Book of the Law (*tôrâ*): "You must purge the evil from among you" (13:5; 17:7; 19:19; 21:21; 22:21, 24; 24:7; cf. 17:12; 19:13; 21:9; 22:22). It is also reflected in the LORD's description of Israel as Jeshurun, "the upright one" (32:15 mg.; 33:5, 26).[6] However, although Deuteronomy stresses the importance of Israel's being righteous, it also allows for the possibility that if Israel fails in this regard, it would still be a witness to God's righteousness (cf. 29:24–28).

Although Israel is the LORD's "treasured possession," this does not give the people a firm guarantee that they will always enjoy divine favor. As we have noted in the previous chapter, the covenant established between the LORD and Israel only guarantees blessing when the people fulfill the obligations placed on them. Failure to meet these obligations will bring on them the curses outlined at the end of the Book of the Law (*tôrâ*). While the Israelites enjoy a unique and privileged position in their relationship with the LORD, they are expected to be especially righteous.

4. The alien, the fatherless, and the widows are mentioned together in the following verses: Deut. 10:18; 14:29; 16:11, 14; 24:17, 19–21; 26:12–13; 27:19. Elsewhere, positive attitudes toward aliens are commended in 1:16; 5:14; 10:19; 14:21; 23:7; 24:14; 26:11. On occasions the Levites, who depended on other Israelites' generosity for their daily needs, are mentioned alongside the alien, the fatherless, and the widows (14:29; 16:11, 14; 26:12–13; cf. 26:11).

5. Deuteronomy assumes that, because these laws are divinely given, they reflect God's righteous nature. It therefore is no surprise that Moses describes God's nature in terms that echo the regulations of the Book of the Law (*tôrâ*): "For the LORD your God is God of gods and Lord of lords, the great God, mighty and awesome, who shows no partiality and accepts no bribes. He defends the cause of the fatherless and the widow, and loves the foreigner residing among you, giving them food and clothing" (10:17–18).

6. Apart from its occurrences in Deuteronomy, the term is used only once elsewhere in the OT (Isa. 44:2).

Israel and the Nations

Thus far we have focused our attention on the LORD's choice of Israel to be his people out of all the nations of the earth. What, however, does the book of Deuteronomy reveal about the LORD's attitude toward other nations? In addressing this question, it needs to be recognized that in Deuteronomy an important distinction is drawn between the nations living in the land of Canaan and those living elsewhere. To appreciate this, it may be best to consider first what Deuteronomy has to say about the nations of Canaan.

Given that the whole movement in the book of Deuteronomy is toward the Israelite occupation of the land of Canaan, it is hardly surprising that considerable attention is devoted to the issue of what should happen to the nations already living there. Since the land is in the possession of seven nations—the Hittites, Girgashites, Amorites, Canaanites, Perizzites, Hivites, and Jebusites (7:1)—how will Israel come to possess it? The response of Deuteronomy is unambiguous. The Israelites are to drive out all those inhabiting the land of Canaan.

To understand why such a policy is adopted toward these nations, three factors should be considered. First, the expulsion of these nations is an act of divine punishment.[7] As Moses emphasizes in 9:4–6, the Israelites are not being given the land as a reward for their own righteousness; rather, "on account of the wickedness of these nations, the LORD your God will drive them out before you" (9:5; cf. v. 4).[8] By worshiping other gods, the nations of Canaan have denied Yahweh the honor and recognition that is due to him alone. Second, the removal of the nations of Canaan is presented as necessary in order to prevent the Israelites from worshiping other gods (20:18). For this reason, Moses commands the destruction of everything associated with foreign gods (7:5, 25–26) and forbids the people from adopting their religious practices (16:21–22; 18:14). The Israelites are to purge the land of anything that might cause them to sin against God. This, however, ought not to be interpreted as being directed only against the foreign nations living in Canaan; the same policy is to be applied toward fellow Israelites (Deut. 13:1–18; 18:9–22; cf. Exod. 22:20). Third, an important distinction needs to be drawn between dispossessing the nations and annihilating them. Various terms are used to describe the process by which the Israelites are to remove the other nations from the land of Canaan. The most striking of these terms are the verb ḥāram (khāram), meaning "to devote something to sacred use," and the related noun ḥērem (khērem), "devoted thing(s)." When these specific terms are used, everything that is captured in battle is to be given over to God; this involves the death of everyone, men, women, and children (e.g., Deut. 2:34; 3:6). While the concept of *ḥērem* comes frequently in Joshua (2:10; 6:17, 18, 21; 7:1, 11–13, 15; 8:26; 10:1, 28, 35, 37, 39, 40; 11:11, 12, 20, 21; 22:20), Weinfeld observes that earlier passages speak of the Israelites as "dispossessing" or "expelling" the nations of Canaan, without necessarily implying that the nations are to be completely destroyed.[9] In the light of this, the concept of *ḥērem* applied to nations is first introduced in the context of the Israelites' being attacked by the Canaanite king of Arad (Num. 21:1–3). Later, Deuteronomy 2:34 and 3:6 apply the same concept to King Sihon of Heshbon and King Og of Bashan, both of whom deliberately attack the Israelites. A survey of the book of Joshua also suggests that *ḥērem* is applied only to those who are actively hostile toward the Israelites. Since such hostility is viewed as being directed against Yahweh, those involved forfeit their right to life.

While total destruction is associated with those who violently oppose the Israelites, the book of Joshua gives special attention to those non-Israelites who do not come under the *ḥērem*. For assisting the Israelite spies to escape from Jericho, Rahab and her family are rescued when the city and its inhabitants are destroyed (2:1–24; 6:25). Similarly, the people of Gibeon are not put to death even though they deceive the Israelites in order to establish a treaty with them (9:1–27). The book of Joshua contrasts the fate of these non-Israelite groups with the destruction that befalls the Israelite family of Achan on account of his disobedience (7:1–26).

While the destruction of the inhabitants of Canaan by the Israelites raises important ethical questions, we should not lose sight of the fact that the Israelites themselves eventually suffer a similar fate at the hand of the Assyrians and Babylonians. At no stage can God be accused of adopting double standards. In all of this we are reminded of the intimate relationship between obedience to God's instructions, divine blessing, and the provision of land.

In spite of the strength of the nations already in Canaan—"seven nations larger and stronger than you" (Deut. 7:1)—the Israelites are assured that the LORD will give them the victory (7:16–24; 9:1–3; 11:22–25; 31:3–8). Although the victory will be decisive, it will also be gradual (7:22). Furthermore, their success is linked to their obedience to God's decrees and laws (11:22–23).

Though the book of Deuteronomy adopts a very negative attitude toward the inhabitants of Canaan, the same is not true of all other nations. This is reflected in a number of ways. First, Moses draws attention to the fact that during their journey to the promised land, the Israelites were not permitted by the LORD to attack certain nations in order to take possession of their land (2:1–23). This was so for the Edomites, Moabites, and Ammonites.

9. M. Weinfeld, *The Promise of the Land: The Inheritance of the Land of Canaan by the Israelites*, TLJS 3 (Berkeley: University of California Press, 1993), 76–98.

Concerning each of these nations, Moses observes that the LORD was responsible for giving them their land (2:5, 9, 19). Since the LORD granted the land to them, the Israelites have no right to take any part of it. Thus Moses observes a number of parallels between the Edomites, Moabites, and Ammonites; all were given land by the LORD,[10] and all overcame powerful enemies in order to take possession of the land (2:10–12, 20–23). Implicit in Moses's comments about these nations is the suggestion that if the LORD has done this for these nations, then the Israelites should have confidence that he will achieve the same for them.

Second, when the Book of the Law (tôrâ) addresses the topic of war against other nations, a clear distinction is drawn between how the Israelites should deal with the nearby nations of Canaan and how they should deal with more-distant peoples. While they are to spare none of the members of the nearby nations who have attacked them (20:16–17)—all are to be put to death, men and women, young and old—a different policy is to be adopted toward other nations. At the start of any conflict, an offer of peace is to be made (20:10). If this is accepted, then no deaths result. If, however, this is refused, the Israelites are to "put to the sword all the men" but spare "the women, the children, the livestock and everything else in the city" (20:13–14).[11]

Third, various minor remarks within Deuteronomy suggest that the Israelites are expected to adopt a positive attitude toward the well-being of the nations outside Canaan. They are commanded not to "despise an Edomite" or "an Egyptian" (23:7). In spite of all that has happened in Egypt, the Israelites are to allow "the third generation of children" born to Egyptians to "enter the assembly of the LORD" (23:8). A positive attitude toward foreigners is also reflected in the numerous references to aliens within the Book of the Law (tôrâ). As noted above, they, like widows and the fatherless, are to be cared for in a special way.

These differing approaches toward foreign nations are in keeping with what we have observed earlier regarding the election of Israel. Since through their wickedness the nations of Canaan have forfeited their right to the land of Canaan, the land is to be given to the Israelites. In this territory Israel is to establish itself as a holy nation. Furthermore, because Israel is to be a light to the nations, it is important that its people reflect in their national life the lifestyle and values that are consistent with the single-minded service of the LORD. This requires that the land be purged of everything that might undermine the divine purpose underlying Israel's election. Hence the Israelites are to completely expel the nations already living in Canaan. However, regarding

10. Moses quotes the LORD as saying, "I have given Esau the hill country of Seir as his own" (Deut. 2:5). Similar statements are made concerning the Moabites (2:9) and Ammonites (2:19).

11. Implicit in the ban against cutting down fruit trees during the siege of a city seems to be a concern to enable life, so that those who survive a siege can return to normality as soon as possible after the conflict has ended. Even in war, the Israelites are to have a humanitarian concern.

other nations, a different attitude is to prevail. At all times Israel is to follow a policy of nonaggression toward them. Only if they threaten the national security of Israel will these nations be in danger of attack.

Election and Responsibility

Although the LORD has chosen the Israelites to be his people, at no stage are they forced against their will to accept him as their God. At Sinai and on the plains of Moab, they are invited to freely enter into a covenant relationship with the LORD. However, once they have entered into such an agreement, they are committed by the terms of the covenant to remain loyal to the LORD. In his speeches Moses emphasizes the benefits available to the Israelites as a result of their divine election; yet the book of Deuteronomy also highlights the serious consequences that will result from a failure to fulfill this calling. If the Israelites are to enjoy the benefits of being the LORD's people, they must keep the obligations placed on them by the covenant.

Although Moses strongly exhorts the people to obey the covenant obligations, Deuteronomy as a whole conveys the idea that the Israelites will fail to keep them. The possibility of failure is introduced as early as 4:25–31, but it is in the concluding chapters that it becomes most prominent. First, the likelihood that Israel will break the covenant obligations is suggested by the space devoted to the curses in Deuteronomy 27 and 28. Twelve verses are given over to outlining the blessings that will reward obedience (28:3–14); the curses occupy sixty-five verses (27:15–26; 28:16–68). By devoting so much attention to the curses, Moses conveys the impression that they are more likely to materialize than the blessings.

Second, although the list of curses does not specifically indicate that the Israelites will fail to keep the covenant obligations, this is stated emphatically shortly afterward in three different speeches.

1. In his final exhortation to the Israelites to keep the covenant with the LORD, Moses clearly envisages a future in which the land will be devastated (29:23) and the people exiled (30:1–4).
2. In one of the few divine speeches recorded in Deuteronomy, the LORD tells Moses: "These people will soon prostitute themselves to the foreign gods of the land they are entering. They will forsake me and break the covenant I made with them. And in that day I will become angry with them and forsake them; I will hide my face from them, and they will be destroyed" (31:16–17). To remind future generations of Israelites of this prediction, the LORD instructs Moses to teach the people a special song (32:1–43).

3. When Moses orders the Levites to place the Book of the Law (*tôrâ*)
   beside the ark of the covenant, he comments:

> For I know how rebellious and stiff-necked you are. If you have been rebellious
> against the LORD while I am still alive and with you, how much more will you
> rebel after I die! Assemble before me all the elders of your tribes and all your
> officials, so that I can speak these words in their hearing and call heaven and
> earth to testify against them. For I know that after my death you are sure to
> become utterly corrupt and to turn from the way I have commanded you. In
> days to come, disaster will fall on you because you will do evil in the sight of
> the LORD and provoke his anger by what your hands have made. (31:27–29)

> Like the song in 32:1–43, the Book of the Law (*tôrâ*) will be a witness
> against the Israelites (31:26; cf. v. 19).

In the light of these developments toward the end of Deuteronomy, it is
clear that the Israelites, due to their disobedience, will experience mixed
consequences from their divine election. Though they will initially enjoy
God's favor in the promised land, in due course this will be replaced by divine cursing, resulting in their expulsion from the land. That Deuteronomy
should envisage such a development is noteworthy. However, even in the
process of being punished by the LORD, the Israelites will still be a witness
to the nations regarding the righteousness of the LORD. When in the future
foreigners ask why terrible disasters have come upon Israel (29:22–24), it
will be stated:

> It is because this people abandoned the covenant of the LORD, the God of their
> ancestors, the covenant he made with them when he brought them out of Egypt.
> They went off and worshiped other gods and bowed down to them, gods they
> did not know, gods he had not given them. Therefore the Lord's anger burned
> against this land, so that he brought on it all the curses written in this book. In
> furious anger and in great wrath the LORD uprooted them from their land and
> thrust them into another land, as it is now. (29:25–28)

Even when divinely punished, the Israelites would be a light to the nations.
Although Israel's election gives them advantages denied to other nations,
in reality, due to their rebellious nature, they will forfeit these. Nevertheless,
in spite of their unfaithfulness, the LORD will not abandon them completely.
If in exile they show remorse for their actions, he will be compassionate
toward them (30:1–10). Significantly, in anticipating the future restoration
of exiled Israelites to the promised land, Moses alludes briefly to the fact
that "the LORD your God will circumcise your hearts and the hearts of your
descendants, so that you may love him with all your heart and with all your
soul, and live" (30:6). Here Moses envisages a time in the distant future when

the LORD will intervene in order to overcome the inability of the Israelites to keep the covenant faithfully.

Old Testament Summary

The book of Deuteronomy highlights why the LORD chose Israel to be his people and the consequences associated with this choice. They are to be a holy nation, keeping the covenant obligations found in the Book of the Law (*tôrâ*) in order that others might know and marvel at the righteousness of God. Yet in spite of the special privileges bestowed on them, Deuteronomy anticipates a future in which the Israelites will rebel against the LORD and break the covenant. As a result, after entering the promised land, they themselves will be exiled and forced to live among other nations.

New Testament Connections

Within the New Testament the issue of Israel's divine election is perhaps most prominent in Paul's Letter to the Romans. Here Paul addresses at length how the gospel has impacted the relationship between Jews and Gentiles. In his discussion Paul highlights the belief of his Jewish contemporaries that "in the law" they have "the embodiment of knowledge and truth" (Rom. 2:20). Such a belief is clearly derived from the way in which the Law (*tôrâ*) is presented in the book of Deuteronomy. While Paul does not dispute this view of the law, he challenges the ability of his contemporaries to keep it. He even suggests that because of their inability to keep the law, "God's name is blasphemed among the Gentiles" (Rom. 2:24, quoting Isa. 52:5; Ezek. 36:22), an idea that may well have its roots in the book of Deuteronomy.

Next Paul focuses on the topic of circumcision and argues that without a circumcision of the heart, implying complete obedience to God, outward circumcision is of no benefit. Although his Jewish opponents are stressing the importance of having the law and being circumcised, Paul argues that they are mistaken in thinking that this makes them more righteous than others: "No one will be declared righteous in God's sight by the works of the law; rather, through the law we become conscious of our sin" (Rom. 3:20). Paul then proceeds to argue that "the righteousness of God . . . is given through faith in Jesus Christ to all who believe" (3:21–22). This righteousness is available to both Jews and Gentiles, to everyone who, like Abraham, exercises faith. By focusing on this "righteousness from God" (3:21–22 NIV 1984), Paul reflects the outlook of Deuteronomy that without a divinely given "circumcision of the heart" (2:29), it will be impossible for the Israelites to keep the covenant.

Later Paul stresses the benefits that belong to the Israelites as God's chosen people: "Theirs is the adoption to sonship; theirs the divine glory, the covenants, the receiving of the law, the temple worship and the promises. Theirs are the patriarchs, and from them is traced the human ancestry of the Messiah, who is God over all, forever praised! Amen" (Rom. 9:4–5). Yet in spite of these things, Paul willingly acknowledges that some Israelites have failed to obtain the righteousness that comes by faith; rather, they have sought to be righteous by keeping the law and have failed. However, Gentiles, "who did not pursue righteousness, have obtained it" (9:30). In the light of this, Paul asks if the LORD has rejected his people, Israel. Though he acknowledges the failure of many Jews to find salvation, he holds out the hope that "all Israel will be saved" (11:26). Although the inclusion of the Gentiles within the people of God is a very significant development for Paul, he does not believe that this implies the complete exclusion of the Jews. Echoing Deuteronomy, Paul sees the divine election of Israel as leading to the salvation of the Gentiles.

24

The Pentateuch
and the Biblical Metanarrative

The Pentateuch is an unfinished story. For this reason, having focused on its contents, in this concluding chapter I shall briefly outline how the opening five books of the Bible provide an essential introduction to the rest of Scripture. By taking a panoramic view, we shall observe how the Pentateuch lays a foundation for the biblical metanarrative that runs from Genesis to Revelation.

The story of God's mission to reconcile humanity and all creation to himself undoubtedly unites the library of books that comprise the Bible.[1] In the face of conflicting master narratives, the Bible offers a radically different account, which claims for itself an authority that rests in the unique Deity, whose existence the entire story presupposes.

From the original creation of the heaven and the earth to the future formation of a new heaven and a new earth, the biblical books of Genesis to Revelation present an incredibly diverse, but nonetheless remarkably coherent, story. At the heart of this story is the grace-inspired redemptive activity of God, with its focus on restoring the broken relationship between himself and wayward humanity, as well as renewing all creation. Fundamental to this whole process is the incarnation of God's unique Son, Jesus Christ, climaxing in his sacrificial death, bodily resurrection, glorious ascension to the right hand of

---

1. Cf. C. J. H. Wright, *The Mission of God: Unlocking the Bible's Grand Narrative* (Downers Grove: InterVarsity, 2006).

the Father, and future return as universal judge. While Christ's first coming to the earth as the God-man is central to the success of God's mission, the whole of Scripture bears witness to an extended program of divine activity that prepares for and follows on from Christ's incarnation.

From Creation to Re-creation, from Garden to City

The biblical metanarrative is framed by two acts of divine creation. Genesis opens by briefly describing how God created the heaven and the earth in the beginning. At the other end of the canon, Revelation concludes by anticipating the divine re-creation of a new heaven and a new earth. Though the beginning (protology) and the end (eschatology) clearly resemble each other, an important difference exists between the first creation and its subsequent re-creation. The opening chapters of Genesis focus on a garden with two human inhabitants; the concluding chapters of Revelation describe a populated city of enormous dimensions. Various features in the opening chapters of Genesis imply that the city of Revelation 21–22, the future new Jerusalem, represents the fulfillment of what God intended when he first created the earth.

The movement from the Garden of Eden to the new Jerusalem underlies all of Scripture. All-important, the biblical metanarrative affirms that this city is designed to be God's dwelling place, shared with humanity. In the Old Testament the tabernacle and the Jerusalem temple point forward to a time when the entire earth will be filled with God's glory. As models of the earth or microcosms, the tabernacle and temple illustrate God's intention that his holy presence should fill the whole world. The establishment of Jerusalem (or Zion) as a temple-city marks an important step toward the fulfillment of God's plan for the earth. However, the city is eventually abandoned by God due to the defilement caused by its imperfect inhabitants. For this reason, the Old Testament prophets envisage the future creation of a new and perfect Jerusalem.

Although the tabernacle and temple function as models pointing forward to the creation of the new earth and the new heaven, they are replaced in the New Testament by a very different kind of temple, one consisting of human bodies. Anticipated by the incarnation of Jesus Christ, the church becomes the new temple of God, extending God's presence throughout the earth. The church is a temple both in use and under construction, with the followers of Jesus Christ being variously equipped by the Holy Spirit as temple builders. While the creation of the church itself is an important part of God's missional activity, the eventual fulfillment of God's plans for the whole earth involves the creation of the new Jerusalem, after Christ's second coming.

The movement from the Garden of Eden to the new Jerusalem involves a process whereby, in stages, God's glorious presence comes to fill the whole world. Not surprisingly, God's presence is directly linked to the expansion of his kingdom throughout the earth. In the Old Testament, God's sovereignty is reflected in the tabernacle and temple, which respectively resemble a royal tent and a palace. In the New Testament, the church is clearly associated with the kingdom of God. Taken as a whole, the biblical metanarrative portrays the expansion by stages of God's sovereign presence on the earth.

To appreciate why the Bible draws attention to the ever-expanding presence and sovereignty of God on the earth, we need to return to the opening chapters of Genesis. As the Lord of creation, God authorizes humanity to exercise dominion on his behalf over all the other creatures of the earth. Though the first human couple are instructed to rule over all the animals, birds, and fish, they betray God by succumbing to the sinister temptation of the "serpent." By obeying a creature rather than the Creator, they submit to its authority. Consequently the "serpent" gains dominion over humans and everything placed by God under their rule. In this way Satan becomes the prince of this world, usurping God himself.

The expulsion of Adam and Eve from the Garden of Eden signifies the end of their special status as God's vice-regents. Exiled from God's presence, with their original nature now corrupted, humans experience the tragic consequences of being alienated from their Creator and the rest of creation. As the opening chapters of Genesis disclose, God's good creation is soon polluted by human violence. Originally tasked with constructing God's holy city upon the earth, sinful humanity ironically builds an alternative city, Babel-Babylon, a monument to humanity's arrogant determination to oust God from the earth and even heaven itself. Although God intervenes to halt the initial Babel-Babylon project by scattering the city's inhabitants throughout the earth, the human ambition to construct an alternative, God-less city remains. As the book of Kings reveals, Babel-Babylon resurfaces in the future to plunder God's chosen city, Jerusalem, destroy its temple, and carry its inhabitants into exile. In the book of Revelation, the city of Babylon continues to be symbolic of human enterprise undertaken in defiance of God. As the Bible repeatedly highlights, there is ongoing human resistance to the construction of God's temple-city upon the earth.

While humanity's rebellion against God jeopardizes the completion of his plan for the earth; God does not abandon humans to their fate. He acts decisively to reinstate as his holy vice-regents those who repent. In a process that spans many generations, God embarks on a mission of rescuing sinful people from the power of Satan, sin, and death. This mission of restoration forms the very core of the whole biblical metanarrative.

The Lion and the Lamb

As the New Testament makes clear, God's mission centers on the coming of Jesus Christ as his unique Son. Through Christ's death, resurrection, and ascension, God establishes the means by which repentant people may be redeemed from the power of evil and restored as royal priests. The Bible uses two images to convey something of the importance of Christ's role: "Lion" and "Lamb" (e.g., Rev. 5:5–6). The former focuses on the royal aspect of Christ's nature; the latter draws attention to the sacrificial dimension of his death. These two aspects are first encountered in the Old Testament, which prepares for Christ's coming.

The significance of Christ's royal nature is clearly related to the vice-regent status that was lost by Adam and Eve. From Genesis onward, the Old Testament anticipates the coming of a special king, from the tribe of Judah and the line of David, who will bring God's blessing to the nations of the earth. As a new Adam, this future king will be entirely obedient to God, eventually establishing God's kingdom of justice and peace on the earth. By being fully human, Christ brings to completion God's original mandate for humanity.

Regarding the sacrificial aspect of Christ's role as "the Lamb of God, who takes away the sin of the world!" (John 1:29), the origins of this are found in the Old Testament account of the exodus from Egypt. As a paradigm of salvation, the divine rescue of the Israelites from slavery under Pharaoh reveals how God in love and mercy delivers people from enslavement to evil. Through the Passover ritual, the Israelite firstborn are redeemed from slavery, ransomed from death, purified from the defilement of sin, and set apart as holy. By participating in the Passover, the Israelites are restored to the status of priest-kings, becoming a holy nation subject to their divine sovereign, the LORD. With the construction of the tabernacle at Mount Sinai, God comes to dwell among the people of Israel, thus partially fulfilling his creation plan. As the prime example of God's salvific activity in the Old Testament, the Passover establishes a paradigm that is later associated with Jesus Christ's sacrificial death. Christ's death, however, benefits people from every nation. With the coming of the Holy Spirit at Pentecost, reversing the confusion of Babel, people "from every nation under heaven" hear in their own native language of God's mighty works. Like the tabernacle and the temple, the new temple of the church is filled with the glory of God's presence.

Priest-Kings and Holy Nation

From Genesis 3 onward, God's actions are clearly designed to restore alienated people to a royal and priestly status so that they may be citizens of God's future temple-city, which will fill the new earth. Although Christ, through his death on the cross, has already defeated Satan, the latter will be fully vanquished from the earth only when Christ returns as universal judge. For the present, God patiently invites people everywhere to repent and acknowledge Christ as Lord and Savior. Until Christ's return, his followers are called to live as citizens of this yet-to-be-revealed city in a world that is antagonistic toward its Creator. As those who have been redeemed from death, purified from sin's pollution, and sanctified, they are expected by the grace of God to live here and now as "a royal priesthood" and "a holy nation," so that they "may declare the praises of him who called" them "out of darkness into his wonderful light" (1 Pet. 2:9).

As the biblical metanarrative clearly sets out, our place within God's purposes has to be understood in the context of God's original plan for the earth. Unfortunately, due to Adam and Eve's betrayal of the trust placed in them, the present world and its inhabitants stand in need of divine redemption. In the light of this, the restoration of the whole of creation from the consequences of human rebelliousness lies at the heart of God's saving activity. While this begins and ends with God, he invites those who have been redeemed to share in his mission.

The task of being a community of believers in the modern world is demanding. Only as we grapple prayerfully and rigorously with God's story of redemption, as it is revealed to us in the whole of the Bible, will we be fully equipped to live out our calling as disciples of Jesus Christ. To this end, it is vital that we recognize the important contribution that the books of the Pentateuch make to the biblical metanarrative of divine salvation.

Recommended Further Reading

Commentaries

Genesis

Aalders, G. C. *Genesis*. 2 vols. BSC. Grand Rapids: Zondervan, 1981.

Alter, R. *Genesis*. New York: W. W. Norton, 1996.

Atkinson, D. *The Message of Genesis 1–11*. BST. Downers Grove, IL: InterVarsity, 1990.

Baldwin, J. G. *The Message of Genesis 12–50: From Abraham to Joseph*. BST. Leicester: Inter-Varsity; Downers Grove, IL: InterVarsity, 1986.

Brueggemann, W. *Genesis*. IBC. Atlanta: John Knox, 1982.

Cassuto, U. *Commentary on Genesis*. 2 vols. Jerusalem: Magnes, 1964.

Coats, G. W. *Genesis with an Introduction to Narrative Literature*. FOTL 1. Grand Rapids: Eerdmans, 1983.

Collins, C. J. *Genesis 1–4: A Linguistic, Literary, and Theological Commentary*. Phillipsburg, NJ: P&R, 2006.

Currid, J. D. *Genesis 1:1–25:18*. EPSC. Darlington, UK: Evangelical Press, 2003.

———. *Genesis 25:19–50:26*. EPSC. Darlington, UK: Evangelical Press, 2003.

Gibson, J. C. L. *Genesis*. 2 vols. DSB. Edinburgh: St. Andrew, 1981–1982.

Gowan, D. E. *Genesis 1–11*. ITC. Grand Rapids: Eerdmans, 1988.

Gunkel, H. *Genesis*. MLBS. Macon, GA: Mercer University Press, 1997.

Hamilton, V. P. *The Book of Genesis: Chapters 1–17*. NICOT. Grand Rapids: Eerdmans, 1990.

———. *The Book of Genesis: Chapters 18–50*. NICOT. Grand Rapids: Eerdmans, 1995.

Hartley, J. E. *Genesis*. NIBCOT 1. Peabody, MA: Hendrickson; Carlisle: Paternoster, 2000.

Jacob, B. *The First Book of the Bible: Genesis*. New York: Ktav, 1974.

Kidner, D. *Genesis*. TOTC. Leicester: Inter-Varsity, 1967.

Maher, M. *Genesis*. OTM 2. Wilmington, DE: Michael Glazier, 1982.

Mathews, K. A. *Genesis 1–11:26*. NAC 1A. Nashville: Broadman & Holman, 1995.

———. *Genesis 11:27–50:26*. NAC 1B. Nashville: Broadman & Holman, 2005.

Rad, G. von. *Genesis*. OTL. London: SCM, 1961.

Ross, A. P. *Creation and Blessing: A Guide to the Study and Exposition of Genesis.* Grand Rapids: Baker, 1988.

Sailhamer, J. H. "Genesis." Pages 21–331 in *Genesis–Leviticus*, edited by R. S. Hess, W. Kaiser Jr., and J. H. Sailhamer. REBC. Grand Rapids: Zondervan, 2008.

Sarna, N. M. *Genesis*. JPSTC. New York: Jewish Publication Society, 1989.

Skinner, J. *Genesis*. 2nd ed. ICC. Edinburgh: T&T Clark, 1930.

Speiser, E. A. *Genesis*. AB 1. Garden City, NY: Doubleday, 1964.

Towner, W. S. *Genesis*. WestBC. Louisville: Westminster John Knox, 2007.

Turner, L. A. *Genesis*. 2nd ed. Sheffield: Sheffield Phoenix, 2009.

Vawter, B. *On Genesis: A New Reading*. Garden City, NY: Doubleday, 1977.

Waltke, B. K. *Genesis: A Commentary*. Grand Rapids: Zondervan, 2001.

Walton, J. H. *Genesis*. NIVAC. Grand Rapids: Zondervan, 2001.

Wenham, G. J. "Genesis." Pages 54–91 in *New Bible Commentary: 21st Century Edition*, edited by D. A. Carson, R. T. France, J. A. Motyer, and G. J. Wenham. Leicester: Inter-Varsity, 1994.

———. *Genesis 1–15*. WBC 1. Waco: Word Books, 1987.

———. *Genesis 16–50*. WBC 2. Dallas: Word Books, 1994.

Westermann, C. *Genesis*. TI. Grand Rapids: Eerdmans, 1987.

———. *Genesis 1–11: A Commentary*. Translated by John J. Scullion. Minneapolis: Augsburg, 1984.

———. *Genesis 12–36: A Commentary*. Translated by John J. Scullion. Minneapolis: Augsburg, 1985.

———. *Genesis 37–50: A Commentary*. Translated by John J. Scullion. Minneapolis: Augsburg, 1986.

Exodus

Alexander, T. D. "Exodus." Pages 92–120 in *New Bible Commentary: 21st Century Edition*, edited by D. A. Carson, R. T. France, J. A. Motyer, and G. J. Wenham. Leicester: Inter-Varsity, 1994.

Ashby, G. W. *Go Out and Meet God: A Commentary on the Book of Exodus*. ITC. Grand Rapids: Eerdmans; Edinburgh: Handsel, 1997.

Bruckner, J. K. *Exodus*. NIBCOT 2. Peabody, MA: Hendrickson; Milton Keynes, UK: Paternoster, 2008.

Cassuto, U. *Commentary on Exodus*. Jerusalem: Magnes, 1967.

Childs, B. S. *The Book of Exodus: A Critical, Theological Commentary*. OTL. Philadelphia: Westminster; London: SCM, 1974.

Coats, G. W. *Exodus 1–18*. FOTL 2A. Grand Rapids: Eerdmans, 1999.

Coggins, R. *The Book of Exodus*. EC. Peterborough, UK: Epworth, 2000.

Cole, R. A. *Exodus*. TOTC. Leicester: Inter-Varsity, 1973.

Currid, J. D. *Exodus 1–18*. EPSC. Darlington, UK: Evangelical Press, 2000.

———. *Exodus 19–40*. EPSC. Darlington, UK: Evangelical Press, 2001.

Dozeman, T. B. *Commentary on Exodus*. ECC. Grand Rapids: Eerdmans, 2009.

Durham, J. I. *Exodus*. WBC 3. Waco: Word Books, 1987.

Ellison, H. L. *Exodus*. DSB. Edinburgh: St. Andrew, 1982.

Enns, P. *Exodus*. NIVAC. Grand Rapids: Zondervan, 2000.

Fretheim, T. E. *Exodus*. IBC. Louisville: John Knox, 1991.

Gispen, W. H. *Exodus*. BSC. Grand Rapids: Zondervan, 1982.

Greenberg, M. *Understanding Exodus*. Teaneck, NJ: Ben Yehuda Press, 2010.

Hamilton, V. P. *Exodus: An Exegetical Commentary*. Grand Rapids: Baker Academic, 2011.

Houtman, C. *Exodus*. Vol. 1, *1:1–7:13*. HCOT. Kampen, Netherlands: Kok, 1993.

———. *Exodus*. Vol. 2, *7:14–19:25*. HCOT. Kampen, Netherlands: Kok, 1996.

———. *Exodus*. Vol. 3, *20–40*. HCOT. Leuven: Peeters, 2000.

Janzen, J. G. *Exodus*. WestBC. Louisville: Westminster John Knox, 1997.

Kaiser, W. C. "Exodus." Pages 333–561 in *Genesis–Leviticus*, edited by R. S. Hess, W. Kaiser Jr., and J. H. Sailhamer. REBC. Grand Rapids: Zondervan, 2008.

Langston, S. M. *Exodus through the Centuries*. BBC. Oxford: Blackwell, 2006.

Larsson, G. *Bound for Freedom: The Book of Exodus in Jewish and Christian Traditions*. Peabody, MA: Hendrickson, 1999.

Meyers, C. *Exodus*. NCBC. Cambridge: Cambridge University Press, 2005.

Motyer, J. A. *The Message of Exodus*. BST. Downers Grove, IL: InterVarsity, 2005.

Noth, M. *Exodus: A Commentary*. OTL. London: SCM, 1962.

Propp, W. H. C. *Exodus 1–18: A New Translation with Introduction and Commentary*. AB 2. New York: Doubleday, 1999.

———. *Exodus 19–40: A New Translation with Introduction and Commentary*. AB 2A. New York: Doubleday, 2006.

Sarna, N. M. *Exodus*. JPSTC. Philadelphia: Jewish Publication Society, 1991.

Stuart, D. K. *Exodus*. NAC 2. Nashville: Broadman & Holman, 2006.

Leviticus

Balentine, S. E. *Leviticus*. IBC. Louisville: Westminster John Knox, 2003.

Bellinger, J. W. H. *Leviticus, Numbers*. NIBCOT 3. Peabody, MA: Hendrickson, 2001.

Bonar, A. A. *A Commentary on Leviticus*. Edinburgh: Banner of Truth, 1966.

Budd, P. J. *Leviticus: Based on the New Revised Standard Version*. NCB. London: Marshall Pickering; Grand Rapids: Eerdmans, 1996.

Currid, J. D. *Leviticus*. EPSC. Darlington, UK: Evangelical Press, 2005.

Gane, R. *Leviticus, Numbers*. NIVAC. Grand Rapids: Zondervan, 2004.

Gerstenberger, E. *Leviticus: A Commentary*. OTL. Louisville: Westminster John Knox, 1996.

Gorman, F. H. *Divine Presence and Community: A Commentary on the Book of Leviticus*. ITC. Grand Rapids: Eerdmans; Edinburgh: Handsel Press, 1997.

Harrison, R. K. *Leviticus*. TOTC. Leicester: Inter-Varsity, 1980.

Hartley, J. E. *Leviticus*. WBC 4. Dallas: Word Books, 1992.

Hess, R. S. "Leviticus." Pages 563–826 in *Genesis–Leviticus*, edited by R. S. Hess, W. Kaiser Jr., and J. H. Sailhamer. REBC. Grand Rapids: Zondervan, 2008.

Kiuchi, N. *Leviticus*. AOTC 3. Nottingham: Apollos; Downers Grove, IL: InterVarsity, 2007.

Knight, G. A. *Leviticus*. DSB. Edinburgh: St. Andrew, 1981.

Levine, B. A. *Leviticus*. JPSTC. New York: Jewish Publication Society, 1989.

Milgrom, J. *Leviticus: A Book of Ritual and Ethics*. CC. Minneapolis: Fortress, 2004.

———. *Leviticus 1–16: A New Translation with Introduction and Commentary*. AB 3. New York: Doubleday, 1991.

———. *Leviticus 17–22: A New Translation with Introduction and Commentary*. AB 3A. New York: Doubleday, 2000.

———. *Leviticus 23–27: A New Translation with Introduction and Commentary*. AB 3B. New York: Doubleday, 2001.

Noordtzij, A. *Leviticus*. BSC. Grand Rapids: Zondervan, 1982.

Rooker, M. F. *Leviticus*. NAC 3. Nashville: Broadman & Holman, 2000.

Ross, A. P. *Holiness to the Lord: A Guide to the Exposition of the Book of Leviticus*. Grand Rapids: Baker Academic, 2002.

Snaith, N. H. *Leviticus and Numbers*. NCB. Grand Rapids: Eerdmans, 1967.

Tidball, D. *The Message of Leviticus*. BST. Downers Grove, IL: InterVarsity, 2005.

Wenham, G. J. *The Book of Leviticus*. NICOT. Grand Rapids: Eerdmans, 1979.

Wright, C. J. H. "Leviticus." Pages 121–57 in *New Bible Commentary: 21st Century Edition*, edited by D. A. Carson, R. T. France, J. A. Motyer, and G. J. Wenham. Leicester: Inter-Varsity, 1994.

Numbers

Ashley, T. R. *The Book of Numbers*. NICOT. Grand Rapids: Eerdmans, 1993.

Bellinger, J. W. H. *Leviticus, Numbers*. NIBCOT 3. Peabody, MA: Hendrickson, 2001.

Budd, P. J. *Numbers*. WBC 5. Waco: Word Books, 1984.

Cole, R. D. *Numbers*. NAC 3B. Nashville: Broadman & Holman, 2000.

Davies, E. W. *Numbers: Based on the Revised Standard Version*. NCB. London: Marshall Pickering; Grand Rapids: Eerdmans, 1995.

Duguid, I. M. *Numbers: God's Presence in the Wilderness*. PW. Wheaton: Crossway, 2006.

Gane, R. *Leviticus, Numbers*. NIVAC. Grand Rapids: Zondervan, 2004.

Gray, G. B. *Numbers*. ICC. Edinburgh: T&T Clark, 1903.

Harrison, R. K. *Numbers*. WEC. Chicago: Moody, 1990.

Knierim, R. P., and G. W. Coats. *Numbers*. FOTL 4. Grand Rapids: Eerdmans, 2005.

Levine, B. A. *Numbers 1–20: A New Translation with Introduction and Commentary*. AB 4. New York: Doubleday, 1993.

———. *Numbers 21–36: A New Translation with Introduction and Commentary*. AB 4A. New York: Doubleday, 2000.

Maarsingh, B. *Numbers*. TI. Grand Rapids: Eerdmans, 1987.

Milgrom, J. *Numbers*. JPSTC. New York: Jewish Publication Society, 1990.

Naylor, P. J. "Numbers." Pages 158–97 in *New Bible Commentary: 21st Century Edition*, edited by D. A. Carson, R. T. France, J. A. Motyer, and G. J. Wenham. Leicester: Inter-Varsity, 1994.

Noordtzij, A. *Numbers*. BSC. Grand Rapids: Zondervan, 1983.

Olson, D. T. *Numbers*. IBC. Louisville: John Knox, 1996.

Philip, J. *Numbers*. CCSOT 4. Waco: Word Books, 1987.

Riggans, W. *Numbers*. DSB. Edinburgh: St. Andrew, 1983.

Sakenfeld, K. D. *Journeying with God: A Commentary on the Book of Numbers*. ITC. Grand Rapids: Eerdmans, 1995.

Snaith, N. H. *Leviticus and Numbers*. NCB. Grand Rapids: Eerdmans, 1967.

Wenham, G. J. *Numbers*. TOTC. Leicester: Inter-Varsity, 1981.

Deuteronomy

Brueggemann, W. *Deuteronomy*. AOTC. Nashville: Abingdon, 2001.

Christensen, D. L. *Deuteronomy 1.1–21.9*. 2nd ed. WBC 6A. Nashville: Thomas Nelson, 2001.

———. *Deuteronomy 21:10–34:12*. WBC 6B. Nashville: Thomas Nelson, 2002.

Clements, R. E. *The Book of Deuteronomy*. EC. London: Epworth, 2001.

Clifford, R. *Deuteronomy*. OTM 4. Wilmington, DE: Michael Glazier, 1982.

Craigie, P. C. *The Book of Deuteronomy*. NICOT. Grand Rapids: Eerdmans, 1976.

Currid, J. D. *Deuteronomy*. EPSC. Darlington, UK: Evangelical Press, 2006.

Driver, S. R. *Deuteronomy*. ICC 5. Edinburgh: T&T Clark, 1895.

Harman, A. *Deuteronomy*. FB. Fearn, Tain, UK: Christian Focus Publications, 2001.

Mann, T. W. *Deuteronomy*. WestBC. Louisville: Westminster John Knox, 1995.

Mayes, A. D. H. *Deuteronomy*. NCB. Grand Rapids: Eerdmans, 1979.

McConville, J. G. "Deuteronomy." Pages 198–232 in *New Bible Commentary: 21st Century Edition*, edited by D. A. Carson, R. T. France, J. A. Motyer, and G. J. Wenham. Leicester: Inter-Varsity, 1994.

———. *Deuteronomy*. AOTC. Leicester: Apollos, 2002.

Merrill, E. H. *Deuteronomy*. NAC 4. Nashville: Broadman & Holman, 1994.

Miller, P. D. *Deuteronomy*. IBC. Louisville: John Knox, 1990.

Munchenberg, R. H. *Deuteronomy*. CRC. Adelaide, Australia: Lutheran Publishing House, 1987.

Nelson, R. D. *Deuteronomy*. OTL. Louisville: Westminster John Knox, 2002.

Payne, D. F. *Deuteronomy*. DSB. Edinburgh: St. Andrew, 1985.

Ridderbos, J. *Deuteronomy*. BSC. Grand Rapids: Zondervan, 1984.

Thompson, J. A. *Deuteronomy*. TOTC. Leicester: Inter-Varsity, 1974.

Tigay, J. H. *Deuteronomy: The Traditional Hebrew Text with the New JPS Translation*. JPSTC. Philadelphia: Jewish Publication Society, 1996.

Weinfeld, M. *Deuteronomy 1–11*. AB 5. New York: Doubleday, 1991.

Wright, C. J. H. *Deuteronomy*. NIBCOT 4. Peabody, MA: Hendrickson; Carlisle: Paternoster, 1996.

Wright, G. E. "Deuteronomy." Pages 331–540 in vol. 2 of *The Interpreter's Bible*, edited by G. A. Buttrick et al. Nashville: Abingdon, 1953.

Selected Bibliography

Only selected books and articles cited in this volume are included here. Fuller bibliographies on each book of the Pentateuch may be found in the commentaries of Mathews, Wenham, and Westermann on Genesis; Childs, Durham, and Propp on Exodus; Hartley, Kiuchi, and Milgrom on Leviticus; Budd and Levine on Numbers; Christensen, McConville, and Weinfeld on Deuteronomy.

Aalders, G. C. *A Short Introduction to the Pentateuch*. London: Tyndale, 1949.

Alexander, T. D. *Abraham in the Negev: A Source-Critical Investigation of Genesis 20:1–22:19*. Carlisle: Paternoster, 1997.

———. "Abraham Re-Assessed Theologically: The Abraham Narrative and the New Testament Understanding of Justification by Faith." Pages 7–28 in *He Swore an Oath: Biblical Themes from Genesis 12–50*, edited by R. S. Hess, P. E. Satterthwaite, and G. J. Wenham. 2nd ed. Grand Rapids: Baker; Carlisle: Paternoster, 1994.

———. "Are the Wife/Sister Incidents of Genesis Literary Compositional Variants?" *VT* 42 (1992): 145–53.

———. "Beyond Borders: The Wider Dimensions of Land." Pages 35–50 in *The Land of Promise: Biblical, Theological and Contemporary Perspectives*, edited by P. Johnston and P. Walker. Leicester: Apollos, 2000.

———. "The Composition of the Sinai Narrative in Exodus xix 1–xxiv 11." *VT* 49 (1999): 2–20.

———. "Exodus." Pages 92–120 in *New Bible Commentary: 21st Century Edition*, edited by D. A. Carson, R. T. France, J. A. Motyer, and G. J. Wenham. Leicester: Inter-Varsity, 1994.

———. "From Adam to Judah: The Significance of the Family Tree in Genesis." *EvQ* 61 (1989): 5–19.

———. *From Eden to the New Jerusalem: An Introduction to Biblical Theology*. Grand Rapids: Kregel, 2009.

———. "Further Observations on the Term 'Seed' in Genesis." *TynBul* 48 (1997): 363–67.

———. "Genealogies, Seed and the Compositional Unity of Genesis." *TynBul* 44 (1993): 255–70.

———. "Genesis 22 and the Covenant of Circumcision." *JSOT* 25 (1983): 17–22.

———. "The Hagar Traditions in Genesis xvi and xxi." Pages 131–48 in *Studies in the Pentateuch*, edited by J. A. Emerton. VTSup 41. Leiden: Brill, 1990.

———. "Lot's Hospitality: A Clue to His Righteousness." *JBL* 104 (1985): 289–91.

———. "Messianic Ideology in the Book of Genesis." Pages 19–39 in *The Lord's Anointed: Interpretation of Old Testament Messianic Texts*, edited by P. E. Satterthwaite, R. S. Hess, and G. J. Wenham. Grand Rapids: Baker; Carlisle: Paternoster, 1995.

———. "The Passover Sacrifice." Pages 1–24 in *Sacrifice in the Bible*, edited by R. T. Beckwith and M. Selman. Carlisle: Paternoster; Grand Rapids: Baker, 1995.

———. "The Regal Dimension of the תלדות־יעקב: Recovering the Literary Context of Genesis 37–50." Pages 196–212 in *Reading the Law: Studies in Honour of Gordon J. Wenham*, edited by J. G. McConville and K. Möller. LHB/OTS 461. Edinburgh: T&T Clark, 2007.

———. "Royal Expectations in Genesis to Kings: Their Importance for Biblical Theology." *TynBul* 49 (1998): 191–212.

———. *The Servant King: The Bible's Portrait of the Messiah*. Leicester: Inter-Varsity, 1998.

———. "The Wife/Sister Incidents of Genesis: Oral Variants?" *IBS* 11 (1989): 2–22.

Alexander, T. D., and S. Gathercole, eds. *Heaven on Earth: The Temple in Biblical Theology*. Carlisle: Paternoster, 2004.

Alexander, T. D., and B. S. Rosner, eds. *The New Dictionary of Biblical Theology*. Leicester: Inter-Varsity, 2000.

Alt, A. *Der Gott der Väter: Ein Beitrag zur Vorgeschichte der israelitischen Religion*. BWANT 12. Stuttgart: Kohlhammer, 1929. Translated by R. A. Wilson as "The God of the Fathers." Pages 3–77 in *Essays on Old Testament History and Religion*. Oxford: Blackwell, 1966.

Alter, R. *The Art of Biblical Narrative*. New York: Basic Books, 1981.

Andersen, F. I. *The Hebrew Verbless Clause in the Pentateuch*. SBLMS 14. Nashville: Abingdon, 1970.

———. *The Sentence in Biblical Hebrew*. The Hague: Mouton, 1974.

Andersen, F. I., and D. N. Freedman. *Hosea: A New Translation with Introduction and Commentary*. AB 24. New York: Doubleday, 1980.

Anderson, B. W. "From Analysis to Synthesis: The Interpretation of Genesis 1–11." *JBL* 97 (1978): 23–39.

Anonymous. "Babel, Tower of." Pages 66–67 in *Dictionary of Biblical Imagery*, edited by L. Ryken, J. C. Wilhoit, and T. Longman. Downers Grove, IL: InterVarsity; Leicester: Inter-Varsity, 1998.

Averbeck, R. E. "Tabernacle." Pages 807–27 in *Dictionary of the Old Testament: Pentateuch*, edited by T. D. Alexander and D. W. Baker. Downers Grove, IL: Inter-Varsity; Leicester: Inter-Varsity, 2003.

Baden, J. S. *J, E, and the Redaction of the Pentateuch*. Tübingen: Mohr Siebeck, 2009.

Baker, D. W. "Source Criticism." Pages 798–805 in *Dictionary of the Old Testament: Pentateuch*, edited by T. D. Alexander and D. W. Baker. Downers Grove, IL: Inter-Varsity; Leicester: Inter-Varsity, 2003.

Bar-Efrat, S. *Narrative Art in the Bible*. Sheffield: Almond, 1989.

Bauer, G. L. *Theologie des Alten Testaments: Oder Abriß der religiösen Begriffe der alten Hebräer: Von den ältesten Zeiten bis auf den Anfang der christlichen Epoche; Zum Gebrauch akademischer Vorlesungen*. Leipzig: Weygand, 1796.

———. *The Theology of the Old Testament: Or, A Biblical Sketch of the Religious Opinions of the Ancient Hebrews*. Extracted and translated by P. Harwood from *Theologie des Alten Testaments*. London: Charles Fox, 1838.

Beale, G. K. *The Temple and the Church's Mission: A Biblical Theology of the Dwelling Place of God*. NSBT 17. Leicester: Apollos, 2004.

Berlin, A. *Poetics and Interpretation of Biblical Narrative*. Sheffield: Almond, 1983.

Bleek, F. *De libri Geneseos origine atque indole historica observationes quaedam contra Bohlenium*. Bonnae [Bonn]: Georgi, 1836.

Blenkinsopp, J. "An Assessment of the Alleged Pre-Exilic Date of the Priestly Material in the Pentateuch." *ZAW* 108 (1996): 495–518.

———. *The Pentateuch*. London: SCM, 1992.

———. "A Post-Exilic Lay Source in Genesis 1–11." Pages 49–61 in *Abschied vom Jahwisten: Die Komposition des Hexateuch in der jüngsten Diskussion*, edited by J. C. Gertz, K. Schmid, and M. Witte. BZAW 315. Berlin: de Gruyter, 2002.

———. "The Structure of P." *CBQ* 38 (1976): 275–92.

Blum, E. *Die Komposition der Vätergeschichte*. WMANT 57. Neukirchen-Vluyn: Neukirchener Verlag, 1984.

———. "Die literarische Verbingung von Erzvätern und Exodus: Ein Gespräch mit neueren Endredaktionshypothesen." Pages 119–56 in *Abschied vom Jahwisten: Die Komposition des Hexateuch in der jüngsten Diskussion*, edited by J. C. Gertz, K. Schmid, and M. Witte. BZAW 315. Berlin: de Gruyter, 2002.

———. *Studien zur Komposition des Pentateuch*. BZAW 189. Berlin: de Gruyter, 1990.

Böhmer, E. *Das Erste Buch der Thora*. Halle: Buchh. des Waisenhauses, 1862.

Breasted, J. H. *Ancient Records of Egypt: The Nineteenth Dynasty*. Vol. 3. Chicago: University of Chicago Press, 1906.

Brichto, H. C. *Toward a Grammar of Biblical Poetics*. Oxford: Oxford University Press, 1992.

Brueggemann, W. *The Land*. Philadelphia: Fortress, 1977.

———. *Tradition for Crisis: A Study in Hosea*. Richmond: John Knox, 1968.

Brueggemann, W., and H. W. Wolff. *The Vitality of Old Testament Traditions*. Atlanta: John Knox, 1975.

Carr, D. M. *Reading the Fractures of Genesis: Historical and Literary Approaches*. Louisville: Westminster John Knox, 1996.

———. "What Is Required to Identify Pre-Priestly Narrative Connections between Genesis and Exodus? Some General Reflections and Specific Cases." Pages 159–80 in *A Farewell to the Yahwist? The Composition of the Pentateuch in Recent European Interpretation*, edited by T. B. Dozeman and K. Schmid. SBLSymS 34. Atlanta: Society of Biblical Literature, 2006.

Cassuto, U. *The Documentary Hypothesis and the Composition of the Pentateuch*. Jerusalem: Magnes, 1961.

Cheyne, T. K. *Founders of Old Testament Criticism*. London: Methuen, 1893.

Childs, B. S. *The Book of Exodus: A Critical, Theological Commentary*. OTL. Philadelphia: Westminster; London: SCM, 1974.

———. *Introduction to the Old Testament as Scripture*. Philadelphia: Fortress; London: SCM, 1979.

Chirichigno, G. "The Narrative Structure of Exodus 19–24." *Bib* 68 (1987): 457–79.

Clements, R. E. *Abraham and David: Genesis XV and Its Meaning for Israelite Tradition*. SBT, 2nd ser., 5. London: SCM, 1967.

Clifford, R. J. *The Cosmic Mountain in Canaan and the Old Testament*. Cambridge, MA: Harvard University Press, 1972.

Clines, D. J. A. *The Theme of the Pentateuch*. 2nd ed. JSOTSup 10. Sheffield: Sheffield Academic Press, 1997.

Coats, G. W. *From Canaan to Egypt: Structural and Theological Context for the Joseph Story*. CBQMS 4. Washington, DC: Catholic Biblical Association of America, 1976.

———. "The Joseph Story and Ancient Wisdom: A Reappraisal." *CBQ* 35 (1973): 285–97.

———. "Redactional Unity in Genesis 37–50." *JBL* 93 (1974): 15–21.

Collins, C. J. "Galatians 3:16: What Kind of an Exegete Was Paul?" *TynBul* 54 (2003): 75–86.

———. "A Syntactical Note (Genesis 3:15): Is the Woman's Seed Singular or Plural?" *TynBul* 48 (1997): 139–48.

Craghan, J. F. "The Elohist in Recent Literature." *BTB* 7 (1977): 23–35.

Crenshaw, J. L. "Method in Determining Wisdom Influence upon 'Historical' Literature." *JBL* 88 (1969): 129–42.

Cross, F. M. *Canaanite Myth and Hebrew Epic*. Cambridge, MA: Harvard University Press, 1973.

Culley, R. C. "Themes and Variations in Three Groups of OT Narratives." *Semeia* 3 (1975): 3–13.

Dahlberg, B. T. "On Recognizing the Unity of Genesis." *TD* 24 (1976): 360–67.

Daube, D. *The Exodus Pattern in the Bible*. London: Faber & Faber, 1963.

DeRouchie, J. S., and J. C. Meyer. "Christ or Family as the 'Seed' of Promise? An Evaluation of N. T. Wright on Galatians 3:16." *SBJT* 14 (2010): 36–48.

Douglas, M. *Purity and Danger*. London: Routledge & K. Paul, 1969.

Dozeman, T. B. *Commentary on Exodus*. ECC. Grand Rapids: Eerdmans, 2009.

———. "The Commission of Moses and the Book of Genesis." Pages 107–30 in *A Farewell to the Yahwist? The Composition of the Pentateuch in Recent European Interpretation*, edited by T. B. Dozeman and K. Schmid. SBLSymS 34. Atlanta: Society of Biblical Literature, 2006.

————. "Geography and Ideology in the Wilderness Journey from Kadesh through Transjordan." Pages 173–89 in *Abschied vom Jahwisten: Die Komposition des Hexateuch in der jüngsten Diskussion*, edited by J. C. Gertz, K. Schmid, and M. Witte. BZAW 315. Berlin: de Gruyter, 2002.

————. *God on the Mountain: A Study of Redaction, Theology, and Canon in Exodus 19–24*. SBLMS 37. Atlanta: Scholars Press, 1989.

Dozeman, T. B., and K. Schmid, eds. *A Farewell to the Yahwist? The Composition of the Pentateuch in Recent European Interpretation*. SBLSymS 34. Atlanta: Society of Biblical Literature, 2006.

Driver, S. R. *An Introduction to the Literature of the Old Testament*. 9th ed. Edinburgh: T&T Clark, 1913.

Dumbrell, W. J. "Genesis 2:1–17: A Foreshadowing of the New Creation." Pages 53–65 in *Biblical Theology: Retrospect and Prospect*, edited by S. J. Hafemann. Downers Grove, IL: InterVarsity; Leicester: Apollos, 2002.

Durham, J. I. *Exodus*. WBC 3. Waco: Word Books, 1987.

Emerton, J. A. "An Examination of Some Attempts to Defend the Unity of the Flood Narrative in Genesis." Pts. 1 and 2. *VT* 37 (1987): 401–20; 38 (1988): 1–21.

————. "The Riddle of Genesis xiv." *VT* 21 (1971): 403–39.

Engnell, I. *Gamla Testamentet: En traditionshistorisk inledning*. Vol. 1. Stockholm: Svenska Kyrkans Diakonistyrelses Bokförlag, 1945.

Engnell, I., J. T. Willis, and H. Ringgren, eds. *Critical Essays on the Old Testament*. London: SPCK, 1970.

Ewald, G. H. A. von. *Geschichte des Volkes Israel bis Christus*. 7 vols. Göttingen: Dieterich, 1843–59.

————. *The History of Israel*. Translated by R. Martineau. 2nd ed. 8 vols. London: Longmans, Green, 1869–85.

————. *Die Komposition der Genesis kritisch untersucht*. Braunschweig, Germany: L. Lucius, 1823.

Fishbane, M. A. "Composition and Structure in the Jacob Cycle (Gen. 25:19–35:22)." *JJS* 26 (1975): 15–38.

————. *Text and Texture: Close Readings of Selected Biblical Texts*. New York: Schocken Books, 1979.

Fokkelman, J. P. *Narrative Art in Genesis*. SSN 17. Assen, Netherlands: van Gorcum, 1975.

Fretheim, T. E. *Exodus*. IBC. Louisville: John Knox, 1991.

Fretheim, T. E., G. M. Tucker, and C. B. Cousar. *The Pentateuch*. IBT. Nashville: Abingdon, 1996.

Friedman, R. E. "Tabernacle." In *ABD* 6 (1992): 292–300.

————. "Torah (Pentateuch)." In *ABD* 6 (1992): 605–22.

————. *Who Wrote the Bible?* Englewood Cliffs, NJ: Prentice-Hall, 1987.

Frymer-Kensky, T. "The Atrahasis Epic and Its Significance for Our Understanding of Genesis 1–9." *BA* 40 (1977): 147–55.

Garrett, D. A. *Rethinking Genesis: The Sources and Authorship of the First Book of the Pentateuch*. Grand Rapids: Baker, 1991.

Gertz, J. C. "The Transition between the Books of Genesis and Exodus." Pages 73–87 in *A Farewell to the Yahwist? The Composition of the Pentateuch in Recent European Interpretation*, edited by T. B. Dozeman and K. Schmid. SBLSymS 34. Atlanta: Society of Biblical Literature, 2006.

Gertz, J. C., K. Schmid, and M. Witte, eds. *Abschied vom Jahwisten: Die Komposition des Hexateuch in der jüngsten Diskussion*. BZAW 315. Berlin: de Gruyter, 2002.

Gooding, D. W. *The Account of the Tabernacle: Translation and Textual Problems of the Greek Exodus*. TS, new ser., 6. Cambridge: Cambridge University Press, 1959.

Gordon, R. P. "Compositeness, Conflation and the Pentateuch." *JSOT* 51 (1991): 57–69.

———. "The Ethics of Eden: Truth-Telling in Genesis 2–3." Pages 11–33 in *Ethical and Unethical in the Old Testament: God and Humans in Dialogue*, edited by K. J. Dell. LHB/OTS 528. London and New York: T&T Clark International, 2010.

———. "The Week That Made the World: Reflections on the First Pages of the Bible." Pages 228–41 in *Reading the Law: Studies in Honour of Gordon J. Wenham*, edited by J. G. McConville and K. Möller. LHB/OTS 461. Edinburgh: T&T Clark, 2007.

Graf, K. H. *Die geschichtlichen Bücher des Alten Testaments: Zwei historisch-kritische Untersuchungen*. Leipzig: Weigel, 1866.

Gray, G. B. *Sacrifice in the Old Testament: Its Theory and Practice*. Oxford: Clarendon, 1925.

Green, W. H. *The Unity of the Book of Genesis*. New York: Scribner's Sons, 1895.

Greengus, S. "Sisterhood Adoption at Nuzi and the 'Wife-Sister' in Genesis." *HUCA* 46 (1975): 5–31.

Gunkel, H. *Genesis*. MLBS. Macon, GA: Mercer University Press, 1997.

———. *Genesis: Übersetzt und erklärt*. 3rd ed. Göttingen: Vandenhoeck & Ruprecht, 1910.

———. *The Legends of Genesis*. Chicago: Open Court, 1901.

Gunn, D. M., and D. N. Fewell. *Narrative in the Hebrew Bible*. Oxford: Oxford University Press, 1993.

Habel, N. C. *Literary Criticism of the Old Testament*. Philadelphia: Fortress, 1971.

Halbe, J. "Erwägungen zu Ursprung und Wesen des Massotfestes." *ZAW* 87 (1975): 325–34.

Hamilton, V. P. *The Book of Genesis: Chapters 1–17*. NICOT. Grand Rapids: Eerdmans, 1990.

———. *The Book of Genesis: Chapters 18–50*. NICOT. Grand Rapids: Eerdmans, 1995.

———. "Genesis: Theology of." Pages 663–75 in *NIDOTTE*, vol. 4. Grand Rapids: Zondervan, 1997.

Haran, M. "Behind the Scenes of History: Determining the Date of the Priestly Source." *JBL* 100 (1981): 321–33.

———. "Ezekiel, P, and the Priestly School." *VT* 58 (2008): 211–18.

———. "The Passover Sacrifice." Pages 94–95 in *Studies in the Religion of Ancient Israel*, edited by G. W. Anderson. VTSup 23. Leiden: Brill, 1972.

————. *Temples and Temple-Service in Ancient Israel*. Oxford: Clarendon Press, 1978.

Hasel, G. F. "The Meaning of the Animal Rite in Gen. 15." *JSOT* 19 (1981): 61–78.

Hess, R. S. "Language of the Pentateuch." Pages 491–97 in *Dictionary of the Old Testament: Pentateuch*, edited by T. D. Alexander and D. W. Baker. Downers Grove, IL: InterVarsity; Leicester: Inter-Varsity, 2003.

Hobbes, T. *Leviathan*. 1651. Reprint, New York: Penguin, 1968.

Hoffmeier, J. K. *Ancient Israel in Sinai: The Evidence for the Authenticity of the Wilderness Tradition*. Oxford and New York: Oxford University Press, 2005.

————. "Out of Egypt: The Archaeological Context of the Exodus." *BAR* 33 (2007): 30–41, 77.

Hoskins, P. M. "Deliverance from Death by the True Passover Lamb: A Significant Aspect of the Fulfillment of the Passover in the Gospel of John." *JETS* 52 (2009): 285–99.

————. "Freedom from Slavery to Sin and the Devil: John 8:31–47 and the Passover Theme of the Gospel of John." *TJ* 31 (2010): 47–63.

————. *That Scripture Might Be Fulfilled: Typology and the Death of Christ*. LaVergne, TN: Xulon, 2009.

Houtman, C. "The Pentateuch." Pages 166–205 in vol. 2 of *The World of the Old Testament*, edited by A. S. van der Woude. Grand Rapids: Eerdmans, 1989.

Hurowitz, V. "The Priestly Account of Building the Tabernacle." *JAOS* 105 (1985): 21–30.

Hurvitz, A. "Dating the Priestly Source in Light of the Historical Study of Biblical Hebrew a Century after Wellhausen." *ZAW* 100 (1988): 88–99.

————. "Evidence of Language in Dating the Priestly Code: A Linguistic Study in Technical Idioms and Terminology." *RB* 81 (1974): 24–56.

————. "The Historical Quest for 'Ancient Israel' and the Linguistic Evidence of the Hebrew Bible: Some Methodological Observations." *VT* 47 (1997): 301–15.

————. *A Linguistic Study of the Relationship between the Priestly Source and the Book of Ezekiel*. CahRB 20. Paris: J. Gabalda, 1982.

Hyatt, J. P. *Exodus*. NCB. London: Oliphants, 1971.

Jackson, B. S. *Wisdom-Laws: A Study of the Mishpatim of Exodus 21:1–22:16*. Oxford: Oxford University Press, 2006.

Jacob, B. *The Second Book of the Bible: Exodus*. Hoboken, NJ: Ktav, 1992.

Jenks, A. W. "Elohist." Pages 478–82 in *ABD*, vol. 2. New York: Doubleday, 1992.

Jenson, P. P. *Graded Holiness: A Key to the Priestly Conception of the World*. JSOTSup 106. Sheffield: JSOT Press, 1992.

Jobling, D. *The Sense of Biblical Narrative*. JSOTSup 7. Sheffield: JSOT Press, 1978.

Johnson, M. D. *The Purpose of the Biblical Genealogies with Special Reference to the Setting of the Genealogies of Jesus*. SNTSMS 8. London: Cambridge University Press, 1969.

Johnstone, W. "The Decalogue and the Redaction of the Sinai Pericope in Exodus." *ZAW* 100 (1988): 361–85.

————. *Exodus*. OTG. Sheffield: JSOT Press, 1990.

———. "Reactivating the Chronicles Analogy in Pentateuchal Studies, with Special Reference to the Sinai Pericope in Exodus." *ZAW* 99 (1987): 16–37.

———. "The Use of the Reminiscences in Deuteronomoy in Recovering the Two Main Literary Phrases in the Production of the Pentateuch." Pages 247–73 in *Abschied vom Jahwisten: Die Komposition des Hexateuch in der jüngsten Diskussion*, edited by J. C. Gertz, K. Schmid, and M. Witte. BZAW 315. Berlin: de Gruyter, 2002.

Kaufmann, Y. *The Religion of Israel, from Its Beginnings to the Babylonian Exile*. Translated and abridged by M. Greenberg. Chicago: University of Chicago Press, 1960.

Kitchen, K. A. *Ancient Orient and Old Testament*. Leicester: Inter-Varsity, 1967.

———. *The Bible in Its World: Archaeology and the Bible Today*. Exeter, UK: Paternoster, 1977.

———. "The Tabernacle—A Bronze Age Artefact." *ErIsr* 24 (1993): 119–29.

Kiuchi, N. *The Purification Offering in the Priestly Literature: Its Meaning and Function*. JSOTSup 56. Sheffield: Sheffield Academic Press, 1987.

Knohl, I. *The Sanctuary of Silence: The Priestly Torah and the Holiness School*. Minneapolis: Fortress, 1995.

Knoppers, G. N., and B. M. Levinson. *The Pentateuch as Torah: New Models for Understanding Its Promulgation and Acceptance*. Winona Lake, IN: Eisenbrauns, 2007.

Koester, C. R. *The Dwelling of God: The Tabernacle in the Old Testament, Intertestamental Jewish Literature, and the New Testament*. CBQMS 22. Washington, DC: Catholic Biblical Association of America, 1989.

Kratz, R. G. "Der Dekalog im Exodusbuch." *VT* 44 (1994): 205–38.

Kraus, H.-J. *Worship in Israel: A Cultic History of the Old Testament*. Oxford: Basil Blackwell, 1966.

Kuenen, A. *An Historico-Critical Inquiry into the Origin and Composition of the Hexateuch*. Translated by P. H. Wicksteed. London: Macmillan, 1886.

———. *Historisch-kritisch onderzoek naar het ontstaan en de verzameling van de boeken des Ouden Verbonds*. 2nd ed. Leiden: Akademische Boekhandel van P. Engels, 1885.

Külling, S. R. *Zur Datierung der "Genesis-P-Stücke," namentlich des Kapitels Genesis XVII*. Kampen, Netherlands: Kok, 1964.

Kuntz, J. K. *The Self-Revelation of God*. Philadelphia: Westminster, 1967.

Lehmann, M. R. "Abraham's Purchase of Machpelah and Hittite Law." *BASOR* 129 (1953): 15–18.

Levin, C. "The Yahwist and the Redactional Link between Genesis and Exodus." Pages 131–41 in *A Farewell to the Yahwist? The Composition of the Pentateuch in Recent European Interpretation*, edited by T. B. Dozeman and K. Schmid. SBLSymS 34. Atlanta: Society of Biblical Literature, 2006.

———. "The Yahwist: The Earliest Editor in the Pentateuch." *JBL* 126 (2007): 209–30.

Levine, B. A. *In the Presence of the Lord*. Leiden: Brill, 1974.

Licht, J. *Storytelling in the Bible*. Jerusalem: Magnes Press / Hebrew University, 1978.

Löhr, M. R. H. *Untersuchungen zum Hexateuchproblem: Der Priesterkodex in der Genesis*. BZAW 38. Giessen: A. Töpelmann, 1924.

Long, V. P. *The Art of Biblical History*. Leicester: Apollos, 1994.

Longacre, R. E. "The Discourse Structure of the Flood Narrative." *JAAR* 47 (1979): 89–133.

Marshall, J. W. *Israel and the Book of the Covenant: An Anthropological Approach to Biblical Law*. SBLDS 140. Atlanta: Scholars Press, 1993.

Martens, E. A. *Plot and Purpose in the Old Testament*. Leicester: Inter-Varsity, 1981.

Martin, W. J. "'Dischronologized' Narrative in the Old Testament." Pages 179–86 in *Congress Volume: Rome, 1968*. By International Organization for the Study of the Old Testament. VTSup 17. Leiden: Brill, 1969.

Mayes, A. D. H. *The Story of Israel between Settlement and Exile: A Redactional Study of the Deuteronomistic History*. London: SCM, 1983.

McCarthy, D. J. "*Bĕrît* in Old Testament History and Theology." *Bib* 53 (1972): 110–21.

McComiskey, T. E. *The Covenants of Promise: A Theology of Old Testament Covenants*. Grand Rapids: Baker, 1985.

McConville, J. G. "Abraham and Melchizedek: Horizons in Genesis 14." Pages 93–118 in *He Swore an Oath: Biblical Themes from Genesis 20–50*, edited by R. S. Hess, P. E. Satterthwaite, and G. J. Wenham. 2nd ed. Grand Rapids: Baker; Carlisle: Paternoster, 1994.

———. *Grace in the End: A Study of Deuteronomic Theology*. Carlisle: Paternoster, 1993.

———. *Law and Theology in Deuteronomy*. JSOTSup 33. Sheffield: JSOT Press, 1984.

———. "The Old Testament Historical Books in Modern Scholarship." *Them* 22, no. 3 (1997): 3–13.

McEvenue, S. *The Narrative Style of the Priestly Writer*. AnBib 50. Rome: Biblical Institute Press, 1971.

McKenzie, S. L. "Deuteronomistic History." Pages 160–68 in *ABD*, vol. 2. New York: Doubleday, 1992.

Merrill, E. H. "The Book of Ruth: Narration and Shared Themes." *BS* 142 (1985): 130–39.

Middleton, J. R. *The Liberating Image: The Imago Dei in Genesis 1*. Grand Rapids: Brazos, 2005.

Milgrom, J. *Cult and Conscience: The Asham and the Priestly Doctrine of Repentance*. Leiden: Brill, 1976.

———. *Leviticus 1–16: A New Translation with Introduction and Commentary*. AB 3. New York: Doubleday, 1991.

———. *Leviticus 17–22: A New Translation with Introduction and Commentary*. AB 3A. New York: Doubleday, 2000.

———. *Leviticus 23–27: A New Translation with Introduction and Commentary*. AB 3B. New York: Doubleday, 2001.

———. "Priestly ('P') Source." Pages 454–61 in *ABD*, vol. 5. New York: Doubleday, 1992.

———. "Response to Rolf Rendtorff." *JSOT* 60 (1993): 83–85.

Millar, J. G. "The Ethics of Deuteronomy: An Exegetical and Theological Study." *TynBul* 46 (1995): 389–92.

———. *Now Choose Life: Theology and Ethics in Deuteronomy.* NSBT. Grand Rapids: Eerdmans, 1999.

Millard, A. R., and D. J. Wiseman, eds. *Essays on the Patriarchal Narratives.* Leicester: Inter-Varsity, 1980.

Moberly, R. W. L. *The Old Testament of the Old Testament: Patriarchal Narratives and Mosaic Yahwism.* OBT. Minneapolis: Fortress, 1992.

Morgenstern, J. "The Mythological Background of Psalm 82." *HUCA* 14 (1939): 29–126.

Muilenburg, J. "Abraham and the Nations: Blessing and World History." *Int* 19 (1965): 387–98.

———. "Form Criticism and Beyond." *JBL* 88 (1969): 1–18.

Mullen, E. T. *Ethnic Myths and Pentateuchal Foundations: A New Approach to the Formation of the Pentateuch.* SemeiaSt. Atlanta: Scholars Press, 1997.

Newman, M. L. *The People of the Covenant.* Nashville: Abingdon, 1962.

Nicholson, E. W. "The Covenant Ritual in Exodus xxiv 3–8." *VT* 32 (1982): 74–86.

———. "The Decalogue as the Direct Address of God." *VT* 27 (1977): 422–33.

———. *Deuteronomy and Tradition.* Oxford: Blackwell, 1967.

———. *Exodus and Sinai in History and Tradition.* Oxford: Oxford University Press, 1973.

———. "The Interpretation of Exodus xxiv 9–11." *VT* 24 (1974): 77–97.

———. *The Pentateuch in the Twentieth Century: The Legacy of Julius Wellhausen.* Oxford: Clarendon, 1998.

Niehaus, J. J. *God at Sinai.* Grand Rapids: Zondervan, 1995.

Noth, M. *Exodus: A Commentary.* OTL. London: SCM, 1962.

———. *A History of Pentateuchal Traditions.* Englewood Cliffs, NJ: Prentice-Hall, 1972.

———. *Überlieferungsgeschichte des Pentateuch.* 1st ed. Stuttgart: Kohlhammer, 1948.

Osumi, Y. *Die Kompositionsgeschichte des Bundesbuches: Exodus 20,22b–23,33.* OBO 105. Göttingen: Vandenhoeck & Ruprecht, 1991.

Otto, E. *Wandel der Rechtsbegründungen in der Gesellschaftsgeschichte des antiken Israel: Eine Rechtsgeschichte des "Bundesbuches" Ex XX 22–XXIII 13.* StudBib 3. Leiden: Brill, 1988.

Pagolu, A. *The Religion of the Patriarchs.* JSOTSup 277. Sheffield: Sheffield Academic Press, 1998.

Parke-Taylor, G. H. *Yahweh: The Divine Name in the Bible.* Waterloo, ON: Wilfrid Laurier University Press, 1975.

Patrick, D. "The Covenant Code Source." *VT* 27 (1977): 145–57.

———. *Old Testament Law.* London: SCM, 1986.

Phillips, A. "A Fresh Look at the Sinai Pericope." Pts. 1 and 2. *VT* 34 (1984): 39–52, 282–94.

329

Pury, A. de. "The Jacob Story and the Beginning of the Formation of the Pentateuch." Pages 51–72 in *A Farewell to the Yahwist? The Composition of the Pentateuch in Recent European Interpretation*, edited by T. B. Dozeman and K. Schmid. SBLSymS 34. Atlanta: Society of Biblical Literature, 2006.

Rad, G. von. *Die Josephsgeschichte*. BibS(N) 5. Neukirchen: Neukirchener Verlag, 1959.

———. "The Joseph Narrative and Ancient Wisdom." Pages 292–300 in *The Problem of the Hexateuch and Other Essays*, translated by E. W. T. Dicken. Edinburgh: Oliver & Boyd, 1966.

———. *The Problem of the Hexateuch and Other Essays*, translated by E. W. T. Dicken. Edinburgh: Oliver & Boyd, 1966.

Redford, D. B. *A Study of the Biblical Story of Joseph (Genesis 37–50)*. VTSup 20. Leiden: Brill, 1970.

Rendsburg, G. A. "A New Look at Pentateuchal HW'." *Bib* 63 (1982): 351–69.

———. *The Redaction of Genesis*. Winona Lake, IN: Eisenbrauns, 1986.

Rendtorff, R. *The Old Testament: An Introduction*. London: SCM, 1986.

———. *The Problem of the Process of Transmission in the Pentateuch*. JSOTSup 89. Sheffield: JSOT Press, 1990.

———. "Traditio-Historical Method and the Documentary Hypothesis." *PWCJS* 5 (1969): 5–11.

———. "Two Kinds of P? Some Reflections on the Occasion of the Publishing of Jacob Milgrom's Commentary on Leviticus 1–16." *JSOT* 60 (1993): 75–81.

———. "The 'Yahwist' as Theologian? The Dilemma of Pentateuchal Criticism." *JSOT* 3 (1977): 2–10.

Reuss, E. *L'histoire sainte et la loi*. Paris: Libraire Sandoz et Fischbacher, 1879.

Riehm, E. C. A. *Die Gesetzgebung Mosis im Lande Moab*. Gotha, Germany: Friedrich Andreas Perthes, 1854.

Robertson, O. P. *The Christ of the Covenants*. Phillipsburg, NJ: P&R, 1980.

Robinson, R. D. "Literary Functions of the Genealogies of Genesis." *CBQ* 48 (1986): 595–608.

Rogerson, J. W. *Old Testament Criticism in the Nineteenth Century*. London: SPCK, 1984.

———. *The Pentateuch*. BibSem 39. Sheffield: Sheffield Academic Press, 1996.

———. *W. M. L. de Wette, Founder of Modern Biblical Criticism: An Intellectual Biography*. JSOTSup 126. Sheffield: JSOT Press, 1992.

Römer, T. C. "The Elusive Yahwist: A Short History of Research." Pages 9–27 in *A Farewell to the Yahwist? The Composition of the Pentateuch in Recent European Interpretation*, edited by T. B. Dozeman and K. Schmid. SBLSymS 34. Atlanta: Society of Biblical Literature, 2006.

Ross, A. P. *Holiness to the Lord: A Guide to the Exposition of the Book of Leviticus*. Grand Rapids: Baker Academic, 2002.

Rost, L. "Weidewechsel und altisraelitischer Festkalendar." *ZDPV* 66 (1943): 205–16.

Rydelnik, M. A. *The Messianic Hope: Is the Hebrew Bible Really Messianic?* NACSBT 9. Nashville: B&H Academic, 2010.

Sailhamer, J. *The Pentateuch as Narrative: A Biblical-Theological Commentary*. Grand Rapids: Zondervan, 1992.

Sandmel, S. *The Hebrew Scriptures: An Introduction to Their Literature and Religious Ideas*. New York: Knopf, 1963.

Sarna, N. M. *Genesis*. JPSTC. New York: Jewish Publication Society, 1989.

Schmid, H. H. *Der sogenannte Jahwist: Beobachtungen und Fragen zur Pentateuchforschung*. Zurich: Theologischer Verlag, 1976.

Schmid, K. *Genesis and the Moses Story: Israel's Dual Origins in the Hebrew Bible*. Winona Lake, IN: Eisenbrauns, 2010.

———. "Die Josephsgeschichte im Pentateuch." Pages 83–118 in *Abschied vom Jahwisten: Die Komposition des Hexateuch in der jüngsten Diskussion*, edited by J. C. Gertz, K. Schmid, and M. Witte. BZAW 315. Berlin: de Gruyter, 2002.

———. "The So-Called Yahwist and the Literary Gap between Genesis and Exodus." Pages 29–50 in *A Farewell to the Yahwist? The Composition of the Pentateuch in Recent European Interpretation*, edited by T. B. Dozeman and K. Schmid. SBLSymS 34. Atlanta: Society of Biblical Literature, 2006.

Schmitt, H.-C. "Das sogenannte jahwistische Privilegrecht in Ex 34, 10–28 als Komposition der spätdeuteronomistischen Endredaktion des Pentateuch." Pages 157–71 in *Abschied vom Jahwisten: Die Komposition des Hexateuch in der jüngsten Diskussion*, edited by J. C. Gertz, K. Schmid, and M. Witte. BZAW 315. Berlin: de Gruyter, 2002.

Schwienhorst-Schönberger, L. *Das Bundesbuch (Ex 20,22–23,33): Studien zu seiner Entstehung und Theologie*. BZAW 188. Berlin: de Gruyter, 1990.

Segal, J. B. *The Hebrew Passover, from the Earliest Times to A.D. 70*. LOS 12. London: Oxford University Press, 1963.

Segal, M. H. "The Composition of the Pentateuch: A Fresh Examination." *ScrHier* 8 (1961): 68–114.

———. "El, Elohim, Yhwh in the Bible." *JQR* 46 (1955): 89–115.

———. *The Pentateuch*. Jerusalem: Magnes, 1967.

Selman, M. "Comparative Customs and the Patriarchal Age." Pages 93–138 in *Essays on the Patriarchal Narratives*, edited by A. R. Millard and D. J. Wiseman. Leicester: Inter-Varsity, 1980.

———. "Comparative Methods and the Patriarchal Narratives." *Them* 3, no. 1 (1977): 9–16.

———. "The Social Environment of the Patriarchs." *TynBul* 27 (1976): 114–36.

Ska, J. L. "The Yahwist, a Hero with a Thousand Faces: A Chapter in the History of Modern Exegesis." Pages 1–23 in *Abschied vom Jahwisten: Die Komposition des Hexateuch in der jüngsten Diskussion*, edited by J. C. Gertz, K. Schmid, and M. Witte. BZAW 315. Berlin: de Gruyter, 2002.

Skinner, J. *The Divine Names in Genesis*. London: Hodder & Stoughton, 1914.

———. *Genesis*. 2nd ed. ICC. Edinburgh: T&T Clark, 1930.

Sklar, J. *Sin, Impurity, Sacrifice, Atonement: The Priestly Conceptions*. HBM 2. Sheffield: Sheffield Phoenix, 2005.

Smith, B. "The Central Role of Judah in Genesis 37–50." *BS* 162 (2005): 158–74.

Smith, G. V. "Structure and Purpose in Genesis 1–11." *JETS* 20 (1977): 307–19.

Smith, M. S. *The Pilgrimage Pattern in Exodus*. JSOTSup 239. Sheffield: Sheffield Academic Press, 1997.

Smith, W. R. *The Old Testament in the Jewish Church: Twelve Lectures on Biblical Criticism*. Edinburgh: A&C Black, 1881.

———. *The Prophets of Israel and Their Place in History*. Edinburgh: A&C Black, 1882.

Soler, J. "The Semiotics of Food in the Bible." Pages 126–38 in *Food and Drink in History*, edited by R. Forster and O. Ranum. Baltimore: Johns Hopkins University Press, 1979.

Soltau, H. W. *The Holy Vessels and Furniture of the Tabernacle*. 1851. Reprint, Grand Rapids: Kregel, 1969.

Sommer, B. D. "Review of *The Pentateuch in the Twentieth Century: The Legacy of Julius Wellhausen*, by E. Nicholson." *RBL* 2 (2000): 184–89.

Speiser, E. A. "'People' and 'Nation' of Israel." *JBL* 79 (1960): 157–63.

———. "The Wife-Sister Motif in the Patriarchal Narratives." Pages 62–88 in *Oriental and Biblical Studies*, edited by J. J. Finkelstein and M. Greenberg. Philadelphia: University of Pennsylvania Press, 1967.

Sprinkle, J. M. *"The Book of the Covenant": A Literary Approach*. JSOTSup 174. Sheffield: JSOT Press, 1994.

Sternberg, M. *The Poetics of Biblical Narrative: Ideological Literature and the Drama of Reading*. Bloomington: Indiana University Press, 1985.

Sun, H. T. C. "Holiness Code." Pages 254–57 in *ABD*, vol. 3. New York: Doubleday, 1992.

Talmon, S. "The Presentation of Synchroneity and Simultaneity in Biblical Narrative." *ScrHier* 27 (1978): 9–26.

Thompson, R. J. *Moses and the Law in a Century of Criticism since Graf*. VTSup 19. Leiden: Brill, 1970.

Thompson, T. L. *The Historicity of the Patriarchal Narratives*. BZAW 133. Berlin: de Gruyter, 1974.

———. "A New Attempt to Date the Patriarchal Narratives." *JAOS* 98 (1978): 76–84.

Tucker, G. M. "The Law in the Eighth-Century Prophets." Pages 201–16 in *Canon, Theology, and Old Testament Interpretation: Essays in Honor of Brevard S. Childs*, edited by G. M. Tucker, D. L. Petersen, and R. R. Wilson. Philadelphia: Fortress, 1988.

———. "The Legal Background to Genesis 23." *JBL* 85 (1966): 77–84.

Turner, L. A. *Announcement of Plot in Genesis*. JSOTSup 133. Sheffield: JSOT Press, 1990.

Van Seters, J. *Abraham in History and Tradition*. New Haven: Yale University Press, 1975.

———. "Comparing Scripture with Scripture: Some Observations on the Sinai Pericope in Exodus 19–24." Pages 111–30 in *Canon, Theology, and Old Testament*

Interpretation: Essays in Honor of Brevard S. Childs, edited by G. M. Tucker, D. L. Petersen, and R. R. Wilson. Philadelphia: Fortress, 1988.

———. "Is There Evidence of a Dtr Redaction in the Sinai Pericope (Exodus 19–24, 32–34)?" Pages 160–70 in *Those Elusive Deuteronomists: The Phenomenon of Pan-Deuteronomism*, edited by L. S. Schearing and S. L. McKenzie. JSOTSup 268. Sheffield: Sheffield Academic Press, 1999.

———. *A Law Book for the Diaspora: Revision in the Study of the Covenant Code*. Oxford and New York: Oxford University Press, 2003.

———. *The Life of Moses: The Yahwist as Historian in Exodus–Numbers*. Louisville: Westminster/John Knox, 1994.

———. "The Place of the Yahwist in the History of Passover and Massot." *ZAW* 95 (1983): 167–82.

———. "The Plagues of Egypt: Ancient Tradition or Literary Invention?" *ZAW* 98 (1986): 31–39.

———. *Prologue to History: The Yahwist as Historian in Genesis*. Louisville: Westminster/John Knox, 1992.

———. "The Report of the Yahwist's Demise Has Been Greatly Exaggerated!" Pages 143–57 in *A Farewell to the Yahwist? The Composition of the Pentateuch in Recent European Interpretation*, edited by T. B. Dozeman and K. Schmid. SBLSymS 34. Atlanta: Society of Biblical Literature, 2006.

Vaux, R. de. *Ancient Israel: Its Life and Institutions*. 2nd ed. London: Darton, Longman & Todd, 1965.

———. *Studies in Old Testament Sacrifice*. Cardiff: University of Wales Press, 1964.

Vervenne, M., and J. Lust. *Deuteronomy and Deuteronomic Literature: Festschrift C. H. W. Brekelmans*. BETL 133. Leuven: Leuven University Press / Peeters, 1997.

Volz, P. *Der Elohist des Erzähler: Ein Irrweg der Pentateuchkritik?* BZAW 63. Giessen: A. Töpelmann, 1933.

Waaler, E. "A Revised Date for Pentateuchal Texts? Evidence from Ketef Hinnom." *TynBul* 53 (2002): 29–55.

Wagner, N. E. "Abraham and David?" Pages 117–40 in *Studies on the Ancient Palestinian World*, edited by J. W. Wevers and D. B. Redford. Toronto: University of Toronto Press, 1972.

———. "A Literary Analysis of Genesis 12–36." PhD diss., University of Toronto, 1965. University of Michigan, Ann Arbor.

———. "Pentateuchal Criticism: No Clear Future." *CJT* 13 (1967): 225–32.

Walsh, J. T. "Genesis 2:4b–3:24: A Synchronic Approach." *JBL* 96 (1977): 161–77.

Walton, J. H. *Ancient Near Eastern Thought and the Old Testament: Introducing the Conceptual World of the Hebrew Bible*. Grand Rapids: Baker Academic, 2006.

———. "Creation." Pages 155–68 in *Dictionary of the Old Testament: Pentateuch*, edited by T. D. Alexander and D. W. Baker. Downers Grove, IL: InterVarsity; Leicester: Inter-Varsity, 2003.

————. "Eden, Garden of." Pages 202–7 in *Dictionary of the Old Testament: Pentateuch*, edited by T. D. Alexander and D. W. Baker. Downers Grove, IL: InterVarsity; Leicester: Inter-Varsity, 2003.

————. *The Lost World of Genesis One: Ancient Cosmology and the Origins Debate.* Downers Grove, IL: IVP Academic, 2009.

Wambacq, B. N. "Les origines de la *Pesaḥ* israélite." *Bib* 57 (1976): 206–24, 301–26.

Warner, S. M. "Primitive Saga Men." *VT* 29 (1979): 325–35.

Weinfeld, M. *Deuteronomy and the Deuteronomic School.* Oxford: Clarendon, 1972.

————. *Deuteronomy 1–11.* AB 5. New York: Doubleday, 1991.

————. *The Promise of the Land: The Inheritance of the Land of Canaan by the Israelites.* TLJS 3. Berkeley: University of California Press, 1993.

Wellhausen, J. *Die Composition des Hexateuchs und der historischen Bücher des alten Testaments.* 2nd ed. Berlin: G. Reimer, 1889.

————. *Prolegomena to the History of Israel.* Edinburgh: A&C Black, 1885.

Wenham, G. J. "The Coherence of the Flood Narrative." *VT* 28 (1978): 336–48.

————. "The Date of Deuteronomy: Linch-Pin of Old Testament Criticism." Pts. 1 and 2. *Them* 10, no. 3 (1985): 15–20; 11, no. 1 (1985): 15–18.

————. "Genesis: An Authorship Study and Current Pentateuchal Criticism." *JSOT* 42 (1988): 3–18.

————. *Genesis 1–15.* WBC 1. Waco: Word Books, 1987.

————. *Genesis 16–50.* WBC 2. Dallas: Word Books, 1994.

————. "Method in Pentateuchal Source Criticism." *VT* 41 (1991): 84–109.

————. "Pentateuchal Studies Today." *Them* 22, no. 1 (1996): 3–13.

————. "Pondering the Pentateuch: The Search for a New Paradigm." Pages 116–44 in *The Face of Old Testament Studies: A Survey of Contemporary Approaches*, edited by D. W. Baker and B. T. Arnold. Grand Rapids: Baker; Leicester: Apollos, 1999.

————. "The Priority of P." *VT* 49 (1999): 240–58.

————. "The Religion of the Patriarchs." Pages 157–88 in *Essays on the Patriarchal Narratives*, edited by A. R. Millard and D. J. Wiseman. Leicester: Inter-Varsity, 1980.

————. "Sanctuary Symbolism in the Garden of Eden Story." *PWCJS* 9 (1986): 19–25.

————. *Story as Torah: Reading the Old Testament Ethically.* OTS. Edinburgh: T&T Clark, 2000.

————. "The Theology of Unclean Food." *EvQ* 53 (1981): 6–15.

Westbrook, R. "Purchase of the Cave of Machpelah." *ILR* 6 (1971): 29–38.

Westermann, C. *Genesis 1–11: A Commentary.* Translated by John J. Scullion. Minneapolis: Augsburg, 1984.

————. *Genesis 12–36: A Commentary.* Translated by John J. Scullion. Minneapolis: Augsburg, 1985.

————. *Genesis 37–50: A Commentary.* Translated by John J. Scullion. Minneapolis: Augsburg, 1986.

————. *Die Geschichtsbücher des Alten Testaments: Gab es ein deuteronomistisches Geschichtswerk?* TBAT 87. Gütersloh: Chr. Kaiser, 1994.

Wette, W. M. L. de. *Lehrbuch der historisch-kritischen Einleitung in die kanonischen und apokryphischen Bücher des Alten Testamentes.* 6th ed. Berlin: G. Reimer, 1845.

Whybray, R. N. *Introduction to the Pentateuch.* Grand Rapids: Eerdmans, 1995.

———. "The Joseph Story and Pentateuchal Criticism." *VT* 18 (1968): 522–28.

———. *The Making of the Pentateuch: A Methodological Study.* JSOTSup 53. Sheffield: JSOT Press, 1987.

Wifall, W. "Gen 3:15—A Protevangelium?" *CBQ* 36 (1974): 361–65.

Williamson, H. G. M. *Ezra, Nehemiah.* WBC 16. Waco: Word Books, 1985.

Williamson, P. R. *Abraham, Israel and the Nations: The Patriarchal Promise and Its Covenantal Development in Genesis.* JSOTSup 315. Sheffield: Sheffield Academic Press, 2000.

Wilson, R. R. *Genealogy and History in the Biblical World.* YNER 7. New Haven: Yale University Press, 1977.

———. "The Old Testament Genealogies in Recent Research." *JBL* 94 (1975): 169–89.

Winnett, F. V. "Re-Examining the Foundations." *JBL* 84 (1965): 1–19.

Winnett, R. V. *The Mosaic Tradition.* Toronto: University of Toronto Press, 1949.

Wolff, H. W. "The Kerygma of the Yahwist." *Int* 20 (1966): 131–58.

Woudstra, M. H. "The *Toledot* of the Book of Genesis and Their Redemptive-Historical Significance." *CTJ* 5 (1970): 184–89.

Wright, C. J. H. "אב ('āb)." Pages 219–23 in *NIDOTTE*, vol. 1. Grand Rapids: Zondervan, 1996.

———. *The Mission of God: Unlocking the Bible's Grand Narrative.* Downers Grove: InterVarsity, 2006.

Wright, D. P. *Inventing God's Law: How the Covenant Code of the Bible Used and Revised the Laws of Hammurabi.* Oxford: Oxford University Press, 2009.

Young, E. J. *An Introduction to the Old Testament.* Grand Rapids: Eerdmans, 1949.

Scripture Index

346

23:18 96
25:4 96
30:1–21 30n72
30:16 96
34:14 96
35:1–19 30n72
35:12 96

Ezra

3:2 96
6:18 96
6:19–22 30n72
7:1–5 138n3
7:6 96

Nehemiah

8:1 96
8:13–14 96
9:17 197
9:23 100
10:34–36 97
13:1 96

Job

14:11 188n2

Psalms

2:8 172
8:6 104n55
32:1–2 160
49 155n10
72 103n47
72:9 104n55
76:2 40
78:59–72 139n5, 158
80:1 227
86:15 197
89:4 104n55
89:5 104n55
89:10 104n55
89:11 104n55
89:20 104n55
89:21 104n55
89:23 104n55
89:24 104n55
89:29 104n55
89:30 104n55
89:36 104n55
89:37 104n55

89:38 104n55
89:39 104n55
95:7–11 285
99:1 227
99:5 227
103:8 197
110:1 104n55
132:7 227
145:8 197

Proverbs

3:19–20 234

Ecclesiastes

2:8 298

Isaiah

7–11 108
9:1–7 109
11:1–5 109
22:20–21 101
37:16 227
41:4 199n19
41:8 153n7
43:10 199n19
43:13 199n19
43:25 199n19
44:2 302n6
46:4 199n19
48:12 199n19
52:5 308

Jeremiah

23:5–6 109
30:8–9 109
31:31–34 222
49 94

Lamentations

4:22 94

Ezekiel

17:22–24 109
25:12–13 94
28:14 127
28:16 127
34:23–24 109
35:15 94

36:22 308
37:24 109
45:21 30n72
47:1–12 124

Daniel

2:43 136n2
9:11 96
9:13 96

Joel

2:13 197

Amos

9:11–12 109

Jonah

4:2 197

Micah

5:2–5 172

Matthew

1:1–17 144
1:16 144n13
1:18–25 144n13
4:1–11 283, 295
4:10 296
5:3–12 160
5:17–48 222
5:18–20 221
5:20 222, 247
5:31 295
5:33–37 221n14
5:38 295
5:43–48 217
5:48 222, 247
6:24 296
8:1–4 248
9:10–11 221
9:18–26 248
9:20–22 248
11:19 221
12:9–14 221
12:42 145
15:1–20 264
15:3–9 221n14
15:4 295

15:10–20 221
15:11 265
15:17–20 246, 265
18:16 295
18:23–35 296
19:3–9 222
19:16–30 296
19:18–19 295
22:35–37 295
22:37–39 221
22:41–46 145
23:23–28 246
24:45–51 296
25:14–30 296
26:17 206
26:27–28 266
26:28 222, 258
27:51 236

Mark

1:24 248
1:40–44 248
2:15–16 221
3:1–6 221
5:24–34 248
5:35–43 248
7:1–8 221
7:1–23 265
7:2 265
7:9–13 221n14
7:10 295
7:15 265
7:18–23 265
7:19 265
7:20–23 246
10:19 295
12:28–34 295n11
12:29–31 221
13:1–2 236
14:12 206
14:23–24 266
14:24 222
14:58 235

Luke

1:42–45 160
1:68–75 144
3:38 258n8
4:1–13 283, 295
4:3 258n8

Name Index

Subject Index